T5-BAV-648

COLERIDGE AND THE CONCEPT OF NATURE

COLERIDGE AND THE CONCEPT OF NATURE

Raimonda Modiano

University Presses of Florida

FLORIDA STATE UNIVERSITY PRESS
Tallahassee

Library of Congress Cataloging in Publication Data
Modiano, Raimonda.
Coleridge and the concept of nature.
Bibliography: p.
Includes index.
1. Coleridge, Samuel Taylor, 1772–1834—Philosophy.
2. Coleridge, Samuel Taylor, 1772–1834—Knowledge—
Natural history. 3. Natural history in literature.
4. Sublime, The. I. Title.
PR4487. P5M63 1985 821′.7 84–8043
ISBN 0–8130–0808–5

University Presses of Florida is the central agency for scholarly publishing of the State c Florida's university system. Its offices are located at 15 NW 15th Street, Gainesville, Fl 32603. Works published by University Presses of Florida are evaluated and selected f publication by a faculty committee of any one of Florida's nine public universities: Florida A&M University (Tallahassee), Florida Atlantic University (Boca Raton), Florida International University (Miami), Florida State University (Tallahassee), University of Central Florida (Orlando), University of Florida (Gainesville), Universit of North Florida (Jacksonville), University of South Florida (Tampa), University of West Florida (Pensacola).

Available outside the United States and Canada from
The Macmillan Press Ltd., Houndmills, Basingstoke,
Hants, RG21 2XS, England.

In memory of my Father
Salomon Modiano

Contents

Preface

The book originates from a question that puzzled me after reading Coleridge's early notebooks and letters. I was struck by the preponderance of landscape description in Coleridge's journals and by his obsessive preoccupation with recording the most minute appearances of nature. Surely, such manifest passion for nature makes it difficult to accept the view that, as some of Coleridge's contemporaries and later critics suggested, he was indifferent to 'Nature's living images'. But equally puzzling was my discovery that in later notebooks Coleridge draws away from a direct contact with nature and that the activity of landscape gazing, formerly a daily and deeply satisfying occupation, is carried on sporadically, if at all, and more significantly, seems to evoke guilt in Coleridge, as if it were illicit. My book is an attempt to provide some explanation for the striking imbalance of an excessive naturalistic zeal in the early Coleridge and his later withdrawal from a direct involvement with nature.

In this study I provide a comprehensive analysis of Coleridge's response to nature at various stages of his career and in various writings – in his poetry, his personal journals and letters, his marginalia to works of German *Naturphilosophen*, his religious and philosophic writings. While like Thomas McFarland and Trevor Levere, I examine the place held by nature in Coleridge's philosophic system, I also follow closely the sources of Coleridge's deep ambivalence to nature. The book is meant to offer a corrective to two equally reductive critical perspectives on Coleridge's interest in nature. According to some critics, nature mattered very little to Coleridge, especially when Coleridge's sentiments for nature are measured against Wordsworth's. Other critics have suggested that Coleridge *always* cared for nature, neglecting the many articulations of his doubts and apprehensions regarding a close association with nature. The view, which Coleridge himself originated, that metaphysics impoverished his receptivity to nature is likewise a simplistic answer to a very complicated question regarding the diminished presence of nature in Coleridge's later writings. Only by examining the convergence between circumstances in Coleridge's private life (his relationship with Wordsworth and Sara Hutchinson) and the moral, philosophical and religious issues he had to resolve in various writings can we begin to appreciate Coleridge's difficulties in sustaining a close kinship with 'outward forms' and his efforts to prevent a complete break with the natural world.

In pursuing various approaches to Coleridge's preoccupation with nature, I found myself at times engaged with new subjects in Coleridge scholarship or familiar topics that, none the less, became increasingly unfamiliar the more I looked at some of Coleridge's private writings. In Coleridge's writings on the symbol, for example, I discovered important connections between his changing view of nature, his philosophy of love and his emerging conception of symbolism. His journal entries in particular reveal more clearly than his statements in published works the philosophical and religious, no less than the psychological bases of his conception of symbolism. Coleridge's notebooks have also made me aware that his relationship with Wordsworth played a crucial role in the development of his response to nature. No matter how much Wordsworth wished to encourage Coleridge's dependence on nature, he merely intensified Coleridge's difficulties in interacting with 'outward forms'.

Coleridge's speculative writings on the subject of nature led me to reevaluate his contribution to the Romantic sublime, including his deft adaptation of Kant's theory of the sublime and his extraordinary feat of passing on to Wordsworth a purer form of Kantian philosophy than Coleridge himself integrated in his work. His interest in science and natural philosophy required an analysis of his advanced philosophy of nature and the works upon which it is based. I go into some detail on the general goals of *Naturphilosophie* in Germany and the systems of some of its proponents (especially Kant, Schelling and Steffens) which influenced Coleridge's speculative concerns in his later years. My analysis of Coleridge's debt to the *Naturphilosophen* attempts to correct the view that Coleridge's conception of the Trinity – the cornerstone of his religious philosophy – represents a rejection of one side of Schelling's philosophy and of pantheistic systems in general. In fact, Coleridge derived his schema for the Trinity from Schelling and other *Naturphilosophen*, and to the end of his life he was unable to cast away Schelling's dynamic model of the coexistence of a triad of powers within an original unity in the Absolute. By refining the Schellingean model in order to purge it of its pantheistic implications, Coleridge tried to reconcile the rival tenets of dynamic philosophy and Christian orthodox thought, and I think in some measure he finally did.

Acknowledgements

Chapter 3 of Part III ('The Kantian Seduction: Wordsworth on the Sublime') appeared in a slightly abbreviated form in *Houston German Studies*, 5 (1984) 17–26, and a shorter version of Chapter 4 of Part IV ('*Naturphilosophie* and Christian Orthodoxy in Coleridge's View of the Trinity') appeared in *Pacific Coast Philology*, 17 (1982) 59–68. I presented some of the material of Part III in 'Coleridge and the Sublime: A Response to Thomas Weiskel's *The Romantic Sublime*', *The Wordsworth Circle*, 9 (1978) 110–20. I wish to thank the editors of these journals for permission to use these articles. I am also grateful to Princeton University Press for permission to quote from *The Notebooks of Samuel Taylor Coleridge*, ed. Kathleen Coburn, Bollingen Series 50, vol. I: *1794–1804* (1957); vol. II: *1804–1808* (1961); vol. III: *1808–1819* (1973).

My work on this book has been supported by a fellowship from the American Council of Learned Societies and a grant from the University of Washington, which enabled me to consult Coleridge's unpublished notebooks and marginalia in the British Library, Dr Williams's Library, the Huntington Library and the Berg Collection of the New York Public Library. I wish to thank the staff of these libraries for their courteous help and to record special thanks to David Paisey of the British Library for his assistance in answering various inquiries connected with my research. In the early stages of writing the book, I was fortunate to join the group of co-editors of Coleridge's marginalia for vols II–V of the *Marginalia* (vol. 12 of the Bollingen edition of *The Collected Works of S. T. Coleridge* [London: Routledge & Kegan Paul; Princeton: Princeton University Press, 1980—]). My editorial work turned out to be a stimulating source of new knowledge of Coleridge's philosophic interests and greatly contributed to my understanding of the development of post-Kantian philosophy in Germany. The section of this study dealing with Coleridge's system of *Naturphilosophie* grew directly out of my work on the marginalia. I am grateful to have had available a typescript of most of the German entries for the *Marginalia*, which has greatly facilitated my work and given me privileged access to one of the most important documents of Coleridge's learning, intellectual resourcefulness, and the originality of his thinking. I wish to acknowledge the late George Whalley's kindness in providing me with material I requested and in granting me respite from my editorial tasks so that I could devote time to writing the book. I am also grateful to Kathleen Coburn for her edition of Coleridge's *Notebooks*, without which there would have been little material for my study of Coleridge's concern with nature, and for lending me a typescript of an unpublished notebook.

Many friends and colleagues have helped with advice, encouragement and useful criticisms during various stages of the composition of the book. I wish to thank Hazard Adams for reading several versions of the manuscript and offering generous suggestions for its improvement. I discussed many of my ideas for the book with my colleagues at the University of Washington, Charles Altieri, Don Bialostosky, Donald Kartiganer and Leroy Searle, who have also read parts of the manuscript and offered useful comments. David Erdman provided his usual insightful suggestions on the manuscript, and I wish to express my thanks to him. For her detailed and illuminating comments on a section of the manuscript I am grateful to Felicity Baker. I wish to thank Michael Cooke and Frederick Garber for reading the manuscript and for their encouraging remarks. I owe a considerable debt to Donald Reiman, whose meticulous reading of the manuscript was invaluable to me in the final stages of its preparation, and to Marshall Brown for his thorough reading and informed comments. I also wish, at long last, to acknowledge my former teacher and mentor, Fred Randel, to whom I owe my earliest interest in Coleridge. For the skilled preparation of the typescript, my thanks to Roberta Pearson, and for her assistance in various administrative matters concerning the manuscript, I am grateful to Betty Feetham. To Edith Baras I owe many thanks for her generous assistance with the proofs. My deepest gratitude goes to my husband, Norman Arkans, with whom I discussed every idea for this book from its inception, and who has helped me overcome every impasse that occurred during the lengthy process of its composition. My work has benefited considerably from his illuminating criticism, his rigorous demand for clarity, and his unfailing support all along. To my mother and brother I am grateful for their patience and sustaining encouragement.

Abbreviations

AP	*Anima Poetae*, ed. E. H. Coleridge (London: Heinemann, 1895).
AR	*Aids to Reflection,* vol. I of *The Complete Works of Samuel Taylor Coleridge*, ed. W. G. T. Shedd (New York: Harper, 1853).
BE	*Biographia Epistolaris*, ed. A. Turnbull, 2 vols (London: G. Bell and Sons, 1911).
BL	*Biographia Literaria*, ed. J. Shawcross, 2 vols (Oxford: Clarendon Press, 1907).
C & S	*On the Constitution of the Church and State*, ed. John Colmer. *The Collected Works of Samuel Taylor Coleridge*, 10, Bollingen Series 75 (London: Routledge & Kegan Paul; Princeton University Press, 1976).
CL	*Collected Letters of Samuel Taylor Coleridge*, ed. Earl Leslie Griggs, 6 vols (Oxford: Clarendon Press, 1956–71).
CM	*Marginalia*, ed. George Whalley. *The Collected Works of Samuel Taylor Coleridge*, 12, Bollingen Series 75 (London: Routledge & Kegan Paul; Princeton University Press, 1980—).
CN	*The Notebooks of Samuel Taylor Coleridge*, ed. Kathleen Coburn, Bollingen Series 50, vols I and II (New York: Pantheon Books; London: Routledge & Kegan Paul, 1957, 1961); vol. III (Princeton University Press, 1973).
The Friend	*The Friend*, ed. Barbara E. Rooke. *The Collected Works of Samuel Taylor Coleridge*, 4, Bollingen Series 75, 2 vols (London: Routledge & Kegan Paul; Princeton University Press, 1969).
Logic	*Logic*, ed. J. R. de J. Jackson. *The Collected Works of Samuel Taylor Coleridge*, 13, Bollingen Series 75 (London: Routledge & Kegan Paul; Princeton University Press, 1981).
L & L	*Coleridge on Logic and Learning*, ed. Alice D. Snyder (New Haven: Yale University Press, 1929).

Misc C — *Coleridge's Miscellaneous Criticism*, ed. T. M. Raysor (Cambridge, Mass.: Harvard University Press, 1936).

N — Unpublished Notebooks.

NTP — *Notes, Theological, Political and Miscellaneous*, ed. Derwent Coleridge (London: Edward Moxon, 1853).

P Lect — *The Philosophical Lectures of Samuel Taylor Coleridge*, ed. Kathleen Coburn (London: The Pilot Press, 1949).

PW — *The Complete Poetical Works of Samuel Taylor Coleridge*, ed. E. H. Coleridge, 2 vols (Oxford University Press, 1912).

Sh L — *Lectures upon Shakespeare and Other Dramatists*, vol. IV of *The Complete Works of Samuel Taylor Coleridge*, ed. W. G. T. Shedd (New York: Harper, 1853).

SM — *The Statesman's Manual*. In *Lay Sermons*, ed. R. J. White. *The Collected Works of Samuel Taylor Coleridge*, 6, Bollingen Series 75 (London: Routledge & Kegan Paul; Princeton University Press, 1972).

TL — *Formation of a More Comprehensive Theory of Life*, in *Selected Poetry and Prose of Coleridge*, ed. Donald A. Stauffer (New York: Random House, 1951).

TT — *Specimens of the Table Talk of the Late Samuel Taylor Coleridge*, ed. H. N. Coleridge (New York: Harper, 1835). Cited by date.

Introduction: Coleridge and the Natural World

> Every season Nature converts me from some unloving Heresy – & will make a *Catholic* of me at last . . . (*CN*, I, 1302)

Writing to his brother George in March 1798, Coleridge disavowed his regrettable involvement in radical politics and announced his decision to devote himself to the much worthier cause of deepening man's sensitivity to nature. He informed his brother that he had given up his concern with revolutions and social reforms, having realized 'the error of attributing to Governments a talismanic influence over our virtues & our happiness'. Governments rise and fall like 'abscesses produced by certain fevers', and they are more likely to stir than cure man's evil inclinations. Nature, on the other hand, instils the love of the good and can gratify one's hopes for moral regeneration, a truth well known to Rousseau and Wordsworth and one that Coleridge wished to perpetuate through his poetry:

> I love fields & woods & mounta[ins] with almost a visionary fondness – and because I have found benevolence & quietness growing within me as that fondness [has] increased, therefore I should wish to be the means of implanting it in others – & to destroy the bad passions not by combating them, but by keeping them in inaction. (*CL*, I, 397)

In catering to the opinions of his elder brother, who did not favour radical politics or unorthodox religious views, Coleridge masked his true political feelings. However, his decision to write about the benefits of a salubrious life spent in the company of nature was not entirely disingenuous. Coleridge's notebooks show that he entertained a good number of poetic projects on the subject of 'the virtues connected with the Love of Nature' (*CN*, II, 2026), both prior to his association with Wordsworth and after the composition of 'Dejection: An Ode', which publicizes the end of his short-lived communion with 'outward forms'. For some of these poems, Coleridge envisioned ambitious philosophic and religious themes unfolding against a grand setting of elemental forces. In 1796 he projected six 'Hymns to the Sun, the Moon, and the Elements', the last of which was to present 'a bold avowal of Berkeley's System' (*CN*, I, 174). The hymns eventually found their way into 'The Rime of the Ancient Mariner' and Coleridge's free adaptation of Stolberg's 'Hymne an die Erde', although the hope of writing a full sequence of poems according to his original design stayed with him for many years, as we can gather from a letter of 1821.[1] Other plans were conceived on a more modest scale in the familiar tradition of loco-descriptive poetry and were frequently inspired by Coleridge's direct contact with a landscape of unusual beauty. In August 1802, during his second tour of the Lakes, Coleridge 'resolved to write under the name of The Soother of Absence' the 'topographical poem' which had long been on his mind and which he tentatively entitled 'The Bards of Helvellin or the Stone Hovels' (*CN*, I, 1225). A month earlier he wrote to Sara Hutchinson about another deeply-cherished plan, which appears to be a localized, quasi-meteorological version of his hymns to the elements.[2] He also proposed to write poems on his experience of *genii loci* (*CN*, I, 1214 and 1241), as well as a separate volume of poetic translations from George Beaumont's landscape drawings in the form of a 'moral Descriptive poem', 'an Inscription' or 'a Tale'.[3] During his voyage to Italy in 1804, Coleridge thought of including similar poems in his collection 'Comforts and Consolations', a work first outlined in 1803 and finally converted into parts of *Biographia Literaria* and *The Friend* (*CN*, II, 1993 and n.).

These and many other projects show how persistently Coleridge relied on nature as a source of new material for his poetry. As late as 1826, when he seemed to have exhausted all resources of poetic survival, he 'was still responding sharply enough to a landscape to feel impelled to write in his notebook a few lines of verse'.[4] And yet to his friends and contemporaries Coleridge did not appear as a man who had a serious attachment to nature, being too engrossed in metaphysical studies to take notice of 'Nature's living images'.[5] This view is not entirely absent in twentieth-century critical opinion. It has been often said that Coleridge 'is less concerned with the phenomena of external nature',[6] and that he turns out minor poetry when he 'attends to the notation of immediate objects and prospects'.[7] He is not, like Wordsworth, 'moved . . . by . . . the process that links nature and mind', and his lyrical effusions on this subject display all the blatant personifications that come 'from the conventional vocabulary of natural influence', which Wordsworth had used only in the most adolescent phase of his career and even then with far greater tact. Coleridge's awkward attempts to speak in 'the language of the sense' demonstrate 'what is plain in the letters of the time', that he 'did not share a "matter-of-factness" that proceeded from Wordsworth's highly personal feelings for nature'.[8] If in speculative matters Coleridge may have had the upper hand over Wordsworth, in that he articulated more cogently the Romantic response to nature, nevertheless 'it was Wordsworth who actually *wrote* the nature – poetry'.[9] It has even been suggested that Coleridge's failure to produce nature poetry was due to the fact that he derived from Schelling a theory of the interaction between self and object too good to be 'translated into the life of a poem';[10] thus, Coleridge's downfall as a poet was the price he paid for his merits as a philosopher.

The trouble with such statements, even when they contain a grain of truth, is that they tend to perpetuate an oversimplified view of Coleridge's dealings with nature. They tell us nothing about the history of Coleridge's involvement with nature, his varied responses to nature at different stages of his career, and, more importantly, the complex problems he faced in maintaining close ties with natural objects. Such problems involve a variety of factors, ranging from personal relationships to philosophic predilections and religious dilemmas. No one would contest the fact that Wordsworth was better versed in 'the vocabulary of natural influence' than Coleridge, or that of the two, Wordsworth was by far the greater poet of nature. But comparisons between Coleridge's and Wordsworth's accomplishments in poetry have consistently worked to Coleridge's disadvantage and have been responsible for a number of critical oversights. Thus, critics have not taken into account the fact that Wordsworth, notwithstanding his lament that Coleridge was alienated from nature, often inhibited his friend from expressing himself in 'the language of the sense'. Coleridge's disenchantment with nature and his frequent confessions in his later poetry that 'outward forms' were 'of import vague / Or unconcerning' to him ('Lines written in the Album at Elbingerode in the Hartz Forest', ll. 19–20) originated in part from the difficulties he encountered in his relationship with Wordsworth.[11] Secondly, comparisons between Coleridge and Wordsworth have generally encouraged critics to look on Coleridge's poetry as the main record of his response to nature. But with a writer of such extraordinary versatility as Coleridge, for whom poetry was only one of many interests and never separate from his philosophical or theological investigations, this approach can only be misleading. In order to determine the full scope of Coleridge's concern with nature, we must consult the many different kinds of writings he left and establish the variants of his utterances in each, as well as their immediate sources. Neither Coleridge's poetry alone, nor a handful of his speculative remarks, can give us an adequate view of his preoccupation with nature. From the poetry we may well conclude that by about 1802 Coleridge's courtship of nature ended definitively. Other works, especially Coleridge's notebooks, indicate on the contrary that in 1802, when Coleridge went on his second tour of the Lake District, and also later, he was deeply absorbed in an exploration of the natural world, which resulted in a record of significant literary value. His descriptions of natural scenery in his journals are frequently more gifted and memorable than those of Dorothy Wordsworth and other celebrated naturalists. On the other hand, some of Coleridge's often-quoted statements about the mutual dependence of subject and object reduce the spectrum of his reactions to nature, concealing in the rhetorical equipoise of seemingly indestructible ideals ('to make the external internal, the internal external, to make nature thought and thought nature'[12]) a vastly troubled history of conflicting attitudes and uncertain aspirations.

The texts that provide a measure of Coleridge's interest in nature are voluminous but scattered and intermixed with a wide range of diverse subjects. They will be found in Coleridge's letters and journals no less than in his poetry, in brief marginal notes no less than in a polished section of his published works, in passages which deal with philosophical and aesthetic questions no less than moral and religious ones. To follow Coleridge through all the stages of his enchantment and disaffection with nature is, in effect, to pursue the complicated path of his career as a whole. We shall see that events of major importance in Coleridge's life, such as his friendship with Wordsworth and love for Sara Hutchinson, as well as concerns which remained central to Coleridge's thinking, directly or indirectly affected his response to the natural world. His conception of symbolism, his religious and moral beliefs, his aesthetic theories, his debt to the German transcendentalists, and not least of all, his difficulties in personal relationships, must all be considered if we are to gain a better understanding of Coleridge's involvement with nature.

In tracing the history of Coleridge's attitudes towards nature, I have tried to combine a chronological method, outlining certain changes that take place in Coleridge's view of nature, with a quasi-dialectical method for structuring the discussion of various aspects of Coleridge's preoccupation with nature. But I should warn the reader from the start that strict adherence either to chronology or dialectics can only misrepresent Coleridge's ideas. It is difficult to find in Coleridge smooth lines of so-called 'development' in his thinking or changes that are clearly earmarked by certain dates. This difficulty is in no small measure due to the fragmentary state of many of Coleridge's writings and the fact that one must always create a text for any of Coleridge's concerns by retrieving relevant passages from an assortment of documents of varied cohesiveness and design. Some of these passages, especially those belonging to Coleridge's journals and marginalia, cannot be dated with precision, even with all the editorial expertise available from very able scholars. Furthermore, in working with Coleridge one discovers sooner or later that one is dealing with an extraordinarily retentive mind and even conservative personality; that although Coleridge is moving forward in time, changing his views, developing new intellectual allegiances, he nevertheless retains ideas and preferences that he developed at an earlier time. (Perhaps one of the greatest virtues of Lowes's study, *The Road to Xanadu*, was to show how impossible it was for Coleridge to forget anything.) In studying Coleridge's relationship with nature, I have found that although certain stages of development can be differentiated, the dividing lines between them are often blurred. Early attitudes resurface in later years and combine with new and sometimes conflicting views on nature. For the sake of analytic clarity I have had to isolate some of these attitudes and present them separately, but, to the extent to which this was possible, I have also tried to point to the complex ways in which early and later reactions to nature coexist in Coleridge.

The dialectical method I pursue here parallels in some way the stages of Coleridge's involvement with nature, from an early period of intense infatuation with its picturesque beauty, to a stage of alienation and grave doubts about the value of encounters with nature, to a later phase of 'higher synthesis' in which nature is given a prominent place in Coleridge's philosophic system. But like the chronological method, this serves merely as a heuristic tool in locating certain problems in Coleridge's complex dealings with nature. There is, I should emphasize, no simple progression from one phase to the next. Coleridge's doubts about nature are present at the time when his passion for nature is at its peak. Similarly, although in his later years Coleridge gives up a direct engagement with external objects for a predominantly speculative interest in nature's dynamic constitution, his attraction to 'outward forms' is still alive, however submerged; and the doubts he entertained about nature surface even at moments of grand intellectual syntheses.

The discussion begins with a chapter that explores the influence of picturesque aesthetics on Coleridge's early perception of nature. I examine the reasons for Coleridge's surprisingly favourable reception of this tradition, a tradition which in his time had already met with severe criticism, and point out the differences between his conception of the picturesque and the theories developed by British aestheticians. In Part II, I turn to the nexus of factors that made it difficult for Coleridge to maintain his preoccupation with landscape viewing and his attachment to nature. For instance, the complex problems Coleridge had to solve in his concept of 'symbol' ultimately dictated a rejection of the natural world. The Coleridgean symbol has an inherently divisive structure, pointing in one direction to the celebration of nature as a medium of divine revelation, yet also in the opposite direction, to a denunciation of nature as a dangerous ground of identification for the self. In later poems and notebooks Coleridge began to draw his symbols from love objects instead of nature. Moreover, he feared that a sensory enchantment with external objects triggered 'eye-given yearnings' which could be transferred to love objects under the form of sexual passion. His great anxiety about maintaining the purity of personal relationships made it imperative that love objects be placed at a great distance from nature.

In Parts I and II the term 'nature', as employed by Coleridge, refers to the external world as an object of imaginative experience (either in immediate encounters by direct observation of the appearances of nature or encounters mediated by poetry) and aesthetic contemplation. In the next two sections, following Coleridge's lead, the word takes on a predominantly abstract meaning, as a philosophic term in his aesthetic theory and system of *Naturphilosophie*. Here I discuss various developments in the intellectual history of the nineteenth century, showing the manner in which Coleridge's early attachment to nature shapes the direction of his speculative concerns. Coleridge systematically rejects doctrines that involve a radical denial of the experiential world. In Part III, I examine Coleridge's conception of the sublime, focusing on his ability to integrate Kant's theory of the sublime within a new formula that no longer requires a sharp conflict between the mind and the phenomenal world. In Part IV, I present Coleridge's system of natural philosophy as it appears in his advanced speculative writings. I begin by introducing the movement known as *Naturphilosophie*, which flourished in Germany at the turn of the nineteenth century, and present a detailed commentary on Kant's, Schelling's and Steffens's systems of natural philosophy, as well as an analysis of Coleridge's response to their works.

I end with a discussion of Coleridge's conception of the Trinity, which was influenced by Schelling and other *Naturphilosophen*, and represents a remarkable synthesis of dynamic philosophy and Christian theology.

My sense of Coleridge's relationship with nature is that it remained in flux till the end of his life, though it clearly went through periods of stability and apparent resolution. I have concentrated on two such stopping points in Coleridge's ongoing reappraisal of nature, namely his conception of the sublime and of the Trinity, when, speculatively at least, Coleridge found a way of safeguarding the importance of nature without jeopardizing the supremacy of the mind and its affiliation with the personal God of Christianity. It is significant that Coleridge achieved such moments of reconciliation in his private writings, in his notebooks and marginalia, which, as critics have long recognized, contain some of his most sophisticated speculations on a wide range of disciplines and topics. For many years Coleridge read voraciously, keeping voluminous notes, with the hope that one day he would develop a grand synthesis, a true 'Logosophia', and present to his contemporaries a philosophic system hitherto unmatched in its originality, scope and logical coherence. But if for several reasons Coleridge was unable to carry out his grandiose ambition, he did achieve some of his finest thinking in fragmentary writings, of which his notes on the sublime and the Trinity are a prime example. This study is intended to show that although Coleridge never managed the public show of intellectual mastery he so keenly desired, he accomplished his most glamorous performance in periods of waiting and private meditation, in interludes leading to but never arriving at the final act.

Part I: Coleridge and the Picturesque

Readers who are familiar with the nineteenth-century view of Coleridge as a man living in a cloud of metaphysical lore may be surprised to find that, as his notebooks convincingly show, he spent countless hours as 'an Eye-servant of the Goddess Nature' (*CL*, I, 658), taking painstaking notes on landscapes. Those looking for signs of Coleridge's conversion to transcendentalist thought in the journals and letters written during his trip to Germany (1798–9) might be disappointed to discover that Coleridge seems to have been more impressed by the look of the German countryside than by the disputes of German philosophers, though, of course, he did not neglect the latter. The sheer bulk of Coleridge's descriptive prose accumulated during the German tour and later travels in the Lake District, Scotland and Italy should by itself dispel the theory that external objects had little bearing on Coleridge's mind and lend support to the view that nature for Coleridge had 'her own *proper* interest'.[1] Wherever he travelled, Coleridge was attentive to the most minute and rapidly changing phenomena in a landscape, patiently describing the diverse appearances of objects both far and near and nervously straining his eyes to encompass the perpetually varying activity of nature, 'an ever industrious Penelope for ever unravelling what she had woven, for ever weaving what she had unravelled'.[2]

Coleridge's preoccupation with landscape views cannot be regarded as unusual in an era that witnessed a massive proliferation of travel literature under the influence of the still widely popular aesthetics of the picturesque. His passion for rugged forms and intricate designs in nature, his habit of judging a landscape according to standards derived from paintings, and the very seriousness he devoted to the activity of landscape viewing indicate that Coleridge, like many of his contemporaries, fell under the spell of the picturesque. But although the impact on Coleridge of a tradition that had infiltrated the perceptual habits and vocabulary of an entire generation should come as no surprise,[3] the extent of his conscious involvement with the picturesque merits special attention. At the time Coleridge began to familiarize himself with the picturesque, many of its assumptions had already been subjected to criticism if not outright ridicule. Satirical literature was plentiful on the subject of the traveller eagerly searching for picturesque sights in order to exercise his expertise in art. Among Coleridge's close friends, Wordsworth voiced a strong opposition to the current 'infection of the age' that had fostered the pernicious habit of applying 'rules of mimic art' to nature.[4] Coleridge never spoke against the picturesque movement as a whole,[5] a curious omission given his sharply critical mind and his characteristic rejection, after an initial wave of enthusiasm, of a widely influential system. Instead of challenging the main claims advanced by writers of the picturesque, Coleridge criticised Wordsworth for dismissing such claims, especially the view that art can unlock the door to nature's hidden riches.[6] Rather than joining the chorus of satirical attacks against the picturesque, Coleridge found it worthwhile to become a serious student of this movement, planning to fill some 128 pages of his pocket-book with notes on 'the Picturesque, & the Pleasures of natural Scenery' from the works of Uvedale Price and Christian Garve, Burke's translator in Germany (*CN*, I, 1676 and n.).

Coleridge was introduced to the picturesque quite early in his career. He was familiar with William Gilpin's works (*CN*, I, 760, 1207, 1755 and nn.) and was drawn into the controversies about Richard Payne Knight's 'Landscape' poem through an anonymous review he wrote for *The Critical Review* in 1796.[7] We know that Coleridge owned a copy of Price's *Essay on the Picturesque*, which Dorothy Wordsworth requested from his wife in 1806,[8] and that, together with Wordsworth, he annotated a copy of Knight's *An Analytical Inquiry into the Principles of Taste*.[9] But even without these references one can observe in Coleridge's landscape descriptions the terminology and taste for particular qualities in nature that stem from the tradition of the picturesque, as the following examples illustrate:

> . . . behind the church flows the River, the Church yard being its bank, which however in another field, slopes down into a flat / – and the other side rises at once, a hill bank . . . shattered, with scattered rockery & sylva. The curve of the River, not indeed the line of exquisite Beauty as at . . . Croft, but wild & more . . . playful, in true keeping with this all lovely Scene – The rocky sylvan Bank is a single Hill, the water deep & smooth in its shadow, then rushes down at once in a rapid – / This Hill bank drops at once & both sides become flat – the left finely wooded – the right a green meadow . . . (*CN*, I, 495)

> . . . Walla Crag – a mountain whose constituent lines with infinite variety yet all in segment of Circles – the whole Crag a rude semicircle . . . On that steep of the Walla crag which terminates your sight . . . a stone wall on the top appears upright like a pillar or watchman – then comes the steep precipice which renders the wall useless & impossible; but 3/4ths down the hill the green recommences, & with the stone wall running in a bold Line straight down into the Lake – 4th View we stand right opposite that narrow part of the Lake which now is a complete River / the simple & tame Beauty of encircled lower Lake, & the wild betongued savage mountained upper Lake – & the pastoral River, on its right bank mirror-smooth enclosed Meadows, the steep mountain its left bank . . . 5th View – ascend the Hill & stand by the waterfall here the upper Lake assumes a character of Beauty, but of a bold many featured original Beauty – the Walla divides itself now into three compartments – the first ending with Sir James' precipice – the second being the bank of the river-reaches the third running slant down into a Lake in a soft tongue . . . then a Hill steep as a nose running behind the embracing Giant's arms . . . then the high black rampart, Mist-covered terminating all – (*CN*, I, 510)

What Coleridge calls a 'lovely Scene' in the first passage due to its 'wild' and 'playful' beauty, Uvedale Price would at a glance identify as picturesque. Again, in Price's terms, the category needed to differentiate a 'bold many featured . . . Beauty' (second passage) from any regular beauty based on symmetry of forms is the picturesque. In *An Essay on the Picturesque* (1794), Price defined the picturesque as an aesthetic category characterized primarily by variety and intricacy of form, the latter being almost automatically implied by the former.[10] He charged Edmund Burke with myopically limiting man's aesthetic perceptions to the beautiful and the sublime. The picturesque, he argued, is qualitatively different from both the beautiful and the sublime. While the beautiful, as defined by Burke, resides in smooth, gradually varying and uniform objects,[11] the picturesque is produced by roughness, irregularity and abrupt changes in scenery. In contrast to the sublime, which thrives on terror, uniformity or shapeless infinity, the picturesque is dependent on visible outlines and objects of a playful rather than a stern character. The picturesque is, in effect, the happy mean between the beautiful and the sublime, or in Price's lovely phrase 'the coquetry of nature', relieving the former of its languor and the latter of its solemnity, and adapting itself with equal ease to 'the grandest and to the gayest scenery'. Thus, it accommodates man's need for pleasure and freedom of expression, making 'beauty more amusing, more varied, more playful, but also "Less winning soft, less amiably mild"', while 'by its variety, its intricacy, its partial concealments, it excites that affective curiosity which gives play to the mind, loosening those iron bonds with which astonishment chains up its faculties' (pp. 86–7).

The two landscape descriptions from Coleridge's notebooks clearly display the qualities that Price attributed to his much prized category of the picturesque. Playfulness,[12] variety, intricacy of design and quick alternation of dissimilar forms are distinct patterns in these and many other notebook descriptions. The second passage in particular (*CN*, I, 510) reveals Coleridge's attraction to 'infinite variety' in a landscape and his habit of pursuing the rapid succession of contrasting objects – the 'simple' and 'tame' with the 'wild' and 'savage', smooth horizontal planes with 'precipitous' elevations – to the point where they dissolve into an all-embracing unity ('Mist-covered terminating all'), which, according to the letter of picturesque aesthetics, is the final harmonizing touch of a successful picture.

Unlike Wordsworth, Coleridge subscribed wholeheartedly to the principle – a commonplace in the aesthetics of the picturesque – that the canons of art provide the means of uncovering the harmony intrinsic to the creations of nature. For Coleridge the term 'picturesque' signified a pleasing arrangement of natural objects such as one finds in a painting, which is the meaning originally assigned to the term by William Gilpin.[13] Coleridge was greatly attracted to landscapes which, through a fortunate combination of colours, contrasts and merging forms, simulated the presence of a highly competent artist at work. He often turned to landscape paintings in order to sharpen his powers of comprehending nature's difficult compositions. 'Painting & Engravings', he wrote, echoing a main tenet of picturesque aesthetics, 'send us back with new Eyes to Nature' (*CN*, II, 1907).[14] His commitment to this principle is attested by his elaborate verbal transcriptions of a number of landscape paintings and drawings by his artist friends Washington Allston and Sir George Beaumont; these appear in his notebooks amid his collection of descriptive notes taken directly from nature.[15] In looking over these notes we find that Coleridge's mode of perceiving a landscape painting resembles very closely his manner of rendering an actual scene in nature; in fact, without the specific references to the painters, it would be difficult to know which of Coleridge's descriptions came from an artistic original and which from a natural one.[16]

Did Coleridge succumb to what was undoubtedly the most commonplace affectation growing out of the vogue of picturesque travel – that of touring to primitive places in order to discover multiple Salvator Rosas and Claude Lorraines lying unattended in the very heart of the wilderness? Did he merely follow in the footsteps of picturesque aesthetics, a tradition that had come under sharp critical review, not least of all among Coleridge's friends? Why did Coleridge maintain such an interest in the picturesque long after Wordsworth became disenchanted with it?

Let me briefly suggest here that Coleridge did not borrow mechanically the picturesque ways of scanning a landscape according to the 'rules of mimic art' (in Wordsworth's phrase). His association with this tradition has roots in a number of areas of interest vital for Coleridge that I shall examine later in Part I. Moreover, Coleridge's landscape writing is very different from the travel literature of his time, easily earning the mark of originality within the picturesque tradition. Coleridge, it appears, is original, not by turning against the picturesque, but by being more doggedly picturesque in his perception of landscape than many of his contemporaries; his vision is picturesque to a point of fine excess. Coleridge, characteristically, chose a conventional medium of expression and plugged it into a most unusual imaginative circuit, just as in 'The Rime of the Ancient Mariner' he chose the lulling metre of a ballad in order to tell one of the most uncanny stories in English literature.[17]

The few critics that have paid attention to Coleridge's descriptions of nature have recognized that they bear little resemblance to the tour guides, topographic charts or personal journals of the period, including those of his intimate friends. Kathleen Coburn observes that Coleridge's 'language for light and colours . . . did not exist elsewhere in English writing in his day; he was seeing the colours of French impressionism a hundred years earlier' (*The Self-Conscious Imagination*, p. 54). Comparing Dorothy Wordsworth's journals with Coleridge's notebook descriptions, George Whalley notes Coleridge's 'superior sense of language, his insistence that language can and must be taken where it had not been before',[18] while Patricia Ball points out that Coleridge is more intensely engaged in capturing 'the momentary shading of light, colour or form' in a landscape than Dorothy Wordsworth.[19]

We are indeed confronted with a record of singular character that does not lend itself to common methods of evaluation. Some of Coleridge's travel notes have the appearance of reliable geographic documents, providing ample data about the configuration of particular spots in a given area, the specific distance between them, the distribution of land and water, woods and mountains, etc. He even appends graphic sketches to many of his descriptions in order to counteract the loss of distinct particularity that is bound to occur when visual objects are represented through the inherently limited medium of language. But despite their topographic richness, Coleridge's notes are of limited use as guides to the various regions he visited, comparing unfavourably with, say, Gilpin's *Observations on the Mountains, and Lakes of Cumberland and Westmoreland*, or Wordsworth's *Guide to the Lakes.* His descriptions accumulate such a large variety of details at such a rapid pace that they tend to overwhelm the reader. Not having been intended for publication,[20] they lack the proper organization, both as regards the sampling of relevant information and authorial directions in the form of rhetorical pauses or emphases, by means of which a reader can comfortably follow the observations of the experienced traveller. Part of the writing is breathlessly cinematic, having an effect on the viewer similar to what in our times would be achieved with a movie camera panning across a crowded landscape. Unlike Dorothy Wordsworth, Coleridge constantly takes us on a chase rather than a leisurely walk.

Measured against standards that emerge from the travel writings of the period, Coleridge's notebook jottings are likely to appear slim in content and idiosyncratic in style, but their divergence from contemporary norms must be evaluated in terms of Coleridge's own purposes and strengths. For instance, one would much rather have Goethe's letters from Italy than Coleridge's Malta journals as a guide to parts of Italy. Goethe takes an active interest not only in the natural environment of various districts of Italy, but also in the mores of the people, their clothing, manner of speech, fireside stories and humour. While conducting an informative discussion on a wide variety of subjects ranging from scientific observations on the mineral composition of the soil and the meteorologic factors in certain regions of Italy, to a study of the artistic profile of particular cities, Goethe is also drawn into the private lives of various people he meets or hears about. In novelistic fashion, he continuously engages the reader's interest by describing a good incident or a striking individual.[21] Although Coleridge, in recounting his experiences in Italy, occasionally turns his gaze towards other people, his notes are generally more introverted, sketchy and discontinuous, and many of his reflections have no connection with a specific place or encounter, but rather originate in the tangled web of his personal anxieties and inner conflicts.

Again, if one would want to learn how Coleridge and the Wordsworths entertained themselves during their tour through

Scotland in 1803, one would have to consult Dorothy Wordsworth's retrospective memoirs of the tour rather than Coleridge's journals, which in the main include a collection of landscape transcriptions and a few hurried references to the itinerary they followed. Dorothy Wordsworth conscientiously records all the events of the journey to the last detail of domestic life, and her interest in the Scottish scenery often takes a secondary place when historical and social subjects or conversations with local people claim her attention. Dorothy was indeed a true child of nature, as her brother portrayed her in 'Tintern Abbey', not because of her need to remain in constant contact with natural objects, but because she can absent herself from watching a fine sunset to focus on William's troubles, an unusual human figure, or her linen. Afterwards she is able to resume her ritual of recording a beautiful view without effort or a sense of loss. The discrete mixture of the human with the natural, of daily trivia with exceptional events, lends her journals the sustained ease and balance admired by many readers.[22] In his notebooks, on the other hand, Coleridge tends to keep landscape notations and the human scene apart, as if the slightest interference of social concerns would impair the concentration needed to decipher the unique code of a panoramic prospect.[23] Coleridge even finds the company of his friends cumbersome and distracting, 'for I must be alone', he writes, 'if either my Imagination or Heart are to be excited and enriched' (*CN*, I, 1610). When people emerge in his descriptions, they usually appear as a detail in a natural setting, equivalent to a brushstroke in a landscape painting:

> Child on Ramparts riding on a saddled goat. – Divine sunset / rich light deeper than sand over the Woods that blackened in the blaze – a brassy mist seemed to float on that part of the wood immediately under the intenser blaze – / The Trees & moving People on the Rampart cut by the brassy splendor – all else obscure – / (*CN*, I, 346)

> Old woman & the Star – all Stars – all of one color – some darker & some lighter (*CN*, I, 756)

> Two Children, in the rain, under one cloak, their arms round each other, their two faces, a pair! – the drapery, &c, very picturesque. – A Fisherman's Hut / the Oar, the one end on the ground, leaning on the Cottage, the broad end rising a few Inches above the little Chimney . . . (*CN*, I, 1468)

> . . . the old Path by the Garrison to the Ferry House by Loch Lomond / where now the Fall was in all *its fury* – & formed with the Ferry Cottage, & the sweet Highland Lass a nice picture . . . (*CN*, I, 1471)

These examples demonstrate Coleridge's habit of looking at a landscape with a painter's eye, intent on grasping the harmonious designs underneath the explosive variety of nature. But unlike other observers of the picturesque, Coleridge did not merely look for paintings in the midst of nature: he literally tried to create paintings in the domain of language. The rapid beat and unusual intensity of Coleridge's descriptions derive from his 'insistence that language can and must be taken where it had not been before'[24] and his stubborn attempts to close the gap between the moment of perception and its subsequent translation into a verbal sign. We often hear in the travel writings of the period a sigh of great frustration when magnificent natural scenes overpower the observer's linguistic resources. Goethe expressed this difficulty when, confronted with a view of Mont Blanc, he remarked: 'My descriptions begin to be irregular and forced: in fact, one wants two persons here, – one to see, and the other to describe.'[25] For Coleridge the great challenge of descriptive writing was to bring the observer and the describer into a happy communion by creating word pictures adequate to his perceptions. Coleridge recognized the difficulties of this attempt, since the act of description can never be 'coinstantaneous' (to use one of Coleridge's favourite words) with the act of perception. The earnest partisan of the picturesque, who attempts to reproduce not a chaotic collection of unrelated objects, but a unified, picture-like assemblage of harmonious forms, faces further obstacles. To recognize or represent a picture means essentially to be able to join parts into a harmonious whole. As Price emphatically puts it,

> If there is any thing in the universal range of arts that is peculiarly required to be a whole, it is a picture: in pieces of music, particular movements may, without injury, be separated from the whole . . . But in a picture, the forms, tints, lights and shadows; all their combinations, effects, agreements, and oppositions, are at once subjected to the eye, all at one glance brought into comparison; and, therefore, however beautiful particular colours may be – however brilliant the lights – if they want union, breadth, and harmony, the picture wants its most essential quality – it is not a whole. (pp. 144–5)

Faced with a panoramic landscape, Coleridge operates under two injunctions: one is to represent each and every object in all its array of diverse appearances and the other is to encompass the whole into which every object fits as a component part. Ideally, one should be able to describe both the particulars of a landscape and its larger frame without damaging either, but in practice this is very difficult to achieve. We watch Coleridge in turn giving way to the pressure of individual objects and patiently cataloguing their minutest forms, or driving directly to the constitutive lines of a landscape without filling in any of its details, as in the following note: 'A circular glade in a forest of Birch Trees, and in the center of the circle, a stone standing upright, twice a tall man's Height – and by its side a stately Ash Tree umbrellaing it' (*CN*, I, 1589). Here, in essence, is one of the characteristic designs in Coleridge's landscape sketches, and a good example of his manner of reproducing visual phenomena in verbal discourse. The description is made up of three distinct units, forming such a simple and vivid geometric pattern that one could easily render it in a drawing. The lines are sparse and closely intertwined; the upright stone meets the circular glade in its very centre, while the ash tree, curving over the stone, effects the final link between the landscape's horizontal and vertical planes. Linguistically, the description is marked by a conspicuous absence of active verbs or subordinate clauses. The objects are placed side by side, like blocks of brick on the foundation of a building, and they become part of a continuum which is neither of a causal, nor of a temporal order, but entirely dependent on spatial connections. These are the 'connections in nature', as Coleridge once observed, looking at a landscape that exhibited numerous arches projected by rocks and various trees, the ash among them (*CN*, I, 753). Like Lessing, Coleridge believed that space is the congealing factor in the construction of visual wholes, whereas time tends to dismember wholes into parts that succeed each other *ad infinitum*. He did not, however, point to language as the province where objects were exclusively perceived in relation to time, but observed that even in nature particular arrangements of corporeal bodies seemed to have been conceived according to a temporal rather than a spatial master-plan. During his trip to Scotland he noticed an unattractive file of larches and firs, appearing as 'a repetition of units of time rather than an Assemblage in Space', that is, 'units without union' or 'character of relationship', and consequently 'without Greatness' (*CN*, I, 1452).

The key to a successful representation of the harmony of outward forms lies, then, in the writer's ability to imitate 'an Assemblage in Space', or objects linked in a 'co-existent multitude', as Coleridge defined space in another context (*CN*, I, 1823).[26] Lessing thought that writers wasted their creative energy in trying to reproduce the spatial totalities of pictures, because 'the coexistence of the body comes into collision with the sequence of words' and by the time all the details of a given scene are listed, 'the reunion of these parts into a whole is made extremely difficult, and not infrequently impossible'.[27] This rule applies to all language, but especially to the language of poetry, and Lessing admonished poets to use descriptions sparingly, reminding them that both Pope and Ewald Kleist were greatly embarrassed by their early efforts to compete with the painters (p. 108). 'The rule is this', he puts it bluntly, 'that succession in time is the province of the poet, coexistence in space that of the artist' (p. 109). Coleridge never doubted that a painter was in a much more advantageous position in dealing with material bodies than a writer, but finally this realization had the effect of heightening rather than hindering his explorations of the pictorial possibilities of descriptive prose.[28] Throughout his descriptions Coleridge uses an elliptical language made of a string of paratactic sentences and dominated by nouns, adjectives or prepositions to define the spatial location of various objects. Coleridge cancels many of the verbal links of normal syntax in order to avoid unnecessary lags in the reproduction of visual phenomena and to approximate in writing the speed with which the eye can take in the widest variety of details in a landscape. As Lessing knew, 'rapidity is absolutely essential to our obtaining an idea of the whole' (p. 102), and Coleridge clearly assumes this principle, trying to modulate his language to the pace of his visual impressions.

But the quick inventory of individual objects is not the only device through which Coleridge assembles parts into a whole. The profuse forms filling his landscapes are usually pinned onto a framework of geometric clarity and simple unity, as in the brief sketch quoted before (*CN*, I, 1589). The landscapes, no matter how different their topography might be, tend to stabilize around a few recurrent patterns that give them the spatial balance required of a picture. Among those found frequently are the contrast between enclosed and bounded objects with bodies soaring freely towards open spaces; the dominance of arches and related arch forms, such as bridges, umbrellas, vaults and semicircles; the use of geometric figures for both static and mobile objects of highly fluctuating shapes; and the joining of a landscape's lower and higher planes through vertical objects that rise out of circular base forms, travelling 'Pillars of Light', water-reflection effects and unified colour tints.[29] To these recurrent features must be added Coleridge's preference for an even mixture of static and volatile objects, and his increasing preoccupation, which is evident in his later Lake District and Italian landscapes, with atmospheric phenomena of a swiftly changing character, such as clouds, travelling mists and light spectra.[30] For Coleridge a successful 'Assemblage in Space' came to mean not any combination of forms, but specifically the union of objects that were either in motion or suggested ideas of motion to the beholder, with stable objects that counteract the tendency of unlimited motion to disperse form.

One of the most successful studies of the relationship between motion and form appears in a poeticised description of a flight of starlings that Coleridge edited from an earlier note:

> . . . Starlings in vast Flights, borne along like smoke, mist – like a body unindued with voluntary Power / – now it shaped itself into a circular area, inclined – now they formed a Square – now a Globe – now from complete Orb into an Ellipse – then oblongated into a Balloon with the Car suspended, now a concave Semicircle; still expanding, or contracting, thinning or condensing, now glimmering and shivering, now thickening, deepening, blackening! (*CN*, I, 1589)[31]

Irving Massey's sensitive analysis of the generic features of descriptive prose provides a relevant gloss to this passage: 'There is a peculiar force in the true descriptive style', he argues, 'which takes over when one surrenders self in favor of the object; it is the force of unbroken continuity. Verb forms, instead of coming to an end, as transitive action, directed from the agent at the world . . . participate instead in a continuum in which every action is reflexive, intermediate between passive and active. The actions, or "verbs" have no objects.'[32] Coleridge's starlings, at once agents of a continuous action and bodies 'unindued with voluntary Power', confirm Massey's sense of the partly passive and partly active character of the performing subjects in descriptive literature; likewise, Coleridge's use at the end of his note of a cumulative string of participles lacking objects corroborates the linguistic formula identified by the critic as the mark of the 'true descriptive style'. And yet we find a distinctly Coleridgean touch in the description of starlings that becomes evident when we compare it with a parallel description of a flight of birds in Chateaubriand's *René*, one of Massey's main exhibits (pp. 44–9). Like Coleridge, Chateaubriand follows the varied movements of the birds, as they chase insects, fly up into the sky, or dive down towards the surface of the lake, but his description is much more difficult to visualize than Coleridge's. By far the most striking feature of Coleridge's note is its sustained graphic quality. We never lose sight of the precise movement of the birds, from the geometric shapes they draw on the sky during their elegant glide, to the shrinking and swelling of their flock. Like Chateaubriand, Coleridge involves us in an action of 'unbroken continuity', but the generating motor of such continuity is specifically the interaction of uninterrupted motion with particularized and perpetually changing forms. The flight of starlings represents 'the perfect experiential embodiment of some of the most cherished ideals that Coleridge discusses in his speculative works: distinction without division, 'Change without loss' (*CN*, II, 2832), the union of being and form, spirit and matter.

We are getting close to the roots of Coleridge's interest in viewing landscape and to his reasons for confining most of his descriptions of nature to his journals. Coleridge was right in thinking that his travel notes brought him forward 'in a *personal* way, as a man who relates little adventures of himself to *amuse* people' (cf. n. 20 above). Extensive transcriptions of natural objects by themselves are not particularly entertaining, and when Coleridge finally decided to publish parts of his German tour, he reduced considerably the number of landscapes he had collected in his journals and added instead an assortment of incidents and humorous conversations for the amusement of the public. After reading 'Satyrane's Letters', we are likely to recall Coleridge's hilarious talk with the Dane on his way to Hamburg, or his meeting with Klopstock, rather than the scenery he observed during his journey. A few of the landscapes recorded in the journals reappear in 'Satyrane's Letters', but dressed in full linguistic garb, and scattered among a host of diverse subjects, they tend to lose the pictorial coherence of his original entries.[33] In his notebooks, on the other hand, Coleridge devotes full attention to natural objects, trying to capture their myriad forms with a scrupulousness that may appear almost obsessive. Coleridge was anything but a casual naturalist or a relaxed observer of picturesque sights. While his landscape descriptions are not all of the same quality or design – some are disorderly and predominantly topographic, others are stylized and visibly artistic; some are sparsely worded, others profit fully from the 'Charm of words'[34] – they share one feature. Coleridge is not merely observing the external appearances of objects. He appears to be studying, instead, patiently and with unabated wonder, 'the marvellous distinctness & unconfounded personality of each of the million millions of forms, & yet the undivided Unity in which they subsisted' (*CN*, II, 2344).

Coleridge's attraction to unity and his need to 'behold and know something *great* – something *one & indivisible*' (*CL*, I, 349) were strengthened by his early contact with the monistic philosophies of Plotinus, Boehme, Berkeley and Spinoza. From his earliest years Coleridge was already seeking to understand how 'there can be *oneness*, there being infinite Perceptions', feeling resolutely that 'there must be a *one*ness, not an intense Union but an Absolute Unity' (*CN*, I, 556). Here we find the deepest springs of Coleridge's interest in the picturesque. The picturesque offered Coleridge the licence to conduct an empirical search for the 'Absolute Unity' he so dearly wished to assert. An essential presupposition of the picturesque was that nature was inherently unified, despite its dazzling variety. 'To examine the face of nature by [picturesque] rules', Gilpin remarked, 'is no more than to examine nature by her most beautiful exertions.'[35] But there is an even more important aspect of the tradition of the picturesque that made Coleridge comfortable in becoming one of its devoted exponents. In the picturesque, the unity of the natural world remained free from religious significance. Writers on the picturesque did not ask whether the natural world is God's temple – that is, whether the harmony one finds in nature springs from an immanent spiritual source, a question which would have inevitably led Coleridge to confront the problem of pantheism.[36] Rather, the main concern of these writers was to show the public how to go about discovering the harmony inherent in nature and how to appreciate more difficult designs than those based on obvious symmetry and regularity of form.[37] For the writers of the picturesque, the question of nature's unity is handled strictly in relation to the perceiver and art, and most of their disputes – such as the controversy between Uvedale Price and Richard Payne Knight on whether the picturesque defines real properties of natural objects or whether it is a mode of vision abstracted from the senses and pertaining exclusively to painting – generally hinge on divergent psychological theories about the process of aesthetic perception,[38] rather than on theological differences. When Coleridge asked, looking at a beautiful vista from a bridge, 'how much of this sense of endless variety in Identity was Nature's – how much the living organ's' (*CN*, I, 1589), he tackled an issue which was of main interest to the British critics and had been formulated during the controversy between Price and Knight. As long as Coleridge remained attached to the pursuits of picturesque writers, he was able to conduct his explorations of nature's abiding unity and of the interchange between mind and object without having to fear pantheism, for the principles of picturesque aesthetics made it totally permissible to take nature's unity for granted without introducing theological questions. The picturesque thus gave Coleridge the privilege of participating in a secure and widely shared tradition, which also satisfied two of his most important needs: to maintain contact with external objects and to experience not just 'an intense Union but an Absolute Unity'.

The aestheticians of the picturesque also advanced psychological theories that were congenial to Coleridge. Oddly enough, they fall within the branch of empirical and associationist philosophy which Coleridge often attacked both in public and private statements.[39] Yet there were good reasons why the notion that the external world controls the associative processes of the mind would at certain times be more of a comfort for Coleridge than a menace. As his opium addiction intensified and revealed to him 'the unfathomable hell within' ('The Pains of Sleep'), Coleridge became more and more prone to entertain theories that emphasized 'man's dependence on some thing *out* of him, on something more *apparently* and believedly subject to regular & certain Laws than his own Will & Reason' (*CN*, II, 2672). The repeated nightmares that Coleridge experienced after 1803 made him aware of a lawless activity within himself that revealed the dangerous influence of the lower regions of consciousness where innocence lies at the mercy of instincts:

> . . . So akin to Reason is Reality, that what I could *do* with exulting Innocence, I can not always *imagine* with perfect innocence / for Reason and Reality can stop and stand still, ~~by~~ new Influxes from without counteracting the Impulses from within, and *poising* the Thought. But Fancy and Sleep *stream on*; and (instead of outward Forms and Sounds, the Sanctifiers, the Strengtheners!) they connect with them motions of the blood and nerves, and images forced into the mind by the feelings that arise out of the position & state of the Body and its different members . . . Thank Heaven! however / Sleep has never yet desecrated the images, or supposed ‡ Presences, of those whom I love and revere. (*CN*, II, 2543)[40]

When innocence can be so easily compromised by the mere position of the body in sleep, one hopes that impulses from without have the power to arouse healthy feelings, irrespective of a person's will or mental condition. In the aesthetic writings of his time Coleridge found the assurance that certain qualities of objects and actions performed in the physical universe automatically release reflex movements within the mind, an assumption which is central to Price's treatise on the picturesque, as well as to Burke's theory of the beautiful and the sublime.[41] 'One of the most noticeable and fruitful facts in Psychology', Coleridge wrote in 1804, 'is the modification of the same feeling by difference of form / The Heaven lifts up my soul, the sight of the Ocean seems to widen it.' One feels 'the same force at work' in 'actual travelling horizontally or in direct ascent' as one experiences 'in fancy' (*CN*, II, 2357). A year earlier Coleridge extracted from Christian Garve's essay 'Über einige Schönheiten der Gebirgsgegenden' ['On Some Beauties of Mountainous Regions'] a similar observation pertaining to the effect of distant and high objects. In mountain regions, he noted, 'you have a continual Inducement to look forward to the distance . . . Now there certainly is an intellectual movement connected with looking forward / a feeling of Hope, a stirring & inquietude of Fancy.' Hence such words as 'to look down upon', to comprehend, to be above, to look forward to, are all metaphors that shew in the original feeling a resemblance to the moral meaning christened thereafter' (*CN*, I, 1675). Coleridge had tried to convince Wordsworth, apparently without much success, that the mere exposure of the mind to a particular spatial setting results in immediate changes of heart; tranquillity arises from contact with broad, horizontal objects, while soaring heights induce excitement and intense emotions:

> One travels along with the Lines of a mountain – / I wanted years ago to make Wordsworth sensible of this – / how fine is Keswick Vale, would I repose? My Soul lies & is quiet, upon the broad level vale – would it act~~ed~~? it darts up into the mountain Tops like a Kite, & like a chamois goat runs along the Ridges . . . (*CN*, II, 2347; cf. *CL*, II, 916)

It may surprise us that Coleridge, who is known to have defended the primacy of the mind over 'outward forms', would have found Wordsworth reluctant to accept his trust in the controlling influence of natural objects. But Coleridge's naturalistic zeal was at times strong enough to put even Wordsworth in a contrary mood. During times of crisis Coleridge relied on nature more desperately and awaited its grace more anxiously than his friend, given that he found little hope that his damaged self could regenerate from within. While climbing Scafell and nearly losing his life, Coleridge still felt 'calm & fearless & confident' in the company of nature and aware of how much worse this experience would have been in a dream, where 'Reason & the Will are away' (*CL*, II, 842). If Coleridge is sometimes found to lean too heavily on nature and expect it to protect his innocence, it is because he knew too well and feared the dark abyss into which the mind can sink when it is 'Compelled to be a life unto herself'.

And yet we cannot ignore the fact that for Coleridge a dependence on nature, however emotionally satisfying it might have been, was ultimately unacceptable if it thwarted the free activity of the mind. We are thus confronted with a new question. Was Coleridge's involvement in the picturesque a mere gratification of emotional needs, basically at odds with his belief in the autonomy of the mind? We recall that Wordsworth looked upon the picturesque as an infectious disease of the age which was responsible for a fateful period in his life when the 'bodily eye' gained 'absolute dominion' over his mind. Are we to look upon Coleridge's own engagement with this tradition as representing a similar capitulation of the mind to the dominion of the senses? As we examine Coleridge's theory of the picturesque, we see that for Coleridge the picturesque did not require an abandonment of the mind to objects of sense. Rather, Coleridge conceived of the picturesque as encouraging an active exchange between the mind and natural objects and preparing the mind for its journey beyond sensory appearances.

The term 'picturesque' appears frequently in Coleridge's landscape notes, and during his early tours in Germany and the Lake District it usually carries traditional associations, designating rugged forms, precipitous heights or objects which embody energetic forces in nature, such as waterfalls (see *CN*, I, 412 f. 25v; 537 f. 41; 541 f. 33v). During his journey to Italy, when Coleridge was thinking more seriously about the meaning of various aesthetic types, such as the beautiful, the grand or the sublime, he developed a concept of the picturesque that is free of its earlier associations. The term 'picturesque' for Coleridge now refers essentially to the manner in which a perceiver apprehends the relationship of parts to the whole. The picturesque still depends on certain physical traits in objects and a combination of contrasting forms, but such objects, while various, are neither rugged nor intricate, and their relationship is marked by balance and proportion, qualities which have been commonly linked with the beautiful.

Coleridge's most elaborate notes on the picturesque appear in an entry written in April 1804 when he was sailing to Malta (*CN*, II, 2012). This entry, like so many other notebook jottings, allows us to follow the process by which Coleridge arrives at his speculative notions from data supplied by immediate experiences and direct observation of particular objects. Coleridge develops his conception of the picturesque by watching closely the component parts of a ship as they form harmonious designs and lines of contact with one another. Among the elements contributing to the 'picturesque effect of a Ship', Coleridge singles out a series of contrasting features – the height of the mast seen against 'a flat surface', the solidity of the hull and the 'strongly felt Lightness & Airiness of the Sails' – which none the less generate an impression of wholeness and not of an 'abrupt or harsh contrast'. This is due to the harmonious geometric shapes, 'the ellipses & semicircles' common to the hull and the sails, as well as to the natural association between the qualities of 'stiffness & determinateness' and 'Straightness', the former being exhibited by the distinct edges of the sails, the latter by the mast. We do not have to read too far into the entry before we discover that Coleridge's main interest is to analyze how the diverse and contrasting elements of the ship form 'one whole of the whole Vessel', and more importantly, how the specific harmony achieved by a ship, a harmony which depends on a clear perception of parts, gives it a 'greater facility of connecting itself . . . with other Ships as Forms, & of forming an interesting part of a common whole: which if it were a complete visual whole in itself, as a circle with its radii, &c it could not so easily do'.

Coleridge appears to differentiate here between two kinds of aesthetic perception, depending on whether particular objects by themselves form a visual whole, or whether they merely hint at the presence of such a whole by combining harmoniously with one another. The former applies to the beautiful, as the subsequent part of the entry and other contexts indicate, the latter to the picturesque. In the case of the picturesque, the lines of a given object do not die 'away into each other' so as to form a 'complete visual whole', as in the example of a circle. They remain distinct even as they interact and form harmonious patterns. This means that an experience of the whole in the picturesque depends on the 'weakening' of 'the *sensuous beauty*', since the idea of a whole is supplied by the mind and not embodied by sense objects. 'Nothing', Coleridge notes, 'more administers to the Picturesque than this phantom of complete visual wholeness in an object, which visually does not form a whole, by the influence ab intra of the sense of its perfect Intellectual Beauty or Wholeness.' Hence, anything that has the effect of 'bringing out and melting down, differences & contrast', be it 'Lights & Shades . . . distance, air tints, reflected Light, and the feeling connected with *the* Object (for all Passion unifies as it were by natural Fusion)' will evoke the 'phantom of complete visual wholeness' that is conducive to the picturesque, 'accordingly as the mind finds it necessary to the completion of the idea of Beauty, to prevent sameness or discrepancy'.

Coleridge conceives of the picturesque as different from the beautiful, but not disconnected from it. In the case of the beautiful, the mind, finding a visual whole already constituted in an object, will remain satisfied contemplating the object itself.[42] The picturesque, on the other hand, opens a greater field of activity for the mind, for it challenges the mind to replace the visual whole produced by objects with an intellectual one. In addition, the mind is not merely forced to reconstitute the unity of a single object, but also that of a larger totality of which the object is a part. The picturesque loosens the sensory boundaries between objects and, as the last part of Coleridge's entry makes clear, takes the mind one step closer to the sublime:

> Proved by the ill look of a large Vessel with bare sails or the greater part of them reefed / unless it be made more than beautiful by becoming the Language of passion & peril / tho' it is most worthy of of Observation, that in such circumstance there is such a wonderful correspondency of the surrounding objects, clouds & billow, & Ships, & their new relations to each other, & to the Stars, the Hull of One to the Masts of the other, &c &c – such a correspondency, I say, either by likeness or counteraction, that the whole Field of Vision becomes sensu~~ally~~ously picturesque, & *the parts* . . . acquire as *parts* a charm which they have not as Things per se. – I mean to say, that divested of the passion that makes such a combination of Forms sublime, it would even sensuously *be grand* / if there be no other & better word . . . & forget not to observe what a vast number of incidents the masts & sails of a Ship can represent, a sort of natural Telegraph, the distinctness of a Signal with the eloquence & absolute unarbitrary appropriateness of passion & reality. (*CN*, II, 2012)

As this entry demonstrates, Coleridge's definition of the picturesque is strikingly different from those current in his time. It appears that all the pains Price took to differentiate the picturesque from the beautiful and the sublime were wasted on Coleridge. For Coleridge the picturesque is not opposed to the beautiful, but complemented by it. Similarly, Coleridge does not insist on fixed boundaries between the picturesque and the sublime. The same group of objects can be 'sensuously' picturesque or sublime, depending on the passion invested in them by the mind. Coleridge's reference to the weakening of sensuous beauty as a condition of the picturesque, and his refusal to divide the picturesque from the beautiful, may suggest that he favoured Knight's aesthetic theory rather than Price's. (Knight contested Price's distinction between the picturesque and the beautiful, arguing that the former 'is merely that kind of beauty which belongs exclusively to the sense of vision; or to the imagination guided by that sense', and which is distinct from sensory impressions, including those triggered by objects of sight.[43]) And yet Coleridge's understanding of the picturesque differs substantially from Knight's assumptions;[44] in a sense he shares greater affinities with Price than Knight. For Coleridge the picturesque is not removed from the realm of sensation, and it still occupies, as in Price's theory, a happy middle ground between the beautiful and the sublime. It represents the middle point of the mind's uninterrupted journey from the defined wholeness of a beautiful object to a kind of indefinite unity leading to the sublime.[45]

Coleridge turns the picturesque into a remarkably flexible concept that is well suited to some of his central values. For Coleridge the picturesque maintains the distinct physical individuality of objects, yet demonstrates that 'distinction is not division',[46] revealing the harmony in which objects coexist by a natural 'likeness or counteraction'. At the same time, the picturesque leaves a significant space open for the contributing action of intellect and feeling. In contrast to Price, Coleridge clearly shifts the weight from specific qualities in objects to the activity of the mind. For Coleridge the mind does not confine itself to the harmony it perceives in the outer world, but by melting differences and looking at 'things' as 'parts' of a whole, it advances towards a higher unity that is imperfectly represented in sense objects. The picturesque involves neither a surrender of the mind to sense impressions nor a disconnection from natural objects, but becomes, in Coleridge's eloquent language, the perfect embodiment of the 'absolute unarbitrary appropriateness of passion & reality'.

In a later classification of various aesthetic types, Coleridge drew more scrupulous distinctions between the picturesque, the beautiful, the sublime and the grand, but the picturesque still ranks high in his esteem, occupying the penultimate step in a hierarchical ladder topped by the sublime (*BL*, II, 309). Yet it would be wrong to conclude from this survey that Coleridge's preoccupation with the picturesque and with viewing landscape remained a permanent interest. After 1806 Coleridge records few landscapes in his notebooks. Coleridge was not able to suppress questions concerning the purposiveness and effects of an intense engagement with nature, nor was he able to brush aside theological questions concerning one's devotion to material and transitory objects. But Coleridge did not, like Wordsworth, abandon the picturesque as a conscious artistic choice and he did not perceive his association with this tradition as a period when, under the 'strong infection of the age', he had given in to the 'absolute dominion' of the 'bodily eye'. His disengagement from the picturesque was the result of a complex process involving a series of conflicting interests and personal problems that I examine at length in Part II. Significantly, the tensions that weakened Coleridge's attachment to viewing landscape did not appear at a time when his interest in the picturesque was waning, but while it was still in bloom. The picturesque was not a phase in Coleridge's development superseded by another phase, but an aspect of a continuous process pointing in Janus fashion to both its beginning and its end.

Part II: The Self and the Receding Landscape

CHAPTER 1 THE DIVIDED PATH

Looking through Coleridge's later notebooks, we seldom come across descriptions of landscape, and of those which crop up sporadically in the midst of biblical exegesis, few, if any, display the exuberance and variety of visual detail of his earlier travel journals. The late tour of the Netherlands with Dora and William Wordsworth appears to have revived Coleridge's passion for picturesque views,[1] but the landscape notes he took during this tour are so sketchy and uninteresting compared to earlier descriptions that, by contrast, they suggest the decline of what had once been a more promising activity. What is more significant and directly related to the scarcity of descriptive material, is that on those rare occasions when Coleridge is moved by a particular scene, he seems uncomfortable dwelling at length on the appearance of natural forms. An unpublished entry in the Folio notebook dated 7 August 1826 indicates that, while in his later years Coleridge may still respond deeply to a landscape, he becomes increasingly reluctant to abandon himself to the contemplation of sensory objects.

The entry begins with the commemoration of a natural event, a beautiful sunset, that offers one more pleasurable evening in a 'wonderful' six-month season. And yet, although Coleridge admits that he is impressed by what he sees around him, he does not immediately linger over the objects which, presumably, he finds so 'overwhelming'. Instead, he is troubled by a more serious question – namely, whether a man caught in 'a sensual trance' would 'attach any practical lively meaning to the Gospel Designation of a Christian as living *a life of Faith*, in the present state' and the belief in 'another world *to come*'. The only mention we get of the scenery viewed by Coleridge appears inadvertently in the middle of the entry and is limited to a few lines. As Coleridge muses on the conflict between a life of sensuous gratification and '*a life of*

Faith', his eyes accidentally fall on 'the lovely Lace-work of those fair fair Elm-trees, so richly so softly black . . . and the deep red clouds & Light of the Horizon, with their interstices of twilight *air* made visible'. Coleridge quickly pulls himself away from the attractive landscape and gears his excitement towards the elaboration of his newly acquired insight into the spiritual nature of 'the intuition of the Beautiful' which he defines, along with Schelling,[2] as 'a silent communion of the Spirit with the Spirit in Nature not without consciousness, tho' with the Consciousness not successively unfolded'.[3]

Why, say, by 1826, does Coleridge not look at a landscape with an easy conscience and why does he feel compelled to postpone, deflect and minimize his direct experience of natural objects? To answer this question we must attempt to identify in Coleridge's fragmented and extremely diversified writings those texts most relevant to his conception of nature, paying special attention to the dilemmas that prevented Coleridge from settling into any one secure attitude towards nature. In the following discussion I want to examine a number of factors that contributed to Coleridge's changing relationship with nature, ranging from intellectual to personal concerns and including such diverse problems as his conception of symbolism and his sexual reticence towards women.

In reviewing Coleridge's attitudes towards nature, we continually receive diverse, if not contradictory impressions. This is so whether we examine individual passages or, more broadly, a collective record over a given period of time. Thus, on the one hand, one finds in Coleridge's work a substantial number of instances where he appears as a sworn devotee of nature, as passionately moved by 'the speaking face' of this universe as Wordsworth is in his most exalted moods. Undoubtedly, Coleridge believed that nature was an invaluable reservoir of material for poetry and that unless a 'Poet's *Heart & Intellect*' were '*intimately* combined & *unified*, with the great appearances in Nature', he would be confined to exercise his fancy at the expense of the imagination and produce artificial works of the kind written by William Lisle Bowles (*CL*, II, 864). He remarked that Shakespeare's supreme excellence as a dramatic poet was due in part to his 'affectionate Love of Nature & Natural Objects, without which no man could have observed so steadily, or painted so truly & passionately the . . . beauties of the external world' (*CN*, III, 3290). In his own poems, Coleridge explored the possibilities of imaginative experience and self-fulfilment within the realm of the natural world, and when his 'genial powers' began to flag, he frequently sought in nature a source for their replenishment. Finally, we might mention what may well be the most radical testimony of Coleridge's appreciation of nature, namely his claim that nature is in effect 'the greatest of Poets', endowed with a creative spirit and the power to exert a unifying action upon the mind equivalent to the imagination. What makes this statement particularly powerful is the fact that Coleridge grants nature the highest order of creativity in the context of a discussion about Shakespeare's superior gifts, specifically the strength of his imagination.[4]

But what does this evidence prove? To avoid hasty conclusions, one must look at another series of documents – some of which are contemporaneous with Coleridge's expressed passion for nature in his writings on the picturesque – which show that nature did not always occupy a prominent place among Coleridge's interests, nor did it enjoy the privilege of being ranked on a par with the imagination. While it is true that Coleridge often derived the stimulus to write poetry when he was engaged in a close study of the natural world, most of the collections of poetry he projected during his excursions in the countryside were never realized. The last important poems where nature still holds a central role were published in 1802 ('Dejection: An Ode', 'The Picture', 'Hymn before Sunrise'). Coleridge's late notebooks, where landscape description is a rare occurrence, likewise confirm the diminishing presence of nature in his experience. It must also be noted that some of Coleridge's most eloquent statements regarding nature's indispensable influence on man are permeated by a mood of hopelessness and despair that certainly detracts from the overall force of such statements. The following notebook entry written in 1809 will serve as a good example:

> O! Heaven! one thousandfold combinations of Images that pass hourly in this divine Vale, while I am dozing & muddling away my Thoughts & Eyes – O let me rouse myself – If I even begin mechanically, & only by aid of memory look round and call each thing by a name – describe it, as a trial of skill in words – it may bring back fragments of former Feeling – For we can live only by feeding abroad. (*CN*, III, 3420)

If we were to separate the last sentence from the rest of the passage we might place it in the first group of statements confirming Coleridge's deep-seated faith in nature. But this is just how an account of Coleridge's relationship with nature can become distorted, by recording only the end product of a particular process, rather than its origins, contextual bearings and full emotive content. The passage just quoted carries two messages, both of which we must acknowledge: one is that Coleridge was keenly aware of the necessity of maintaining a strong foothold in the external world; the other, equally important, is that by 1809 Coleridge had grown so isolated from the natural world that the attempt to reestablish communication with it required all the skill necessary to relearn a language once known but almost forgotten.

The signs of a potential disconnection from nature appear quite early in Coleridge, long before a self-conscious initiative to counteract this tendency took place or seemed necessary. We may begin by singling out one factor that had a direct bearing on this process. It concerns Coleridge's strong commitment to the life of the intellect and the value he placed on a 'mind preserved watchful & *inward*' (*CN*, I, 193), free from the rule of the senses. From early childhood, Coleridge wrote to Poole in 1797, 'I never regarded *my senses* in any way as the criteria of my belief. I regulated all my creeds by my conceptions not by my *sight* . . . I know of no other way of giving the mind a love of "the Great", & "the Whole"' (*CL*, I, 354). The belief in the supremacy of the mind does not preclude an attachment to sensory objects, and Coleridge himself offered a number of attractive formulas integrating mind and nature in a communal bond under the safe dominion of the former. But looking beyond optimistic solutions, we notice that Coleridge's great fondness for nature was often undermined by his need to assert and give full sway to man's higher intellectual and spiritual faculties. Late in life Coleridge admitted in a memorable letter to James Gillman that the mind's relationship with nature is not one of peaceful communion but of intense rivalry and 'sharp conflict of Conjuration' (*CL*, V, 496). Nature's competitive force in this contest remains uncertain, subject to Coleridge's fluctuating scale of values and immediate concerns. At times nature takes the upper hand, particularly when an enfeebled self, tormented by nightmares, guilt and disappointment with friends, seeks in the outside world a principle of stability and order;[5] at other times nature falls to the bottom of the ladder, when the more pressing imperative is to cultivate the mind's 'love of "the Great", & "the Whole"'.

This instability comes into full view in notebook entries where both positions are asserted in one sweeping reflection, as in an October 1803 entry arising from a dispute Coleridge had with Hazlitt and Wordsworth:

> But surely always to look at the superficies of Objects for the purpose of taking Delight in their Beauty, & sympathy with their real or

> imagined Life, is as deleterious to the Health & manhood of Intellect, as always to be peering & unravelling Contrivances may be to the simplicity of the affections, the grandeur & unity of the Imagination. – O dearest William! Would Ray, or Durham, have spoken of God as you spoke of Nature? (*CN*, I, 1616 f. 74)

There is nothing particularly unusual about Coleridge's statement here, not even the fact that he unfairly accuses Wordsworth of surrendering the mind to objects of sense, for the two friends are notorious for their biased view of each other's failings or strengths. What captures our attention is that within the same notebook entry Coleridge practises the very doctrine he preaches against, being engaged in an activity which involves intense, some might say obsessive, poring over 'the superficies of Objects'. And while he is watching closely the various appearances of a skyscape, the one self-critical remark he makes about his occupation is not that it endangers the potency of his mental faculties, but rather that he is not sufficiently equipped to pursue it properly, lacking a resourceful vocabulary to describe the rich shapes he perceives around him: 'Sadly do I need to have my Imagination enriched with appropriate Images for Shapes – /Read Architecture & Icthyology—'.

Although Coleridge maintains his observations about Wordsworth and about himself as separate and unrelated, their appearance in the same entry, however coincidental, reveals none the less the roots of an inherent ambivalence towards the natural world. On the one hand, Coleridge finds that the self needs and profits from a continuous engagement with outward objects; on the other hand, he perceives that this activity, while stimulating the imagination to seek new forms of expression can, if pushed too far, cripple man's intellectual progress, just as an excessive preoccupation with casuistry and abstruse research can injure the viability of his affective and creative faculties. To a great extent Coleridge's criticism of Wordsworth reflects his own anxiety that the mind is liable to be carried away in seeking empathic relations with external objects, thus compromising its intellectual authority. Clearly, if the mind is to develop its full capacity for reflection, it must keep firm control over its tendency to be seduced into a passive contemplation of sensory objects. It was Coleridge's great hope that Wordsworth would eventually take on the task of teaching his generation that the mind rules over and is not ruled by the senses.[6]

Wordsworth figures prominently in Coleridge's dilemmas about the natural world, and before pursuing the diverse articulations of Coleridge's divided allegiance to nature and the life of the mind, it is worth reviewing, however briefly, some episodes of his literary association with Wordsworth. As I will show in the following discussion, the relationship with Wordsworth and the frictions resulting from their collaboration on the *Lyrical Ballads* seriously hampered Coleridge's ability to express himself in the 'language of the sense'. One notices a number of revealing links between Coleridge's deteriorating friendship with Wordsworth and his increasing alienation from nature. This aspect of the Coleridge–Wordsworth association has been generally neglected by critics who have been more interested in studying the impact the two friends had upon each other's poetic career or the differences between their approach to nature.[7] My purpose is to show that Coleridge's attitude towards nature and his fortune as a poet are related issues that cannot be treated separately from one another, or from the psychic entanglements of his personal relationship with Wordsworth.

CHAPTER 2 CHIVALRY OR CONTEST? COLERIDGE, WORDSWORTH AND 'THE GODDESS NATURE'

It is well known that Coleridge's opinion of himself depended excessively on how others viewed him and that he continuously regarded himself through the eyes of powerful men on whom he bestowed more affection than he would or could hope to get in return. He was given to idolizing his friends and easily disappointed when he sensed the slightest breach of loyalty. He was also easily persuaded of his own worthlessness by comparison with the creative stamina and successful lives he attributed to his friends, while at the same time he knew that he possessed extraordinary powers that, potentially at least, far exceeded those of his rivals. Of all the men Coleridge successively chose as his idols, none engaged his admiration more and none caused him as much anguish and perilous self-doubt as Wordsworth. From the early stages of their collaboration on the *Lyrical Ballads* and even after their quarrel in 1810, 'The Giant Wordsworth' (*CL*, I, 391) remained for Coleridge an intimidating example of personal success that far outweighed anything Coleridge thought he had accomplished. While Wordsworth's poetic star was rising, his was setting, and Coleridge saw himself increasingly pushed into the inferior role of a metaphysician. While Wordsworth's private life, after the turbulent episode with Annette Vallon, was finally settling into a peaceful marriage, Coleridge's was disintegrating due to his aggravated opium addiction, increasing marital tensions, and his passionate but hopeless love for Sara

Hutchinson. While the women of the Wordsworth household all flocked around his friend, obviously attracted by his masculinity, Coleridge had to struggle for their attention, and he even suspected, to his utmost despair, that Sara Hutchinson was in love with Wordsworth.[8] Wordsworth was constantly in the way, conquering and appropriating more of the territory Coleridge felt should have been his but which he had no power to withhold.

It is apparent that among their friends Wordsworth enjoyed the reputation of being best acquainted with 'Lady Nature' and that Coleridge would have liked to have some recognition on this score. Thus, Coleridge often engaged in competition with Wordsworth – directly, by claiming to perceive more clearly the identity of some misty phenomenon in a landscape they were both observing, or to understand more profoundly the impact of natural forms upon the soul;[9] and indirectly, by trying to impress upon his friends the extent of his passion for nature. To Sara Hutchinson, for instance, he described in great detail his adventurous second tour of the Lakes (1802) and his nearly fatal descent from Scafell, which left him with shaking limbs but a 'fearless' spirit and an even greater confidence in the safe abode of nature, provided one's 'powers of Reason & the Will' were in order (*CL*, II, 842). Two years earlier Coleridge wrote to Francis Wrangham about a less risky, though still slightly sacrificial activity stirred by his great attraction to nature: 'I seldom shave without cutting myself. Some Mountain or Peak is rising out of the Mist, or some slanting Column of misty Sunlight is sailing cross me / so that I offer soap & blood daily, as an Eye-servant of the Goddess Nature' (*CL*, I, 658).

This light and somewhat jocular remark should not mislead us. It is not a casual remark but reflects Coleridge's acute anxieties, voiced earlier in the letter, that in relationship to Wordsworth he was no more than an inferior sort of metaphysician: 'As to our literary occupations they are still more distant than our residences – He [Wordsworth] is a great, a true Poet – I am only a kind of Metaphysician. – He has even now sent off the last sheet of a second volume of his *Lyrical Ballads*' (*CL*, I, 658). In his subsequent confession of his daily sacrifice to nature, Coleridge is clearly trying to subvert the validity of his self-portrait as a metaphysician. He is not, as Charles Lamb fondly remembered him at Christ's Hospital, a man removed from reality by his metaphysical pursuits, but, on the contrary, irresistibly drawn to nature to the point of becoming oblivious to his daily occupations. Coleridge's confession is by no means inauthentic. As his passionate explorations of picturesque scenery attest, he had every right to present himself as a devotee of nature. But the confession betrays a sense of embarrassment. Coleridge, it appears, cannot speak to Francis Wrangham, a friend of Wordsworth, about his interest in nature, except by way of a joke. No doubt Coleridge was sufficiently wary of the mind's surrender to sense objects to resist a complete identification with nature. But the irony injected into his declaration of subservience to 'the Goddess Nature' has more complex sources. At this time Coleridge wanted very much to assert his passion for nature as a testimony that he was not exclusively preoccupied with metaphysics, and by implication, still capable of becoming a 'true Poet'. Coleridge perceived a direct link between one's communion with natural objects and poetic power, a link fully and somewhat painfully confirmed by Wordsworth's fortunes as a poet. Wordsworth was at once completely integrated in his natural environment at Grasmere – a place, Coleridge wrote to Wrangham, 'worthy of him, & of which he is worthy' – and happily productive completing the second volume of the *Lyrical Ballads*.

The cooperation with Wordsworth on the *Lyrical Ballads* left Coleridge with a huge complex of poetic inferiority, fostered to a great extent by Wordsworth's insinuation that the supernatural strangeness of 'The Rime of the Ancient Mariner' was largely responsible for the poor reception of the volume as a whole.[10] It is significant that in the letter to Wrangham Coleridge referred to the *Lyrical Ballads* as Wordsworth's sole property, even though the volume contained some of Coleridge's own poems and was conceived as a joint literary endeavour. But the letter to Wrangham is suggestive in another respect: it shows that Coleridge's feelings of poetic inferiority in relationship to Wordsworth also affected his self-image as a lover of nature. It is as if, having failed to prove himself as a great poet, Coleridge could not seriously claim a great attraction to nature, but only a fated passion for metaphysics. Coleridge's confession of loyalty towards nature has a double edge to it. It serves as a protection against a full surrender to the natural world, which Coleridge found dangerous to the life of the mind. It also allows Coleridge to express his passion for nature by way of self-mockery, thus saving himself from possible ridicule for striking the pose of a devotee of nature, a pose as improbable for Coleridge as that of a successful poet.

The link between Coleridge's sense of poetic failure *vis-à-vis* Wordsworth and his conflicting desire to attach himself to nature and yet to remain detached from it is not incidental and bears further scrutiny. When Coleridge left for Germany after the publication of the *Lyrical Ballads*, he had, supposedly, also left behind his career as a poet, returning fully dressed in the garb of a philosopher. This view, to which Coleridge himself gave currency, cannot be taken at face value,[11] though the psychological toll it took of Coleridge cannot be underestimated either. Furthermore, his reputation as a poet had been severely wounded by the publication of 'The Rime of the Ancient Mariner', a work which one reviewer characterized as a 'rhapsody of unintelligible wildness and incoherence'[12] and about which Wordsworth himself had expressed serious reservations. In Wordsworth's eyes Coleridge's experiment in the species of poetry 'directed to persons and characters supernatural' (*BL*, II, 6) had failed, and Wordsworth was hardly diplomatic in conveying his dissatisfaction with the contribution of his partner, as shown by the apologetic note to the poem he included in the second edition of the *Lyrical Ballads*. Wordsworth also refused to include 'Christabel' in the second edition of the *Lyrical Ballads* on the grounds that it was 'disproportionate both in size & merit, & as discordant in it's [*sic*] character' (*CL*, I, 643).

The impact on Coleridge of Wordsworth's disappointment with his supernatural poems was devastating and long-lasting. It virtually maimed the poet in him, as I. A. Richards put it.[13] Wordsworth's rejection of 'Christabel', a poem in which Coleridge was nearer to realizing his ideal, at least in his own estimate (*BL*, II, 6), brought him to the verge of a physical breakdown.[14] Coleridge did not publish 'Christabel' until sixteen years after he had begun it, and then only perhaps because Byron urged him to do so.[15] It was also not until 1817 that Coleridge included the revised version of 'The Rime of the Ancient Mariner' in a volume of his own poetry (*Sibylline Leaves*). That after the *Lyrical Ballads* Coleridge no longer wrote 'Christabels and Ancient Mariners', as Charles Lamb deplored,[16] is not, therefore, surprising. Coleridge could not bring himself to repeat the creative effort which, in Wordsworth's opinion, resulted in a poetry of questionable quality and taste. Already the composition of 'Christabel' proved to be extremely difficult, and Coleridge left the poem unfinished.

In the period following the publication of the *Lyrical Ballads*, Coleridge, despite his protestations to the contrary, was still very much concerned with his prospects as a poet and planned to write a good number of poems and collections of poetry. Many of these projects, interestingly enough, mark a complete break from the supernatural poetry Coleridge undertook to write as part of the *Lyrical Ballads* experiment. The plans Coleridge frequently announced after 1800 concern topographic poems, poems celebrating the daily performance of nature in the vale of Keswick, or transcriptions of landscape drawings in the form of a 'moral Descriptive poem', 'an Inscription' or 'a Tale'.[17] Consistently, Coleridge's privileged subject for future poetry turned on 'the virtues connected with the Love of Nature' (*CN*, II, 2026), a choice less peculiar than it may seem when we take into account Coleridge's extreme vulnerability to Wordsworth's opinions and his instinct to emulate his influential friend.[18]

When 'Christabel' was dropped from the *Lyrical Ballads*, Coleridge was to replace it with a group of poems on 'the Naming of Places' – a project that Wordsworth seemed to encourage, making a special trip to Keswick in mid-October 1800 to acquire the poems for the *Lyrical Ballads*.[19] Coleridge never produced the promised poems,[20] but the plan is itself symptomatic of his willingness to substitute naturalistic poems for a supernatural tale and to produce the kind of poetry that he thought Wordsworth would approve. The poems on 'the Naming of Places' fit in with the characteristic projects on topographic or moral–descriptive subjects Coleridge envisioned writing after 1800. One other project, perhaps the most ambitious of all, should be mentioned here, as it reveals poignantly the extent to which Coleridge felt compelled to imitate the Wordsworthian canon. The plan was conceived during a walk Coleridge took through Borrodale in October 1803 and appears to be no less than an intended replica of *The Prelude*, which Wordsworth was working on at the time. The immediate occasion that prompted Coleridge to devise this plan was his discovery in Borrodale of a magnificent spot that deserved to be marked with a 'Cross or Heap of Stones' and honoured in verse. Just before announcing his projected poem in his entry, Coleridge drops a casual reference to an argument he and Wordsworth had about the size of 'Bowder Stone' compared to two other rocks in Borrodale. This trivial argument introduces a far more serious battle with Wordsworth that Coleridge does not openly acknowledge – the battle of a dispossessed poet trying to regain his status by borrowing his rival's own means of success. Here is how Coleridge conceives of *his* autobiographical poem:

> Go & build up a pile of three [stones], by that Coppice – measure the Strides from the Bridge where the water rushes down a rock in no mean cataract if the Rains should have swoln the River . . . from this Bridge measure the Strides to the Place, build the Stone heap, & write a Poem, thus beginning – From the Bridge &c repeat such a Song, of Milton, or Homer – so many Lines I ~~will~~ must find out, may be distinctly recited during a moderate healthy man's walk from the Bridge thither – or better perhaps from the other Bridge – so to this Heap of

> Stones – there turn in – & then describe the Scene. – O surely I might make a noble Poem of all my Youth nay *of all my Life* – One section on plants & flowers, my passion for them, always deadened by their learned names. (*CN*, I, 1610)

As much as we can infer from this brief description, it appears that Coleridge's 'noble Poem' was to be written in the high style of an epic or perhaps an ode and grafted onto the Wordsworthian topos of adherence to natural spots. It was to be a poem celebrating Coleridge's passion for nature and, possibly, tracing the history of his relationship with nature throughout his life. Coleridge would have found a model for such a poem in 'Tintern Abbey', and from talks with William and Dorothy he might have also anticipated the kind of project Wordsworth was engaged in at the time.[21] There is, however, something altogether peculiar about the way Coleridge proceeds to lay out his poem. It is as if Coleridge is trying not just to evoke a certain place in a poem, but virtually to tailor his composition according to the physical pattern provided by the place. There is a deliberate binding of poem to place or, borrowing one of Coleridge's own phrases in another context, what I would like to call spot fixation 'with a vengeance'.[22] Thus, Coleridge's preliminary concern is to count the number of strides from the bridge to the discovered spot and to schedule the length of his poem accordingly. The writing of the poem is presented as an activity that is continuous with and undifferentiated from the purely mechanical parts of the project: 'measure the Strides to the Place, build the Stone heap, & write a Poem'.

It is to be expected that no *Prelude* ever emerged from such tight measurements. Coleridge's 'noble Poem', so far as we know, was never written, just as the other projects in the naturalistic mode never materialized. This evidence seems to corroborate the opinion of some critics that Coleridge is not concerned with external objects and incapable of writing good nature poetry because for him the main source of inspiration came from 'the life within', from fantasy and dream. Wordsworth summarized this view best when he told Henry Crabb Robinson in 1812 that Coleridge was addicted to 'his own extraordinary powers summoning up an image or series of images in his own mind' and thus given to 'a sort of dreaminess which would not let him see things as they were' or experience the 'influence of external objects'.[23] But surely this view, while capturing a certain direction in the later Coleridge of which he was himself most critical, is an inadequate description both of his poetry and of his personality as a whole. To say that Coleridge could not write nature poetry or that he was perpetually sleep-walking in an imaginary realm closed to nature's 'living images' is to ignore his having composed a poem like 'This Lime-tree Bower my Prison', and the fastidiously precise observations of various sensory phenomena in his journals. In fact, comparing Coleridge's description of a spot in the hills of Alfoxden in 'This Lime-tree Bower my Prison' with Wordsworth's own account of this place in 'Lines Written in Early Spring', Stephen Maxfield Parrish concludes that 'Coleridge traces the surfaces of Nature with close attention to realistic detail, only unobtrusively committing the pathetic fallacy, while Wordsworth glances at but moves beyond the surfaces, boldly investing Nature with life and feeling, then turns from Nature to man. In the end, Coleridge's poem is more an outright celebration of nature than Wordsworth's, and closer to the matter-of-fact world of eye and ear' (p. 45).

If we accept the premise that Coleridge could – and did – write nature poetry, then his failure to turn out the projected topographic and autobiographic poems cannot be attributed to some constitutional handicap of his temperament or to his reputation as a poet of trance. I would like to advance a speculation here that may shed some light on this matter. The history of Coleridge's early collaboration with Wordsworth shows that the two poets could not engage successfully in the same project and that they wrote some of their best work when dealing with completely different subjects and methods of exploration.[24] Coleridge's and Wordsworth's attempts to collaborate on a single poem, which was the earliest plan for the *Lyrical Ballads*, resulted instead in a more voluminous output of 'two sorts' of poems, one adhering to 'the truth of nature' and lending 'the charm of novelty to things of every day', the other proposing to show 'the dramatic truth' of emotions experienced by 'every human being who, from whatever source of delusion, has at any time believed himself under supernatural agency'. This account given by Coleridge in *Biographia Literaria* (*BL*, II, 5–6) is an accurate description of what came out of the *Lyrical Ballads* venture, but, as Shawcross pointed out, it is not a reliable testimony of how the volume was originally conceived. In a letter to Humphry Davy written in October 1800, Coleridge presents the *Lyrical Ballads* as 'an experiment to see how far those passions which alone give any value to extraordinary Incidents, were capable of interesting, in & for themselves, in the incidents of common Life' (*CL*, I, 631). This version of the project, which approximates the way Wordsworth himself recalled it in his Fenwick note to 'We Are Seven',[25] makes no provision for 'persons and characters supernatural' or 'the willing suspension of disbelief'. From the written evidence we have and from what we know about

Wordsworth's sensibility, it is safe to assume that Wordsworth had in mind a homogeneous volume of poetry by theme and purpose,[26] and not a Coleridgean meeting of extremes, or a synthesis of opposite artistic modes, as his partner presented the case in *Biographia Literaria.*

If we take into account the fact that Wordsworth was by nature averse to the merging of discordant elements, then his decision to exclude 'Christabel' on the grounds that the poem was 'in direct opposition to the very purpose for which the Lyrical Ballads were published' (*CL*, I, 631) is understandable, particularly if his expectations of the volume were those conveyed by Coleridge's letter to Davy. When Wordsworth, for the purpose of minimizing the discrepancies in the projected second edition of the *Lyrical Ballads*, encouraged Coleridge to produce his poems of 'the Naming of Places', he in effect invited Coleridge to surrender his sovereign territory and join in a truly communal enterprise. But in so doing Wordsworth presented Coleridge with a dangerous challenge that Coleridge accepted with determination, though not without some foreboding. Wordsworth held out for Coleridge the attractive prospect of becoming a successful poet, acceptable to his partner, if he abandoned the supernatural ideal and concerned himself instead with the feelings which grow from 'little Incidents' among 'rural Objects'. The extent to which Coleridge accepted the Wordsworthian challenge is evident from the number of naturalistic poems he kept on devising. As much as one might sympathize with Charles Lamb's regret that Coleridge stopped writing 'Christabels and Ancient Mariners', it is important to realize that after 1800 Coleridge tried very hard to do just that, to move away from a supernatural poetry that had incurred Wordsworth's opprobrium. But by giving in to the pressure of becoming a naturalistic poet, Coleridge was forced into an impossible competition on his rival's home ground. In this context, his inability to complete his topographic poems and the obvious self-defeating mechanism ingrained in his formula for a *Prelude* of his own become increasingly comprehensible.

It was not uncharacteristic of Coleridge to take on unsuitable projects of various magnitude and kinds, especially during times of personal unhappiness, which would usually deepen his feelings of inadequacy, guilt and self-reproach. His failure, therefore, to write poems in the naturalistic vein cannot be seen simply as externally induced by Wordsworth's demands, but as related to Coleridge's personality as well as his fluctuating views regarding the value of nature poetry. In this respect one may recall that Coleridge vigorously encouraged Wordsworth to write philosophical poetry, and was most critical of his friend's unwise devotion to small projects of the kind he produced for the *Lyrical Ballads*. If this reflects at all Coleridge's ideal of high poetry, then his attitude towards poems set in a rural setting and dealing with commonplace incidents could only be unenthusiastic if not downright disparaging. It is as if Coleridge were willing to assume the burden of writing minor poetry in order to allow Wordsworth to devote himself to the great task of becoming 'the first & greatest philosophical Poet' (*CL*, II, 1034).[27] The fact that Coleridge did not go ahead with his projected naturalistic poems reveals the limits of such self-sacrificial generosity in this literary relationship and of Coleridge's own capacity for self-denial.

In a later notebook entry, recalling the painful, humiliating reception that his supernatural poems received from the Wordsworths, Coleridge reflected on their 'cold praise and effective discouragement of every attempt of mine to roll onward in a distinct current of my own' (*CL*, I, 631 n.2). Although this statement may be more indicative of Coleridge's excessive need for approval than of the total disapproval he met with in his relationship with the Wordsworths, it offers, none the less, a valuable insight into the nature of the crisis of poetic power Coleridge encountered during the years of his literary association with Wordsworth on the *Lyrical Ballads*. Coleridge's supernatural poems, which clearly signalled a 'distinct current' of his own, were not appreciated by the Wordsworths. On the other hand, naturalistic poems of the kind Wordsworth seemed to like did not fully satisfy Coleridge's standards for good poetry. Coleridge's disorientation as to what should be his own direction in poetry accounts to a large extent for the feelings of creative paralysis he experienced especially in 1802 and dramatized in 'Dejection: An Ode'. Though this perspective does not offer a full explanation of how Coleridge lost his poetic momentum after 1800, it provides a useful corrective to the view enunciated by Coleridge in 'Dejection' that metaphysics killed the 'shaping spirit' of his imagination, and with it, his sensitivity to nature.

Coleridge's relationship with Wordsworth thus had a direct influence on his ambivalent response to nature and his damaged confidence regarding his prospects as a poet. In the early stages of their association, while mutual admiration and love were still the overriding sentiments between them, Coleridge's interest in nature was undoubtedly stimulated by the spirited nature talk they conducted during their walks and travels. His successful composition of 'This Lime-tree Bower my Prison' might owe something to a more relaxed attitude towards nature that Coleridge derived from his communication with the Wordsworths and that helped him to overcome the feelings of guilt fostered by earlier encounters with the natural world, as conveyed in 'Reflections on having left a Place of Retirement' or 'The Eolian Harp'. By March 1798, in a letter to his brother George, Coleridge already presents himself as a poet of nature, inspired by 'fields & woods & mountains with almost a visionary fondness' and seeking to 'elevate the imagination & set the affections in right tune by the beauty of the inanimate impregnated, as with a living soul, by the presence of Life' (*CL*, I, 397). Coleridge illustrates his position by quoting some lines from 'The Ruined Cottage', thus showing his eagerness to align his poetic goals with those of Wordsworth, though, of course, the sentiment and theme of 'the one Life' were indigenous to Coleridge. It is worth remembering that at the time Coleridge assumed the identity of a poet of nature, 'The Rime of the Ancient Mariner' was for the most part written. This, as well as the close proximity between the composition of 'This Lime-tree Bower my Prison' and 'The Rime of the Ancient Mariner', indicates that before his relationship with Wordsworth deteriorated, Coleridge could function successfully as a poet both of nature and of the supernatural, just as prior to 1800 he was tormented neither by his identity as a metaphysician nor by the conviction that metaphysics was detrimental to poetry.[28]

While the relationship with Wordsworth in its early, benevolent phase greatly spurred Coleridge's passion for nature, it also had the opposite effect of turning Coleridge's rapport with nature into a highly complicated affair. Two related matters show how a weakening of Coleridge's ties with nature can be linked to the increasing tensions caused by his collaboration with Wordsworth. The first pertains to Coleridge's tormented struggle for poetic survival after Wordsworth assumed sole authorship of the *Lyrical Ballads*. We have already seen that Coleridge, despite frequent announcements to friends that he had surrendered poetry to Wordsworth, tried to keep a low profile as a naturalistic poet. Moreover, he continued to look on nature as a revitalizing source of creative energy. In a sense, as the relationship with Wordsworth became less reassuring, Coleridge transferred his dependency from his friend to nature, from a stern father-figure to a more forgiving, motherly guardian.[29] This transference is most clearly seen in a notebook entry written around the time of Coleridge's severe rift with Wordsworth in 1810. Here, adapting a consoling passage from Richter's *Geist*, Coleridge speaks of nature as a steadfast and loyal companion, lulling one's grief and extending generous protection and sympathy 'even when all men have seemed to desert us'. While the 'Love of Nature is ever returned double to us', the love of man appears to Coleridge as a one-way, inconstant and disappointing affair (*CN*, III, 4040). In his rift with Wordsworth, Coleridge experienced the reversal of the Wordsworthian mythos 'love of Nature leads to love of Man'. Instead, love of man leads, *via negativa*, to an appreciation of nature.

The transference of dependency from Wordsworth to nature took place much earlier than the time of the quarrel in 1810 and caused, as relationships of dependency normally do, a disquieting awareness of an imperfect guardianship. When his prospects as a poet became uncertain after his banishment from the *Lyrical Ballads*, Coleridge often turned to nature with hopes of finding an immediate stimulus for poetic productivity. His expectations of the bountiful gifts nature held in store for him and his mode of gaining possession of such gifts are best represented by a few lines from Coleridge's free translation of Stolberg's 'Hymne an die Erde':

> Thrilled with thy beauty and love in the wooded slope of
> the mountain
> Here, great mother, I lie, thy child, with his head on thy bosom!
> Playful the spirits of noon, that rushing soft through thy tresses,
> Green-haired goddess! refresh me; and hark! as they hurry or linger,
> Fill the pause of my harp, or sustain it with musical murmurs.
> (ll. 7–11)

What Coleridge found, however, is that while nature might perform miraculous acts of benevolence for a loving and needy child, it does not fill those pauses of the poetic lyre with a steady voice 'but half its own'. Consistently, Coleridge discovered that the strategy of courting nature to gain instant poetic recovery did not succeed.[30] As his notebooks show, Coleridge's repeated efforts to provoke inspiration by dwelling on 'outward forms' finally convinced him that, while his sensitivity to nature was ample and visitations of 'poetic feeling' *did* occur in the midst of natural objects, without 'the combining Power, the power to do, the manly effective *Will*' (*CN*, II, 2086), such visitations finally dissipated into nothingness. This experience differs from the crisis Coleridge dramatizes in 'Dejection: An Ode'. It is not the failure of responding to the natural world, but the very amplitude of this response that makes the absence of the 'genial spirits' so much more evident and painful to endure. While Coleridge could persuade himself (as he tried to persuade Francis Wrangham) that his love of metaphysics by no means overshadowed his devotion to the 'Goddess Nature', he could not thereby also prove that he was, like Wordsworth, a great poet. In the decline of a poetic career, Coleridge recognized that encounters with the natural world that merely tease but do not satisfy the 'genial spirits' were hopelessly defective and self-defeating.

Coleridge's growing alienation from nature also originated from his need, contrary to the dependency drive, to dissociate himself from Wordsworth's values. Several small incidents show that Coleridge found Wordsworth's nature worship irritating, just as he began to find fault with his friend's self-involuted personality and artistic principles. In a letter of August 1801, Coleridge invited Francis Wrangham for a visit to the Lakes, mentioning in a tone of light mockery that Wordsworth would undoubtedly introduce him to nature's 'best things in all her mollissima tempora – for few men can boast, I believe, of so intimate an acquaintance with her Ladyship' (*CL*, II, 750). There is here a covert criticism of Wordsworth's engagement with the transitory 'superficies of Objects', an activity which, as Coleridge remarked, is bound to weaken 'the Health and manhood of Intellect' (*CN*, I, 1616). We find again that during their tour through Scotland Coleridge conducted a silent battle with the Wordsworths on an issue most likely pertaining to the picturesque, referring specifically to the authority of the mind in its dealings with nature:

> Those who hold it undignified to illustrate Nature by Art – how little would the truly dignified say so – how else can we bring the forms of Nature within our voluntary memory! – The first Business is to subjugate them to our Intellect & voluntary memory – then comes their Dignity by Sensation of Magnitude, Forms & Passions connected therewith. (*CN*, I, 1489)

We are familiar with Wordsworth's aversion to applying the 'rules of mimic art' to nature and can infer from Coleridge's note that he must have spoken vehemently against a standard presupposition about the picturesque. Coleridge privately replies to Wordsworth that the dignity of nature depends upon man's intellectual mastery, and that the function of art is therefore to provide the medium through which the mind can assimilate, control and retain the forms of nature, thereby endowing them with the 'life and passion' they do not by themselves possess. The view that the mind must be granted dominion over the world of the senses is not unusual in Coleridge, but the recommendation that nature must be 'subjugated' by the mind, which would undoubtedly have irritated Wordsworth, has a more extreme edge to it that comes from the controversial dispute with Wordsworth. Such origins are important to bear in mind. As a way of asserting his independence from Wordsworth, Coleridge is likely to make radical claims that are not fully representative of his view of nature at a given time.[31]

During the years of growing disaffection with Wordsworth, Coleridge identified an area of difference between himself and his friend where he could, comfortably, prove Wordsworth to be in the wrong. It concerned Wordsworth's tendency to place the mind in a relationship of servitude to the great 'Green-haired goddess'. (This is not, of course, the Wordsworth we know, though Coleridge's interpretation of Wordsworth's cult of nature is not different from the view of other contemporaries, such as Blake or Shelley.) It concerned, moreover, Wordsworth's taste for the accidental and transitory aspects of nature, his stubborn matter-of-factness and unwillingness to devote himself to 'great objects & elevated Conceptions' (*CL*, II, 1013). Coleridge used this line of criticism in *Biographia Literaria*, where he adopted in opposition to Wordsworth's views the Aristotelian notion that 'poetry is essentially *ideal*, that it avoids and excludes all *accident*' (*BL*, II, 33). Earlier, before he could turn his disagreement with Wordsworth into a fully-fledged literary theory, he charted out a private region of sensibility in which he took great pride. But in sorting out his differences from his partner, Coleridge found himself in an ambivalent position as to how prominent a place he should allot to nature. A good example of Coleridge's dilemma in this regard is provided by a notebook entry written during his Malta journey in April 1804 (*CN*, II, 2026).

The entry commemorates Coleridge's first sight of the coast of Africa and his discovery that the continents of Europe and Africa, so distinct by names, are in nature nothing but two undivided 'Mountain Banks, that make a noble River of the interfluent Sea'. The discovery prompted Coleridge to meditate on the 'Power of Names to give Interest' to certain objects or places and on his inability to derive more than light amusement from contingent associations such names might carry. 'Of all men, I ever knew', Coleridge writes, 'Wordsworth himself not excepted, I have the faintest pleasure in things contingent & transitory. I never, except as a forced Courtesy of Conversation, ask in a ~~Coach~~ Stage. whose House is that . . . I am not certain, whether I should have seen with any Emotion the Mulberry Tree of Shakespeare.' The knowledge that Shakespeare planted the tree would in effect intrude upon any 'unity of Feeling' he might have experienced otherwise, preventing him from losing himself 'in the flexures of its Branches & interweaving of its Roots'. There are, however, 'conceivable circumstances', Coleridge adds, where 'the contrary would be true', where the knowledge that

Giordano Bruno or Milton inhabited a certain 'Rock by this Sea' or 'Bank' would greatly enhance one's experience of the place. Coleridge explains the difference as follows:

> At certain times, uncalled and sudden, subject to no bidding of my own or others, these Thoughts would come upon me, like a Storm, & fill the Place with something more than Nature. – But these are not contingent or transitory / they are Nature, even as the Elements are Nature / yea, more to the human mind / for the mind has the power of abstracting all agency from the former, & considering as mere effects & instruments, but a Shakespere, a Milton, a Bruno, exist in the mind as *pure Action*, defecated of all that is material & passive / . – And the great moments, that formed them – it is hard & an impiety against a Voice within us, not to regard as predestined, & therefore things of Now & For Ever and which were Always. But it degrades this sacred Feeling; & is to it what stupid Superstition is to enthusiastic Religion, when a man makes a Pilgrimage to see a great man's Shin Bone found unmouldered in his Coffin . . .

On the surface Coleridge's argument is fairly clear and consistent. Coleridge distinguishes between an artificially programmed association of a place with a famous person or incident in history and a completely spontaneous train of thought that transcends the immediate material object or circumstantial event which provoked it. His point is that by trying to induce some heightened thrill through linking Shakespeare to the mulberry tree he planted, one does neither the tree nor Shakespeare any service. On the one hand, one could not immerse oneself in a fully empathic experience of the tree due to the expectations of what an experience of Shakespeare's tree should be, along with the ensuing disappointment when the actual feelings were found to be ordinary. On the other hand, to link Shakespeare to his tree is in effect to confuse a spiritual presence, a thing of the mind existing as '*pure Action*' in the mind, with a material object. The failure to distinguish between 'things of Now & For Ever' and 'contingent or transitory' things is at the root of all idolatry and superstition. So far Coleridge's argument proceeds evenly and seems sure-footed. But it is by no means completed. Towards the end of his entry Coleridge's tone becomes more vehement as he launches an attack against the 'mass of mankind' who 'whether from Nature or . . . Error of Rearing & the Worldliness of their after Pursuits, are rarely susceptible of any other Pleasures than those of *amusement*, gratifications of curiosity, Novelty, Surprize, Wonderment from the Glaring, the harshly Contrasted, the Odd, the Accidental: and find in the reading of Paradise Lost·+·a task, somewhat alleviated by a few entertaining Incidents'. Next follows an attack on Johnson, both for his lack of interest in nature and his view of Milton, and finally, a brief memorandum on the subject of 'the virtues connected with the Love of Nature' for Coleridge's projected volume of poetry 'Comforts and Consolations'.

There is something intriguing about the closure of Coleridge's entry. The last three steps in Coleridge's line of argument have a distinctly Wordsworthian genealogy. Wordsworth himself had severely chastised the public for its 'craving for extraordinary incident' and 'degrading thirst after outrageous stimulation' to the extent that the 'works of Shakespeare and Milton, are driven into neglect'.[32] It is unclear whether Coleridge had Wordsworth's Preface to the *Lyrical Ballads* in mind towards the end of his entry. If, however, we assume (and this must remain a tentative speculation) that the reference to Wordsworth at the beginning of the entry is not a casual one but a stimulus for the whole entry, then the final part of Coleridge's argument acquires added significance. By suggesting that Wordsworth was not free from the love of the 'contingent' and by linking such habits with the vulgar taste for novelty, Coleridge has in effect included Wordsworth in the very category of people he criticized in the Preface to the *Lyrical Ballads*. At the same time, Coleridge has located himself within the sacred circle of those who respect the pure act of the mind – a circle which excludes 'all that is material and passive'. The nice Wordsworthian touch at the end of the entry concerning the 'virtues connected with the Love of Nature' does not cancel the fact that midstream in his argument Coleridge identified certain forms of nature worship as superstitious idolatry[33] and circumscribed the area of the sacred as that which contains 'something more than Nature', the spirituality of the human mind itself.

Characteristically, Coleridge's ambivalent feelings of dependence on and rejection of the Wordsworthian canon were not confined to private utterances in his journals but left their mark on his published works as well. I shall refer here to one example from Coleridge's poetry, namely 'Dejection: An Ode', and deal briefly with only a few moments in the dramatic development of the poem.[34] It need hardly be emphasized that the relationship with Wordsworth was at the heart of the crisis of imaginative inhibition that Coleridge analysed in 'Dejection'. As de Selincourt pointed out, 'the root idea of "Dejection"' was 'a conscious and deliberate contrast' between Coleridge and his more fortunate friend.[35] Predictably, in Coleridge's case such comparison led to a painful and debilitating complex of inferiority. By following the textual variants of the poem we can almost follow chronologically the effects of Coleridge's subordination to and gradual liberation from Wordsworth's commanding authority.

An examination of the several versions of 'Dejection' clearly reveals Coleridge's uncertainty in deciding whom he wanted to address in the ode. Coleridge successively changes the form of address from Sara ('Letter——', *CL*, II, 790–8) to William (Letter to William Sotheby of 19 July 1802 and to Sir George Beaumont of 13 August 1803 [*CL*, II, 815–19, 970–2]), to 'Edmund' (the *Morning Post* text published on 4 October 1802), and finally to the anonymous 'Lady' of the 1817 *Sibylline Leaves* version. Beverly Fields attributes this uncertainty to Oedipal tensions that made it difficult for Coleridge 'to separate his feelings for men from his feelings for women'. This is why the 'object of his emotions' in the poem can be interchangeably a male or a female.[36] But there is a significant difference in the ending of the various versions of the poem, depending on whether a man or a woman is the intended love object. As the closing lines in the following four versions indicate, Coleridge assumes a much more subordinate role towards his friend when he addresses Wordsworth or Edmund (a 'transparent sobriquet for Wordsworth', as de Selincourt puts it [p. 8]), than towards Sara or the anonymous 'Lady':

1. 'Calm stedfast Spirit guided from above, / O Wordsworth! friend of my devoutest choice, / Great Son of Genius! full of Light & Love / Thus, thus *dost thou rejoice*. / To thee *do* all things *live* from pole to pole . . .' (Letter to Sotheby)
2. 'O EDMUND, friend of my devoutest choice . . . Joy *lifts* thy spirit, joy *attunes* thy voice, / To thee *do* all things *live* from pole to pole . . .' (*Morning Post*)
3. 'By the Immenseness of the Good & Fair / Which thou see'st every where – / Thus, thus *should'st* thou rejoice! To thee *would* all Things live from Pole to Pole . . .' (Letter to Sara)
4. 'Joy *lift* her spirit, joy *attune* her voice; / To her *may* all things *live*, from pole to pole . . .' (*Sibylline Leaves*) [my italics]

In the first two versions, the poet-friend is presented as positively possessing the joy that ensures poetic creativity and, therefore, hardly needing protective prayers from the speaker. The *Morning Post* version makes clear that the friend is capable not only of maintaining his 'genial spirits', but also of teaching the speaker how 'to rejoice' with 'his lofty song'. The speaker's prayer in the end that his friend be visited by 'gentle Sleep, with wings of healing' seems incongruous, because there is no indication that things are other than 'good and fair' for the friend. In the early versions where Coleridge unfolds his doleful tale under the imagined scrutiny of Wordsworth, he virtually pushes himself into a position of complete uselessness. Years later when Coleridge revised the poem for his collection *Sibylline Leaves*, at a time when he experienced a period of significant productivity and, through the writing of *Biographia Literaria*, defined more clearly his differences with Wordsworth, he replaced Wordsworth with the anonymous 'lady' and at the same time granted the speaker a much more meaningful role in the end. This change is marked by a subtle shift from the present indicative of the letter to Sotheby and *Morning Post* versions to the optative mood that was present in the original letter to Sara.[37] Thus, it no longer appears that the friend is in full possession of joy as a *fait accompli*, and by implication more dependent on the speaker's selfless guidance and prayers.[38]

There is in 'Dejection' another Wordsworthian moment that also reveals Coleridge in the typically helpless role he assumed towards his friend: the story of the little lost child in Part VII, which alludes to Wordsworth's 'Lucy Gray'. As Irene Chayes notes, 'partly seeking a similar lyric inspiration from without and partly coming on it unexpectedly during his impromptu literary survey, the poet of "Dejection" begins in his reverie to re-compose another man's poem and for the moment become a poet again'.[39] As we have seen, Coleridge was in the habit of imitating Wordsworth in a desperate attempt at poetic survival, and such attempts usually failed. In a similar fashion, in 'Dejection' the very act of reformulating another man's work points to the absence of radical creativity on the part of the speaker, confirming his worst fears about the state of his 'genial spirits'.[40] The one revision Coleridge introduced in his version of 'Lucy Gray', namely the change of focus from the parents' to the child's despair, indicates Coleridge's own self-projection as a dependent and helpless being, rather than an actual rebirth of poetic vigour at the heels of his poet-master.

But dependency is not the only mood voiced in 'Dejection'. We have seen previously that Coleridge's sense of inferiority towards Wordsworth was invariably accompanied by a strong drive towards self-assertion. The speaker of 'Dejection' repeatedly slips in and out of two roles that closely parallel Coleridge's divided reactions to Wordsworth: one is the role of a defeated poet, opening his wounds, so to speak, to dwell on his despair and to invite the pity and protection due to the defenceless; the other is that of a man who finds considerable power in speculative insights and the benediction of a friend. It is certainly not from a position of a defenceless and injured poet that Coleridge formulates the doctrine of creative joy in stanzas IV and V. The tone here is as assertive as it is confident, and as Suther sensed, it is even a little overly insistent.[41] The speaker is aware that he is in possession of a precious gift, the knowledge of nature's complete dependence on the life of the mind, a knowledge that is not given to the 'sensual and the proud' and, evidently, needs to be preached even to the 'pure of Heart'. In effect, Coleridge holds before Wordsworth the bright torch of higher knowledge, which he is willing to pass on to his friend in order to protect him from the dark passage of dejection where Coleridge remains imprisoned and alone. Coleridge thus achieves a double victory on both intellectual and moral grounds. He becomes the enlightened philosopher–poet, teaching, as he had hoped Wordsworth would, that the mind rules over and is not ruled by the senses. At the same time Coleridge presents himself in the flattering posture of a disinterested poet, seeking nothing for himself and keeping nothing to himself, but caring only for the well-being of another.

The partial record I have reconstructed here of the progressive alienation of Coleridge and Wordsworth shows all the conflicting attitudes and desires that are at the heart of such separations. Coleridge's inclination to surrender both poetry and nature to Wordsworth often brought him into the arena where courteous chivalry gave way to contest, just as his desire to subordinate his artistic goals to those of his partner merely intensified his need for independence. In his effort to locate a 'distinct current' of his own, Coleridge found it imperative to reject Wordsworth's cult of nature and isolate himself in the magic sphere of the mind which contained '*pure Action*, defecated of all that is material & passive'. It is difficult to tell whether Coleridge's existing ambivalence towards nature led to his disagreement with Wordsworth, or whether the Wordsworthian challenge provoked a much more radical denial of nature than would otherwise have occurred. But the difficulty itself suggests that much of the text of Coleridge's love song and breach of loyalty to the 'Goddess Nature' is buried in the psychic history of a most extraordinary literary friendship.

CHAPTER 3 SELF AND NATURE: THE EARLY POETRY

In this chapter I shall examine primarily some of Coleridge's early poems but also works from a later period ('Dejection: An Ode' and related prose passages) in which an encounter with nature becomes the central event and leads to various reflections on the possibilities and dangers of a close intimacy with natural objects and, conversely, on the incapacitating effect of a complete separation from them. Some of these poems ('The Eolian Harp', 'Reflections on having left a Place of Retirement') give us a better sense of the difficulties Coleridge had in establishing a relationship with nature prior to the period when he developed close literary and personal ties with Wordsworth. Other works indicate the existence of intellectual influences, such as Schelling's natural and aesthetic philosophy, that compounded Coleridge's dilemmas in sustaining a balanced interaction with external objects. Coleridge, it appears, either surrenders the self to nature to such an extent that he must face the consequences of broken domestic and social ties, or he protects so firmly the independent power of the mind that he finds himself deprived of the nourishing contact with nature. By moving too close to nature Coleridge also approaches positions that are pantheistic and at odds with orthodox Christian belief; by giving the self full priority over nature Coleridge encounters the threat of subjective idealism of the kind advocated by Berkeley, which breeds solipsism and destructive desires. In order to mediate between these two equally unsettling extremes, Coleridge developed a philosophy of symbolism which aimed at establishing the coexistence of nature with a fully independent and imaginative mind sustained by transcendent aspirations. But, as we shall see, the symbol for Coleridge in the end heightened rather than settled the tensions that beset his amorous courtship of 'Lady Nature'.

There are few poems in the early Coleridge in which a communion with nature, however intense and fulfilling it may be, does not involve the poet in a conflict of rival desires and uncertain resolutions. In 'Lines: Composed while climbing the Left Ascent of Brockley Coomb' (1795), the poet's increasingly exuberant response to the panoramic mountain landscape ends, none the less, in disappointment, as he finds his joy incomplete without sharing it with his beloved. In 'Reflections on having left a Place of Retirement', the difficult mountain ascent offers the speaker the rewarding experience of nature's divine unity and the integration of self and objects. But even such an experience, which leaves no wish unsatisfied and allows the speaker to immerse himself in a unique 'luxury' of pure being, appears to be of limited value in the face of social commitments that require the abandonment of individualistic pursuits.

There is, moreover, considerable ambivalence in the early Coleridge regarding the way in which a union of self and nature should occur. Coleridge explored two main possibilities of reaching the desired oneness of subject and object, placing in each case a different emphasis on the part contributed by the two agents of this complex transaction. At one end of the spectrum it appears that the mind partakes of an all-embracing unity by journeying towards nature and by learning to interpret its varied alphabet of 'shapes and sounds'. (In this alternative, harmony is presumed to lie within nature, and the self merely accomplishes the task of finding an entry into the organic unity of the outer world.) At the opposite end, priority is given to the self, which is represented as the originating voice of all of nature's melodious language.

The first alternative, in its most optimistic form, is best illustrated by 'This Lime-tree Bower my Prison'. The speaker of this poem is able to overcome his initial feelings of deprivation and resentment at being confined to his bower by reconstructing in his mind the itinerary taken by his more fortunate friends. As he follows his friends' journey from the narrow dell to the gradually expanding landscape 'Beneath the wide, wide Heaven', his sense of confinement disappears, his attitude towards his friends changes from envy to a more generous disposition of empathy and, energized by what Keats would call a rising 'pleasure thermometer' of imaginative participation in the life of objects, the speaker reaches a climactic experience of the spiritual oneness of nature:

So my friend
Struck with deep joy may stand, as I have stood,
Silent with swimming sense; yea, gazing round
On the wide landscape, gaze till all doth seem
Less gross than bodily; and of such hues
As veil the Almighty Spirit, when yet he makes
Spirits perceive his presence. (ll. 37–43)

Intense perception of outward objects thus provides the means by which the mind accomplishes its feat of grasping the presence of a spiritual power in the world of sense. In turn, this visionary expansion nourishes a more refined and a richer sensory awareness. Returning to the bower, the speaker discovers a plenitude of visual and aural delights in the very place he had earlier regarded as a barren desert; his conclusion, that nature always offers its bounty to those 'Awake to Love and Beauty' (ll. 59–64), reflects the progress he has made towards a deeper understanding of nature.

'This Lime-tree Bower my Prison' gives us the most optimistic version of one viable strategy in bringing about the harmony of self and nature that clearly grants priority to the latter. The mind is by no means passive in its interchange with outer objects, perception itself being an activity which is sustained by feeling and imagination. But the presupposition remains, none the less, that unity is inherent in the natural world and it is the mind's task to uncover it. The psychological forces that are at play in this poem, directing the subject towards his climactic vision of the mountain landscape, correspond to some observations Coleridge developed about the picturesque regarding the immediate effects of spatial bodies upon the mind.[42] Thus, the first signs of a change of disposition in the speaker appear when he confronts the extended landscape stretching as far as the 'wide Heaven' and the open sea. From then on, the roads are open for the speaker to experience the natural world more intensely and to understand its laws more fully. The assumption conveyed by this poem is straightforward enough: in order to escape from unproductive self-confinement, the subject must place itself in nature's hands and grant nature the prerogative of setting down the rules of their mutual commerce. From nature's side the ground rule, as Emerson phrased it, is: 'he [man] is my creature, and maugre his impertinent griefs, he shall be glad with me'.[43]

Perhaps the clearest presentation of this point of view appears in the opening section of 'The Nightingale', a poem Coleridge included among his compositions for the *Lyrical Ballads*. The poem begins with a refutation of the traditional association of the nightingale with melancholy, which provides the speaker with the opportunity of reflecting on the differences between a genuine and a false rapport with nature. The false approach is to project one's sorrows onto nature and to view everything in the outside world merely as a mirror of personal moods and desires. The temptation exists for man to fill 'all things with himself' (l. 19) and thus become impervious to any influence from the outside. Just this error caused some distant poet of the past to represent the nightingale as a melancholy bird and 'profane / Nature's sweet voices, always full of love / And joyance!' (ll. 41–3). Coleridge's advice to future poets is to rid themselves of old conceits and begin to experience nature on its own terms:

> When he [the Poet] had better far have stretched his limbs
> Beside a brook in mossy forest-dell,
> By sun or moon-light, to the influxes
> Of shapes and sounds and shifting elements

Surrendering his whole spirit, of his song
And of his fame forgetful! so his fame
Should share in Nature's immortality,
A venerable thing! and so his song
Should make all Nature lovelier, and itself
Be loved like Nature!

(ll. 25–34)

The proper encounter with nature requires a renunciation of self-assertiveness on the part of the subject. The poet must give up his ambition to increase his productivity and acquire more fame until he has made contact with a higher power, which is the source of all enduring artistic expressions. Physical relaxation is an initial step towards achieving a state of receptivity to external influences, and the poet is invited to lie down in a 'mossy forest-dell', the Romantic version of a psychiatric couch. By surrendering the self to nature, the poet can hope to create a viable work of art that will render a truthful image of nature.

'The Nightingale' is an important exhibit of Coleridge's view of nature, not only because it spells out unambiguously the terms of a successful interaction between the mind and external objects, but also because it provides a revealing point of contrast to Coleridge's further elaborations of this problem. Elsewhere, Coleridge claims that the submission of the self to nature is a fruitless course to take since nature's own life and one's 'genial' powers depend entirely upon the mind. 'Dejection: An Ode' comes to mind as the obvious example, but I shall postpone, for the moment, an examination of the poem and turn instead to a speculative document where Coleridge's changed attitude towards nature receives its fullest philosophic treatment. This occurs in a passage from the thirteenth lecture ('On Poesy or Art') of the 1818 course, in which Coleridge discusses, among other topics, the concept of imitation in art, following closely the arguments of Schelling's essay 'Über das Verhältniss der bildenden Künste zu der Natur' (*CN*, III, 4397). Here Coleridge points out that the familiar proposition 'Art is the imitatress of Nature' is valid only in so far as the object of imitation is the spiritual essence of nature (*natura naturans*) and not its external appearance (*natura naturata*).[44] If the artist copies nature blindly, he engages in 'an idle rivalry' which can only result in the creation of lifeless masks; similarly, if he starts with a preconceived idea of beauty, he will produce empty forms devoid of reality. The artist must grasp the spirit of nature (*Naturgeist*) which 'presupposes a *bond* between *Nature* in this higher sense and the Soul of Man'. It is precisely the realization of this bond which defines the Genius in the arts. The 'Man of Genius' contains within him both unconscious activity of the order of nature and conscious activity which belongs to man and thus becomes 'the Link that combines the two'. Coleridge recommends the following steps concerning the way in which artists must go about the business of rendering nature in their works:

> This is true Exposition of the Rule, that the Artist must first *eloign* himself from Nature in order to return to her with full effect. – Why this? – Because – if he began by mere painful copying, he would produce Masks only, not forms breathing Life – he must out of his own mind create forms according to the several Laws of the Intellect, in order to produce in himself that co-ordination of Freedom & Law . . . which assimilates him to Nature . . . He absents himself from her only in his own Spirit, which has the same ground with Nature, to learn her unspoken language, in its main radicals, before he approaches to her endless compositions of those radicals – Not to acquire cold notions, lifeless technical Rules, but living and life-producing Ideas, which contain their own evidence / and in that evidence the certainty that they are essentially one with the germinal causes in Nature, his Consciousness being the focus and mirror of both – for this does he for a time abandon the external *real*, in order to return to it with a full sympathy with its internal & actual . . .

The first step towards a *rapprochement* with nature is, despite all apparent paradox, a movement away from nature. The ethic that must guide the artist in his pursuit of nature is renunciation and temporary postponement of his desired intimacy with outward forms. To find nature means, essentially, to discover the basis of its affinity and link with man, that is, nature at its highest point as self-realization. This link exists only within man's consciousness, which must become the primary field of artistic exploration. Only after the artist has mastered the alphabet of nature as spelled by the laws of the intellect can he return to nature with a full appreciation of its inner life. The 'speaking face of earth and heaven', by itself, does not yield knowledge of nature's language, contrary to what Coleridge had previously taken to be the most trustworthy tool for his son's education.[45] The book of nature may be inscribed on 'lakes and shores / And mountain crags' ('Frost at Midnight', ll. 57–8), but the key to its intelligibility is possessed solely by the mind. We notice here a complete reversal of the premises that inform the dialectic between self and nature in Coleridge's conversation poems.

The assumption conveyed by these poems is that nature's grammar can be inferred from its vocabulary of shapes and sounds and that nature itself is the 'prime teacher' that turns man into a competent reader of its works. In his lecture, on the other hand, Coleridge argues that nature's grammar must be known prior to, and not derived from, its 'endless compositions'.

The conversation poems share with Coleridge's essay the notion that nature has affinity with and permeates man's unconscious life, as exemplified by the models of interaction presented in 'The Nightingale', such as the birds' spontaneous production of songs and the child's instant change of mood at the sight of the moon (ll. 75–82; 98–105). But the difference is that while in the former instance the artist is advised to move towards nature in order to commune with the unconscious wells of his being, in the latter he is taught to turn his attention away from nature and direct it to the mind, which is the harbour and true mirror of nature's spirit. While the coalescence of subject and object, of conscious and unconscious activity, is in both instances regarded as the source of authentic art, in the former the unifying power rests with nature, in the latter with the mind.

Coleridge's tendency to assert the priority both of nature over the self and of the self over nature reflects a common problem in English Romanticism, namely the coexistence of a strong penchant for subjective idealism with an equally powerful attraction to naturalism. Clearly, Romanticism is neither subjective idealism exclusively nor a return to naturalism; both attitudes exist in nearly all of the authors of the period and are continually qualified by being played off against one another.[46] The power and complexity of *The Prelude* depend on Wordsworth's ability to keep both alternatives alive and to compose a poem which is at once a love song about nature and a massive epic of the self. In Shelley's *Alastor*, to refer to another example, the spotlight falls on the manner in which a narrator of Wordsworthian sentiments for nature confronts a solipsistic character fully committed to an inward dream. The narrator's overdrawn descriptions of the natural scenery traversed by the youthful poet during his journey, to which the hero himself is mostly oblivious,[47] show the excesses that a too-zealous worshipper of nature is liable to commit. On the other hand, seen through the narrator's ambivalent attitude towards his hero, and the tenuous moral viewpoint upheld by the speaker in the preface to the poem, the young poet appears in turn as a potentially tragic hero at war with forces beyond his control, and as a deluded idealist, as a man to be commended for his unswerving pursuit of an ideal or to be despised for his lack of love for real human beings. If the Romantics seem to swing too readily from one pole to the other in their handling of the dialectic between subject and object, it is not for lack of clear-sighted understanding of the problem, but because they are too sensitive to the possible risks of any one position to recommend it with full and steady confidence.

In Coleridge's case the risks are pantheism and the loss of individuality and freedom at one end of the spectrum, and subjective idealism and loss of contact with external objects at the other. Coleridge saw both the luminous and the dark side of the two strategies for achieving the ideal communion of self and nature discussed above. Thus, if nature is to be given priority and the self is to be 'sent . . . abroad' to partake of a higher realm of being, the danger exists that it could be swept away by an external force and rendered a passive link in an infinite chain of interconnected parts. By surrendering his spirit to nature, as the speaker of 'The Nightingale' advises, man may not only fail to supply a sizeable contribution to the commerce with outward objects, but may also lose control over his inner world of thoughts and feelings and begin to entertain highly suspect speculations and modes of action. These anxieties appear in sharper focus in 'The Eolian Harp', a poem that reveals the irresolutions and conflicts over which in 'This Lime-tree Bower my Prison' Coleridge achieved a one-time victory. In the second part of the poem the speaker journeys to a nearby hill and executes to the letter the instructions Coleridge later codified in 'The Nightingale'. Stretching on a slope of the hill in a comfortable position, the speaker abandons himself to a state of passive receptiveness to nature's 'shapes and sounds'. Gradually, the speaker becomes mesmerised by the reflection of the sunbeams on the sea to the point where he can no longer exert any control over his train of thoughts and 'flitting phantasies' that move across his 'indolent and passive brain / As wild and various as the random gales / That swell and flutter on this subject Lute' (ll. 40–3). The speaker is aroused from his trance by a bold speculation imaging the world as a system of 'organic Harps diversely fram'd, / That tremble into thought, as o'er them sweeps / Plastic and vast, one intellectual breeze, / At once the Soul of each, and God of all?' (ll. 45–8). The speculation, as soon as it is phrased, is shot down by a mere glance of disapproval from his chaste wife and dismissed as an unworthy product of 'the unregenerate mind'.

Many readers have found the end of 'The Eolian Harp' anticlimactic and have been bothered by Coleridge's self-flagellating confession of guilt and his hasty adoption of Christian faith.[48] The artistic debility of the last section of the poem has less to do, however, with Coleridge's poor selection of a substitute for his personal metaphysics than with the fact that a substitute is needed at all when the entire energy of the speaker has been channelled into the act of constructing this metaphysics around a progressive experience of the harp. Clearly, something much more compelling than a 'mild reproof' from his chaste companion causes the speaker's final repudiation of his reflection on the universe of animated harps.[49] As Paul Magnuson points out, Coleridge's repeated revisions of the poem indicate that he was never at ease with the symbol of the harp as a model for the mind's union with nature.

> The obvious problem is that if the mind is like an eolian harp, it is completely passive, and its products do not depend upon the active powers of the mind itself. . . . If the soul, the 'I' is like a tune, then the mind as it appears in the poem has no control over itself. The tune is 'wild,' 'various,' and 'random.' Coleridge recognized that the theology was heretical because the 'I' would be irrationally and capriciously constructed. Furthermore, there is the hint that he was afraid that in his own case his speculations on the 'I' might be true, that his self was merely an indefinite collection of random notes, unpredictable, unconnected, and without a unifying consciousness.[50]

Aside from presenting a direct threat to the independent activity of the mind, the speculation entertained by the speaker also implicates him in a more serious heresy due to the metaphoric equivalence established between God and nature *via* the unifying 'intellectual breeze', a position that bears, unavoidably, the stigma of pantheism.[51] To purge the symbol of the harp of its pantheistic residue, Coleridge added in the *Errata* to the 1817 edition of his poems (*Sibylline Leaves*) a new version of his meditation on the organic unity of nature, which he maintained in subsequent editions of the poem. The function of lines 26–9 ('O! the one Life within us and abroad, / Which meets all motion and becomes its soul, / A light in sound, a sound-like power in light, / Rhythm in all thought, and joyance every where') is to tighten the loosely phrased speculation of lines 44–8 into a more controlled argument that leaves God out of the picture and cancels any overt suggestions that the mind is a passive instrument played upon at random by an external power. The syntax of the passage is so carefully constructed as to make it difficult to determine which is the originating voice of the harmonious union of life and which the echo, thus leaving open the possibility that the self, the 'Life within', might be that voice. The passage also conveys a greater sense of interiority than of spatial expansiveness that dominates the speaker's metaphoric presentation of universal harmony in lines 43–

8. The accent in lines 26–33 falls on a unifying centre which holds things together. Objects move into each other, converging, as it were, at one and the same point; light is present in sound, sound in light, spirit is contained in motion, while motion is incorporated in 'all thought'. The suggestion that the territory of this marvellous confluence of the inner with the outer world might be the mind itself is implanted in the section of the poem immediately preceding lines 26–33. As the harp becomes the object of an inner fantasy, transporting the speaker into a fairy-land of bewitching melodies, its meaning as a symbol for the mind's relationship with an external agency begins to alter (ll. 13–25). The wind which strikes the strings of the harp produces within not a 'correspondent breeze', but, in Wordsworth's words, a veritable tempest, 'a redundant energy, / Vexing its own creation' (*The Prelude*, Bk I, ll. 37–8). The music made by the harp takes on a life of its own, unconfined and self-perpetuating, as illustrated by the vivid image of the birds of Paradise, 'footless' and 'wild', which neither 'pause, nor perch, hovering on untam'd wing!' (ll. 24–5). By implication, the mind is projected as having bottomless energies of its own, independent of an external power.

Coleridge undoubtedly chose the right segment of the poem to transplant his later metaphysics of the 'one Life', which subtly shifts the emphasis to the active powers of the mind.[52] But while the new part accords well with the neighbouring body of the earlier text, it throws out of balance the latter section of the poem,[53] and, in the view of some commentators, it invalidates the speaker's repudiation of his metaphysics at the end. On the one hand, it is difficult to see how a firm and more mature enunciation of the doctrine of the 'one Life' would precede rather than follow a tentative and less safe speculation on the same subject. On the other hand, as some critics have argued, since the later formulation of this doctrine does not confuse God with nature but 'uses the less complex "Life" and "motion" to intimate their greater counterparts', Coleridge's fears about pantheism and his final rejection of the symbol of the harp on this ground are insubstantial.[54] This may be true, but it is also possible to see that Coleridge's closing remarks apply, though to a lesser degree, to his statement of lines 26–33. The theory of the 'one Life' is not foolproof. While God is not brought down to the level of nature, no serious attempt is made to assert the separate authority of a divine agency in legislating the extent of its involvement in the sweeping unity of life. Yet, the suggestion that the mind plays an active role in its interaction with nature is never made explicit but kept in suspense by the tight syntax of the statement, which conveys a relationship of perfect equivalence between mutually inclusive entities.

Thus, Coleridge's later formula, however deftly phrased, leaves enough leeway for an unsympathetic auditor to misread his intentions and beliefs.

In 'Dejection: An Ode' Coleridge quite predictably moves towards a much more radical position concerning the primacy of the mind in its dealings with the world of sense. But 'Dejection' is itself rife with paradoxes and ambiguities. The theory giving radical priority to the mind over nature does not emerge out of a set of firmly-established beliefs, but as an alternative to an older doctrine that is first explored and then found to be obsolete. And no sooner is the new theory asserted than some life begins to stir in the corpse of the old one.

As the poem opens, the speaker's attention is once again caught by the eolian harp, but this time the harp no longer pours forth 'delicious' music like a 'coy maid half yielding to her lover' ('The Eolian Harp', l. 15), since the wind has changed from a caressing partner to a violent, tempestuous and savage force, destroying the inner balance of the instrument. The harp, as Wordsworth picked up the image in *The Prelude*, 'Was soon defrauded, and the banded host / Of harmony dispersed in straggling sounds, / And lastly utter silence' (*The Prelude*, Bk I, ll. 97–9). The 'defrauded' harp signals portentously the end of the poet's faith in a guaranteed interaction between self and nature predicated by the unifying 'intellectual breeze'. The change to a new creed cannot be made suddenly, however, or without undergoing a severe crisis, as suggested by the poignant image of the new moon with the old moon in her lap, 'foretelling / The coming-on of rain and squally blast' (ll. 13–14).[55] Thus, in the first two parts of the poem the speaker still holds on to familiar habits and beliefs, hoping, as was the good fortune of the persona in 'This Lime-tree Bower my Prison', to overcome his 'wan and heartless' mood by sending his soul 'abroad'. But the stubborn attempt to provoke an eruption of feelings by keeping his eyes fixed on the beautiful appearances of outer objects proves to be pointless and leads to the realization that this activity no longer holds the promise of bringing about miraculous cures for a sickly self.[56] The speaker's first reaction to this realization is complete desolation, since, according to the code presupposed by the old doctrine, if nature withdraws its favours, the imagination is doomed to die:

> My genial spirits fail;
> And what can these avail
> To lift the smothering weight from off my breast?
> It were a vain endeavour,

> Though I should gaze for ever
> On that green light that lingers in the west:
> I may not hope from outward forms to win
> The passion and the life, whose fountains are within.
>
> (ll. 39–46)

At the end of stanza III the speaker makes a subtle accommodation to his unhappy situation by perceiving that it may be related to a mistaken assumption as to where the healing power for the self lies. Not the outward forms but the inner forces of the self are the source of the 'passion and the life' one may experience in the neighbourhood of nature. The insight, as soon as it is grasped, grows to full bloom in the next two sections, engaging the speaker in the act of elaborating the doctrine regarding the interaction between self and nature that temporarily liberates him from the burden of dejection. The new doctrine is announced in celebratory language; its components are well known. It is the soul which imparts life to what otherwise would remain an 'inanimate cold world', and 'from the soul itself must issue forth / A light, a glory, a fair luminous cloud / Enveloping the Earth' (ll. 53–5). More precisely, it is joy which, first nourished within the soul, becomes 'the spirit and the power, / Which wedding Nature to us gives in dower / A new Earth and new Heaven'; and 'thence flows all that charms or ear or sight, / All melodies the echoes of the voice, / All colours a suffusion from that light' (ll. 67–75).

Critics commonly quote these lines out of context to illustrate either Coleridge's or the Romantic poet's characteristic way of regarding the commerce between mind and nature. Abrams finds in the fourth and fifth stanzas of 'Dejection' a cluster of metaphors that best express the Romantic conception of the mind as an active power projecting, like a lamp, its own radiance into the inanimate world.[57] But, as Suther cautioned, the theory concerning the primacy of the mind over nature is voiced in the language of protestation and is repeated rather too insistently for us not to wonder about the psychological pressures behind Coleridge's assertive stance.[58] Even if we take the theory for granted,[59] it still represents only a phase in the speaker's formulation of his beliefs and less conscious desires. Thus, as the speaker tests this theory upon himself, he discovers that it provides little encouragement and is hardly a comfortable faith by which to live. Looking over his past and present state of imaginative power, the speaker finds that he is subject to an irreversible process of decay. If the regeneration of the self cannot be helped by nature and if the self does not appear to possess a mechanism of auto-regeneration, then the final result will indeed be complete emotional stasis, the 'stifled, drowsy, unimpassioned grief' the speaker described in the second stanza. But the speaker makes a further adjustment to his situation, turning his attention away from painful self-analysis to the wind which 'long has raved unnoticed' (l. 97). In effect, the speaker appeals once again to an external force as a rescue measure for his impaired self, a gesture that represents a clear departure from his earlier affirmation of nature's total subordination to the mind. Perhaps, as Harold Bloom has suggested, the speaker's presentation of the wind as a 'bad actor, overplaying, or a worse poet, raving bombast' is an implicit acknowledgement of his own overly dramatic stance in stanzas II–VI (*The Visionary Company*, p. 225).

By identifying himself with the wind, the speaker is able to overcome his crisis of emotional paralysis and regain a healthier state, though not one approximating a full imaginative recovery.[60] He can at least feel cleansed enough of 'viper thoughts' to articulate his prayer for the well-being of his friend. As at the end of 'Tintern Abbey', the speaker expresses his hope that his friend will be protected from the ills of his own fate, that what for one was violent storm would turn out to be but a 'mountain birth' of joy and gaiety for the other.[61] But unlike Wordsworth, whose prayer for Dorothy was linked with hopes of personal salvation, Coleridge merely extends the protection of his good wishes to his friend, without entertaining any illusions of thus regaining the 'language of' his 'former heart' and 'former pleasures'.[62]

'Dejection' remains the record of a profound crisis of identity, complicated by Coleridge's relationship to the Wordsworth circle. To the extent that we can separate Coleridge's conception of nature from the web of personal problems with which it is intimately connected, it is fair to say that 'Dejection' postulates not one but two points of view regarding the relationship between man and nature.[63] The view that the self is the sustaining, life-giving force of nature is prominently expressed, and it is the reaffirmation of this position which brings the poem to a more serene end. On the other hand, the speaker's conclusion in stanza III, that outward forms cannot influence the life of the self, is premature when tested against his subsequent response to the wind and his need to believe that the self is dependent, like a child, upon the protective magnanimity of outside forces. When Coleridge sent a copy of 'Dejection' to William Sotheby, he particularly wanted to emphasize the latter approach. Concluding his letter to Sotheby with an apology for sending 'such a long verse-cramm'd Letter', Coleridge wished that he had sent instead an 'Image' of a 'glorious' skyscape that he proceeds to describe with obvious emotional involvement and vivacity. It is as if Coleridge, by way of a covert commentary on 'Dejection', tries to deny that the activity of sending his soul 'abroad' means as little to him as he claimed in the first part of the poem (*CL*, II, 819).

In an article on Coleridge's view of nature, Douglas Brownlow Wilson argues that 'Dejection' 'embodies a major thrust of Coleridge's thinking – the dominion of the human mind over its vassals the senses', but the poet 'achieves this dominion at the painful expense of forfeiting his healing relationship to nature'. Wilson points out that Coleridge found a much more satisfying position in a symbolic approach to nature that 'firmly establishes the lordship of the mind over nature, but without the sacrifice of health' and without 'denying a life in nature'.[64] Although, in my view, 'Dejection' neither forfeits completely a healing relationship with nature nor asserts exclusively the supremacy of the self over nature, it is worth pursuing Wilson's suggestion and examining the components of a symbolic approach to nature. This is, in essence, the apprehension of nature as it relates to law and to the faculty of reason; that is, nature as the receptacle of the universal. According to Wilson, the distinction between *natura naturans* and *natura naturata* supplied Coleridge with a philosophic basis for his theory of symbolism and a viable strategy of maintaining the doctrine of the 'one Life' while keeping pantheism at a safe distance. This distinction has already appeared in the passage from Coleridge's lecture on 'Poesy or Art' I examined earlier (pp. 54–6 and n. 44 above) and I want to return to it and follow a bit more closely Coleridge's argument. We have seen before that in his definition of art as an imitation of nature, Coleridge adopts Schelling's notion that the artist must seek to become acquainted with nature as an active force participating in the life of reason rather than as a mere collection of external phenomena available to the senses and the understanding. Schelling's theory undoubtedly presented Coleridge with a number of attractive features, the most important one being the presupposition that nature and the human mind share the same ground and are thus permanently wedded to one another. The theory also establishes the rule that the marriage between mind and nature takes place within the territory of the mind which, as Coleridge puts it, is 'the focus and mirror of both' and the place where nature achieves its highest 'moment of *self-exposition*'. Thus, Schelling's formula appears to validate both the priority of the mind over nature (as *natura naturata*) and its oneness with nature (as *natura naturans*); it maintains therefore the hierarchy of spirit over matter without presenting them as heterogeneous entities. This should be, then, an ideal theory for Coleridge to embrace. But as Coleridge elaborates Schelling's doctrine, he begins to encounter difficulties in accepting the philosopher's system. After following Schelling's essay up to a point, Coleridge, in characteristic fashion, redirects what had appeared to be a perfectly satisfactory argument. This is evident in a brief interpolation immediately following the passage quoted on p. 55 above, where Coleridge appears to discover certain directions in Schelling's theory that approach dangerously the tenets of radical idealism:

> Of all, we see, hear, or touch, the substance is and must be in ourselves – and therefore there is no alternative *in reason* between the dreary (& thank heaven! almost impossible) belief that every thing around us is but a phantom, or that . . . Life which is in us is in them likewise – and that to know is to *resemble*. When we speak of Objects out of ourselves, even as within ourselves to learn is, according to Plato, only to *recollect*. – The only effective Answer to which (that I have been fortunate enough to meet with) is that which Mr. Pope has consecrated for future use in the Line–
>
> And Coxcombs vanquish Berkley [*sic*] with a *Grin*. (*CN*, III, 4397)

This passage has no analogue in Schelling's essay. Schelling makes no reference to Plato or Berkeley and feels no need to rescue his system from the ghost of subjective idealism. After presenting his thesis that the artist must distance himself from nature as product in order to 'regain it a thousandfold', Schelling calmly expands his argument, stating that the artist should imitate the 'indwelling spirit of nature' that is within all forms of the phenomenal world, a line which Coleridge himself resumes after the passage just quoted.[65] Why, then, does Coleridge consider it necessary to invoke Berkeley at all and finish him off hastily with a derisive line from Pope?[66]

In his appropriation of Schelling's thesis, Coleridge veers off from the original and finally finds himself pushed into a position that resembles ominously the language of radical idealism. As Kathleen Coburn points out, Schelling, in the true spirit of Platonism, regards the artist's departure from nature as 'a metaphysical flight of the spirit to the realm of pure idea', while 'Coleridge thinks of the mind's own need of forms, shown by the artist's willing acquiescence in the requirements of the medium'.[67] Coleridge conceives of the artist's course as a flight not so much upward as inward, into the centre of his own being, the crossroads where the human and the natural intersect. The statement that 'Of all, we see, hear, or touch, the substance is and must be in ourselves' logically extends the changed course taken by Coleridge in his elaboration of Schelling's thesis; it means quite simply that the essence and life-giving power of nature reside within the self, or, to quote 'Dejection', that 'in our life alone does Nature live'. It does not necessarily follow from this proposition that the external world has no separate existence apart from the self, since the 'substance' Coleridge talks about pertains to *natura naturans* and not to *natura naturata*. Yet, the phrasing of the argument in the language of the senses, coupled with the emphasis on the self, must have alerted Coleridge to the fact that he was coming close to Berkeley's position that 'there is not any other Substance than *Spirit*, or that which perceives'.[68] What comes with Berkeley is the unpalatable reduction of the physical world to a collection of ideas and sensations which exist solely in the perceiver's mind,[69] a notion that did not fare well with Coleridge. As he pointed out in *Biographia Literaria*, Berkeley's idealism is no better than materialism in that both doctrines remove 'all reality and immediateness of perception', and place us 'in a dream world of phantoms and spectres, the inexplicable swarm and equivocal generation of motions in our own brains' (*BL*, I, 92).

The unwelcome appearance of Berkeley in the midst of Schelling's argument indicates that even a symbolic approach to nature based on the affirmation of the primacy of the mind did not settle all of Coleridge's anxieties and doubts. A vague fear still lingers in Coleridge's mind and is obliquely expressed in his invocation and hasty rebuttal of Berkeley. By seeking nature in his own spirit, the artist may end up conversing solely with himself rather than holding a genuine dialogue with outward forms. The return to nature after an interval of decontamination from its sensory products might be difficult, and we recall Coleridge's entry of 1809 (*CN*, III, 3420 cited on p. 30 above), where the disconnection from nature is seen as producing a partial amnesia of what the outward objects and the feelings associated with them might signify. Schelling believes that the artist's initial flight from nature secures for him a bountiful and unproblematic gain, and he phrases his argument in a few even-paced and straightforward sentences. Coleridge articulates a similar viewpoint, but in an expansive and meandering rhetoric that becomes more insistent when Coleridge has to explain the rationale for the artist's departure from nature. Finally, the rhetoric collapses under its own weight as Coleridge, turning Schelling's thesis inside out, perceives that what begins as an elevated conception of nature ends as a reduction of nature to an imaginary projection of the self.

Without further difficulty, Coleridge resumes the path traced by

Schelling past this halting point. The interpolation on Berkeley is, in a sense, incongruous if only because an attack on idealism is out of place in a context where the immediate concern is the subject of imitation in art. Coleridge, in effect, pushes Schelling's argument out of the area of aesthetics into that of epistemology. The leap here is much more marked than in *Biographia Literaria* where in my view Coleridge does not depart as drastically from Schelling as critics have generally claimed. By constructing an ontology out of what in Schelling appears to be a strictly epistemological treatment of self-consciousness, Coleridge merely makes explicit the fact that Schelling's arguments hover around an infinite 'I AM', albeit not the personal God of Christianity.[70]

The Berkeley episode shows that a heavy emphasis on the primacy of the mind, which is a prerequisite of what Wilson calls a symbolic approach to nature, is not free from the threat of a potential devaluation of the physical world and the collapse of the mind's dialogue with nature into a spurious dialogue with itself. In Coleridge's personal experience a retreat into subjectivity often meant not a purifying ascent to a spiritual ideal, but a descent into 'the unfathomable hell within' that led to progressive isolation and artistic sterility. Paradoxically, the way Coleridge mapped his escape from the trap of subjectivity was precisely by following the path of a symbolic relationship with outer objects. We are thus obliged to circle back to the same issue with which we began. It should be clear from the previous discussion that for Coleridge a symbolic approach to nature was both a highly promising solution to the unification of self and objects and a problem in itself; to see this in its entirety, however, we must examine more closely the main components of Coleridge's conception of symbolism.[71]

CHAPTER 4 COLERIDGE'S PHILOSOPHY OF SYMBOLISM

Although Coleridge left relatively few statements on the symbol, critics have generally paid special attention to his philosophy of symbolism. Undoubtedly, Coleridge gave the symbol privileged status in his writings, and regarded it not only as a literary trope, superior to allegory, but as an elevated means of attaining self-knowledge and moral values. For Coleridge the symbol made possible the fellowship between the sensible and the super-sensible world, man and nature, the self and other individuals. All this is evident in Coleridge's often-quoted definition of the symbol in *The Statesman's Manual* (*SM*, p. 30). But I am primarily interested in a different record, composed of several notebook entries that precede *The Statesman's Manual* definition and reveal more clearly the psychological and philosophical underpinnings of Coleridge's emerging conception of symbolism. These entries show that the idea of the symbol grew out of Coleridge's experience of love and helped him work out personal problems in his relationship with Sara Hutchinson. Moreover, they indicate that nature loses much of its importance for Coleridge the more he links the symbol with increasingly higher goals, such as the unity of consciousness and the mind's quest for an ideal model of perfection in the Absolute. For Coleridge the symbol ultimately requires a free activity of the mind that finds its sustenance in human agents rather than nature. The ideal symbol for Coleridge becomes one that is dislodged from its middle position between the universal and the particular and moves closer to its point of destination in the Absolute, which is also the place of its extinction. Coleridge found such ideal symbols more readily among love objects than natural objects.

Perhaps the most general thing that can be said about the Coleridgean symbol is that at all times it is conducive to a unity of some kind. From the moment a particular object acquires symbolic functions, it loses its separate identity and becomes part of and modified by a whole; thus, it is no longer identical with its corresponding counterpart in the physical world, being lifted onto an ideal plane of existence. In a sense, the symbol represents the means by which the phenomenal world can be redeemed of its otherness and its forbidding physicality and brought into closer communication with the self. As objects are permeated by a higher power and absorbed into a spiritual totality, they are recognized by the self as kindred entities and transformed into characters from which the self composes the language of its own aspirations. We recall the passage from *The Statesman's Manual* where, gazing at a flowery meadow and meditating on the process of organic growth in plants, Coleridge finds in nature's symbolic intimation of the 'higher life of reason' a model for the mind's ideal relationship to the divine creator (*SM*, pp. 71–3). And we recall, of course, the often-quoted notebook entry where, somewhat more hesitantly though no less eloquently, Coleridge explores the way in which the self finds meaning in objects of nature:

> In looking at objects of Nature while I am thinking, as at yonder moon dim-glimmering thro' the dewy window-pane, I seem rather to be seeking, as it were *asking*, a symbolical language for something

> within me that already and forever exists, rather than observing any thing new. Even when that latter is the case, yet still I have always an obs~~cure~~cure feeling as if that new phaenomenon were the dim Awaking of a forgotten or hidden Truth of my inner Nature / It is still interesting as a Word, a Symbol! It is <u>Λογος,</u> the Creator! and the Evolver! (*CN*, II, 2546)

Coleridge begins his meditation in a faltering language, punctuated by such qualifying words as 'seem', 'rather', 'as it were', 'even if', 'yet still', 'as if'. The assertive tone at the end of the entry indicates that Coleridge reaches some conclusive resolution, but we must not overlook the tentative turns of Coleridge's reflection, lest we miss much of what the resolution is all about. The centre of uncertainty appears to be related to the status of Coleridge's activity of reading symbolic meanings in natural objects. Is Coleridge 'seeking' or merely 'asking' for a 'symbolical language' for the self? The haste with which he confronts the possibility that the latter might be the case indicates that he is sufficiently worried about the distinction between seeking and asking. It is possible to infer from Coleridge's note that he involuntarily stumbled onto the question as to whether a link between the outer and inner world exists in actuality or is fabricated by the self to satisfy its own needs.

We have already seen enough instability in Coleridge's positions regarding the interaction between self and nature to suspect that at the time the entry was written (1805) this issue could be unsettling. To seek in nature a vocabulary for a subject's self-knowledge would, in effect, imply that an essential rather than arbitrary connection exists between 'perishable Things' and 'imperishable Thoughts' (*CN*, I, 1575), and that objects of nature constitute, therefore, an authentic mirror through which a subject can regard the 'forgotten or hidden' truths of its 'inner Nature'. On the other hand, to *ask* for a symbolical language (that is, to *desire* it) would automatically place on the self the burden of validating its subjective needs, thereby casting some doubt upon the manner in which the self uses objects of nature. Coleridge resolves this dilemma by removing the issue altogether from the realm of 'obscure feeling' and by collapsing the distinction between seeking and asking. Coleridge finally diverts attention from the relationship between objects of nature and the self and, instead, directs it to the relationship between these objects and the Absolute.

The move is urgent enough to generate a syntactical equation between physical objects, symbols and the Absolute,[72] a position that Coleridge later would have found untenable on both philosophical and religious grounds. For, according to Coleridge's definition in *The Statesman's Manual*, a symbol can never be confused either with the object that serves as its sensory carrier, or with the greater reality it designates. A symbol is from the very start a mixture of the individual and the general, of the temporal and the eternal, and a synthetic unit is always different from any of its components. Even according to earlier statements made by Coleridge, the symbol, while it is consubstantial with the higher power it embodies, or rather *because* it is, still 'tends towards it ever' (*CN*, II, 2540); that is, it always points to but never reaches completely the fullness of an absolute unity. But leaving aside all the tangles in which Coleridge implicates himself at the end of the entry, he clearly succeeds in removing all uncertainty regarding the authenticity of his quest. By showing that objects are united with a divine *logos*, Coleridge implicitly asserts that 'asking' and 'seeking' are equivalent acts that are part of a meaningful process of self-discovery. The self can never go wrong in seeking the symbolical language it desires. Through natural objects, the self will discover not only the hidden truths of its own being but also the ultimate source of those truths, which is 'the Creator! and the Evolver!'

Coleridge's meditation, despite its brevity and the underlying currents of uncertainty so characteristic of his notebook writing, provides us none the less with rich information regarding his philosophy of symbolism, virtually isolating its main constituents. Coleridge ultimately binds the symbol to the Absolute, a direction that brings us to *The Statesman's Manual* passage and that we shall observe in other instances. We also notice that the external objects which enter Coleridge's meditation compose a sparse landscape, devoid of physical details. These objects are, notably, a celestial body which is a source of light (the moon) and a transparent medium through which light filters into a room (the dewy window-pane). From the very beginning the landscape is apparently not a purely external environment but a largely emblematic one. The moon and window-pane embody two essential qualities that characterize symbolic objects in the Coleridgean scheme – light and translucency. Objects which generate light naturally intimate divine light, thus projecting the human mind's highest destination. Similarly, translucent objects do not attract attention to themselves, but form a discrete ladder conducting the mind towards the greater reality they represent. The remarkable thing about Coleridge's notebook entry is that in the process of inquiring about the nature of symbols Coleridge has in effect constructed them.[73] In addition, this very confluence of direct experience and conscious reflection (which marks so many of

Coleridge's notes) comments on and reinforces a main part of his philosophy of symbolism. As Anthony Harding aptly puts it, for Coleridge the symbol 'has no *intrinsic* meaning. It acquires meaning, it exists as symbol, only when it is part of the process of knowing.'[74] Only when symbols are linked with the activity of a 'Being seeking to be self-conscious' (*CN*, II, 3026) can they be saved from lapsing into empty figures of speech.

Several other elements can be discerned in Coleridge's note which further clarify his thinking on the symbol. First, the natural objects of Coleridge's symbolic landscape, though not depending on the life of the self for their existence, depend on it for their relative worth and power. According to Coleridge's meditation, an external phenomenon becomes 'interesting' – that is, acquires meaning – to the extent that it reveals to the perceiver a particular fact of consciousness of which he had previously no distinct awareness or recollection. However 'new' and undiscovered an object might appear, it cannot in fact feed the mind any information it did not already possess, albeit unconsciously. Through natural objects the mind does not learn a new language but merely recovers the innate language it was born with. Thus, all perception of outer objects is basically an act of recollection of inner, pre-existent and eternal truths. There are obvious Platonic echoes in Coleridge's note that, as other examples will show, usually accompany his reflections on the symbol. In this instance, one is reminded of Plato's dictum (which Coleridge was fond of reiterating) that all knowledge is recollection,[75] though it is important to bear in mind that for Plato the process of recollection either by-passes phenomenal objects or employs them only as a demonstration of their imperfection and inadequacy.[76]

Coleridge's use of Plato here, with one essential difference, not only illustrates his characteristic way of handling the systems of other philosophers, but also reveals directly his divided feelings towards the natural world. By insisting that external objects cannot add to the already existent repository of the mind's ideas, Coleridge undoubtedly has restricted whatever power the natural world holds over the self. Yet, at the same time, by implicating natural objects in the process of self-discovery, he has also granted such objects more value than they would have in a Platonic system. Implicit in Coleridge's note is the statement that the self would have no way of recognizing its own activity without physical objects that externalize or lend 'outness', to use a Coleridgean term,[77] to the self's internal landscape. In the absence of sensory signs the truths that lie hidden in the deepest recesses of consciousness would remain forever buried, while various thoughts and impressions rising to the surface would be forced to return to the silent regions of the self. As Jean Paul Richter wrote in an eloquent passage of *Vorschule der Aesthetik*, 'There are feelings in the human breast that remain inexpressible until one uses all the physical attributes of nature in which they arose like perfumes, as words to describe them.'[78] In his notebook meditation, Coleridge, while ostensibly subordinating the natural world to the self, also presents the self as utterly dependent on that world and unable to know itself without it. Thus, the natural world appears at once as subservient to and vitally needed by the self, at once of limited and far-reaching power.

In later notebook entries, Coleridge tested further the mind's need for external objects as a means of grasping its own activity and the origin of ultimate truths. By way of private experience and his inveterate habit of self-analysis, Coleridge came to realize the absolute necessity of symbols to the most rudimentary act of thinking and cognition in general. No 'generous mind', Coleridge wrote in 1808, can either think or live without a symbol (*CN*, III, 3325). The mind's self-originating thoughts have a tendency to proliferate rapidly to the point where they 'crowd each other to death'. As often as 'one thought leads to another', Coleridge observed, musing on a deficiency of his memory, 'so often does it blot out another' (*CN*, III, 3342). The only thing that saves the mind from losing itself in the vertigo of unarticulated impressions, too faint to recollect, is its ability to find some sensory medium through which it can externalize its ideas and regard them from a distance, as it were. As Ernst Cassirer writes, spelling out in a comprehensive philosophy of symbolism some of Coleridge's own insights, the very highest and purest spiritual activity 'is known only by and in the aggregate of the sensible signs which it uses for its expression'. For the mind the symbol represents

> the first stage and the first demonstration of objectivity, because through it the constant flux of the contents of consciousness is for the first time halted, because in it something enduring is determined and emphasized . . . For the sign, in contrast to the actual flow of the particular contents of consciousness, has a definite ideal *meaning*, which endures as such. It is not, like the simple given sensation, an isolated particular, occurring but once, but persists as the representative of a totality, as an aggregate of potential contents, beside which it stands as a first 'universal'.[79]

There is nothing in Coleridge's entry of 1808 that approximates any such coherent definition of the symbol as given by Cassirer. It is rather in the later *Statesman's Manual* assessment of the symbol as abiding 'itself as a living part in that Unity, of which it is representative' that we recognize more distinctly the affinity between Coleridge's and Cassirer's views. And yet it is important to examine closely Coleridge's notebook entry, for here Coleridge makes greater claims regarding the psychic necessity of symbol-making than is evident in *The Statesman's Manual* passage. Coleridge turns the symbol into a psychic imperative indispensable to an individual's survival, just as for Cassirer the symbol represents a cultural imperative, the very means by which myths and other forms of human creativity come into being and are preserved.[80]

> All minds must think by some *symbols* – the strongest minds possess the most vivid Symbols in the Imagination – yet this ingenerates a *want*, <u>ποθον</u>, *desiderium*, for vividness of Symbol: which is something that is *without*, that has the property of *Outness* (a word which Berkley [*sic*] preferred to 'Externality') can alone fully gratify / even that indeed not fully – for the utmost is only an approximation to that absolute *Union*, which the soul sensible of its imperfection in itself, of its *Halfness*, yearns after, whenever it exists free from meaner passions, as Lust, Avarice, love of worldly power . . . I say, every generous mind not already filled by some of these passions feels its *Halfness* – it cannot *think* without a symbol – neither can it *live* without something that is to be at once its Symbol, & its *Other half* . . . Hence I deduce the habit, I have most unconsciously formed, of *writing* my inmost thoughts – I have not a soul on earth to whom I can reveal them – and yet
>
> 'I am not a God, that I should stand alone'. (*CN*, III, 3325)

We notice from the very beginning that Coleridge regards symbol-making as an innate function of the mind coinstantaneous with the act of thinking. The faculty of the imagination is not the sole generator of symbols, inasmuch as symbols are already present at the earliest stages of mental activity. Yet the imagination plays a very important role in that it intensifies the vividness of symbols to the point where the mind is overstimulated, as it were, by its own energy and seeks for a richer vividness outside itself which stabilizes and satisfies its desires. Coleridge speaks of two different kinds of symbols here that are mutually dependent on one another. The mind possesses symbols of its own that arise prior to and independent of linguistic expression or other forms of externalization. But the mind also finds in its own store of symbols an absence which only 'something that is *without*' can fill. There are, then, inner and outer symbols, symbols which have their origin in the self and symbols which are derived from an external source. Much depends on the latter, for while inner symbols might sustain some form of mental or imaginative activity, outer symbols alone sustain the soul and life itself. The outer symbols provide what the mind can never have or achieve by itself, namely the means of perfecting itself through union with an external object and, in more ordinary terms, companionship. At the end of the entry, Coleridge shows that the need to verbalize inner thoughts is directly related to the mind's inability to subsist without extending itself outward in an effort to escape the utter solitude of the self. As Coleridge put it earlier, 'Language & all *symbols* give *outness* to Thoughts / & this the philosophical essence & purpose of Language' (*CN*, I, 1387). Language becomes therefore a primary source of symbolic expression, as readily productive of outer symbols as thinking is of inner symbols.

Yet Coleridge makes it clear that man searches for a higher and more gratifying symbol than language can provide and, therefore, depends on language only as a last resort when other means of self-realization are not available. What man desires most is a symbol which in a sense is bigger than itself, is more than a symbol, i.e. an object which is at once the mind's 'Symbol, & its *Other half*'. Language relieves solitude in so far as, by externalizing thoughts, it turns the mind into its own companion, but this is ultimately an exchange of one form of solitude for another. Language is not something one seeks actively but something one falls into 'unconsciously'. But the ideal symbol Coleridge speaks of is one which impels the mind to undertake a quest for an 'absolute *Union*' in the course of which it perfects itself, even though it can only come nearer to and never fully reach its goal. Such a symbol does not merely reflect like a mirror what the mind already possesses within itself, but also embodies what the mind ought to have and to yearn for. While it shows the mind's 'imperfection', the symbol offers itself as the '*Other half*' the mind needs to become whole; it destroys itself as symbol at the very point where the mind reaches its desired perfection.

Coleridge's ideal symbol, we can infer, is a human being, and the complicated relationship of mind and symbol he describes is no other than human love. Moreover, the 'absolute *Union*' Coleridge refers to, compared to which the union of two beings is only 'an approximation', must be the divine *logos* itself. Two other notebook entries contain a more explicit confirmation of these inferences. In the first, written in 1807, Coleridge reflects on the relationship of love to duty and inclination and then goes on to define the relationship of love and self-consciousness:

> Deeply important that Incarnation & Transfiguration of Duty as Inclination,? when it is that a sense of Duty lessens inclination – from what imperfection in the sense this arises – & how a perfect sense makes it impossible to will aught else. This height of Love / – Reality in the external world an instance of a Duty perfectly felt. How to make Duty add to Inclination. The necessary tendency of true Love to generate a feeling of Duty by increasing the sense of reality, & vice versâ feeling of Duty to generate true Love. All our Thoughts all that we abstract from our consciousness & so form the Phaenomenon Self is a Shadow, its whole Substance is the dim yet powerful sense that it is but a Shadow, & ought to belong to a Substance / but this Substance can have no marks, no discriminating Characters . . . it is simply Substance – & this deepliest felt during particular phaenomena with a consciousness that the phaenomenon is in us but *it* not in the phaenomenon, for which alone we yet value the phaenomenon, constitutes the craving of True Love. Love a sense of Substance / Being seeking to be self-conscious, 1. of itself in a Symbol. 2. of the Symbol as not being itself. 3. of the Symbol as being nothing but in relation to itself – & necessitating a return to the first state, Scientia absoluta. – Discontent, when pain, when joy – when is it quieted? In virtuous *action* – Sensuality itself a symbol of this or counterfeit action / (*CN*, II, 3026)

This entry marks an important stage in the development of Coleridge's conception of the symbol. It shows that Coleridge connects the symbol with a specific philosophy of love relationships and ethical behaviour. Nature is conspicuously (and not accidentally) absent in this entry. Coleridge is primarily interested in establishing the identity of a moral, fully self-conscious 'I AM', which frequently involved the severance of his ties with nature. From the very start Coleridge attempts to formulate a different view of morality to that he found in Kant's ethical theory.[81] Unlike Kant, who insisted on the incompatibility of duty and natural inclinations, Coleridge is interested in the affinity between the two and their convergence in love.[82] In Coleridge's view, Kant made a major error when he restricted the meaning of moral acts to an agent's performance in accordance with the principles of duty, making no allowance for a state of being which is independent of 'mere *Actions*, in the vulgar sense'.[83] Coleridge wanted a moral theory that would validate not merely man's stoic fortitude against his natural self, but also feelings of sympathy and love, which were themselves 'actions', though distinct from performance in a Kantian sense (*CN*, I, 1705).

In his notebook entry Coleridge evades the Kantian dichotomy between duty and inclination by introducing a middle category, love, and by shifting significantly the meaning of the two terms. Duty, as defined by Coleridge here, does not involve exclusively a rational act or an absolute ethical standard. It is a quality, a mode of feeling, that reaches its highest perfection at the time it assumes the identity of inclination. Coleridge next redefines the meaning of inclination in such a way that the 'Incarnation & Transfiguration of Duty as Inclination' would appear to be the fulfilment of duty and not its sacrifice. He resorts to another equation, that between inclination and love, which, in turn, requires a careful definition of love, for lurking in the background is Kant's view that love and inclination are equivalent and therefore outside the moral sphere. Indeed, the delicate framework of a reconstituted system of morality now rests entirely on Coleridge's ability to elevate love to a function that even a supporter of Kant would have difficulty dismissing.

We notice that Coleridge immediately links love with an individual's quest for a unified, substantive self, raising love to as high a level as Kant and his followers would reserve for 'apperception' and 'self-consciousness'. But for Coleridge love, in contradistinction to a unified self for Kant or Schelling, increases a subject's sense of 'Reality in the external world', and with it, one's feelings of duty towards other beings.[84] Only by acknowledging 'the action of kindred souls on each other' (*CL*, II, 1197), the fact that other beings modify our thoughts, will an individual attain self-consciousness and behave morally towards others. (In effect, from a Kantian perspective, love for Coleridge fulfils both a theoretical and a practical role.) The symbol appears in this context as a valuable reminder that the mind by itself can never overcome its 'halfness' and is doomed to a shadowy, imperfect existence. Yet, while revealing the mind's incompleteness, the symbol also provides the mind with the means of acquiring a 'sense of Substance', that is, the knowledge that substance, which has no sensory marks, can never reside in any one phenomenon but only in the state of union between two agents 'Intensely similar, yet not the same' (*CN*, I, 1679). Just as the mind would be condemned to a purely phenomenal existence without symbols, the symbol would have no meaning apart from a self-conscious being. Thus self and symbol are mutually dependent on one another and their particular bond is established by love. This enables Coleridge to introduce an even more striking revision of Kant's ethical theory by presenting sensuality as a form of symbolic expression for love and as connected therefore with 'virtuous action'. To admit sensuality into the sphere of moral action is to stretch the allowance for inclination to its limits.[85] Yet Coleridge insisted that sensuality can be redeemed of all impurity if one learns to regard another being not as an object of physical desire but as a symbol pointing to a state of wholeness. The important thing is to view sensuality 'in the symbolic sense', as a way of allowing the self to become 'great and good' by 'spreading thro' and combining with all things'.[86]

We have come a long way from Coleridge's earlier understanding of the symbol as the means of recovering some forgotten truths of one's being or of making thinking and cognition possible. Here Coleridge establishes the symbol as the bastion of morality, securing a mode of behaviour that saves man from sinking into a shadowy existence, selfishness or animal desires. From the symbol as a vehicle of moral purification to the symbol as an instrument of religious fulfilment is but a short step, which Coleridge willingly takes:

> The best, the truly lovely, in each & all is God. Therefore the truly Beloved is the symbol of God to whomever it is truly beloved by! – but it may become perfect & maintained lovely by the function of the two / The Lover worships in his Beloved that final consummation of itself which is produced in his own soul by the action of the Soul of the Beloved upon it, and that final perfection of the Soul of the Beloved, ⟨which is in part⟩ the consequence of the reaction of his (so ameliorated & regenerated) Soul upon the Soul of his Beloved / till each contemplates the Soul of the other as involving his own, both in its givings and its receivings . . . and thus still keeping alive its *outness*, its *self-oblivion* united with *Self-warmth*, & still approximates to God! Where shall I find an image for this sublime Symbol ⟨which ever⟩ involving the presence of Deity, yet . . . tends towards it ever! (*CN*, II, 2540; April 1805)

This entry may well be regarded as the single most comprehensive notebook record of Coleridge's conception of the symbol, bringing together the individual strands we observed in the other examples. Here Coleridge clarifies fully the role played by symbols in love relationships and a subject's search for self-perfection. There is at the core of each person, Coleridge claims, an ideal self constituted by the noblest parts of one's being, which maintains the status of man as originally created in God's own image.[87] For Coleridge the ideal self is not the product of a private vision that endures as long as that vision is sustained; nor does it come into being in any one individual except as a mere potentiality awaiting fulfilment. The ideal self is created through the interaction of two agents who are intent on attaining ultimate self-knowledge and offer themselves to one another as a mirror in which each can perceive 'two Souls as one, as compleat . . . as the *ever-improving* Symbol of Deity' (*CN*, II, 2530). In love relationships, which represent the purest form of such a partnership, two beings independently act on and receive the influence of the other to the point where each contemplates 'the Soul of the other as involving his own'. The lover is engaged in a double act of self-finding and 'self-oblivion', seeking not only his own perfection but also the perfection of the beloved and ultimately achieving the former through the latter. Conversely, the beloved, herself a 'Being seeking to be self-conscious' through a symbol, remains completely receptive to the influence of her partner and thus projects for the lover an image of his own soul as enshrined within hers with the added halo of unity. For Coleridge the ideal self is forged and maintained only in the ongoing process of 'givings' and 'receivings' between two 'Intensely similar' beings.[88] It is here that one must look for the origins of a 'pure Will' and the principles of moral conduct.

While Coleridge relaxes the boundaries of the ethical realm to include acts that are not of a purely rational nature, he makes the acquisition of a moral being every bit as exacting as Kant's 'categorical imperative'. The laws of the heart can be as rigorous and demanding as the laws of reason, and fit for saints rather than ordinary men. Coleridge's frequently voiced feelings of incompleteness and his choice of utterly deprived and companionless figures as embodiments of his habitual self[89] testify that Coleridge has placed the principles of morality beyond the scope of ordinary human possibilities. There is first the matter of connecting the ideal self with the will of two individuals rather than one. From Coleridge's model we can infer that if one of the partners were to falter or withdraw from the quest for self-knowledge, even temporarily, the entire effort of the other partner directed towards self-improvement would collapse. The ideal self is not something given once and for all, but something that needs to be continually formed by two individuals whose souls must remain attuned to one another, like two clocks set to keep perfect time with one another.[90] The difficulties inherent in the realization of Coleridge's ideal self are perhaps best seen from the very inappropriateness of the mechanical analogy to the workings of the human psyche.

By being associated with the somewhat precarious though fully desirable attainment of the ideal self, the symbol is already charged with a complicated function. Coleridge puts an even greater burden on the symbol by expecting it to connect with a transcendent 'I AM' in such a way that it does not violate either the permanent distance between the Absolute and an individual being, or their kinship. Evidently, the successful realization of the ideal self depends entirely on the adequacy of the symbol to represent the deity. This is evident in the question Coleridge raises towards the end of the entry: 'Where shall I find an image for this sublime Symbol which ever involving the presence of Deity, yet . . . tends towards it ever!' The uncertainty as to whether Coleridge can find his ideal symbol is undoubtedly related to the difficult task he expects it to perform. For Coleridge the symbol must render divinity as simultaneously immanent and transcendent. This aspect of the Coleridgean symbol has not been clearly seen by critics, who emphasize either Coleridge's attachment to the transcendental source of the symbol at the expense of its material existence, or his belief in the full power of the particular to embody the universal (see n. 71 above). The example before us illustrates that Coleridge tries to sustain a much more comprehensive, albeit tenuous concept. For Coleridge, the symbol must indeed always partake 'of the reality which it renders intelligible', but not to the extent that it fully constitutes this reality. Coleridge believes that the symbol can generate a closer proximity between the Absolute, the eternal 'I AM' and man's individual existence in the world of phenomena. That much the symbol must accomplish. But at the same time, the symbol is meant to preserve a distance between the two levels of being, which is as vital to man as the air he breathes. There are, of course, obvious theological reasons which explain Coleridge's unwillingness to do away with this distance. With divinity brought too close to the surface of things, pantheism threatens to erupt. But there are also equally compelling psychological reasons. For Coleridge man is capable of perfecting himself as long as there are goals to pursue and as long as such goals are yet to be accomplished. The quest for an ideal self must, therefore, remain a quest without a finite boundary, an activity with a determinate destination but without a point of arrival. Man's humanity lies in his capacity for continuous growth and his ability to yearn for the betterment of his condition. What ultimately nourishes man's desire for self-improvement is the existence of an absolute model of perfection which is God himself, the 'purely & absolutely ONE' (*CN*, I, 1680), a being the scholastics defined as 'actus purissimus sine ulla potentialitate' (*BL*, I, 94; *CL*, II, 1195). As Coleridge put it, without God 'Man ceases to be Man, and either soars into a Devil or sinks into a Beast.'[91]

In this context, we can better interpret Coleridge's stringent rule that the symbol must 'involve the presence of Deity' only to the degree that it can still tend 'towards it ever'. Only if a symbol projects a point of destination for the mind does it carry out its appointed function. In a symbol, substance is simultaneously present and absent, and it is just this void within each representational sign which goads the mind to seek the fullness of a supreme reality. An effective symbol gives man a foretaste of wholeness but not wholeness itself and thus stimulates his desire 'to *totalize* – to make a *perfectly congruous whole* of every character' (*CN*, I, 1606). In all of the entries on the symbol I have discussed there is a recurrent language of yearning and desire, coupled with the metaphysics of a partly immanent, partly transcendent substance, that appears to provide for Coleridge the proper ambience to sustain desire. Every time Coleridge comes too close to asserting that an ideal totality is within the reach of two beings who have achieved oneness, he makes an immediate qualification. The symbol can never 'fully gratify' one's desire for complete unity, for to gratify would mean to destroy desire itself and with it any incentive for self-improvement; nor can the union of two beings amount to more than an 'approximation to that absolute *Union*' (*CN*, III, 3325) towards which the soul is 'driven by a desire of Self-completion with a restless & inextinguishable Love' (*CN*, I, 1680). The symbol's special function is not only to relate substance to phenomena, but also to keep them apart and teach the mind that approximation cannot be mistaken for identity.

Coleridge insists on this distinction in another entry concerned not with religious matters but with aesthetics:

> Hard to express that sense of the analogy or likeness of a Thing which enables a Symbol to represent it, so that we think of the Thing itself – & yet knowing that the Thing is not present to us. – Surely, on this universal fact of words & images depends by more or less mediations the *imitation* instead of *copy* which is illustrated in very nature *shakespearianized* / – that Proteus Essence that could assume the very form, but yet known & felt not to be the Thing by that difference of the Substance which made every atom of the Form another thing / – that likeness not identity – an exact web, every line of direction miraculously the same, but the one worsted, the other silk. (*CN*, II, 2274)

The Shakespearean example of a protean spirit equally capable, as Keats put it, of 'conceiving an Iago as an Imogen',[92] provides Coleridge with the opportunity to meditate on the difference between genuine mimesis and mechanical imitation[93] and, in this context, to examine the principles of symbolic representation. The relationship between symbol and substance remains basically the same as in previous entries, but we are given here a new set of terms and metaphors that display Coleridge's views from a fresh angle. As usual, Coleridge begins his meditation by raising a problem that is puzzling at first but to which he finds a satisfactory solution in a few succinct propositions. The issue at hand is to understand how symbols in general and language in particular signify a reality that is never present to us as such, and yet, like a powerful magnet, draws our entire attention to itself. What, in symbols, Coleridge asks, invites us to by-pass their physical immediateness, to look through them as it were, and to think only of 'the Thing itself' which is, after all, an absent entity with no distinguishing marks? (We can already perceive in Coleridge's inquiry the germinating seeds of his later emphasis on the necessary transparency of the symbol as a condition of its embodiment of the Absolute.)

Coleridge finds the best answer to this question provided by Shakespeare himself, the capacious genius who could pass 'into all forms of human character and passion' and become 'all things, yet for ever remaining himself' (*BL*, II, 20). Shakespeare demonstrates through the inexhaustible characters and roles he assumes that the most viable artistic form never duplicates but merely resembles its original source, be it an internal or external one. If form is to remain a true imitation of substance, it must always look both like and unlike substance 'by that difference of the Substance which made every atom of the Form another thing'.[94] Clearly, what safeguards the vitality of a work of art for Coleridge is its power to return continually to its own origins and point beyond itself to an essence, an informing idea, that is 'above Form', since that which 'puts the forms together can not be itself form' (*CN*, III, 4397 f. 53). As Coleridge explained in 'On Principles of Genial Criticism', the most enduring art forms that cannot be substituted by any others are those which 'in the least possible degree, distract the attention, in the least possible degree obscure the idea of which they . . . are the symbol' (*BL*, II, 238). By extension, all language and symbols are effective to the degree that they become unobtrusive, creating an 'empty doorway' pointing to the infinite, an absence which most nearly expresses 'the Thing itself'. (Pushed to its extreme implication, this stance would suggest that the purest symbol is the symbol that destroys itself in order to merge with the inexpressible, just as the most eloquent page of writing would be the page that becomes blank.) In aesthetics, as in matters concerning morality and religion, Coleridge wanted to secure the sanctity of a spiritual power by keeping it distinct from its manifestations. Just as for Coleridge the ideal self is independent of any actions it might perform in the world of practical ends, similarly, the generative power in art, the productive imagination, is prior to and never equivalent with its products. This is not to say that between essence and form, substance and its symbolic language, 'poetry' and 'poems' (*BL*, II, 8–13) there exists an intrinsic disparity that cannot be transcended. Coleridge merely suggests here that distinction does not necessarily imply division,[95] just as likeness is not equal to identity, or, to use Coleridge's metaphor, fine silk is not the same as worsted cloth. The existence of a difference between spirit and form is precisely what stimulates the rebirth of creative activity, for all activity, like any physical journey, requires a point of destination distinct and at a distance from the departure point. The success of artistic forms and of symbols in general depends on their power to intimate a reality that they cannot fully embody and to project a space for a mental journey from the particular to the universal, from the finite to the infinite, from a specific image to the informing idea or 'free life' behind it.

The sampling of Coleridge's statements given thus far should suffice to provide us with some of the representative assumptions and norms that govern his thinking on the symbol, but the implications of Coleridge's views bear further scrutiny, especially with reference to their effect on his engagement with nature. As we re-examine Coleridge's notebook entries, we can distinguish several indications of a potentially divisive element at the heart of the Coleridgean symbol. On the one hand, Coleridge seems firmly committed to the idea that without sensible mediation of some kind, ultimate truth is inaccessible – be it God's word in the religious sphere, the truth of one's 'inner Nature' and the ideal self in the psychological and moral sphere, or the artist's originating intuitions in the aesthetic domain. From this position Coleridge is bound to emphasize not just the need for the symbol but, more importantly, the symbol's miraculous fitness to the tasks it is meant to perform, and, by extension, the adequacy of language, as of nature, to represent the world of the spirit. It is in this context that we are likely to hear claims about the consubstantiality of the symbol with the reality it designates, about the 'living continuity' between '*Words* and *Things*' or the sacramental character of nature. As Coleridge writes in *The Statesman's Manual*, nature should be regarded as 'the other great Bible of God', and like the Bible itself, should be read figuratively, as 'the expression, an unrolled but yet glorious fragment, of the wisdom of the Supreme Being' (*SM*, p. 70 and n. 3). Such claims originate from Coleridge's belief that ideas of reason are, as Kant demonstrated, not merely regulative, but constitutive, being present in the world of experience as unifying 'energies', and as accessible to intuitive organs of reflection as the material world is to organs of sense.[96] Ultimately such claims, as so many other of Coleridge's fundamental tenets, centre on the belief in a personal, loving God, who does not hide from but communicates with man by revealing himself through all forms of nature, the meanest object not excluded, and by having endowed man with the capability of 'beholding, or being conscious of, the divine light' through the power of reason.[97] In a universe where ultimate truth is not regarded as a delusive ambition of reason (as in Kant) and where the spirit of God, in whom all truth resides, is '*Overflowing*' through the entire creation 'by its communicativeness' (*SM*, p. 91), the symbol acquires a well-defined and important role, as the very means of actualizing the desired communication between lower and higher levels of being.

And yet we also find in Coleridge's reflections a visible strain that presses against, or at least qualifies, the version of the symbol presented above. We have seen from previous examples that Coleridge takes great care to place the symbol at a remove from the Absolute, so as not to reduce substance to any of its manifestations but to hold out for a subject the prospect of continuous self-improvement. While Coleridge clearly subscribed to the Christian view of a loving and intelligible God, he was equally intent upon maintaining the sense of God's mystery and incomprehensibility,[98] for to presume complete knowledge of God would be to commit the religious heresy of equating God with the created world, and the equally unpardonable heresy of overestimating the capacity of human reason. The more Coleridge emphasized the transcendence of the infinite 'I AM' and the craving of a self-conscious subject to attain access to, if not full knowledge of, the Absolute, the more likely it is that he would tend to divest the symbol of its ties with the phenomenal world and ultimately discard the symbol altogether. Since the symbol always remains somewhere behind substance, the being who wishes to communicate with the Absolute must, while employing the symbol at some stage, eventually by-pass it. As Shawcross observed, looking at some passages from 'The Destiny of Nations', for Coleridge the phenomenal world, being symbolic of a spiritual reality, represents the medium through which 'spirit meets spirit; but in that contact the symbol is forgotten, the means is discarded in the attainment of the end; or if it still abides in consciousness with the reality which it figures forth, yet its presence is secondary and subordinate'. This means that the symbol is 'only co-present with the direct consciousness of the ideal', but neither 'co-existent with' the ideal itself, 'nor yet an essential medium to its fruition' (*BL*, I, Introd., pp. xix–xx). And this also implies that access to the ideal can be gained through a direct, inner intuition without the mediation of either sensory objects or rational and linguistic categories, a notion that Coleridge often found attractive and that has an entangled ancestry in Neoplatonic, mystical and Schellingian thought.[99] Such a notion clearly renders the symbol dispensable, or if it does not do away with the symbol altogether, validates only such symbols as are utterly transparent and 'in the least possible degree obscure the idea' they represent. Thus, Coleridge writes approvingly of the mystics' conception of beauty as 'the subjection of matter to spirit so as to be transformed into a symbol, in and through which the spirit reveals itself', and their sense that an object is '*most* beautiful, where the most obstacles to a full manifestation [of spirit] have been most perfectly overcome' (*BL*, II, 239).[100] This definition suggests that the most successful symbol is that which is least in the way of the march of spirit and so nearly transforms matter into spirit as to destroy its own material existence.

It is evident from the potentially self-annihilating tendencies of the Coleridgean symbol and its progressive distance from the material world that the activity of symbol-making does not secure for Coleridge, as Wilson believes, a healthy relationship with nature, but may in fact put this relationship in greater jeopardy. The place occupied by nature in Coleridge's symbolic schema is problematic at best, and this is perhaps felt even more strongly in those passages where Coleridge openly points to nature as the repository of symbolic material for the self or of the sacred language of God. We have already seen Coleridge limiting the role of natural objects to that of aiding the self in recollecting its own knowledge, which comes from sources other than the immediate world of experience (p. 70 above). Similarly, if we turn to the most outspoken celebration of nature as an ideal receptor of divine light and pregnant with symbolic meaning – I refer, of course, to Coleridge's extended meditation on the symbol in *The Statesman's Manual* (*SM*, pp. 71–3) – we find that even here Coleridge exhibits uncertainties in locating the degree to which the mind can participate in, or must keep its distance from, the universal harmony embodied by nature.

From the very moment that Coleridge rests his gaze on a flowery meadow, he discovers himself on the other side of nature, neither integrated nor at peace with it. The sight of the meadow provokes an immediate awareness of the difference between the serene life of nature and the far less blissful life of the mind, which cannot escape 'guilt or anguish'. Nature appears to Coleridge as showing no sign of inner conflict, 'no lamenting word', and as untroubled as a 'beautiful infant that has fed itself asleep at its mother's bosom'. By contrast, the mind is subject to 'aching melancholy' and mixed feelings of aspiration and defeat, particularly as it views itself through the harmonious and self-satisfied spectacle of nature. What the mind discovers in nature is a state of fulfilment through unobstructed receptivity to the divine laws of reason – a discovery which sadly points to the mind's fallen condition and the hard road it must travel to recover its lost innocence. For the mind is not, like nature, privileged to respond spontaneously to divine light 'by an act not its own'; rather, the mind must engage in a strenuous effort to orient its acts 'in the light of conscience' through vigilant prayer and 'a watchful and unresisting spirit'. While nature, by virtue of its mere existence, partakes of the 'transmitted power . . . of God', the mind must strive continually to make itself 'permeable to a holier power' and become that which nature already is.

Coleridge's experience of the meadow clearly evolves into a complex awareness both of the ideality of nature as a model of receptivity to divine light and of the limitations of such a model with regard to the workings of the mind. His meditation carries an ambiguous message regarding the prospects of intimacy between the mind and nature in the act of symbol-making.[101] Part of the problem lies in Coleridge's inability to sustain a stable hierarchical order in the analogy he sets up between nature and the mind. The assumption that nature is further from the Absolute than the mind becomes increasingly dubious the more Coleridge investigates with unabated wonder the miracle of organic growth in the plant (*SM*, p. 72). As his awe at nature's remarkable capacity to transform external influence into inner growth increases, he is less certain that the mind can surpass nature's accomplishments or even match them. If anything, Coleridge's meditation proves persuasively that the mind will always trail behind nature in that it cannot 'open out . . . to that holier light' as the plant opens 'to the orient beam' (*SM*, p. 73). The hovering sentiment of anxiety and guilt that pervades the opening of Coleridge's discourse on 'the vegetable creation' might be seen as a presentiment of the uncomfortable, if not heretical, conclusion he is forced to suggest in the end; namely, that nature is a far more trustworthy messenger of God than is man. It is not surprising that when Coleridge reviewed his meditation at a later time he felt embarrassed by his 'very imperfect and confused' views 'of *Nature*', and thought that '*una litura* would be the best amendment' to his recommendation that man should strive to become like nature and imitate nature's ways of communicating with the deity (*SM*, p. 71, n. 6). Coleridge must have sensed that he allowed himself to be carried away by his attraction to the meadow to the point of deifying nature, and that he compromised the stature of human spirituality by toppling it from its hierarchical standing. Nature must find its ideal completion in man and not vice versa.

If, in such passages, nature is both exalted and found to be a faulty model for the mind, nature is not represented at all in most of Coleridge's reflections on the symbol. It is important not to deduce from the passionate celebration of nature's organic unity in *The Statesman's Manual* that Coleridge will systematically draw his symbols from natural objects. Most of Coleridge's statements on the symbol, as well as the evidence presented by Coleridge's later poetry and notebook writing, support a quite different conclusion. Coleridge shows an increasing preference for love objects, which displace natural objects as the means of fulfilling the self's aspiration of unity with the divine. We have seen from a number of notebook entries that Coleridge progressively raises the symbol to such a high status, placing upon it the task not only of making cognition possible but also of securing the acquisition of a moral being, that he effectively narrows the choice of symbolic objects to one option only: another human being. Coleridge came to realize that, if the self is to achieve wholeness by union with an external object, this object 'must be itself a subject – partially a favorite dog, principally a friend, wholly God, *the* Friend'.[102] But even in the sphere of human relationships Coleridge further reduces the choice of symbols to one kind, for unique and exacting qualities are obviously required of a person who is to become the self's symbol. Such a person must be 'intensely similar, yet not the same' and possess an unyielding passion for self-perfection as well as an unblemished spiritual purity; furthermore, this person must be fully 'permeable' to divine influence so as to send it off to others 'not like the polish'd mirror by rejection from itself, but by transmission thro' itself' (*CN*, II, 2435).

Among Coleridge's close friends, only Sara Hutchinson could meet these requirements, and it is she who became Coleridge's prototype of the ideal love object in the quest for a unified self. As Coleridge refines his model of human partnership, he confers on Sara such profoundly spiritualized qualities that she begins to look less and less like an actual physical being and approximates as closely as possible a 'pure soul', a disembodied essence free from the constraints of earthly life. The best example of Coleridge's ideal love object in its perfected form appears in the poem 'Phantom':

> All look and likeness caught from earth,
> All accident of kin and birth,
> Had pass'd away. There was no trace
> Of aught on that illumined face,
> Uprais'd beneath the rifted stone
> But of one spirit all her own; –
> She, she herself, and only she,
> Shone through her body visibly.

As Edward Kessler states, this poem 'is perhaps Coleridge's purest apprehension of unified Being'.[103] It shows, moreover, that Coleridge's substitution of love objects for natural objects fulfils his tendency to uproot the symbol from its material existence and push it firmly towards its transcendent abode. In this poem, as in many notebook entries, Sara appears as a spiritual presence, devoid of any physical particularity, as ethereal as light itself. She represents in the fullest sense the 'subjection of matter to spirit so as to be transformed into a symbol'. And if such an 'unsculptured image' (Shelley, 'Mont Blanc', l. 27) is to be the high destination of the Coleridgean symbol, we should not be surprised to find that the predominance of the symbolic perspective brings with it a devaluation of sensory objects.

CHAPTER 5 EROS AND NATURE: THE LATER POETRY

Coleridge's progressive withdrawal from the natural world and his corresponding attachment to love objects appear most clearly in his later poetry, a record showing that the tendencies heretofore noted have a much more encompassing reach than the specific instance of Coleridge's theory of symbolism. One of the noticeable changes that occurs in Coleridge's later poetry is the gradual disappearance of the journey motif, and its accompanying engagement with nature. One might describe Coleridge's journey poetry (exhibited in Coleridge's conversation poems and, with grimmer overtones, in 'The Rime of the Ancient Mariner' and 'Christabel') as a poetry of encounter or confrontation: between man and nature; the private and the public world; the imaginative artist and conventionally-minded auditors; the limited though safe life in a familiar, home environment (the cot, the harbour, the castle) and the vastly larger experience, of either joyous or devastating possibilities, gained through contact with the external world. Along with the disappearance of the journey pattern in Coleridge's later poetry, we also notice the change to a poetry of private meditation, which avoids dramatic confrontations.[104]

A poem such as 'Lines written in the Album at Elbingerode in the Hartz Forest' (1799) shows the breakdown of a mode of experience that in earlier poems led to an intense interaction with objects of nature. The poet who in 'Reflections on having left a Place of Retirement' (1795) forced his way up a 'stony Mount' with 'perilous toil' and thereby gained the luxury of a unique moment of fulfilled existence is here dragging his way down from the summit of Brocken with much difficulty and an obvious lack of enthusiasm for the scenery he perceives. A number of perceptual details apprehended by the speaker during his tiresome journey hint at the possible awakening of a sublime mood, but the potentially awesome aspects of the landscape he views (the panoramic scene of woods and hills extending into infinity, the 'solemn murmur' of the breeze, the sound of waterfalls) are undercut by playful, down-to-earth touches, such as the sight of the 'dingy kidling with its tinkling bell' or of the 'old romantic goat' waving its 'white beard'. The speaker cannot, consequently, make any visionary contact with the surrounding landscape and cannot outgrow his 'low and languid' disposition. He finds instead supporting evidence to justify his failure to 'feel', not just 'see', the beautiful in nature, in the claim, familiar to us from 'Dejection', that 'outward forms the loftiest still receive / Their finer influence from the Life within'. In addition, the speaker provides another, more powerful explanation for his lack of response to the mountain landscape, namely that, in Blake's words, 'where man is not nature is barren'. No matter how 'fair' natural objects might be, they are 'of import vague / Or unconcerning, where the heart not finds / History or prophecy of friend, or child, / Or gentle maid, our first and early love, / Or father, or the venerable name / Of our adored country!'

Coleridge's rejection of a personal experience of nature in favour of a relationship with another human being or patriotic sentiment in general is certainly nothing new in his poetry. His dissatisfaction with experiences of nature that, however enlightening, exclude other beings is evident as early as his sonnet 'Lines: Composed while climbing the Left Ascent of Brockley Coomb', composed in 1795, and is also prominently voiced in his conversation poems. But the important difference between a poem like 'Reflections' and 'Lines written in the Album at Elbingerode' is that in the former the rejection of a solitary experience of nature does not detract from the vitality and imaginative power of the experience as such, but points to an unresolved conflict between the poet's private desires and social responsibilities.[105] In 'Lines', on the other hand, no such conflict ever emerges, because the speaker's encounter with nature remains to the end an empty and disillusioned one, leading to no significant growth of awareness.

'Lines written in the Album at Elbingerode' is not one of Coleridge's outstanding poems after the *annus mirabilis* of his career, but it brings together in the clearest, least complicated and most comprehensive way the main directions of his later poetry. Coleridge is moving towards a poetry that will emphasize the 'finer influence from the Life within' and resist the influence of 'outward forms'. As a result, absent or ethereal objects, made from the fine texture of desire, longing and the 'life of dreams' ('Phantom or Fact' [1830], l. 18) are given a powerful sway over and finally eliminate immediate objects of direct experience. In 'Lines', the poet's 'longing eye' turns away from the mountain landscape, 'shaping in the steady clouds' the absent landscape of his distant homeland (ll. 25–7). In 'Apologia pro Vita sua' (1800), which may be regarded as the literary manifesto of the later Coleridge, the poet shows no interest whatsoever in undertaking adventurous journeys into the outer world but draws his inspiration from an activity far removed from all 'accidents' of the phenomenal world:

> The poet in his lone yet genial hour
> Gives to his eyes a magnifying power:
> Or rather he emancipates his eyes
> From the black shapeless accidents of size –
> In unctuous cones of kindling coal,
> Or smoke upwreathing from the pipe's trim bole,
> His gifted ken can see
> Phantoms of sublimity.

Sublimity is no longer to be gained through an intense interaction with natural objects, but only through an individual act of the mind, shaping to itself 'phantoms' of its own liking. The poet must exert himself to avoid surrendering to mechanical habits of seeing and train his eyes to project with 'magnifying power' that which the mind imagines. We find a good example of this activity in 'Fancy in Nubibus' (1817), a poem in which Coleridge fancies himself a 'traveller', but one who has clearly learned that imaginary journeys are the only ones worth pursuing. Having 'emancipated' his eyes from their dependence on visual objects, the poet knows how to 'make the shifting clouds be' what he wishes or 'let the easily persuaded eyes / Own each quaint likeness issuing from the mould / Of a friend's fancy' (ll. 3–6). Thus, the poet can turn clouds into 'a gorgeous land' of mountains or even allow himself the considerable fantasy of projecting himself as Homer, 'the blind bard' whose creativity came solely from inner sources.

As 'Apologia pro Vita sua' and 'Fancy in Nubibus' illustrate, Coleridge's interest in how the mind attends to the production of ideal, inner landscapes is accompanied by a displacement of natural objects. If we return to 'Lines written in the Album at Elbingerode', we find a second source for this displacement in the growing rivalry of love objects with nature. Though not an entirely new aspect of Coleridge's poetry, there is in 'Lines' a much more radical perspective on the necessary participation of other human beings in all encounters with nature. The poet does not merely suggest here how much more exhilarating his experience of the mountain would be in the company of another being as in 'Lines: Composed while climbing the Left Ascent of Brockley Coomb', but recognizes that in the absence of such company no exhilaration can occur at all. The journey in the later 'Lines' is a failed journey that never gets off the ground; the denial of a solitary encounter with nature is not contradicted by the imaginative expansion and sheer ecstasy of the experience as such, as in 'Reflections', but is fully confirmed by the futility of the journey itself.

In some of the later poems that still maintain the pattern of a journey, Coleridge continually introduces human beings in a natural environment and uses nature as the background for a quest for a love object, usually one that is absent. In 'The Keepsake' the poet wanders 'By rivulet, or spring, or wet roadside' seeking to relive the memory of a scene of blissful love in a verdant bower. In 'A Stranger Minstrel' we find the poet stretched on 'Skiddaw's mount' in a 'repose divine', indulging in a pleasant receptiveness to the influence of the natural environment. Yet the close interaction with nature leads to no metaphysical insight into some unifying organic breeze, but to an awareness that the more the soul has had, the more insatiable it becomes. As the poem continues, it is apparent that the real object of the speaker's desire is not nature at all, but a 'lady of sweet song' and 'soft blue eye' who had died, and that in the beginning the speaker avoided confronting his loss by seeking for a surrogate partner in nature.

By far the most complex treatment of the journey motif and of the intricate exchange between natural and love objects appears in 'The

Picture' (1802). Here Coleridge creates two personae, a self-conscious narrator and a foolish, love-yearning youth, the alter ego of the former. This method allows Coleridge to explore with unprecedented comprehensiveness the problems involved in various forms of imaginative activity, nature worship and the pursuit of constantly elusive love objects. For the narrator of the poem, external objects frequently recede into a shadowy existence while ideal objects created through purely imaginative means move into the foreground. The natural world no longer carries the power to propel the mind towards an encounter with the omnipresent life behind mere appearance but loses its significance for man's inmost desires and needs.

In 'The Picture' the 'love-lorn' youth acts out the errors and delusions that the narrator is trying to resist; although the narrator repeatedly declares his triumph over the follies of the youth, he is in fact drifting dangerously close to the very traps he thinks he can escape. We follow the narrator through a long journey with many stops in different physical surroundings, which become not so much places of encounters with nature but turning points in the narrator's progressive recognition of the kinds of delusions to which one is liable when nature and Eros are brought closely together. From the beginning of the journey we are made aware that the narrator is struggling to control some 'master-passion' that comes upon him as suddenly and powerfully as a 'summer gust'. In his first confrontation with the youth, the narrator is in fact testing what happens when some inner passion is turned loose upon the world. The result appears to be a form of nature worship which not only threatens to destroy any core of personal identity, but also leads to a false representation of nature. The youth 'Worships the spirit of unconscious life / In tree or wild-flower' and not knowing what 'he is' or should be, disperses his being 'In winds or waters, or among the rocks'. In a way, the youth of this poem commits the same error that Coleridge had censored in 'The Nightingale', namely that of filling 'all things with himself' and making nature 'tell back the tale' of his melancholy heart. But in 'The Picture' Coleridge isolates a different, though equally mystifying, aspect of the projective imagination. The youth does not, as his counterpart in the earlier poem, evade his sorrow by attributing it to an external object, but diffuses it completely by viewing an idealized, animistic landscape. While the 'night-wandering' lover of 'The Nightingale' will falsely perceive a perfectly happy bird as a melancholy one, the 'love-lorn' youth will mistake a path of 'weeds and thorns' for 'myrtle-walks' through enchanted 'groves' populated by mythological figures and will undoubtedly wake up from his imagined journey with sore, bleeding feet. Coleridge hardly conceals his mockery of the animistic imagination, which is the origin of pagan myth, a mockery that touches not only the youth but also the narrator as well.

Throughout the poem the narrator affirms his moments of victory over his 'master-passion' and the delusions accompanying it by a renewed contact with his physical surroundings. It is as if the narrator tries to maintain the posture of a man who believes in firmly-rooted visual experiences rather than in imaginary projections of any kind. But no sooner does the narrator find a comfortable place that seems protected from man, such as the place by the river beneath a 'weedy oak', than he drifts into reverie. The breeze that 'visits' him brings associations of an absent maiden, and of a 'wanton' love game which the breeze plays upon the 'tendril ringlets' and 'snowy bosom' of the beloved. These pleasurable associations become so compelling that the narrator falls deeper into reverie and soon sees in the surface of the river the reflection of the maiden. His efforts to resist reverie are, however, as evident as the reverie itself, for the narrator constructs his fantasy through a series of denials (the breeze, he claims, never performed the wanton love play with the maiden, nor did the river host the reflection of the virgin's 'form divine') that, ironically enough, have the opposite effect, drawing him into the vortex of his visions with magnetic force. Furthermore, as his consecutive negations reinforce his imaginary projections, the narrator imperceptibly switches from the first person to the third, attributing to the youth the more extreme form of his fantasy. This confirms our suspicion that the youth is not a separate character but a facet of the narrator's own personality, the 'fool' within him which the narrator is trying to exorcise through self-analysis. The youth acts out another delusion that the narrator is trying to escape, which is a different form of idolatry originating from the same inclination towards self-projection. The youth now worships not the unconscious life of nature but a 'watery idol' made from the 'fleeting' and 'vain' material of 'dreaming hopes / Delicious to the soul' (ll. 83–4). He becomes further and further engrossed in his 'phantom-world' and is doomed to waste his 'manly-prime' imprisoned in a world created by his own fantasies and 'sickly thoughts' (ll. 106–11).

We are by now familiar with the narrator's strategy of letting the youth fall into dangerous modes of self-deception, thereby recovering his own sanity and freedom. We have also seen that the narrator's way of emancipating himself from 'Passion's dreams' is to situate himself firmly in a natural environment and separate fantasy from reality. Indeed, after the episode of the maiden by the stream, the narrator restores the river to its own identity as a gloomy, wild and loveless 'desert stream' (ll. 112–17), and seeks a new spot in nature 'of deeper shades and lonelier glooms', which would be more fully protected from the intrusion of human imagination. From here on, the youth disappears completely from the narrative, which is a clear indication that the speaker has overcome his worst fears and can proceed confidently on his own. The last part of the journey (ll. 118–86) is indeed quite different from the earlier phases. The narrator still alternates natural and love scenes, but he no longer confuses one with the other, nor does he succumb to reverie.[106] The best test of the narrator's new development can be seen in the last and main event of the journey when he finds the picture left behind by his beloved. The episode forms an interesting parallel to the earlier encounter with the phantom of the maiden (ll. 68–117) in that we again discover that the narrator imperceptibly slips from one kind of reality into another. Thus, before we are even aware of it, the narrator is describing the content of a picture, a human artefact (ll. 152–8), instead of a varied external landscape (ll. 135–52). And there is an essential difference between the narrator's activity in the two episodes. In the latter (ll. 118–86) he is not drifting into reverie but merely focusing on another object of sight. The picture is not the narrator's fantasy in any way but has an independent, objective existence, being the product of a separate human being and not of a fictitious youth who is the narrator in disguise. The blurring of the lines dividing the external landscape and the scene in the picture serves not so much as a reminder of the narrator's capacity for self-deception as an affirmation of the kind of imaginative activity which the picture embodies. The realism of the picture indicates that the artist was engaged in a conscious reproduction of an objective reality and not in a self-indulgent play with her own fancies. It thus reinforces the objective that the narrator himself has been trying to attain throughout his various trials.[107] Yet the narrator has to pass still another test. He is tempted to 'keep the relique' to himself (ll. 181–2), to worship it as an idol and dream about the maiden who made it, in which case he would be in no better shape than the youth staring at his own projections in the river.[108] But the narrator quickly realizes that such idolatry, even directed to an object of art, will only 'feed / The passion that consumes' him, and his final resolution is to find the author of the picture, his beloved Isabel, restore the picture to her, and accompany her on the possibly treacherous path towards her father's house. His journey, which began as a purposeless climb through 'weeds and thorns, and matted underwood' (l. 1), finally acquires a true destination, the reunion with another human being.

'The Picture' is the last of Coleridge's poems in which encounters with nature are given any prominence,[109] although the poem raises serious questions about the value of such encounters. As in 'Dejection: An Ode', a poem completed in the same year as 'The Picture', the narrator is subject to conflicting responses to nature. He is by no means indifferent to nature, for he repeatedly tries to remain faithful to nature's true identity and protect it from the misrepresentations and myths that man attaches to it. But at the same time, the side of nature that is revealed in the absence of human projections is often so harsh and unappealing that it almost invites personal fantasy.[110] Even where the physical surroundings are pleasant, the narrator does not gain any powerful experiences from them but uses such encounters to stabilize his emotions and cast away his deceptions. And even in this respect nature has a limited role, for clearly the only thing that breaks the endless cycle of his fall into and recovery from 'Passion's dreams' is an encounter with a human artefact.

In later poems Coleridge no longer tests the complex meeting and parting of ways between natural and love objects, but merely makes explicit what in 'The Picture' is presented as a gradual process of discovery, namely that only encounters with human beings matter. In 'Constancy to an Ideal Object' he shows that even when personal relationships are entertained solely 'in the brain' in a purely abstract fashion, there is nothing in 'Nature's range' of temporal phenomena that should divert one's devotion from such relationships. The role of nature in this poem is confined to that of providing an occasional metaphor for the definition of the ideal love objects.[111] Similarly, in 'The Blossoming of the Solitary Date-tree' Coleridge presents through a cumulative series of emblems (the date tree which cannot bear fruit until it receives a branch from another date tree, the mountain peaks which despite the tropical sun remain 'Thrones of Frost, through the absence of objects to reflect the rays', the lonely, blind Arab, the mother with a still-born child on her knee) and direct prose statements ('What no one with us shares, seems scarce our own') the utter desolation of the self in the absence of human companionship, a desolation for which nature has no cure. It is not that nature does not provide luxurious enjoyment for the senses and the imagination but 'It is her largeness, and her overflow' (ll. 56–7) which, paradoxically, deepen 'the ache of solitariness', for all of nature's riches dissolve like a 'bubble into idle air' when man is deprived of direct contact with other beings. In 'The Blossoming of the Solitary Date-tree' Coleridge does not allow the speaker the illusion of finding a temporary harbour in nature, as in 'The Picture'. Rather, he confronts with painful clarity the unredeemed solitude of the unloved self. Encounters with the natural world thus become of minor importance in Coleridge's later poetry. When an experience of nature occurs, it is presented either as a visionary experience mediated by an artistic product ('The Garden of Boccaccio'),[112] or as an incongruous and illusory experience, such as that of the old, blind man who gazes at the moon in 'Limbo'.[113] More often than not, Coleridge concentrates on inner landscapes, on visions, sublime or spectral, which bear no relation to an external environment but arise directly from 'Passion's dreams' ('Phantom or Fact', 'Love's Apparition and Evanishment').

Through 'The Picture', we gain insight into a private aspect of Coleridge's personality. His deep anxieties about his liability to entertain sexual desires towards love objects and thus taint their intrinsic purity give us further clues regarding his reluctance to maintain a close association with both natural and love objects and his need to abandon the former. As so many of his notebook entries reveal – especially those written in connection with his relationship to Sara Hutchinson – Coleridge was obsessively preoccupied by the distinction between love and lust, one which he subjected to a rigorous process of analysis (see n. 85 above). His struggle to control his habitual daydreams and reveries, as well as his utter abhorrence of the 'unfathomable hell within' released during sleep, were in part motivated by his awareness that when the mind is lost to an uncontrollable stream of fancies, love can easily degenerate into meaner passions (see *CN*, II, 2543). Coleridge accepted some measure of sensuality as congenial to love and consistent with moral conduct, but in those entries where Coleridge seems particularly tolerant about the manifestation of physical desires, he establishes, none the less, two rather strict contingencies: that such desires have the sanction of matrimony and that they be expressed in a direct action, a gesture of caress towards the beloved (see *CN*, II, 2495). The circumstances of Coleridge's private life, however, afforded neither the possibility of matrimonial bliss nor extended contact with Sara Hutchinson or any other woman he loved.[114] Thus, Coleridge was left with a host of untoward desires that needed the vigilant exercise of the will to be chastened into longings of a more spiritual nature. In this respect, Coleridge came to regard the action of natural objects as detrimental to the objectives of a self that wanted very much to protect the purity of love relationships. In 'The Picture' we see how, in the absence of love objects themselves, natural objects stimulate erotic reveries, which take a rather obviously 'wanton' turn. The breeze becomes an 'accomplice' to man's physical desires. It is not by chance that the narrator tries to temper his all too sensuous reverie (ll. 58–67) by slipping into a sobering Platonic language and concentrating on the virginal qualities, the 'form divine', 'stately' appearance and 'Contemplative' look of the maiden (ll. 74–6). We might also recall a similar situation in 'The Eolian Harp', where the breeze playing upon the harp evokes associations of 'some coy maid half yielding to her lover' (ll. 14–17). In contrast to the loose sensual dimensions of the 'Fairy-land' of the poet's fancies, the environment of the cot exudes an atmosphere of controlled sensuality that fully accords with the principles of chastity, 'Innocence and Love' (ll. 1–5). As long as the poet is situated imaginatively in the cot and fully conscious of the physical presence of the beloved, he can enjoy nature without falling into 'unregenerate' sexual fantasies. Undoubtedly, more is involved in the speaker's apology to his beloved at the end than the embarrassment about his 'vain' intellectual 'babbling' or his unorthodox theological views.

Two notebook entries written by Coleridge in 1803 and 1810 respectively illuminate Coleridge's understanding of the tensions and threats posed by one's association with sensory objects, be they natural or artistic.

> In looking at Knorr's Shells felt the impulse of *doing* something– pleasures of gazing not sufficient – if I can *do* nothing else with the beauty, I can *show* it to somebody. Sympathy itself perhaps may have some connection with this impulse to embody Feeling in action. The accumulation of these eye-given pleasure-yearnings may impel to energetic action / but if a woman be near, will probably kindle the passion of sexual Love. (*CN*, I, 1356)

> Sometimes when I earnestly look at a beautiful Object or Landscape, it seems as if I were on the *brink* of a Fruition still denied – as if Vision were an *appetite*: even as a man would feel, who having put forth all his muscular strength in an act of prosilience, is at that very moment *held back* – he leaps & yet moves not from his place. (*CN*, III, 3767)

The following passage from Goethe provides a useful gloss to Coleridge's notes:

> I lately had a present of a basket of fruit. I was in raptures at the sight of it, as of something heavenly, – such riches, such abundance, such variety, and yet such affinity! I could not persuade myself to pluck off a single berry: I could not bring myself to take a single peach or fig.

> Most assuredly this gratification of the eye and the inner sense is the highest, and most worthy of man: in all probability it is the design of Nature, when the hungry and thirsty believe that she has exhausted herself in marvels merely for the gratification of their palate. Ferdinand came and found me in the midst of these meditations. He did me justice and then said, smiling, but with a deep sigh, 'Yes, we are not worthy to consume these glorious products of Nature: truly it were a pity. Permit me to make a present of them to my beloved?' How glad was I to see the basket carried off! How did I love Ferdinand! How did I thank him for the feeling he had excited in me, for the prospect he gave me! Ay, we ought to acquaint ourselves with the beautiful: we ought to contemplate it with rapture, and attempt to raise ourselves up to its height. And, in order to gain strength for that, we must keep ourselves thoroughly unselfish: we must not make it our own, but rather seek to communicate it, indeed, to make a sacrifice of it to those who are dear and precious to us.[115]

In both his entries Coleridge examines the psychological effects of an intense engagement with objects of stimulating sensory beauty, finding in each case that such an engagement leads either to a compromising moral situation or to a frustrating complex of desire and inability to act. Coleridge perceives that the 'accumulation' of 'eye-given pleasure-yearnings' derived from objects of art or of nature causes an increase of psychic energy that demands release in some form of humanistic or creative action. Yet we see that in the first instance the natural impulse to share beauty with another person is hindered by the distinct possibility that the stimulus gained from sensory objects will be transferred to a love object in the form of sexual passion, while in the second example the 'pleasures of gazing' turn into a virtual appetite that feeds the desire for action but brings action to a standstill. Goethe is caught in a similar dilemma upon receiving a basket of splendidly arranged fruit, but he manages to steer clear of the difficulties experienced by Coleridge in a way that is worth examining, for it is in fact congruent with a perspective Coleridge himself would have shared.

Like Coleridge, Goethe is faced with a most inviting spectacle of visual beauty but finally comes to regard the 'pleasures of gazing', as insufficient unless they are communicated to 'those who are dear and precious to us'. His initial dilemma is also, like Coleridge's, that of being caught in a suspended action, but part of the suspense comes from Goethe's attempt to prevent 'Vision' from turning into 'an *appetite*'. As he contemplates the extraordinary richness and variety of the fruit,

Goethe cannot bring himself to consume 'a single peach or fig', even though the present was probably intended for just such a purpose. But to remove any fruit from the basket would in effect imply the disruption of the 'heavenly' harmony and diversity of the original arrangement, and the sacrifice of the 'gratification of the eye and the inner sense', which is 'most worthy of man', for the gratification of the palate. Goethe's choice thus seems perfectly reasonable in that the enjoyment he derives from the contemplation of beauty matters more to him than the satisfaction of an immediate appetite. But from the scene that follows, it is evident that the 'pleasures of gazing', while presumably delivering one from purely physical desires, constitute another form of entrapment from which Goethe is luckily saved through the beneficial intervention of a friend. As we watch Goethe's overly enthusiastic response to Ferdinand's proposal to offer the basket of fruit to his beloved, we begin to suspect that his activity of contemplating the beautiful might not have been as innocent and 'worthy' as it had appeared earlier. The flagrant relief and gratitude experienced by Goethe when the basket of fruit is carried out of his sight indicate that all along the basket had been an object of great temptation and anxiety.

Much of the increasing dramatic momentum gathered by the scene of Goethe's attraction to the basket of fruit comes from hovering associations with man's original fall from Eden, though the biblical myth is tailored according to the circumstances of a domestic occasion. Peaches and figs replace the infamous apple, 'Eve' happens to be at a safe distance and becomes the beneficiary of man's successful struggle against temptation, while the intermediary is no longer a beguiling serpent but a trustworthy friend who offers truthful and salutary help. Similarly, knowledge is not gained through a fall into error but through a timely deliverance from it. What Goethe comes to realize is that he had mistakenly located virtue in his preference for visual enjoyment over oral satisfaction. He had failed to see that a personal 'gratification of the eye' by itself is in fact equivalent to the gratification of the palate in that, like ingestion, it is expressive of our instinct to appropriate an object, to make it 'our own'. Goethe's true insight and his final salvation is his understanding that virtue lies in man's capacity to sacrifice personal enjoyment for the benefit of others, and that only when spiritual pleasures are shared and turned over from one being to another as a gift, can they survive deterioration into selfishly possessive physical instincts.

Like Goethe, Coleridge knew the insufficiency of the 'pleasures of gazing' and the absolute need to make such pleasures a communal property. He would have agreed with Goethe that the good offices of a friend are instrumental to one's ability to engage in moral action and triumph over temptations. But in matters concerning relationships with women, Coleridge was far less sure that the Goethean rapture over beautiful objects could be transferred to objects of love without transmitting at the same time 'eye-given pleasure-yearnings' of a less innocent and disinterested kind. This is why Coleridge prefers to remove love objects completely from the presence of sense objects and keep them close to the realm of thought or divine light where their purity can be protected. The one gift Coleridge can confidently entrust to love objects is to give them a purely mental abode, a temple of worship such as the one described in 'Love's Sanctuary', where the poet's 'thoughts all stand ministrant night and day / Like saintly Priests, that dare not think amiss'. One might say that for Coleridge nature becomes too sensuous a partner and a threat to his relationship with other beings. His need to abandon nature, as well as his tendency to desensualize love objects to the point where they turn into a pure transparent symbol for the divine, cannot be fully understood without some sense of the intransigent moral standards Coleridge set for himself in his relationship with women (and I refer especially to Sara Hutchinson, Coleridge's ideal love object) and the erotic tensions he experienced that made these standards difficult to maintain and that strengthened his determination to enforce them. Coleridge's attachment to nature is seriously affected by the competing authority of love relationships, and grows considerably weaker, as was the case in his relationship with Wordsworth. In effect, in Coleridge sensuality is deflected from love objects to nature, which is then spurned as a dangerous ground of identity for the self, mirroring the self's darkest and most compromising passions. If love objects are to remain an ideal mirror of the self's moral integrity, they must be placed at a safe distance from the impurity of natural objects and the 'eye-given pleasure-yearnings' they inspire.

If we now return to Coleridge's late notebook entry, with which I began this chapter, we can recognize in it familiar problems regarding his precarious engagement with the natural world. Although Coleridge is powerfully drawn to a summer scene of 'overwhelming' beauty, he is immediately alerted to the 'impossibility that a mind in his sensual trance could attach any practical lively meaning to the Gospel Designation of a Christian as living a *life of Faith*'. His visible attraction to the external landscape is undermined by stern reminders that a 'Sensualist' who abandons himself to visual objects will derive as little meaning from what he sees as 'an unalphabetic Rustic' presented with 'a fine specimen of Calligraphy', and that to a spiritually-minded person a 'fine landscape' cannot be a mere object of sight but an inner 'Music – the intelligible Language of Memory, Hope, desiderium / the rhythm of the Soul's movements' (pp. 28–9 above). Here, as well as in the other examples we have examined, too many forces work against Coleridge's attraction to nature's sensory appearances, making it uncomfortable and ultimately unfeasible for him to pursue his activity as an observer of the picturesque, or to maintain his interest in nature as a poetic subject. His suspicion that the 'pleasures of gazing' produce a passively complacent individual who might lose control over his mental processes and fall into crass sensuality or spurious philosophic speculations; his difficulties in sharing such pleasures with other beings; his aspiration for a pure state of being for the attainment of which only love objects are appropriate mediators; his fears that a devotion to nature conflicts with the principles of a committed Christian;[116] his developing study of Platonic, mystical and transcendentalist philosophers who in diverse ways insisted on the necessity of freeing the mind from the confines of the material world; and, not least of all, Coleridge's complicated personal relationships with male and female guardians – all point to the inevitable weakening of his attachment to nature. And yet, it is difficult to imagine that the intensity of Coleridge's activity of viewing landscape that we observed earlier, his fine sensitivity to sensory phenomena, or his enthusiasm over the marvel of organic growth in nature, could simply disappear from his work without a trace. If anything, in the late notebook entry of 7 August 1826, his attraction to nature is just as evident and his eye for sensory details as remarkable as are the forces that prevent Coleridge from abandoning himself to the life of a 'Sensualist'.

We must not expect to find in Coleridge any one fixed or completely predictable attitude towards nature but a multiplicity of reactions feeding into an ever-expanding and varying stream. It would also prove futile to attempt to sort out Coleridge's response to nature by means of some clear chronological landmarks. It is true that between 1798 and 1806 approximately, Coleridge was more keenly involved in an exploration of nature's picturesque sights than at any later time, due in part to the fact that this was a period of travel and sojourn in the Lake District and of various trips to Germany, Scotland and Italy. But this is also the period in which Coleridge's relationships with Wordsworth and Sara Hutchinson matured, in which his philosophy of symbolism was born, all of which, as seen before, contributed to his alienation from nature.

Coleridge is liable to assert conflicting attitudes towards nature in roughly contemporaneous texts or even in the same text. He may find that nature safeguards man's innocence, or that it compromises his moral standing;[117] that nature is an inferior companion to man compared to other beings, or that it is a far more dependable friend; that nature cannot revitalize the poetic imagination, or that it alone can rekindle the dying sparks of poetic power. Moreover, although in his later years Coleridge no longer devoted his attention to natural scenery or wrote nature poetry, a concern with nature did not disappear but is present in his writings on aesthetics, natural philosophy and even theology. In Parts III and IV I shall leave aside Coleridge's poetry and personal relationships and concentrate exclusively on his speculative writings. I shall focus on Coleridge's use of nature not in the sense of a body of external objects available to direct imaginative experience but as an aesthetic term related to the faculty of taste, or as a purely abstract concept signifying the objective world as opposed to the subjective. I shall not document further Coleridge's ambivalence towards nature, which I have already discussed, but point out instead the resolutions he sought and the strategies he adopted in establishing a secure place for nature in his philosophic system. I shall examine in particular Coleridge's reactions to German transcendentalists and his attempts to utilize some of their concepts in a significantly altered system that accommodates both his interest in nature and his Christian beliefs. Orsini once marvelled at the extent to which Coleridge became converted to the doctrines of German transcendentalists, Kant and Schelling in particular.[118] In my view the real marvel about Coleridge is the extent to which he remained temperamentally rooted in the external world while at the same time practising idealism in an even more refined and in some aspects more radical form than his German peers. In the following chapters I take up this complex history of Coleridge's mixed propensities towards philosophic idealism and empirical thought.

Part III: Coleridge's Conception of the Sublime

CHAPTER 1 THE TYPOLOGY OF THE SUBLIME IN ENGLISH AND GERMAN AESTHETICS

At the centre of the Romantic sublime is the belief that man can transcend the boundaries of the phenomenal world and discover the divine power and freedom of the mind. As Schiller wrote, in the 'presence of the sublime we feel ourselves sublime, because the sensuous instincts have no influence over the jurisdiction of reason, because it is then' that 'the pure spirit . . . acts in us as if it were not absolutely subject to any other laws than its own'.[1] For Kant, too, the sublime marks the stage of consciousness when one becomes aware of '*a faculty of the mind surpassing every standard of sense*' and pointing to man's supersensible destination.[2] The German sublime, as presented by Kant and Schiller, gives a clear warranty to the supremacy of the mind over nature. Coleridge was keenly interested in the sublime and followed closely the radical developments in German aesthetics. But although Coleridge found the German sublime preferable to Burke's empirically-based doctrine, he was not as eager to abandon nature as Kant or Schiller, or to use a confrontation with nature as a means of bolstering the mind's sense of its own power. In his representation of the sublime Coleridge tried to grant nature a positive role, without denying the subjective origin of the sublime or its relationship to a transcendent world, as maintained by Kant and Schiller. Coleridge devised a formula for the sublime that mediates between an empirical and transcendental philosophy. It also combines in a new synthetic version two typologies of the sublime that were current at the time. The first is what, for lack of a better term, I shall call the sublime of crisis. It is best seen in the theories of Burke, Kant and Schiller, and it presupposes a trauma of consciousness that disrupts a subject's habitual relationship with the external world and leads to a mixed emotion of pleasure and pain, variously defined as a 'delightful horror' (Burke), a 'negative pleasure' (Kant) or a 'paroxysm' of shudder and joy (Schiller).[3] In the other typology (formulated by John Baillie and Richard Payne Knight in England and by Johann Gottfried von Herder and Jean Paul Richter in Germany) the experience of sublimity is neither disruptive nor painful and leads to a pure elevation of spirit. A brief examination of both typologies will illuminate the kinds of choices Coleridge made in shaping his own, distinctly individual conception of the sublime.[4]

Burke was the first who conceived of the sublime as originating in a crisis of consciousness and explored in detail the emotional trauma produced by it. While Kant and Schiller are less interested in the crisis engendered by the sublime than in the adaptations and responses by which the crisis is resolved, Burke spends the bulk of his treatise analysing the specific qualities in sensible objects and the associative train of ideas which cause 'that state of the soul, in which all its motions are suspended, with some degree of horror' (p. 51). For Burke the sublime occurs when man finds himself face to face with threatening objects of overwhelming power which suggest the idea of pain, danger and death, and which fill the mind with a sensation of paralysing horror. Part of the intensity and traumatic impact of the sublime arises because the experience short-circuits, as it were, all possibility of rational defence or rescue through active resistance to the might of the opposing agent. As Burke puts it, the sublime 'anticipates our reasonings, and hurries us on by an irresistible force'. It 'effectually robs the mind of all its powers of acting and reasoning' (p. 51). Burke insists that for the sublime to succeed one must always feel completely helpless in the face of an external power and at no point doubt 'its ability to hurt' (pp. 57–62). If the balance of power is at all upset, if the weak party senses that the strength of the opponent is not absolute, the latter becomes not an object of sublime feelings, but of contempt.[5]

Burke was well aware that, having made terror 'the ruling principle of the sublime', he would have to explain at some length 'how any species of delight can be derived from a cause so apparently contrary to it' (p. 112). His most coherent analysis of delight involves him in rather primitive physiological speculations which even in his time were regarded with suspicion.[6] He argues that terror is a form of labour for the mind, which strengthens the 'more delicate' parts of our system, just as physical exercise strengthens the body. The exposure of the sublime either in nature or art protects man from falling into mental relaxation leading to 'melancholy, dejection, despair and often self-murder' (p. 113). The crisis of terror, which from one perspective may have appeared as debilitating for man, forcing him into a complete subjection to an external agent and suspending all of his 'powers of acting and reasoning', proves to have restorative effects that ultimately condition man's psychic well-being. And yet, for Burke, the resolution of the crisis of terror, however energizing in the long run, does not leave a subject with an immediate feeling of increased vigour or self-esteem, and it does not alter his original position of powerlessness in relation to an external agent. On the contrary, the feeling of 'delight', which is basically the relief experienced when one escapes from an 'imminent danger' (p. 35), always carries along the memory of the traumatic event of terror; that is, it maintains the power balance which led to the original crisis. As Burke puts it, the 'delight which arises from the modifications of pain confesses the stock from whence it sprung, in its solid, strong, and severe nature' (p. 35).[7]

While for Burke the sublime inspires feelings of terror and awe in response to an external power which has full dominance over man, for Kant and Schiller no sublime feelings can ever emerge as long as man finds himself in passive subjection to a power controlling his destiny. The absolute condition of sublimity for both writers is that 'humanity in our person remains unhumiliated' ('Analytic of the Sublime', p. 101), no matter how severe a threat a given individual may be faced with from the outside. The German sublime is distinctly a sublime of resistance to power and requires a full affirmation of man's capacity to prove himself larger than and independent of an external agency. This is possible only in an advanced state of culture when man is able to form judgements according to the supersensible ideas of reason and develop a 'mental disposition which is akin to the moral' ('Analytic of the Sublime', p. 109).[8] As Kant explains, 'without development of moral ideas, that which we, prepared by culture, call sublime presents itself to the uneducated man merely as terrible. In the indications of the dominion of nature in destruction, and in the great scale of its might, in comparison with which his own is a vanishing quantity, he will only see the misery, danger, and distress which surround the man who is exposed to it' (p. 105).

The result of moving the sublime out of nature into the state of culture and moral education is to give it a finality and uniqueness it could not achieve within the premises of Burke's system. Because Burke distrusts any form of mediation in the experience of the sublime and bases it on the direct impact of physical objects on the passions, there can be no way in which any individual encounter with the sublime can be retained in the mind long after the exciting cause has disappeared. Hence, the experience of the sublime must, according to Burke's principles, be repeated continually to keep the soul fit, just as physical exercise must be performed regularly. This means that no individual encounter with the sublime has any unique value, or more than a merely temporary influence on the mind. For Kant and Schiller, on the other hand, the attitude of the mind corresponding to the sublime is either acquired absolutely or not at all and it does not require the constant repetition of the process whereby it was initially attained. While for Burke the sublime moment cannot be retained in the mind, for Kant and Schiller it cannot be annihilated.[9]

In Kant the sublime experience has a much more complex structure than in Burke, including not only a direct response to an external power but also a self-conscious evaluation of that response and a significant growth of reflective awareness. The Kantian sublime is based on a sharply defined turning point in man's consciousness of his relationship to nature and the world of physical necessity. In the beginning man falls into error by entertaining a powerful attraction towards the infinity and force displayed by nature. By a certain 'subreption', Kant explains, 'we attribute to an object of nature' the sublimity which in fact belongs squarely and exclusively to the mind (p. 96). Kant locates the cause of this error in the faculty of the imagination which summons all its resources to encompass nature's magnitude ('the mathematical sublime'), or to resist its might ('the dynamical sublime'). The effort leads to complete failure, for the imagination cannot help exhausting itself in trying to attain through phenomenal objects an idea of totality, which, belonging to reason, admits of no sensory representation. But the inadequacy of the imagination to carry out its goals is the very means by which the mind becomes aware of an inner faculty beyond and far greater than nature. The mere fact that the mind can think of nature as a unified whole without contradiction at the time when the imagination fails to comprehend it indicates the presence of a supersensible faculty. The turning point in the experience of the sublime occurs at the moment when the error of entertaining respect for an object becomes 'intuitively' evident to the mind and when reason allows man to recognize that, compared to his own power, everything in nature's range is small or a 'mere nothing'. It is reason, finally, that 'makes us judge as *sublime*, not so much the object, as our state of mind in the estimation of it' (p. 94).

The Kantian sublime requires the double activity of both imagination and reason, an activity which involves conflict but which furthers a common goal.[10] Without the imagination, reason, its supremacy and potency notwithstanding, would have no intuitive ground through which to reveal itself to the mind. To put it in Coleridgean terms, the defeat of the imagination is what provides 'outness' to the ideas of reason. Only by denying itself on one level of experience can the mind awaken to its full essence. On the other hand, without reason, the imagination may well push the mind to the brink of an abyss. The imagination needs reason to remain undamaged even in its defeat. In effect, for Kant the negative phase of the sublime, when the imagination confronts its powerlessness, never reaches the seriousness of a real crisis. The mind seems almost to know of its capacity to overcome defeat and joins in a single perception the viewpoint of the imagination, which regards its failure as painful, with the viewpoint of reason, which sees pain as purposive and therefore pleasurable. Reason unobtrusively supports the mind at the very moment when it contemplates the abyss through the imagination. Hence Kant can go on describing the doomed struggle of the imagination with complete serenity, for, according to his premises, this struggle can never touch deep levels of anxiety in man or lead to an acute and frightening crisis.

The differences between the way Burke and Kant represent the negative phase of crisis in the sublime are nowhere more evident than in the section where Kant deals with the 'dynamical sublime' and has to account for the presence of fear in an encounter with nature conceived as might. Kant makes it clear that the fear associated with the dynamical sublime is quite distinct from any 'terror seriously felt', which is what Burke means by fear. 'He who fears', Kant says unequivocally, 'can form no judgment about the sublime in nature, just as he who is seduced by inclination and appetite can form no judgment about the beautiful' (p. 100). To experience the sublime, man must at no time doubt his security or contemplate seriously the possibility of injury. Hence, when Kant speaks of fear, he has in mind a response to an imagined danger, not a real one. This response can best be described as 'fearless fear', which is, of course, a paradox. Kant claims that we 'can regard an object as *fearful* without being afraid *of* it'. We merely conceive of a situation in which, when wishing to resist a power, we find that 'all resistance would be altogether vain' (p. 100).

There is, then, no exposure to real danger in the Kantian sublime. Rather, the sublime is staged solely within the arena of the mind, and danger as such becomes a mental fantasy which has the effect of waking the mind to the reality of its safety from all danger and uncontested might. As in the case of the mathematical sublime, the mind allows itself to entertain a fiction in order to discover the truth. It attributes to objects of nature a power that renders them sublime in order to undo the sublimity of nature and claim it all to itself. We 'willingly call these objects [of nature] sublime', Kant points out, 'because they raise the energies of the soul above their accustomed height and discover in us a faculty of resistance of a quite different kind, which gives us courage to measure ourselves against the apparent almightiness of nature' (pp. 100–1). For Kant the salvation of man's humanity (i.e. his freedom from external necessity) during the experience of the sublime is never a problem. Man is never really in the hands of nature. Rather, man allows nature to participate in a free play of his faculties to the extent that the mind can profit from it. In a sense, nature represents a form of entertainment for the mind in that it becomes a grand fiction in which for an instant the mind 'willingly' suspends disbelief. But for the same reason, nature cannot pose a threat to man; the mind ultimately has control over its faculties and can unravel the fictions it creates. Kant has too much faith in the mind ever to have to worry about nature.

To pass from Kant's to Schiller's sublime is in a way to watch how the tight logical structure of Kant's system comes apart at its seams. The collapse of Kant's sublime is the more spectacular the more Schiller insists on retaining it. Schiller faithfully adheres to the main constituents of the Kantian sublime, including the distinction between the mathematical and the dynamical sublime and the structure of transcendence predicated by the defeat of the imagination and the triumph of reason. He believes, like Kant, that in order to discover the 'absolute grandeur which is in ourselves', we 'willingly allow our imagination to find something in the world of phenomena that passes beyond it' ('On the Sublime', p. 133). And he also subscribes to Kant's notion that the sublime depends on a moral education that teaches man to regard himself as absolutely free (see note 8 above). But this is as far as the similarities between the two writers can be drawn. Schiller differs from Kant most strikingly in making the sublime a tragic choice for man, involving him in a permanent strife between his physical and spiritual existence. The serenity with which Kant looked on the glorifying march of the intellect to its proper destination gives way in Schiller to a restless rhetoric laden with deep anxieties. This is because for Schiller nature has a much more immediate reality, in both its benevolent and malefic possibilities, than for Kant.[11]

Schiller is keenly aware, in a way that reminds one of Burke, of the violence and devastation that the world of physical necessity can inflict on man. As long as man remains subject to forces of nature, he is exposed to an unbearable threat, which is 'nothing less than' the violation of his 'humanity' (p. 129). When Schiller writes that 'Man is in the hands of nature, but the will of man is in his own hands' (p. 134), he attaches much more reality to the first part of the sentence than Kant ever would. While Kant treats nature ironically, Schiller takes it seriously. The challenge which nature poses to man is a radical one and must be met with a corresponding radical gesture, which in some cases may involve suicide (see note 13 below). For Schiller the imperative of transcending the world of sense thus acquires a desperate urgency which is completely missing in Kant's treatise. If there is *'a single case'*, Schiller writes nervously, in which man 'is forced to what he does not wish', then this 'single terrible exception, to be or to do what is necessary and not what he wishes, this idea will pursue him as a phantom . . . His boasted liberty is nothing, if there is a single point where he is under constraint and bound' (p. 129). When Schiller enacts the stage of crisis in the sublime, during which reason snatches the mind away from the grip of the imagination, he turns it into a heightened drama of fearful proportions. The mind is not merely faltering at the brink of an abyss, as in Kant, but virtually hangs unsupported over it. The rescue initiated by reason must therefore be extremely prompt, for one moment of hesitation might irrevocably compromise man's humanity.

Having made the sublime dependent on a radical and unhesitating separation between nature and spirit, Schiller is forced to admit that if we were to commit ourselves wholeheartedly to the sublime, 'we should be strangers to this sphere of life'. The sublime inevitably condemns us to 'an eternal strife between our natural and rational destiny' (p. 141). Schiller, who in a curious way combines Burke's sense of the immediacy of nature's impact on man with Kant's belief in man's freedom from nature, perceives acutely the tragic foundation of the sublime. Although Burke often draws his examples from tragedy, real or literary, and establishes many connections between tragedy and the experience of the sublime, for him man is without exception a spectator of tragic events, not a victim of them. For Kant, tragedy as such has no relation to the sublime; it is only the limited perspective of one faculty which stirs up in the mind some rudimentary sense of the tragic. But for Schiller, man confronts tragedy in every instance in which he approaches the sublime. The sublime implicates man in an insoluble conflict, which is, after all, what all good tragedy thrives on. He can either choose to remain a slave to nature and suffer ignominy at its hands, or take the path of the free spirit and become a permanent stranger 'to this sphere of life'. Although in his essay Schiller clearly prefers the latter, he forces us to question whether the complete alienation from life itself is a fair price to pay in exchange for a heroic pose of freedom. Schiller is himself aware of this problem, though his final solution of uniting the sublime with the beautiful is as hasty as it is improbable.[12]

With Schiller we reach the most pessimistic phase of what I have called the sublime of crisis.[13] This influential model had its impact on Coleridge's views on the sublime but also presented a number of difficulties. In the theories of Burke, Kant and Schiller, nature appears as a threat, albeit one that is conducive to a certain schooling of the soul that eventually leads to greater strength. But Coleridge did not relish the darker side of nature and did not value at all the competitive measuring of power between man and nature which is at the centre of the sublime of crisis. Although Coleridge had his own anxieties regarding a close attachment to nature and found it important to liberate the mind from a debilitating dependence on sense objects, he did not find nature either overpowering, like Burke, or ultimately insignificant like Kant and, to a lesser degree, Schiller. Of the three writers discussed, Kant exerted the most enduring influence on Coleridge's views on the sublime. But Kant's theory presupposed a discontinuity between the sensible and super-sensible worlds and a blunt power play between man and nature which did not suit Coleridge's beliefs. Coleridge tried to work out a conception of the sublime which, while liberating the mind from its subjection to the senses, did not thereby result in a tragic predicament for man, as in Schiller, or in a supreme assertion of individual might, as in Kant. Moreover, Coleridge was searching for a different kind of sublime experience that did not involve a dramatic crisis or any form of therapy by fear and shock. In this he was not alone. There were in England and Germany a number of writers who developed a less gloomy version of the sublime free from any traumatic experiences. It is worth examining briefly the views of these writers in order to evaluate more accurately Coleridge's individual conception of the sublime.

Ten years before the appearance of Burke's *Inquiry*, John Baillie's 'An Essay on the Sublime' was published posthumously (1747). It did not attract much attention until Alexander Gerard referred to it in his *Essay on Taste* (1759).[14] Baillie questions whether danger and fear can be considered sources of the sublime, but his conclusions differ radically from Burke's views. For Baillie, anything that agitates the mind, be it fear of powerful objects of nature, or the exposure to an overwhelming variety of 'a thousand different Objects', belongs to the category of the

'Pathetic'. By contrast, the sublime 'rather composes than agitates'; it is not 'hurrying us from Object to Object', but presenting us with a uniform object of infinite dimensions which fills the mind with 'one *vast and uniform Idea*'. Baillie rejects the idea of conflict within the mind during the experience of sublimity. Instead of emphasizing the contrariety between pain and pleasure, defeat and victory, Baillie stresses the complete homogeneity of the process leading to the acquisition of sublimity. 'The sublime', Baillie remarks, 'when it exists *simple* and unmixed, by filling the *Mind* with one *vast and uniform Idea*, affects it with a solemn *Sedateness*; by this means the Soul becomes, as it were, one *simple grand* Sensation' (p. 33). Whatever duality of experience is implied in the expression 'solemn *Sedateness*', it is clearly not of a divisive kind, as in the case of Burke's 'delight', but presupposes a harmonious relationship of intrinsically complementary feelings.

One might wonder whether this serene and visibly simplified sublime could generate the same psychic energy and accelerated growth of mental power that the sublime of crisis unmistakably promised. For Baillie, evidently, it does. The sublime, Baillie writes, 'raises the Mind to Fits of *Greatness*, and disposes it to soar above *Mother Earth*' (p. 4). As for Kant and Schiller, the sublime involves a reflective stage when the mind develops a 'lofty Conception of her own Powers'. 'Whatever the *Essence* of the *Soul* may be', Baillie explains, 'it is the *Reflections* arising from *Sensations* only which makes her acquainted with Herself, and know her *Faculties*' (p. 7). But this statement also draws the line between Baillie and the German philosophers, for it betrays Baillie's firm roots in empirical thinking and his manner of conceiving the mind as dependent on sensations. For Baillie there is a perfect continuity between the stage when the mind is merely responding to sensory stimuli and the stage when it makes significant progress towards a self-conscious assessment of its superior might. 'Vast Objects occasion vast Sensations, and vast Sensations give the Mind a higher Idea of her own Powers' (p. 7). This simple faith in the cooperation of sense and the mind allows Baillie to see the sublime as a smooth progression 'without contraries', and without any crisis or disruption. In contact with vast and uniform objects, the imagination finds 'no Limits of its vastness, and the Mind runs out into *Infinity*, continually *creating* as it were from the *Pattern*'. As the 'Eye loses the vast Ocean, the Imagination having nothing to arrest it, catches up the Scene and extends the Prospect to *Immensity* . . .' (pp. 9–10). The imagination, then, is not subjected either to extraordinary labour or to painful defeat and the transcendence it accomplishes is not felt as a separation from the phenomenal world. Keats would call the experience the repetition of earthly life 'in a finer tone' (Letter to Benjamin Bailey, 22 November 1817).[15]

Baillie aligns himself with the tradition of Longinus's sublime in emphasizing the purely positive feelings of exaltation and pride that the mind experiences in contact with vast objects (p. 7). Years later Richard Payne Knight invoked the same tradition rather vociferously in an attempt to restore the orthodox meaning of the sublime as signifying the '*high* or *exalted*' exclusively. In his treatise *An Analytical Inquiry into the Principles of Taste* (1805), Knight undertakes a fiercely polemical dialogue with Burke's conception of the sublime, specifically his notion that terror is 'the ruling principle of the sublime'. He bluntly rejects this principle as being peculiarly 'strange and unphilosophical', and finds Burke's physiological explanations without scientific foundation, as well as leading 'directly to materialism' (pp. 374, 377). For Knight, fear represents 'the most humiliating and depressing of passions; and when a person is under its influence, it is as unnatural for him to join in any sentiments of exaltation with that which inspires it, as it would be for a man to share in the triumph of the feast of the lion, of which he was himself the victim and the prey' (p. 364).

Knight agrees with Burke on only one basic assumption about the sublime, namely, that it appeals to the passions, not to man's reason. But Knight conceives of a split sensibility during the experience of the sublime, a contrariness of feeling and knowledge, which is quite different to what Burke had in mind in dismissing rational mediation. Knight argues that it is possible to 'know an object to be terrible; that is I may know it to possess the *power* of hurting or destroying: but this is *knowledge*, and not *feeling* or *sentiment* . . . and all agree that the effect of the sublime upon the mind is a sentiment of feeling, and not a result of science' (p. 368). In other words, Knight assumes that there is no necessary relationship between what one knows to be true and how one reacts to a given event. We can experience positive sympathy with the power projected by a terrible object, even while we distinctly apprehend the possibility of danger. For Burke such a situation would, of course, never arise. What Knight calls knowledge of danger would in Burke's terms become instant emotional response. For Kant and Schiller, on the other hand, the phase of knowledge means the discovery of our immunity to all external force, not of our vulnerability to it. Knight's notion that a rational assessment of the danger involved in a given circumstance can elicit no fear whatsoever seems odd, for it implies that the apprehension of danger is a rational response, whereas the avoidance of terror is instinctual; conversely, the positive emotions we experience by repressing the knowledge of imminent danger may well prevent us from averting disaster and deliver us nicely as viands to the feast of the lion. Thus, Knight can go so far as to say that someone caught in a violent storm or shipwreck, while plainly recognizing danger, can still experience the sublime by not feeling the danger, an argument that Wordsworth and Coleridge found 'extravagant',[16] and which, less generously, can be called absurd. At least Burke, whatever limitations his theory of the sublime might have, did not falsify the ordinary human reaction to catastrophe.

Knight essentially takes over Burke's classification of the sensible qualities which generate the sublime, but divests them of their association with terror. Thus, darkness, vacuity, silence, etc. inspire exalted feelings, not because they suggest frightening privation, but because they are linked with infinity, which stimulates the mind to expand itself 'in the same manner; and in expanding itself, [the mind] will of course conceive of grand and sublime ideas'. Similarly, violent phenomena of nature 'impress sublime sentiments', only in so far as they convey energy and power, not terror (p. 367). Knight's sublime is strictly a positive experience of mental expansion and elevated feelings. He dissociates the sublime not only from the 'terrible', but also from its dependence on physical measurements. He argues that in art a great number of objects can be rendered sublime, from a swarm of bees to minute and deformed objects, regardless of how one might react to such objects in reality. Likewise, soft feelings of tenderness and love can generate as much rapture as 'terrific images of war'. Knight is quite restrictive about the kind of response the sublime produces, yet by desensualizing the sublime, he leaves room for an open-ended multiplicity of subjects. While attempting to liberate himself from Burke's empiricism, he does not succeed in escaping the associationist presuppositions of this theory, remaining liable to the charge of making the sublime a matter of individual, inherently subjective taste.[17]

In England Knight's rejection of the sublime of crisis resulted not only in the rejection of pain as a component of the sublime, but also in the distancing of the sublime from the sensory world. By contrast, in Germany the rejection of the sublime of crisis had the effect of returning the sublime to the world of nature. Both Jean Paul Richter and Gottfried von Herder, in opposition to Kant's and Schiller's theories, turn part-way towards Burke, looking for an empirical foundation for the sublime, without, however, adopting an extreme form of empiricism, or the principle of 'pain with every instance of the sublime', as Richter put it. Richter opens his discussion on the sublime in *Vorschule der Aesthetik* with a direct attack on Kant's and Schiller's notion that the imagination and the senses fail to grasp sublimity, which is accessible only to reason. He argues that the sublime 'cannot be beyond the reach of the senses' or of the imagination, because 'they embrace the object in which the sublime itself resides'. For Richter the sublime is 'always bound to some sensuous *sign* within or without us', and while it may involve transcendence, only 'nature, not an intermediate idea, makes the immense leap from the sensuous as sign into the immaterial as thing signified'. As this statement illustrates, for Richter the sublime partakes of the nature of the symbol, employing a sensory vehicle in order to reach a supersensible essence. A particular object of nature thus becomes, as in Coleridge's conception of symbolism, the carrier of the universal.

Richter takes over Kant's and Schiller's distinction between the mathematical and the dynamical sublime, but diversifies the sublime by introducing other categories such as the moral sublime, or the sublime of action, which 'may not engage the powers of the imagination and the senses', and stands in inverse relation to the prominence of the sensory symbol. Thus, for Richter, as for Knight, small objects or discrete signs, such as a 'soft, faint breeze', can be messengers of the grandest sublimity. 'Jupiter's eyebrows', he notes, 'move much more sublimely than his arm or than he himself.'[18] Towards the end of his essay Richter strongly objects to Kant's inclusion of pain in the sublime on the ground that it leads to the heretical notion that 'the greatest instance of the sublime, namely God, will give the greatest pain' (p. 76). He also opposes Kant's view that compared to the sublime 'everything else is small', which fails to acknowledge the existence of degrees within the sphere of the sublime. This Kantian precept also intrigued Herder and Coleridge, but for different reasons.

By comparison with Richter's arguments, Herder's response to Kant's sublime of crisis is at once fuller and more coherent, though far less charitable. In Part III of *Kalligone* Herder undertakes a systematic, point by point critique of Kant's 'Analytic of the Sublime', and consistently denies the validity of Kant's claims.[19] Like Richter, Herder begins by opposing Kant's notion that the sublime does not reside in objects of nature and is beyond the grasp of the imagination. His main claim, which becomes the leitmotiv of his discussion of Kant, is that there can be no sublime outside the realm of nature and that art itself depends on nature for its supply of sublime forms. Herder does not understand how the sublime can be divorced from sensible objects since only such objects can generate feelings, and the sublime, as Kant himself admits, pertains to feelings. He also thinks he perceives a logical fallacy in Kant's statement that although the ideas of reason do not allow for an adequate sensory presentation, this very inadequacy 'admits of sensible presentation' through the trial of the imagination. In other words, Herder does not comprehend how negativity can signify and how ideas which cannot be represented in sensible objects can none the less be 'aroused and summoned into the mind' ('Analytic of the Sublime', p. 84). There is, of course, no logical inconsistency in Kant's argument; as Coleridge well knew, it is not in matters of logic that one can find shortcomings in Kant. But if the metaphysics of *a priori* ideas is unacceptable, as it is for Herder, none of Kant's claims, regardless of their impeccable cogency, could possibly make much sense.

Herder finds that the ideology of the supersensible in Kant's theory of the sublime rests on an insensitivity to and misunderstanding of nature, as well as a self-serving philosophy of personal aggrandizement. To say that there can be nothing sublime in nature is to declare oneself as the 'only, absolute and all sublime'. If in the experience of sublimity one must abandon sensibility altogether in order to engage oneself with the ideas of reason, one might as well remain on land rather than confront the spectacle of a raging sea. Nature is not, as Kant presented it, chaotic or devoid of purpose, but shows in its rudest objects a striving for form. Indeed, Herder argues, chaos and nature are incompatible with one another. Herder is particularly antagonized by Kant's definition of the sublime as '*that in comparison with which everything else is small*'. This definition again results from Kant's denial of nature which, according to Herder, gives us measures of comparison. In Herder's view this principle involves a form of despotism and self-deification that did not exist even during the era of Roman emperors. Herder also objects to Kant's claim that the imagination must deny itself in order to project reason's higher might, a point to which Weiskel himself is also sensitive. This notion is as tyrannical as the previous one and can only result in a crippling conflict within the mind. Like Blake, Herder insists that the Absolute can be contained by the imagination; otherwise, the sublime would move one 'as little as the man on the moon'. For Herder the sublime does not subject the mind to convulsive movements or give rise to pleasure fraught with pain, but consists in a pure, unadulterated and completely fulfilling enlargement of the spirit. Finally, Herder makes a sharp turn away from the Kantian sublime by denying its radical difference from the beautiful. Like the beautiful, the sublime is connected with sensible objects and depends on our discovery of the finality of nature. The sublime may be regarded as the highest form of the beautiful, with which it coexists as the stem and branches of the same tree.[20]

Coleridge was quite receptive to Herder's idea of a continuity between the beautiful and the sublime, and to the view that the sublime does not loom over a threatening abyss between the sensible and supersensible world and does not involve fear, a view also shared by Baillie, Richter and Knight. He was predisposed to entertain the notion that the sublime could be achieved through a smooth transition between sense objects and a transcendent world, but not from a position of naive empiricism, as in Baillie. For Coleridge, as for Richter, this transition presupposed a structure of symbolic mediation, and, as we shall see, there are many points of similarity between his conception of symbolism and of the sublime. The sublime also tends, like the Coleridgean symbol, towards an infinite 'I AM' as its highest destination. Like Herder and Richter, Coleridge wanted to give nature a much more positive role in the experience of sublimity than it has in Kant. He probably did not mind at all Herder's criticism of Kant's view that, for the most part, 'nature excites the ideas of the sublime in its chaos or in its wildest and most irregular disorder and desolation . . .' ('Analytic of the Sublime', p. 84).[21] But Herder's wholesale rejection of Kant's metaphysics of *a priori* ideas was thoroughly distasteful to Coleridge and tended to strengthen Coleridge's pro-Kantian leanings.[22] Coleridge felt that Herder, in reacting to Kant, centred the sublime too firmly in nature, thus jeopardizing the mind's necessary flight towards a transcendent realm. On the whole Coleridge found Kant's theory of the sublime much more rigorously conceived than Herder's. Of particular appeal to Coleridge was Kant's view, to which Herder objected, that the sublime suspends all comparison within the mind, securing the subjective identity of the sublime object and its location in a transcendent abode to which no objective measures of comparison with other objects apply.[23] But Coleridge, although attracted to Kant's version of the sublime, had a number of objections to it. These objections led Coleridge to transform the Kantian sublime into a new structure which suited both his sensitivity to nature and his Christian beliefs.

CHAPTER 2 COLERIDGE'S CONCEPTION OF THE SUBLIME

Some of Coleridge's most important statements on the sublime appear in his marginalia to Herder's *Kalligone*, and this is a good place to begin an analysis of his views.[24] For Coleridge, Herder's definition of the sublime was imprecise and faulty. Herder, he complained, 'mistakes for the Sublime sometimes the *Grand*, sometimes the *Majestic*, sometimes the *Intense*', without realizing that a visual whole as such 'cannot be sublime'.[25] Thus, 'A Mountain in a cloudless sky, its summit . . . hidden by clouds and seemingly blended with the sky, while mists and floating vapours encompass it, is sublime'.[26] Elsewhere Coleridge provided a literary illustration which sheds further light on his objection to Herder's confused use of the term sublime. He argued that the description of the Messiah in Milton's lines 'Onward he moved / And thousands of his saints around' is marked by 'grandeur, but it is grandeur without completeness'. However, when Milton adds the line 'Far off their coming shone', he achieves the 'highest sublime. There is *total* completeness. So I would say that the Saviour praying on the Mountain, the Desert on one hand, the Sea on the other, the City at an immense distance below, was sublime. But I should say of the Saviour looking towards the City, his countenance full of piety, that he was majestic, and of the situation that it was grand.'[27]

From these examples encompassing the natural and the rhetorical sublime, we may infer that for Coleridge the essential qualities which occasion the sublime are boundlessness and indefiniteness. Yet Coleridge's emphasis is not so much on infinite extension as on the quality of perceptual indistinctness which allows certain objects to lose their individual form and blend with one another into a whole, though not one that can be grasped visually. As Wlecke observes, commenting on Coleridge's note to Herder, 'it is not the vastness as such of the mountain which occasions the experience of sublimity. Instead, it is the fact that the perceptual boundaries of the mountain are obscured which allows for the experience . . . It seems that for Coleridge the intended object of sublime consciousness must be in some way undefined, lacking in observable limits, and therefore not exhibiting a precisely delineated spatial identity' (pp. 73–4). This is true, but with one important addition: the lack of distinct boundaries and spatial specificity serves as the means of conveying to the mind an impression of unity, of 'total completeness'. Wlecke's statement may be rephrased, therefore, as follows: for Coleridge the 'intended object of sublime consciousness' must be undefined physically so as to intimate a unity of the highest order which is vaguely present in phenomenal reality. Unity of an indeterminate character, which cannot be localized in physical forms, yet is hazily apprehended through them, is the foremost quality of Coleridge's sublime object, to which all others are subordinated. What makes the clouded mountain sublime is not just the fact that its boundaries are obscured, but that by virtue of this obscurity it is '*seemingly* blended with the sky' (my italics). The union of the mountain with the sky is merely guessed at, not seen, since the combined effect of mists and clouds makes it impossible to perceive an outline of harmonious shape. Similarly, in the example from Milton, the line 'Far off their coming shone' conveys through the uniform impression of light a sense of oneness which subsumes the multiplicity of particulars previously suggested by the image of the Messiah moving onward with 'thousands of his saints around'. Here light serves the same function as the clouds and mists in the mountain passage, smoothing over the separate edges of particular objects and communicating to the mind a single impression of wholeness.

In insisting on the indefinite and loosely harmonious texture of the sublime object, Coleridge clearly intends to emphasize the mind's freedom from the phenomenal world in the experience of sublimity. The reason why a mountain summit projected against a clear sky fails to arouse sublime feelings is that its commanding presence enthrals the mind completely, blocking its flight beyond the world of physical objects. By contrast, the misty and clouded mountain nowhere arrests or intrudes upon an observer; its physicality is so discrete, so 'translucent', one might say, using a loaded, though, as we shall see, quite appropriate term, that it hints at a spiritual essence, leaving the mind free to explore its origins. For Coleridge the sublime object appears to be an invitation to an experience of transcendence, nourishing the mind's longing to reach out for the '*total* completeness' which is only hazily intimated by shadowy images in the phenomenal world. Coleridge's sublime landscape implies, however vaguely, a relationship between a subject and an infinite 'I AM'. This is supported indirectly by a passage from *The Friend* in which Coleridge is concerned with the susceptibility of 'deep feelings' to 'combine with obscure ideas, in preference to distinct and clear notions'. He notes that while it is important to accustom the intellect to develop clear conceptions of things, it is likewise essential to 'reserve deep feelings' to objects which are sublime, that is, objects 'which their very sublimity renders indefinite, no less than their indefiniteness renders them sublime' and which 'belong, as by a natural right to those obscure ideas that are necessary to the moral perfection of the human being'. Coleridge identifies such objects as 'the Ideas of Being, Form, Life, the Reason, the Law of Conscience, Freedom, Immortality, God'.[28]

It appears that for Coleridge an idea is a source of sublimity to the extent that, like the misty and clouded mountain landscape, it remains indefinite. Phenomenal shapelessness and conceptual indistinctness are thus directly related,[29] just as there is a fundamental affinity between delimited objects of sense and 'distinct and clear notions'. To express this differently, it is not the understanding – a faculty which 'concerns itself exclusively with . . . *particulars* in time and space' and which organizes such data into distinct notions (*SM*, p. 59) – that supplies the mind with ideas of sublimity. By simple exclusion, we may deduce that it is the imagination and reason which play a part in the experience of sublimity, though I hasten to add that Coleridge's terms are distinct from what at a mere glance may appear as Kantian concepts. An idea, as an object of sublimity, must be 'an educt of the Imagination actuated by the pure Reason' (*SM*, p. 113). As an offspring of the imagination, that 'esemplastic' power which dissolves all 'fixities and definites'[30] in order to recreate an ideal unity, an idea betrays its heritage by breaking out of the confines of form; it is itself a dynamic power, rather than a form in the Aristotelian sense. At the same time, through its very indefiniteness, an idea becomes susceptible to the influence of a higher power, and becomes the means through which an absolute essence, be it life, reason, immortality or God, reveals itself to the mind. An idea is never to be confused with the Absolute itself; it merely points to it, as a sign to a thing signified. Its final point of destination is an infinite 'I AM', without which its indefiniteness would fail to signify and become mere emptiness. In short, an idea is born out of the womb of the imagination, but is baptized and given a purpose by pure reason (*SM*, pp. 60–1 n. 2).

A structure of symbolic signification is at the root of Coleridge's representation of the sublime whether by means of a natural or conceptual object. The obscure harmony present in the mountain landscape, which as Coleridge put it elsewhere 'is more a Feeling than a Sight' (*CN*, II, 2453), suggests the presence of a higher unity of which it is the symbol, just as an indefinite idea, itself linked with deep feeling, is a symbol of pure being.[31] There is a striking resemblance between the physiognomy of Coleridge's symbolic and sublime objects. Both share the qualities of light and translucence[32] and both are centred in a subject, not in an object. Just as the Coleridgean symbol has no meaning apart from a mind seeking to become self-conscious 'of itself as a subject', through the process of coming to unity with another being, so Coleridge's sublime object is a mere void if separated from an activity which involves 'the whole soul of man' and is directed towards the attainment of an ideal unity. But Coleridge himself neatly establishes the connection between the symbol and the sublime, as the following two related passages indicate:

> We call an object sublime in relation to which the exercise of comparison is suspended: while on the contrary that object is most

beautiful, which in its highest perfection sustains while it satisfies the comparing Power . . . It is impossible that the same object should be sublime and beautiful at the same moment to the same mind, though a beautiful object may excite and be made the symbol of an Idea that is truly [sublime. A] Serpent in a wreath of folds bathing in the sun is beautiful to Aspasia, whose attention is confined to the visual impression, but excites an emotion of sublimity in Plato who contemplates under that symbol the Idea of Eternity. (Shawcross, 'Coleridge's Marginalia', p. 341)

. . . the difference of the Sublime and the Beautiful is a *diversity* . . . I meet, I *find* the Beautiful – but I give, contribute, or rather attribute the Sublime. No object of Sense is sublime in itself; but only as far as I make it a symbol of some Idea. The circle is a beautiful figure in itself; it becomes sublime, when I contemplate eternity under that figure – The Beautiful is the perfection, the sublime the suspension, of the comparing Power. Nothing not shapely . . . can be called beautiful: nothing that has a shape can be sublime except by metaphor *ab occasione ad rem*. So true it is, that those objects whose shape most recedes from Shapeliness are commonly the exciting occasions.[33]

These passages contain the essence of Coleridge's philosophy of the sublime and the most elaborate version of it to be found in his work. They spell out what we have already inferred from Coleridge's previous illustrations, namely, that the sublime consists in a mode of symbolic contemplation and pertains to the mind, not to an object. A sense object may possess in itself qualities which make it fit for the sublime, the most important of which appears to be shapelessness. Yet, it is clear from Coleridge's examples of the serpent and the circle that even a shapely object can be the occasion of an experience of sublimity, which means that the mind essentially creates sublimity out of any object by lending it purely subjective qualities. In the process of seeking to grasp an idea of eternity that is intrinsically obscure and 'shapeless', the mind can dissolve the shapeliness of an object and transform it into a diffuse texture approximating the indefiniteness of the conceptual sign. As Wlecke explains, 'Whenever anything is grasped as sublime, it necessarily takes on the characteristic of appearing "indefinite," whether or not it possesses this characteristic in itself apart from any relation to a subject.' The circle in Coleridge's example, 'though retaining its purely objective shape, does indeed recede from shapeliness to the extent that it comes to function as a phenomenon symbolic of the obscure and indefinite idea of eternity . . . The circle comes to be seen not for what it is, but for what it represents as a symbol; as a phenomenon, therefore, its objective shape sinks away into the indefiniteness of its symbolic dimension. It takes on a kind of subjective shapelessness, and thus is rendered sublime' (pp. 79–80).

Much of Coleridge's definition of the subjective origin of the sublime is based on a distinction between the beautiful and the sublime which is, of course, central to Kant's aesthetic theory. In the *Critique of Judgement* Kant argues that in the case of the beautiful we always 'seek a ground external to ourselves' in objects of nature, whereas for the sublime we seek it 'merely in ourselves and in our attitude of thought, which introduces sublimity into the representation of nature' (p. 84). Coleridge's point that one '*finds* the beautiful' in objects of sense but one must 'contribute, or rather attribute the sublime' to them seems to approximate closely Kant's argument. Clarence D. Thorpe, the earliest critic who examined Coleridge's philosophy of the sublime, considers Coleridge's distinction between the beautiful and the sublime to be identical with Kant's. In the case of the beautiful, Thorpe argues – providing an accurate synopsis of Kant's views, but not, as I shall show, of Coleridge's – 'the mind goes out to its object, and, finding a definite form which can be grasped and held in its unity, it rests there and takes its pleasure in the sensible image'. In the sublime, on the other hand, the mind, 'baffled by an inability to grasp the object, yet conscious of a totality which fascinates while it eludes, recoils upon itself, finding its pleasure in elevated ideas that rival the greatness of the object, but which center in itself rather than in the object' (p. 197). In the experience of the sublime the mind 'tends to expand indefinitely, seeking a unity which it feels but cannot perceive, until it is lost in a sort of pleasing bewilderment in intuitions of endless power and greatness' (p. 196). Thorpe ploughs through the vast descriptive material accumulated by Coleridge during his travels and sorts out passages which fall under the category either of the beautiful or of the sublime. He identifies as sublime those descriptions which show Coleridge in a state of mental tension, unable to rest his eyes in a particular scene. I would like to quote one passage where, according to Thorpe, 'though the word is not mentioned, the conditions of sublimity are all satisfied' (pp. 201–2):

> And now we arrived at Hartsburgh – Hills over by our sides, in all conceivable variety of forms and garniture – It were idle in me to attempt by words to give their projections and their retirings and how they were now in Cones, now in roundnesses, now in tonguelike

> lengths . . . or how they now stood abreast . . . now rose up behind each other, or now . . . presented almost a Sea of huge motionless waves, too multiform for Painting, too multiform even for the Imagination to remember them – yea, my very sight seems *incapacitated* by the novelty and Complexity of the Scene. Ye red lights from the Rain Clouds! Ye gave the whole the last Magic Touch! (*CL*, I, 513)

One could easily make a case that Coleridge's description is picturesque rather than sublime, since what dominates the landscape is infinite variety, while at the same time the 'parts are seen and distinguished', to quote from Coleridge's own definition of the picturesque (*BL*, II, 309). But this is a minor objection. The more important point here is that the assumptions which lead Thorpe to regard the Hartsburgh landscape as sublime are difficult to accept in full, or at least require finer tuning. Although Thorpe is on the whole quite sensitive to the differences between Kant's and Coleridge's sublime and in the latter part of his essay goes to some length pointing them out, none the less, in his exposition of Coleridge's views he often slips into a Kantian language, thus attributing to Coleridge beliefs that were foreign to his thinking. What convinces Thorpe that the Hartsburgh landscape is sublime is undoubtedly Coleridge's confession that his visual, imaginative and verbal powers were '*incapacitated* by the novelty and Complexity of the Scene', which suggests to the critic a parallel with the breakdown of imaginative comprehension in Kant's theory. Thorpe repeatedly identifies sublime passages in Coleridge by markers stemming from Kant: 'mental tension or exertion' rather than pure enjoyment, an object which 'tends to baffle the imagination', an experience where the mind 'recoils upon itself', being forced to 'flee from sensible imagery'.

It is one thing to say that Coleridge's sublime object is elusive, but quite another to imply that this elusiveness generates the kind of mental stress and bafflement which in Kant's sublime arises from the unsuccessful effort of the imagination to comprehend infinity. For Coleridge the elusiveness of the sublime object is not a sign of the representational inefficacy of the imagination, which in turn signals reason's higher finality; rather, it is a guarantee that the imagination is alive, since such phenomenal elusiveness is the work of the imagination in the first place. Furthermore, it is risky to equate whatever restlessness Coleridge may have felt when facing a landscape of overwhelming variety with the dramatic journey of the imagination towards 'an abyss in which it fears to lose itself', as described by Kant. What Coleridge saw out there was not nature's chaos but luxurious richness. Hence, the threat of being engulfed by the external world was certainly less real for Coleridge than it was for Schiller, and to a lesser degree for Kant. Nowhere in his statements on the sublime did Coleridge mention nature's formless chaos or aimless violence as a condition of attaining the triumph of man's ascent into the world of absolute freedom. Coleridge was, accordingly, not as anxious as Kant or Schiller to 'flee from' the phenomenal world. Rather, he felt much more comfortable with a form of sublimity which, while originating in the mind, allowed for an intense imaginative engagement with a sense object, such that the object itself becomes 'a living part in that Unity, of which it is the representative'.

Thorpe's emphasis on the bafflement of the imagination in Coleridge's theory has the effect of representing the Coleridgean sublime as a dual experience based on conflict, and we are naturally led to think of the conflict at the centre of Kant's sublime between the imagination and reason. Yet Coleridge nowhere speaks of such a conflict, nor does he identify directly the presence of two faculties. Coleridge's sublime is an homogeneous structure without any visible breaks or discontinuities. Furthermore, Coleridge does not seem to posit an actual moment when the experience of sublimity is consummated as such, which would produce the kind of release Thorpe speaks of. The sublime, like the Coleridgean symbol, is a relational term, which, like a discrete ray of light, merely maps out a path of travel, a point of destination, not one of arrival. Its main dimension is the amorphous experience of 'allness' in which the self is completely absorbed, and from which it does not emerge, as in Kant, with a sense of having reached a point of divine superiority and might, '*in comparison with which everything else is small*'.

This brings me to another point of disagreement with Thorpe's interpretation of Coleridge's sublime. In defining Coleridge's experience of sublimity as one in which the mind 'recoils upon itself finding its pleasure in elevated ideas' of 'endless power and greatness', that 'rival the greatness of the object', Thorpe again extrapolates ideas from Kant's treatise which do not fully represent Coleridge's views. The pattern of 'rivalry' between nature and the mind is indeed endemic to Kant's theory of the sublime, but it does not apply to Coleridge's. We recall that for Kant the mind willingly allows nature to present itself as an object of sublimity, displaying all its magnitude and might, so that the mind can then discover within itself a power that puts all of nature's greatness to shame. But we will be hard-pressed to find in Coleridge's statements on the sublime any suggestions regarding a power play between nature and the mind. In fact the rhetoric of power, which is so prevalent in eighteenth-century treatises on the sublime, is conspicuously absent in Coleridge. Unlike Kant, Coleridge does not refer to sublimity as a moment when the mind seizes upon its God-like might. On the contrary, in one instance where Coleridge is more articulate than usual in defining the culminating emotional response to sublimity, he speaks of an intense feeling of self-annihilation, and not one of self-aggrandizement. 'Gothic art', Coleridge writes, 'is sublime. On entering a cathedral, I am filled with devotion and with awe; I am lost to the actualities that surround me, and my whole being expands into the infinite; earth and air, nature and art, all swell up into eternity, and the only sensible impression left is, "that I am nothing"' (*Misc C*, pp. 11–12, quoted by Thorpe, p. 207).

Wlecke, who has provided an excellent analysis of this passage, perceives Coleridge's experience in the Gothic cathedral as involving the 'dissolution of the spatial identities of the objects of perception', which leads to 'a dissolution of a sense of a fixed spatial identity on the part of the subject'. By 'becoming "lost to the actualities that surround" him', Wlecke points out, 'he also loses his sense of the way in which his presence is delimited or defined in space. Hence the subject can feel his "whole being" expanding "into the infinite"' (pp. 74–5). The notable point here is that for Coleridge the self's expansion 'into the infinite' is not followed by a recognition of its superior power, but by a feeling of nothingness. What Coleridge seems to suggest is that in the experience of sublimity the self grows out of any determinate form and is swallowed up by an indefinite 'allness'. The term 'nothing' does not 'deny the existing reality of the "I"', but merely indicates that the self 'now lacks the means to define itself as any precisely limited "thing"'.[34] Coleridge, then, expects from the sublime not the attainment of personal power but the absorption into a higher unity. Moreover, Coleridge's experience in the Gothic cathedral shows no sign of a rivalry with nature. It appears that Coleridge wants to take nature along in the experience of the sublime, rather than leave it behind in order to look down upon it from the insurmountable height of the supersensible world. The mind's sense of infinite expansion is dependent on the concomitant swelling of the phenomenal world 'into eternity'. It is as if Coleridge wants to make the experience of sublimity all-inclusive without exception, embracing 'earth and air, nature and art'. At no point in this experience does Coleridge establish comparisons between the relative greatness of the physical world and the absolute greatness of 'elevated ideas'.

In his marginal comments on Herder and Solger and elsewhere as well, Coleridge explicitly rejects the 'exercise of comparison' as having any bearing on the sublime. What Coleridge had in mind by the 'exercise of comparison' is not entirely clear, and since Coleridge fails to provide additional information, one can only speculate. On this point Thorpe is not very helpful. He quotes all the important passages where Coleridge refers to the principle of comparison, but assumes that the premises of Coleridge's argument and the meaning attached to the term 'comparison' remain the same in each instance. I believe that a few discriminations can be made and that there are at least two different ways in which Coleridge formulates the principle of comparison. The first, which appears in a piece written from Ratzeburg in 1799, betrays the influence of Burke's notion of the sublime:

> About a month ago, before the thaw came on, there was a storm of wind; during the whole night, such were the thunders and howlings of the breaking ice, that they have left a conviction on my mind, that there are sounds more sublime than any sight can be, more absolutely suspending the power of comparison, and more utterly absorbing the mind's self-consciousness in its total attention to the object working upon it. (*The Friend*, I, 367)

This is one of the few instances where Coleridge's sublime is selected from among the more violent and potentially fearful manifestations in nature. Burke comes immediately to mind, not only his unshaken belief in terror as a 'ruling principle of the sublime', but especially his description of the sublime experience as one in which 'the mind is so entirely filled with its object, that it cannot entertain any other, nor by consequence reason on that object which employs it' (p. 51). Burke also claimed that 'The eye is not the only organ of sensation by which a sublime passion may be produced' and that 'Sounds have a great power in these as in most other passions.' 'Excessive loudness alone', he argued, 'is sufficient to overpower the soul' (p. 72). Although Coleridge does not make a case about terror as an emotional response to the sublime, he implies a structure of experience parallel to the one articulated by Burke. In effect, Coleridge states that one is so entirely given over to and possessed by an object of sublimity that one loses all consciousness of other objects, and of oneself as a separate, thinking being. Burke's definition of astonishment as 'that state of the soul, in which all its motions are suspended', is a rough equivalent of what Coleridge may mean by the suspension of the 'power of comparison'.

In looking at this passage, Thorpe concludes that Coleridge's sublime involves a blatant paradox, for 'while it is characterized by a flight of mind from the sensuous reality to its own conceptions, the object giving rise to it so compels and enchains the attention that no comparison with other objects is possible' (p. 197). The paradox, however, is not to be found in Coleridge's Ratzeburg description, but emerges only if one assumes, like Thorpe, that the underlying structure of Coleridge's sublime is without fail some form of Kantian experience of transcendence. This is, though, highly suspect. Neither in the Ratzeburg description, nor in the previously quoted passage from Coleridge's letter to Poole (quoted on pp. 119–20 above), does Coleridge indicate 'a flight of mind from the sensuous reality'. On the contrary, he is so engrossed in the immediate objects of perception as to lose all awareness of himself, not to mention the mind's elevated ideas. In 1799 Coleridge, we must recall, was quite receptive to modes of thinking which are closer to the English empirical tradition than to German transcendentalism. During his travels through the countryside in various places in England and abroad, Coleridge, as we have seen in the chapter on the picturesque, often found objects of nature in themselves as 'absorbing' as the sounds heard during a stormy night in Ratzeburg. If in such instances Coleridge referred to a particular landscape as sublime, he had in mind an experience that was deeply connected to natural objects in a way that is quite foreign to Kant's philosophy.

Yet, if we turn to Coleridge's definition of the principle of comparison in his marginalia to Herder, which were probably written in 1804, it seems quite appropriate to use Kant's metaphysics as a frame of reference, since here Coleridge is directly engaged with the tenets of Kant's theory of the sublime, as Herder interprets them. However, we immediately encounter difficulties. Coleridge's rejection of the principle of comparison in the sublime appears to be an attack on Kant, rather than an endorsement of his views. Thorpe reads Coleridge's comments thus, but there is also another possibility which should be considered. In rejecting the principle of comparison Coleridge may very well have intended to undermine Herder's position and to reinforce Kant's. Kant, after all, despite the fact that the process whereby sublimity is reached in his system involves a structure of comparison – between the capability of the imagination and that of reason, between the power of nature and the superior power of the mind – isolates the actual moment of sublimity itself as that in which all comparison ceases to exist. 'We call that *sublime*', Kant claims, which is 'not only great, but absolutely great in every point of view (great beyond all comparison).' Kant's point is that the standard of comparison is operative in the world of sense, where something can always appear to be greater or smaller than something else. Since the beautiful is linked with objects of sensible intuition, it can be characterized as great or small according to the object to which it refers. On the other hand, since the sublime pertains to ideas and not to objects of nature, it is not subject to a principle of comparison based on an 'objective measure'. The sublime object is therefore simply great 'beyond all comparison'. It is defined by standards which are purely subjective and its logical structure is a proposition of identity: A = A ('Analytic of the Sublime', pp. 86–8).

Coleridge, too, like Kant, uses the principle of comparison in order to establish the mental abode of the sublime and the objective location of the beautiful. It was Herder who, in response to Kant's *Critique*, argued that 'nothing is absolutely great', that in every experience of sublimity an act of comparison is involved, even though it is not consciously realized, and that finally to separate the sublime from objects and inevitably from standards of comparison is to rob it of its own basis (*Kalligone*, pp. 62–4). It appears, then, that Coleridge's arguments regarding the principle of comparison stand firmly on the foundation of Kant's sublime and are directed against Herder. Coleridge understood the substance of Kant's thesis and did not accept the premises of Herder's denial of it.

This example shows how careful one must be in tracing the meandering path of Coleridge's involvement with Kant's philosophy, for Coleridge, in typical fashion, simultaneously moves towards and away from the eddy of Kantian ideas. In defending the suspension of the principle of comparison, Coleridge reinforces Kant's distinction between the beautiful and the sublime; yet, in providing the subsequent illustrations of the serpent and the circle, Coleridge empties Kant's distinction of much of its significance. It is important to keep in mind that for Kant the sublime cannot have its starting point in a beautiful object which always has a definite form and conveys to the mind an idea of nature as purposive in itself. Rather, the sublime 'is to be found in a formless object, so far as in it or by occasion of it *boundlessness* is represented, and yet its totality is also present to thought' (p. 82). Coleridge clearly moves out of Kant's orbit when he asserts that a beautiful object may become the occasion of an experience of sublimity, provided that the mind lends this object a symbolic content. His argument in favour of Kant's distinction between the beautiful and the sublime slips into an argument stressing not the divergence but the intrinsic compatibility between the two aesthetical judgements.

In other writings Coleridge also tends to represent the beautiful as a category which, as Elinor Shaffer suggests, 'more and more resembles the sublime', being defined according to the principle of 'free life' rather than form ('Coleridge's Revolution in the Standard of Taste', p. 219). In fact, Coleridge's sense of the continuity between the beautiful and the sublime has much in common with Herder's claim that the sublime is merely the culmination of a process which begins with the beautiful. We recall that Herder described the beautiful and the sublime as 'the branches and stem of one tree'. The best testimony of Coleridge's interest in the affinity between the beautiful and the sublime is a notebook entry written from Malta in 1804, the same year when Coleridge may have written the commentary on Herder's *Kalligone*:

> O that Sky, that soft blue mighty Arch, resting on the mountains or solid Sea-like plain / what an aweful adorable omneity in unity. I know no other perfect union of the sublime with the beautiful, that is, so that they should both be felt at the same moment tho' by different faculties yet each faculty predisposed by itself to receive the specific modification from the other. To the eye it is an inverted Goblet, the inside of a ~~gold~~ sapphire Bason; = perfect ⟨Beauty in shape and colour⟩; to the mind ⟨it is⟩ immensity, but even the eye ⟨feels as if it were to⟩ look *thro*, with dim sense of the non ~~differ~~resistence . . . the eye itself feels that the limitation is in its own power not in the Object, but pursue this in the manner of the Old Hamburgh Poet. (*CN*, II, 2346)

This passage maintains the same basic features of Coleridge's conception of the sublime as the marginalia on Herder. We see again that the essence of the sublime for Coleridge is the experience of a complete unity, of the dissolution of 'omneity' or multiplicity of parts into an absorbing feeling of 'allness'. And we also recognize the familiar distinction between the beautiful and the sublime: the former refers the mind to the 'shape and colour' of objects, the latter inspires the mind to contemplate an 'immensity' that transcends individual objects. And yet on one important issue Coleridge's notebook reflection contradicts his theory of the sublime, as expounded in the commentary on Herder. In the latter he argues, apropos of the difference between the beautiful and the sublime, that 'It is impossible that the same object should be sublime and beautiful at the same moment to the same mind, though a beautiful object may excite and be made the symbol of an Idea that is truly [sublime].' In his notebook, on the other hand, Coleridge describes just what had appeared to be impossible, the simultaneous perception of the beautiful and the sublime in the same object, by the same mind. Despite this discrepancy, there is a basic similarity in structure and syntax between the two passages. In both examples Coleridge establishes distinctions between the beautiful and the sublime with one hand and removes them with the other. His argument moves towards sharp analytic focus and distinction and towards indistinction at the same time. The syntax in both passages is marked by subordinate clauses which qualify and ultimately change the direction of the argument introduced in the main clause. Thus, in the marginalia to *Kalligone* the main clause ('It is impossible that the same object should be sublime and beautiful at the same moment to the same mind') pronounces the beautiful and the sublime to be separate, while the subordinate clause ('though a beautiful object may excite and be made the symbol of an Idea that is truly [sublime]') clearly bridges the gap between the two. In the notebook entry, the syntax is more elaborate and shows more clearly the characteristic form of Coleridge's utterance, halting as it does, and winding backward and forward, gathering a string of qualifying 'yets', 'buts' and 'thoughs'. Here Coleridge begins by asserting the 'perfect union of the sublime with the beautiful', a perception which immediately triggers his opposite concern to chart the differences between the two categories. He notes that the faculties involved in the perception of the beautiful and the sublime are distinct, even though both may 'be felt at the same moment'. Yet as soon as this point is made, it becomes amplified in exactly the opposite direction, for we are invited to consider not how different the faculties are, but how such 'distinction is not division', as 'each faculty' is 'predisposed by itself to receive the specific modification from the other'. We thus return to the original perception of the harmonious coexistence of the beautiful and the sublime. This ample argument, by the way, is developed by Coleridge in one long, meandering sentence. In the latter part of the notebook entry, Coleridge recapitulates the same movement towards and away from the starting point of his reflection. He begins by identifying the faculties which pertain to the beautiful and the sublime and by showing how, viewed through each faculty, the same object will appear differently to a perceiver. Yet by the end of the same sentence, the focus has clearly shifted again to the manner in which the two faculties may converge and perceive the same object in the same way. The eye, which perceives the beautiful, itself appears to strive for a mode of vision which is not attached to sensible objects, but looks through them. Coleridge describes here an experience where sight changes imperceptibly into feeling, and sense becomes, as it were, mind. We can see from this example why Coleridge could not subscribe to Kant's conception of the sublime, even as he tried to uphold Kant's system against Herder's objections. Coleridge is not interested in exploring the strife between nature and mind, sense and reason; rather, he is interested in the process whereby one merges with the other in an 'adorable' image of 'omneity in unity'. His concern is finally not with the dichotomy between the beautiful and the sublime, but with their intrinsic affinity to one another. For Coleridge the sublime represents the highest form of unity, towards which the beautiful tends and to which it can be elevated.

Curiously enough, Wordsworth seems to have understood that the basic meaning of the sublime for Coleridge was an experience of total unity. Whether by choice or an inability to resist the force of Coleridge's influence, Wordsworth, in a fragmentary essay on the beautiful and the sublime, integrated, among a variety of other perspectives, Coleridge's ideas on the sublime. This essay shows how Wordsworth responded to Coleridge's views and provides us with an example of a flexible and richly constructed theory of the sublime against which we may be able to draw more clearly a synthetic composite of Coleridge's conception of the sublime.

CHAPTER 3 THE KANTIAN SEDUCTION. WORDSWORTH ON THE SUBLIME

In his well-known study *The Sublime*, Samuel Monk argues that Kant's critical philosophy captured the 'fundamental contrasts between the romantic age and the early eighteenth century'. Although 'Argument by analogy is confessedly weak', Monk writes, 'it is possible to maintain that there is a general similarity between the point of view of *The Critique of Judgment* and the *Prelude*; and that the *Prelude* differs from the *Essay on Man* in a manner vaguely analogous to the way in which *The Critique of Pure Reason* differs from *An Essay on Human Understanding*' (p. 5). Monk's overly cautious and somewhat embarrassed suggestion regarding the convergence between Kant's and Wordsworth's views is indicative of a general reticence among critics to entertain the possibility that Kant exerted a direct influence on Wordsworth and that the 'vaguely analogous' modes of thought in both writers are not merely coincidental. Admittedly, it may seem rather indecorous to link the poet who made no secret of his distaste for books and formal training and who often criticized Coleridge for his devotion to metaphysics instead of nature, with as radical a thinker as Kant. But Wordsworth's little-known essay written about 1811 ('The Sublime and the Beautiful')[35] strongly suggests that he was familiar with Kant's 'Analytic of the Sublime' in *The Critique of Judgement*. No evidence, however, has surfaced to date which indicates that Wordsworth had read Kant's *Critique*. What we do know is that Wordsworth frequently discussed the subject of the sublime with Coleridge,[36] who was, of course, well versed in Kantian philosophy. Ironically, in his theory of the sublime Coleridge assimilated fewer components of Kant's system than Wordsworth. If Coleridge was in fact Wordsworth's instructor in transcendental philosophy, he managed to turn Wordsworth into a far more faithful disciple of Kant than he was himself.

The full impact of Kant's conception of the sublime becomes evident only in the latter part of Wordsworth's essay. In the beginning Wordsworth attempts to clear the ground of conventional definitions of the sublime, staging a battle against various unnamed opponents, among whom Coleridge wins a prominent place. Wordsworth's first strategy is to subvert the privileged hierarchical status given to the sublime by most aestheticians, including Burke, Kant and Coleridge, by suggesting that the beautiful represents a subtler and more mature aesthetic perception which develops after the mind is able to shake off its early infatuation with the sublime.[37] The sublime, he argues, in a confessedly 'ungracious' observation, is likely to appeal to the immaturity and natural impressionability of children or to newcomers in a mountain country who respond merely to the obtrusive and sensational features of a landscape (ll. 26–31).

And yet Wordsworth himself cannot withstand the fascination with the sublime that dominated the sensibility of his contemporaries, for he spends the rest of his essay defining and redefining the sublime and nearly forgets the beautiful altogether. In his first attempt to provide a definition of the sublime, Wordsworth again takes an anti-Coleridgean stance. He argues that the sublime is a composite sensation made of three elements: 'a sense of individual form or forms; a sense of duration; and a sense of power' (ll. 67–9). Owen and Smyser, the editors of Wordsworth's *Prose Works*, remark that the emphasis on individual form does not appear in any discussions on the sublime.[38] This observation needs an important qualification. The issue of whether or not individual form pertains to the sublime is not foreign to the aesthetical controversies of the time; on the contrary, it figures prominently in Kant's and Coleridge's theory. We recall that Coleridge unequivocally rejects individual form as a basis for the sublime, arguing that formal shapeliness belongs to the beautiful, not to the sublime.[39] Wordsworth's inclusion of individual form as a component of the sublime experience may have originated as a response to Coleridge's theory and is symptomatic of Wordsworth's desire to work out a definition of the sublime that would be radically different from that of his friend.

It appears that Wordsworth intended to accomplish several things by making individual form the 'primary requisite' for the sublime (ll. 218–19). First, he is able to maintain the association of the sublime with a certain obtrusiveness of impression and thus downplay its hierarchical status in relation to the beautiful. Second, Wordsworth seems to have regarded individuality of form as a vehicle through which the idea of power could be evoked more vividly in the mind, and it is clear from the latter part of his essay that he is far more interested in power as a determinant of the sublime sensation than in the other two components (individual form and duration) or their interaction.[40] Finally, by maintaining individual form Wordsworth may have wished to reinforce the connection between the sublime and sensible objects and thus resist the temptation of advancing in the direction of the Kantian sublime, advocated, though substantially revised, by Coleridge. This is evident in a passage where Wordsworth tries to mitigate the empirical premises of his system by claiming that the sublime depends not so much on the sensible qualities of objects, as 'upon the state or condition of the mind, with respect to habits, knowledge, & powers' (ll. 108–14). But lest one think that, like Coleridge, he is moving the sublime out of nature, he makes a hasty qualification. 'It is to be remembered that I have been speaking of a visible object' (ll. 114–15), to which one may add: 'It is to be remembered that for Coleridge no visible object as such can be sublime.'

And yet Wordsworth appears to have mixed feelings about the part played by individual form in the sublime, just as he is unable to maintain a firm anti-Coleridgean position throughout the essay. He wants at once to establish individual form in its most prominent aspects and at the same time mitigate its obtrusiveness. Accordingly, duration, the middle component of the sublime impression, becomes an important element for Wordsworth, in that it has the effect of minimizing the prominence of form by transforming a spatial structure into a temporal one. He argues that the only way in which a mountain ridge can become an object of sublimity is 'when the faint sense which we have of its individuality is lost in the general sense of duration belonging to the Earth itself. Prominent individual form, must, therefore, be conjoined with duration, in order that Objects of this kind may impress a sense of sublimity' (ll. 82–7). After a brief description of the operation of power in the sublime, Wordsworth returns once again to the relationship between individual form and duration, evidently feeling that his argument required further elaboration (ll. 115–16). He points out that during childhood 'the milder influence of duration' is absent and consequently the child's sense of sublimity depends exclusively on the fear and awe evoked by 'precipitous' forms (ll. 116–31). As the argument unfolds, though, we begin to see that certain terms in the essay conflate to the point where their separate functions become indistinct. Wordsworth states that familiarity with objects 'tends very much to mitigate & to destroy the power which they have to produce the sensation of sublimity as dependent upon personal fear or upon wonder' (ll. 131–4). But this is just what duration is meant to accomplish, and we wonder whether for Wordsworth a sense of duration develops only as a result of repeated exposure to the same objects. Moreover, at the beginning of the essay Wordsworth attributes to the beautiful a similar function to that performed by duration within the sublime. He defines the beautiful as being rooted in the love and gentleness that nourish our 'daily well being' rather than in the 'exaltation' inspired by the 'obtrusive qualities' of sublime objects (ll. 10–20). We are thus left wondering whether through the 'milder' element of duration Wordsworth intended to pull the beautiful within the sublime (a practice not foreign to Coleridge) so as to domesticate and tame the latter.[41]

But if this is not enough, we have a new piece of the puzzle to consider, for suddenly and rather unexpectedly, in the midst of the discussion on the child's manner of apprehending the sublime, Wordsworth introduces a new definition of the sublime that is unmistakably Coleridgean: 'For whatever suspends the comparing power of the mind', he writes, '& possesses it with a feeling or image of intense unity, without a conscious contemplation of parts, has produced that state of the mind which is the consummation of the sublime' (ll. 140–4).[42] Unfortunately, the editors of the essay missed an opportunity to set this development in its appropriate context. They have traced this definition to Burke and Alexander Gerard, but not to Coleridge and Kant, where it originates.[43] 'We call an object sublime', Coleridge wrote, 'in relation to which the exercise of comparison is suspended' (Shawcross, 'Coleridge Marginalia', p. 341). 'The Beautiful is the perfection, the Sublime the suspension, of the comparing Power' (Raysor, 'Unpublished Fragments in Aesthetics', p. 533).

Wordsworth's reference to the suspension of the comparing power represents the first clear signal that he is approaching the Kantian–Coleridgean perspective on the sublime. From here on Wordsworth drops all discussion of individual form or duration and repeatedly asserts that the 'head & front of the sensation' of sublimity 'is intense unity' (ll. 159–60). Intense unity of indeterminate bounds is, as I mentioned earlier, the most important constituent of Coleridge's sublime. But Wordsworth is interested in the way in which unity can be experienced after the mind has confronted an external power that threatens its supremacy. In this he is clearly closer to Kant than to Coleridge. He points out that 'Power awakens the sublime either when it . . . calls upon the mind to grasp at something towards which it can make approaches but which it is incapable of attaining – yet so it' imparts force to the very power 'which is acting upon it; or, 2ndly, by producing a humiliation or prostration of the mind before some external agency which it presumes not to make an effort to participate . . .' (ll. 149–55). Wordsworth's distinction between a sublime in which the mind labours in vain to contain something too vast for its capacity and a sublime that involves consciousness of an 'external Power at once awful & immeasurable' bears a vague resemblance to Kant's differentiation between the mathematical and the dynamical sublime.[44] But the most important Kantian moment is yet to come. Wordsworth is properly struck by the problem of explaining how in the case of the sublime of submission or prostration to power the mind can still attain a feeling of 'intense unity'. The problem is essentially one of showing how an initial sense of humiliation can lead to an exhilarating state 'that is truly sublime'. 'The cause of this', Wordsworth explains, 'is either that our physical nature has only to a certain degree been endangered or that our moral Nature has not in the least degree been violated'.

> [With] respect to power acting upon our moral or spiritual nature . . . it may be confidently said that, unless the apprehensions which it excites terminate in repose, there can be no sublimity, & that this sense of repose is the result of reason & the moral law. Could this be abstracted & the reliance upon it taken away, no species of Power that was absolute over the mind could beget a sublime sensation; but on the contrary, it could never be thought of without fear and degradation. (ll 196–211)

It is difficult to think of a more plausible source than the German sublime for Wordsworth's explanation of how tranquillity follows the original shock of humiliation by an external agency. For both Kant and Schiller the sanctity of one's moral nature during the negative phase of the sublime is of utmost importance, and man's immunity to fear and degradation is secured by the *a priori* ideas of reason. Moreover, as Wordsworth begins to employ a vocabulary of transcendence, he also introduces a new variant of the sublime which presupposes resistance to power, rather than participation or submission. The German sublime is characteristically a sublime of resistance to power. In defining the sublime in which power is 'contemplated as something to be opposed or resisted' (ll. 223–4), Wordsworth refers to a 'twofold agency of which the mind is conscious', and one wonders whether this is an allusion to the dialectic of the imagination and reason in Kant's sublime. He also states that 'there is no sublimity excited by the contemplation of power thought of as a thing to be resisted & which the moral law enjoins us to resist, saving only as far as the mind . . . conceives that that power may be overcome or rendered evanescent, and as far as it feels itself tending towards the unity that exists in security or absolute triumph' (ll. 228–34). This passage is replete with Kantian concepts. Wordsworth locates the moment of sublimity in the mind's 'absolute triumph' over an external power, which is dictated by 'the moral law'. For the first time Wordsworth explicitly dissociates unity from an external power. Unity is reached only after the mind overcomes an external agency and is fully secure in its supremacy.[45]

All that is needed to complete Wordsworth's Kantian sublime is a firm statement that the sublime resides in the mind, not in objects of nature. Finally, after many overtures to Kant's system, Wordsworth takes this last step. He points out the 'difficulties & errors' incurred by those whose attention was 'chiefly fixed upon external objects' and 'not upon the mind itself'. 'To talk of an object as being sublime or beautiful in itself', Wordsworth claims, 'is absurd.' Like Kant, he criticizes empirical philosophy as encouraging relativity of taste and as being unable to explain why men 'in different states of civilization & without communication with each other' have been affected 'with similar sensations either of the sublime or beautiful'.[46] He argues that the business of the philosopher is not 'to grope about in the external world' and identify 'such or such a quality' that renders an object beautiful or sublime, but to 'look into his own mind and determine the law by which he is affected'. Finally, Wordsworth defines the sublime as based on the mind's 'transcendent sympathies' that can be fulfilled by reason and the moral law (ll. 256–82).

In looking over Wordsworth's essay as a whole, one could easily conclude that its main argument is inconsistent; that Wordsworth begins by cataloguing the sensible qualities of sublime objects and then goes on to assert that the sublime pertains to the mind; that he introduces new terms at every turn of his argument, some of which he drops along the way; and that his philosophical bearings are unsteady as he moves back and forth from empirical to transcendental principles.[47] But arriving at this conclusion yields only part of the tale, for as I have suggested, there lies behind Wordsworth's essay a complex process of developing a system of thought, a process that was complicated by his competitive relationship with Coleridge. At one point in his essay, just before his argument takes a significant swing towards Kant's theory, Wordsworth begs forgiveness for having allowed himself to be 'seduced to treat the subject' of the sublime 'more generally' than he 'had at first proposed' (ll. 212–14). Indeed, Wordsworth allowed himself to be tempted by the Kantian–Coleridgean perspective on the sublime, which he had at first resisted, and his seduction, with all its awkwardness and timidity, constitutes a rare episode in the intellectual history of the nineteenth century, showing the diverse ways in which Kant's influential philosophy reached English writers.

CHAPTER 4 COLERIDGE AND THE ROMANTIC SUBLIME

One of the most instructive things to be learned from this episode of Wordsworth's entanglement with Coleridge is how their respective theories of the sublime were conceived in reaction to each other's views. Coleridge's image of Wordsworth as a man who was in the habit of surrendering the mind to objects of sense and as one in need of more ample philosophic training must have affected Wordsworth enough for him to try to compensate for the deficiency that displeased his friend. Kant's philosophy thus presented Wordsworth with a unique opportunity to prove to himself and his friend that the 'mind of Man' was what finally mattered. On the other hand, Wordsworth's image of Coleridge as a stranger to 'Nature's living images', who was more interested in the mind than in nature, left Coleridge insecure about his actual ties to nature and in need of reinforcing them. As much as Coleridge was attracted to Kant, he approached Kant's philosophy cautiously, particularly where he perceived that taking a Kantian position meant a radical denial of the natural world. Although Coleridge firmly supported Kant's view that the sublime resides in the mind and not in objects, he stretched and adjusted Kant's theory to the point where he could maintain a link with nature without compromising the mind's transcendent aspirations. Moreover, unlike Wordsworth, he was careful not to make the least allusion to the presence of a 'double agency' in the mind as a means of attaining the sublime, for any such allusion to the

Kantian dialectic of the imagination and reason would have automatically introduced a discontinuity in the experience of sublimity and signalled the mind's rupture from sensible forms. To put it differently, Wordsworth was secure enough in his self-image as a lover of nature to take a more radical plunge in the direction of Kant's doctrines than Coleridge. He was also less threatened by discontinuity and less worried about the problem of re-establishing 'intense unity' once the mind has experienced a moment of disorientation and arrest. For Wordsworth, the mind's confrontation with a 'dark abyss' or 'unknown modes of being' was not without 'ample recompense' and the promise of 'future restoration'.

In comparison with Wordsworth's conception of the sublime, as well as the doctrines of other writers I have examined, we are struck by how different Coleridge's elegantly simple formula is. Coleridge did not root the sublime in a dialectic of contrariety or a mixed experience of pleasure and pain. He did not seem to tolerate any form of crisis as part of the sublime experience and had no sympathy for the dominant attitude in the German sublime of 'resistance to Fate & Nature, and the rest of the hyper-tragic histrionic Stoicism borrowed from the late Theories of the Greek drama'.[48] He remained unresponsive to the fascination with power which was so widespread among the proponents of the sublime. He did not seem to believe that one's spiritual energy would be aroused by exposing oneself to a threatening external force, as did Burke, or for that matter by finding within the mind an absolute power which no other agent could rival, as did Kant and Schiller. Partly, Coleridge's unwillingness to 'go the way of so many eighteenth-century theorists and characterize the culminating intensity of sublime self-consciousness as a kind of apotheosis, an exhilarating sense of the mind's quasi-divine power and capacity',[49] is related to his religious sensitivity and the religious shading he gives to the sublime. Christianity, Coleridge once remarked, is of all religions most suitable to the sublime, in that 'the Imagination is kept barren in definite Forms and only in cooperation with the Understanding labours after an obscure & indefinite Vastness' (*CL*, I, 466). Clearly, from a Christian standpoint, the deification of man above all powers, as celebrated by eighteenth-century proponents of the sublime, was an heretical attitude which could only lead to excessive pride and disobedience to the Supreme Deity. It has often been said that the prominence achieved by the aesthetics of the sublime in the eighteenth century was a direct result of the breakdown of orthodox Christian values. As Weiskel writes, 'in the history of literary consciousness the sublime revives as God withdraws from an immediate participation in the experience of men' (p. 3). Yet for Coleridge the sublime was not an antidote to Christianity, but compatible with its fundamental beliefs. The proper response to an encounter with sublimity, which was at the same time sanctioned by Christian dogma, was the feeling of nothingness Coleridge described upon entering a Gothic cathedral, a feeling which is akin to 'atonement', in the sense in which Coleridge understood the meaning of this word, namely 'at-one-ment' with a higher being (*SM*, p. 55 and n. 4). Finally, the absolute unity which is the crown of the sublime experience for Coleridge is not equivalent with the abstract supersensible totality which is accessible to reason in Kant's sublime, but implies an infinite 'I AM', the living and personal God of Christianity.[50]

All this is not to say that Coleridge's conception of the sublime is idiosyncratic or cut off from the mainstream of current views circulating in his time. Many strands and traditional ideas come together in Coleridge's theory of the sublime, some by influence and some by coincidence, some from writers he liked and some from writers he disliked. Like Baillie, he conceived of the sublime as a uniform experience, with no breaks or discontinuities, which did not produce agitation in the mind. Like Richter, he believed that certain objects, such as the stars, were naturally fit to represent sublimity,[51] and like Richter and Richard Payne Knight, he thought that the sublime did not depend upon large gestures or the prominence of the sensuous symbol. While Schiller had to set a whole town on fire to produce the sublime, Shakespeare drops a handkerchief and achieves a much greater effect.[52] Coleridge shared Burke's notion that during the sublime the mind is fully occupied with an object and can entertain no other,[53] but against Burke's as well as Kant's theories, he supported Herder's view that the sublime is not radically separated from the beautiful, that it coexists with it, sometimes even in the same object at the same time. Like Kant and Schiller, Coleridge believed that the sublime originates in the mind, not in objects, but he upheld Richter's and Herder's objection to pain and fear as a basis of the sublime, an objection also raised by Knight against Burke. Coleridge maintained that terror and all such related emotions were destructive of the sublime, and he was pleased to discover a link between this concept and the unavoidable fallacies of associationist doctrines, which Coleridge rarely failed to denounce.[54]

To a large extent, however, Coleridge's uneasiness with the sublime of crisis stemmed from temperamental propensities and personal problems, regardless of how clearly he could demonstrate the theoretical deficiencies of the writers who embraced this type of the sublime. For

Coleridge, imaginative defeat, danger, fear and pain were much too real to be played with or indulged in. Coleridge did not have Kant's faith in the power of the mind both to initiate a pseudo-crisis and to resolve it without suffering any damage. Nor did he share Kant's and Wordsworth's faith that the scars left by disruptive experiences of 'visionary dreariness' can be healed and that man is fortified by facing up to such experiences. How pain can be turned into joy, how discontinuities and ruptures can foster a sense of 'intense unity', were clearly not issues that Coleridge, unlike Wordsworth, felt he could resolve. For Coleridge, fear and pain signalled all too often the 'unfathomable hell within' with which he was well acquainted. Coleridge was neither fond of nor capable of finding recompense in loss, and stoicism was not his forte. Temperamental proclivities, then, as well as intellectual commitments, explain why Coleridge, as Weiskel observes, 'never could manage the egotistical sublime' or the Kantian sublime.[55] But this does not mean that, as Weiskel implies, Coleridge falls outside the Romantic sublime. Coleridge succeeded in formulating a new and remarkably subtle version of the Romantic sublime. By denying the necessity of a crisis in the sublime, Coleridge was able to avoid an abrupt rupture from sensible objects and maintain nature in the role of a benevolent power, aiding the self towards achieving the desired experience of transcendence. Conversely, by removing the apotheosis of personal power from the structure of the sublime, Coleridge significantly narrowed the gap between the sublime and the Christian ethos. The essential and unique character of Coleridge's conception of the sublime rests on the integration of nature in an experience of transcendence tending towards a Christian 'I AM'. The same attempt to retain the importance of nature and of Christian values also dominates Coleridge's advanced speculative writings on natural philosophy, but, as we shall see in Part IV, it took Coleridge many years and far greater labour to devise as flexible a formula for such a synthesis as that of the sublime.

Part IV: Coleridge's System of *Naturphilosophie*

CHAPTER 1 COLERIDGE AND NATURAL PHILOSOPHY

Coleridge's early devotion to a close observation of the external appearances of nature was superseded in later years by a no less passionate and steady interest in the inner constitution of nature and its laws of development. For a decade after 1815 Coleridge immersed himself in a systematic study of various branches of science and works of German philosophy in order to gain comprehensive knowledge of the evolution of nature from mineral forms to plant and animal life. His concern with natural science and philosophy pervades his later writings and remains dominant to the end of his life. It converged with Coleridge's efforts to complete his 'Logosophia' or *magnum opus*, which was to contain the results of some '20 years' incessant Thought, and at least 10 years' positive Labor' and present 'a compleat and perfectly original system of Logic, Natural [Philosophy] and Theology' (*CL*, IV, 736). In one projected version, the 'Logosophia' was to include a separate treatise on 'the Dynamic or Constructive Philosophy as opposed to the Mechanic' and another on 'the Systems of Giordano Bruno, Behmen, and Spinoza' (*CL*, IV, 687). Although Coleridge's *magnum opus* turned out to be no more than a 'poignant illusion', as McFarland put it,[1] some of its component pieces appear in various documents. (His extensive marginalia to the works of Jakob Boehme, for instance, offer as thorough a commentary on pantheistic and mystical systems of thought as one would hope to find in a formal treatise on Bruno, Boehme and Spinoza; see *CM*, I, 553–696.) Coleridge's writings on natural philosophy reveal the lineaments of the system Coleridge hoped to present in his projected 'Logosophia' and fulfil some of the expectations he entertained about this most ambitious work. In these writings Coleridge provides a far-ranging analysis of German metaphysics, of the 'LOGOS, divine and human', of dynamical principles of philosophy, and of major Christian dogmas.[2] He achieves a remarkable synthesis of religion, philosophy and science, drawing freely on the latest discoveries in chemistry, botany, zoology, comparative anatomy, geology, optics, astronomy and physiology.[3]

There is no single place in Coleridge's writings where one can find a sketch of his system of nature as a whole. Coleridge never composed a comprehensive treatise on natural philosophy like Kant, Schelling, Heinrich Steffens or Lorenz Oken, among others. A fairly coherent version of the earliest form of his system appears in his *Theory of Life*[4] and the letters to C. A. Tulk of September 1817 and January 1818 (*CL*, IV, 767–76, 804–9). But the greater part of Coleridge's writings on natural philosophy is scattered throughout his notebooks and marginalia written from about 1818 onward and other fragments, some of which still await publication.[5] Coleridge developed his system of nature gradually, over many years, through careful readings of the works of the *Naturphilosophen*, among them Johann Friedrich Blumenbach, Adam Karl August Eschenmayer, Kant, Fichte, Schelling, Hegel, George August Goldfuss, Johann Christian Heinroth, Hans Christian Oersted, Oken, Gotthilf Heinrich von Schubert and Steffens. Of these Kant, Schelling and Steffens had the greatest impact on Coleridge's emerging views on nature.

From the *Naturphilosophen* Coleridge derived a dynamic model of the constitution of nature that asserted the primacy of ideal powers interacting according to a principle of polarity. He was also influenced by the view, of which Schelling was the primary spokesman, that nature was a productive force through and through, activated by a ceaseless movement that stemmed from an opposition of polar powers. But unlike Schelling, Coleridge could not regard nature as self-subsistent, for this conflicted with the biblical account of the creation of the world. As much as Coleridge was attracted to the dynamic view of nature formulated by various *Naturphilosophen*, he remained apprehensive of the pantheistic pitfalls of their system. Coleridge tried to devise a system in which a dynamic conception of nature's polar activity and intrinsic unity could be maintained side by side with the belief in a Christian God. This led Coleridge to Trinitarian theology which he integrated in his philosophy of nature. Coleridge relied on the Trinity not only as a corrective to the pantheism he detected in the *Naturphilosophen*, but as a foundation for a new version of dynamic philosophy.

Naturphilosophie remained for Coleridge both an attractive and inherently problematic tradition, supplying him with new ways of thinking about nature, the self and the deity, but also enhancing his difficulties in establishing a philosophic system of his own. Coleridge took a hard look at the underside of the most appealing concepts proposed by the *Naturphilosophen*. He saw, for example, that due to their unqualified exuberance for the notion of organic unity and polarity, the *Naturphilosophen* elevated sameness of essence over important hierarchical differences between lower and higher forms of life and consciousness. In interpreting the works of his predecessors, Coleridge was undoubtedly helped by his Christian beliefs, although he also stretched them far enough to include the tenets of dynamic philosophy. Christianity provided Coleridge with a model for establishing the unity of life which was different from the philosophy of identity between the real and the ideal that he found, among others, in Schelling. Coleridge attempted to construct a system in which he could demonstrate not the identity but the continuity between the ideal and the real based on a structure of mediation which preserved their hierarchical separateness and their mutual dependence.

In the following section I examine the goals and constitutive features of Coleridge's philosophy of nature. Because so many of Coleridge's elaborations of a dynamic system of nature are based on the works of the *Naturphilosophen*, I begin with a brief introduction to the development of natural philosophy in Germany at the turn of the nineteenth century, followed by an account of the views of three of its main proponents, Kant, Schelling and Steffens.[6]

CHAPTER 2 THE DEVELOPMENT OF DYNAMIC PHILOSOPHY: THE PROBLEM OF HIERARCHY AND UNITY

It is almost as difficult to characterize succinctly the phenomenon of *Naturphilosophie* in the nineteenth century as it is to find an adequate definition of Romanticism. In Germany the two movements were intimately connected, to the extent that, as one critic notes, Goethe's age as a whole 'can be profitably approached from the standpoint of natural sciences', just as his 'scientific work can supply the key to all of his thought' (von Aesch, pp. 4–5). Moreover, there was such a close interaction among German intellectuals in the nineteenth century that it would be inappropriate to confine the term *Naturphilosoph* either to philosophers such as Schelling and Kant, or physical scientists such as

Johann Wilhelm Ritter and Oersted. Speculative philosophers based many of their theories on recent advances in the sciences, while in turn, their doctrines affected the development of scientific investigations that led to important discoveries. Historians of science have long recognized that Oersted's discovery of electromagnetism or Ritter's discovery of ultraviolet light were born out of speculations drawn from Kant's and Schelling's philosophy, with which both scientists were well acquainted.[7] At the same time, ideas expounded by philosophers and scientists alike bear the mark of a distinct Romantic heritage. In a sense, *Naturphilosophie* can be viewed as one among many forms in which Romanticism manifested itself. It was perhaps, as one commentator put it, merely 'one extreme systematization' of Romantic ideas (Snelders, p. 195).

The *Naturphilosophen*, notwithstanding their extremely diversified and complex intellectual careers, shared a number of concerns which guided their investigations of various phenomena of nature. They were all animated by the hope that their research in a particular field of inquiry would yield knowledge not just about an isolated element of nature, but about the essence of natural processes and of life as a whole. Consistently, these writers were labouring to uncover the final piece of evidence, speculative as well as experimental, that would explain how all of the phenomena of nature were organically related, stemming from a common source which was yet to be identified. When Coleridge hailed Davy's discovery of 'the identity of electricity and chemical attractions' and his hypothesis 'that there is only one power in the world of the senses' as a prophetic anticipation of the time when 'all human Knowledge will be Science and Metaphysics the only Science' (*CL*, III, 38), he was voicing quite accurately the sentiments and expectations of a generation of German writers.

The *Naturphilosophen* generally conceived the universe as a complicated web of polar forces, operating in distinct though related modes, in both inorganic and organic nature, matter and spirit. They commonly rejected the Newtonian atomistic conception of nature, proposing instead a dynamic theory which explained the manifestations of given phenomena on the basis of original forces opposed to one another. The view that matter was composed of indivisible atoms whose moving force depended on their shape was largely discredited at the time. As Kant wrote in *Metaphysical Foundations of Natural Science* (1786), any theory that explains 'the specific variety of matters by the construction and composition of their smallest parts' leads to '*mechanical natural philosophy*'. By contrast, '*dynamical natural philosophy*' does not regard material bodies as 'machines, that is, mere tools of external moving forces', but explains their diversity by means of the 'moving forces of attraction and repulsion originally belonging to them'.[8] This model of interactive forces allowed Kant to explain the diversity of matter and dispense with Newtonian theories widely shared by eighteenth-century scientists, such as the notions that matter was absolutely homogeneous with regard to inertial mass; that absolute impenetrability was an essential property of matter; and that, given the original homogeneity of matter, the differences in the density of given bodies cannot be explained without positing an empty space between solid particles.[9]

Although a dynamic conception of interactive forces was not foreign to Newton,[10] many nineteenth-century *Naturphilosophen* singled out Newton as the arch enemy of dynamic philosophy. His *Opticks* in particular came under sharp attack. Goethe, Schelling, Steffens and Oken, among others, severely criticized Newton's corpuscular theory of light and colour, showing that these phenomena could be explained scientifically only by referring them to ideal forces interacting with one another according to the principle of polarity.[11] In *Erste Ideen zur Theorie des Lichts, der Finsterniss, der Farben und der Wärme* (1808), Oken launched one of the most vituperative attacks on Newton's *Opticks*, arguing that this work is filled with 'the most absurd hypotheses ever conceived by man', and is the single most 'untrue and pernicious book' since 'the reinstatement of the sciences'. He found all of Newton's claims to be false, even those based on experiments rather than his characteristically bizarre and incomprehensible hypotheses.[12]

According to Oken, light is 'nothing material' and does not take place through a 'mechanical vibration of a very fine matter', as Newton claimed. Light is merely the outward manifestation of a polar tension originating in the ether[13] and propagated by the interaction between the sun and the planet, the two primary poles of nature. All optical phenomena for Oken, such as transparency and colour, are the result of a 'genuine light process' connected with a polar activity in various entities. 'Just as the tension in the ether constitutes light, the tension in earthly matter constitutes colour' (p. 35). Oken interprets the diversity of colours as the expression of varied degrees of tension in the ether. He argues that there are two primal colours, white and black, which are the earthly counterpart of light and darkness in the cosmic sphere, that is, of ether existing either in tension or at rest. The middle point between these two poles is occupied by red, the central colour of the spectrum (*Grundfarbe*) and the 'noblest of all', from which all others are constituted. The other main colours are merely the result of the particular inclination of red towards the two primal colours. By this dynamic explanation of colours Oken thought that he had opened a new course in the scientific investigation of optical phenomena, which had long been dominated by Newton's 'absurd' theories. Moreover, he believed that his analysis of light also provided a full clarification of how the solar system came into existence, viewing the 'dispersion of light into colours' as the 'visual symbol of the formation of the heavenly bodies' (p. 42).[14]

Such claims undoubtedly meet with scepticism among readers, and scientists may disclaim the validity of Oken's explanation of the phenomena of light and colour. Oken's diatribe against Newton seems overbearing, as Coleridge himself noted (marginal note to *Erste Ideen*, p. 14), for his notions that light and colour originate from the tension between primal poles in nature are no less 'bizarre' than Newton's corpuscular theories. None the less, Oken's treatise tells us much about a particular way of looking at nature that dominated the scientific investigations of the *Naturphilosophen* and generated the kinds of extravagant claims we have just observed. Clearly, for Oken the only acceptable explanation of nature is that which reveals nature's unity and its perpetual activity generated by the interaction of polar forces. What fascinates Oken about the phenomenon of light is the fact that it establishes a seamless continuity between earthly and cosmic forces, between the sun and the planet, both of which originate from a common source and thus share a common essence. His is a universe that has no empty spaces or heterogeneous substances, for the universe is nothing but a plenum of activity, stemming from the original dispersion of primal matter into centre and periphery which spreads downward and outward into the entire cosmos. Hence every phenomenon in the physical world is the result of a dynamic process; it is itself an activity which mirrors the division of primal matter into interactive poles. Every manifestation of polarity in nature is a living symbol of the primordial unity of the cosmos.

The view that matter was a continuous activity sustained by polar forces did not, though, originate with Oken. As we have seen, in *Metaphysical Foundations of Natural Science* Kant had already exposed the inadequacies of a mechanical theory of matter, arguing that matter was constituted by the forces of attraction and repulsion. This dynamic model was further developed by Schelling, who, refining Fichte's concept of the infinite activity of the self, showed that nature was itself an infinite process with the same source as the activity of the self, namely an original polarity in the absolute act of self-consciousness. By the time

Oken wrote his treatise on light, the principle of polarity had been widely accepted by scientists and philosophers as the most viable direction of scientific research, promising to effect a radically new conception of the laws of nature.

Kant's and Schelling's dynamic theories did not, of course, arise in a vacuum of scientific speculation, but were indebted to important discoveries in the physical and medical sciences of the last decades of the eighteenth century. The experiments in electricity conducted by Volta and Galvani, the progress made by chemists such as Lavoisier, Cavendish, Priestley, Black and Scheele in isolating the function of various gases, and the physiological theories of irritability developed by John Brown and Albrecht von Haller, all supplied empirical evidence that vital powers were at work in the inanimate and the animate world, and that hitherto unanticipated connections existed between the two realms of being. Galvani's discovery of animal electricity through his experiment with frog legs (1789) gave rise to the wildest speculations regarding the existence of a vital force in organic nature that was similar to the power of electricity in the physical world.[15] Brown's theory of excitability as the property of living matter,[16] Haller's view that animation depended on the sensibility of the nerves and the irritability of the muscles and Mesmer's discovery of animal magnetism likewise encouraged many German scientists and philosophers to identify the existence of a single force as the cause of all life in nature.[17]

The *Naturphilosophen* were particularly interested in seeking out similarities between various phenomena and processes of life.[18] No experiments were as rewarding to individual scientists and stirred as much excitement among their contemporaries as those which provided new evidence regarding the abiding unity of the cosmos. In his *Autobiography* Oersted singled out the year 1820 as the 'happiest' in his 'scientific life'. It was the year when he finally discovered the relationship between magnetism and electricity and the law of electromagnetism. This discovery fulfilled a long-cherished belief to which Oersted adhered throughout his career on philosophical grounds, namely that 'magnetism and electricity were produced by the same forces', which might be merely different forms of one original power.[19] Oersted's experiments in electromagnetism were widely acclaimed by scientists of many countries, and he received many honours and awards from distinguished scientific societies. 'During all these testimonials of approval', Oersted writes, 'the inventor could not but feel deeply that even those discoveries which we have sought industriously are not the fruit of our efforts alone, but are conditioned by a series of events and a situation in the scientific world which are subject to a law higher than all those he is seeking' (p. 50).

The situation in the scientific world was indeed partly responsible for discoveries such as Oersted's or Ritter's, for under the spell of Schelling's philosophy of nature and the ideal of an organic world entertained by many Romantic writers, scientists were predisposed to find evidence of a universal sympathy between various phenomena of nature. The tendency to locate in every phenomenon analogous structures based on a principle of polarity resulted in a breakdown of hierarchical barriers between man and God, man and animal, the physical and the spiritual forms of life. An organic view of the world modelled on an interaction of polar forces clearly disrupts a traditional chain of being, conceived as an ascending ladder, strictly ordered, from the lowest forms of nature to the highest order of God. If, for example, the body and the soul are regarded as opposites in the way in which the negative and positive poles of a magnet are opposites, then the difference between them can no longer be hierarchical but merely functional. Each is equally vital to the existence of the other and, according to the law of polarity, both must share the same essence.[20] Again, if we examine another model of interaction quite common in the works of the *Naturphilosophen*, namely the circle,[21] the obvious conclusion is that between centre and periphery, or between the various points of the circumference, the difference is merely relational. The periphery, as Oken wrote, 'is the centre itself, placed everywhere'. Should the world of nature be represented as a vast circle, all of its phenomena would become points on the periphery connected with a central generative force. It would be absurd to determine which of these phenomena are 'higher' or 'lower', according to some hierarchical standards, since every phenomenon is an indispensable part of the whole and equal to all others, just as every point of a circle is equidistant from the centre.

We can better observe the effects of employing such emblems of organic unity by examining the way the *Naturphilosophen* classify the senses. Traditionally, the senses were divided into two separate groups: the higher senses (sight and hearing), which were connected with man's soul and mind, and the lower senses (smell, taste and touch), which pertained to the body. In Platonic, Neoplatonic and Christian thought, in works of literature, philosophy or science, this distinction was strictly maintained well into the eighteenth century. In the latter part of the eighteenth century and the early nineteenth century several factors, some of which I have discussed elsewhere,[22] led to a reevaluation of the lower senses and a relaxation of the boundaries between the two groups.

Touch, which had been commonly regarded as the lowest of the senses and 'most ignoble', came to be seen as a vital sense, sharing affinities with man's spiritual faculties. The *Naturphilosophen* played an important role in bringing about this change in man's understanding of the senses, showing that the senses were part of a dynamic system of nature and that all were activated by polar powers which originated from a common source. There are 'as many types of sense experiences', Heinroth wrote in *Lehrbuch der Anthropologie*, 'as there are powers in nature' (p. 66). The sense of touch, for example, is connected with one of the primary powers of nature, the power of magnetism or cohesion, which outwardly determines the degrees of expansion and contraction in bodies. Given the link between touch and 'the deepest order of natural phenomena' (pp. 42–3), it would appear that a rejection of this sense on account of its incompatibility with man's spiritual being would carry as little validity as a denial of magnetic phenomena in nature.

The *Naturphilosophen* did not abandon the traditional grouping of the senses into two distinct classes, but the differentiation of sight and hearing from the other senses was not established on the basis of hierarchical principles. In 'Kritische Fragmente', Schelling places sight and hearing in one class, representing the ideal side of nature, and touch, taste and smell in another class, representing the objective order of nature as present in material things.[23] This distinction seems to echo the traditional view that the higher senses are related to man's spiritual being, and the lower ones to man's physical existence. Such orthodox associations are not, however, congruent with Schelling's system of the senses and the general principles of his philosophy of nature. It is true that sight and touch correspond to the ideal and real forms of nature (*natura naturans* v. *natura naturata*), but that makes them true opposites, essentially related to one another, and not the highest and lowest end of two heterogeneous classes. Nature, Schelling reminds us, is neither an ideal essence exclusively, nor a multitude of outer products, but 'the absolute identity of both' (p. 291). Steffens was well aware that Schelling's classification of the senses did not confer upon the so-called 'lower senses' a stigma of inferiority. In adopting Schelling's notion that touch represents the real pole of nature, as opposed to the ideal one, Steffens emphasized that touch should not be regarded as the 'last' of the senses and therefore the 'lowest'. It is, rather, 'the first sense' which appears in nature, and becomes most distinct in insects, the order which marks a significant progress in nature's development towards higher 'individuation'.[24]

In his system of the senses Schelling allows for rich possibilities of interaction between all the senses. Once polarity is introduced as the basic principle of the sensory existence of the organism, the particular grouping of the senses becomes extremely flexible and varied. Thus, viewed in relation to the three powers of nature (magnetism, electricity and galvanism, or chemical activity), the senses fall into the following polar pairs: touch v. hearing, smell v. sight and taste v. the sense of warmth (*Wärmesinn*), the last group representing the synthesis of the two, just as the power of galvanism is the synthesis of magnetism and electricity. On the other hand, different sets of senses can be established when the criteria of classification become the relationship between the soft and hard parts of the body (the flesh and the bones), between space and time, or between the power of light and gravity. Accordingly, hearing, smell and taste belong to the class of the hard senses, whereas sight, touch and the sense of warmth belong to the soft senses. The former are dominated by gravity, the latter by light. It is apparent that with a slight variation of polar forces, sight and touch, traditionally regarded as the two most incompatible senses, can emerge as members of the same group. For Schelling the development of higher forms of life depends on the development of all the senses and on their close interaction. Man, who embodies the apex of nature and the fulfilment of its laws, is the 'most felicitous union of the most perfect hearing and feeling animal'. He is at once an 'inner and an outer' being ('Kritische Fragmente', p. 289).

Other *Naturphilosophen* devise different classifications of the senses and offer different explanations regarding the way in which the senses interact with one another, but they commonly adopt a principle of polarity and implicitly affirm the basic unity of all the senses. K. C. Wolfart, Mesmer's interpreter and supporter, appears to hold on more strenuously than others to orthodox notions granting a privileged status to sight and hearing, but in typical fashion he employs a dynamic model for his schema of the senses, which suggests close ties between all the senses. He argues that sight and hearing are the more developed and finer senses, forming two poles of an outer circle. This circle encloses an inner circle made up of smell, taste and touch. The inner circle becomes the point of indifference for the two primary poles of the sensorium. The equilibrium and harmonious development of sight and hearing thus depend fully on an interaction with the other senses. Finally, Wolfart finds the true centre of both circles in the inner sense, which orders and brings to oneness the diverse impressions received through the two concentric circles of the sensorium.[25]

Like Wolfart, Eschenmayer at once follows a traditional ordering of the senses, placing sight at the top of the ladder as the 'most spiritual sense', and touch at the bottom, as the most 'mechanical' sense, and at the same time insists on the unity of all senses. He shows that the senses can be differentiated according to the time it takes to perceive a given object or the distance from which an object can be apprehended. The eye registers an object at farthest distance in the least amount of time, whereas touch can only distinguish an object upon contact in the longest period of time. In the former, time disappears and space becomes boundless; in the latter, space disappears and time becomes immeasurable. The other senses represent various moments in the gradual shrinking of space and the corresponding expansion of time. From this observation Eschenmayer deduces that the sense of sight is the most intense and active sense (and consequently the most spiritual), whereas the sense of touch is merely 'spiritless extension' (*geistlose Extension*).[26]

Although this view of the senses sounds orthodox, we notice that Eschenmayer does not conceive of a break between sight and hearing and the lower senses, but arranges the senses in a continuum. Sight and touch appear as the opposite poles of one, essentially unified stream of sensory impressions, differing merely in degrees of intensity. Furthermore, Eschenmayer takes for granted the notion that in consciousness all the senses are assimilated in an undifferentiated unity. Consciousness is homogeneous and one; it becomes the centre from which all sensory impressions originate and to which they return, like radii of a circle. The tags 'spiritual' and 'spiritless', then, by which Eschenmayer distinguishes between sight and touch do not carry the same weight as in earlier classifications of the senses. Eschenmayer's system does not allow for a dichotomy between the higher and the lower senses. The terms 'higher' and 'lower' signify primarily forms of energy and differences between the intensity of sensory activities. Finally, for Eschenmayer the specificity of various senses leaves unaltered and dissolves into the absolute unity of consciousness.

The classification of the senses is merely a small part of a much larger system of nature developed by the *Naturphilosophen*, but in keeping with the principles of an organic world-view, this part is a truthful representation of the whole. It is not incidental that, in the theory of the senses offered by Wolfart and Eschenmayer, traditional hierarchies emerge side by side with and are finally superseded by dynamical models of interaction. The *Naturphilosophen* did not wish to deny the hierarchical priority of God over the created world, man over animal, the spiritual over the physical modes of being. In their works they consistently adhere to strict distinctions between lower and higher forms of life and demonstrate the evolution of nature towards its consummate point of achievement, which is man (cf. von Aesch, chs VI and XI). But at the same time, the *Naturphilosophen* are so intent on proving the organic unity of the cosmos, so fascinated by analogies between different phenomena, and so committed to dynamic principles of philosophy that they often end up closing the gaps and removing the hierarchical distances between various orders of being. The highest and lowest ends of a particular chain of phenomena close before our eyes into a circle, and what seems to have been a difference in kind between these phenomena turns out to be, as in Eschenmayer's system of the senses, a difference in degree. The many conflicts and reconciliations present in the works of the *Naturphilosophen* between organicism and hierarchical values constitute a rich and as yet unexplored subject, one too large to be treated here. I shall merely offer one other example to illustrate both the inability of the *Naturphilosophen* to sustain hierarchical distinctions between various orders of being and Coleridge's unwillingness to sacrifice such distinctions for the sake of the ideal of organic unity.

In *Psychologie*, Eschenmayer tackles the subject of the differences between the act of procreation in animals and man (pp. 93–7). He is first of all properly struck by the possible objections to the treatment of this subject in a work of psychology. Since the act of procreation is purely organic, having to do with the fertilization of an egg by a male sperm, isn't this process the business of the physiologist? Eschenmayer argues that the act of procreation in man belongs to the area of psychology because it is not purely physical, but involves a spiritual component. Otherwise, there can be no adequate explanation as to why out of an organic seed there emerges a spiritual being and why under the same conditions of reproduction, animals always beget other animals, whereas men always beget other human beings. We must therefore assume, Eschenmayer points out, that during the act of procreation 'a spiritual principle connects with the organic and that the body and soul are thus fused into one at the inception of life'. This spiritual principle originates from the faculties of feeling which form the 'central part of the spiritual organism'. These faculties generate an overflowing of emotion that passes through the body all the way down to the organic seed with which it unites. Hence, in the act of procreation the spiritual part of man plays as much of a role in the generation of new life as the organic. In it, 'the moment of beauty and love mingles with the sexual urge'. The 'intensity of pleasure that accompanies every reproductive act' is not an 'accidental phenomenon', but its 'essence', for it expresses the complete union of the physical and the spiritual part of man (p. 95).

We observe here a typical junction in the work of a *Naturphilosoph* when hierarchical distinctions are forcefully defended and brushed aside at the same time. Ostensibly, Eschenmayer's purpose in explaining the process of human reproduction is to show through a magnifying glass the difference between man and animal. But by trying to establish a barrier between man and animal, Eschenmayer ends up removing another, that between man's body and soul, which, paradoxically, has the effect of narrowing the distance between man and the animal world. In his enthusiasm over the unity of body and soul in the act of procreation, Eschenmayer seems unaware that he has not elevated the spiritual over the purely organic part of man, or man over the animal, but in fact has rendered the soul as functioning like a reproductive organ. The soul, as it were, ejaculates a seed in a moment of 'overflowing feelings' and this seed travels to and fertilizes 'the organic seed of future life'. The soul thus appears to be of a corporeal nature with corporeal functions. Its most intense pleasure is mixed with the satisfaction of a physical urge. Eschenmayer, in effect, demonstrates the closeness between man's physical and spiritual being and, by implication, between man and animal.

In his marginal comments to this section of *Psychologie*, Coleridge ridiculed Eschenmayer's notion of the unity between body and soul in the act of procreation. His witty parody of Eschenmayer's argument ('Um das Wundervolle (i.e. in the production of such d——n'd Nonsense) wegzuräumen, we have *only* to assume, that in, with and thro' the Author a nonsensical Spirit passed into combination with the first Drop of Ink, after its entrance into a *Quill* with a *Slit* in it. *Ein geistiger Keim sich ablöse*!!') shows that he grasped fully the fact that Eschenmayer lowered the spiritual to the level of the corporeal. The intensity Eschenmayer refers to, Coleridge noted, is not one of feeling, but of 'Ejaculation' (marginal note to pp. 94–5 of *Psychologie*). Coleridge was remarkably alert to errors in the tenets advocated by the *Naturphilosophen* which resulted from their all too zealous need to affirm the unity of the cosmos, with its many 'wooings, and retirings and nuptial conciliations' and 'marriages'.[27] Although he too was greatly attracted to the ideal of organic unity, he knew that such an ideal could not be acquired at the expense of meaningful differences between distinct hierarchical orders of being. He saw that the *Naturphilosophen* often tended to ascribe physical causes to spiritual activities, that in their attempt to locate the one dynamic power at the root of all phenomena of nature, they confused ideal forces with material substances, and that by seeking to establish a general principle of polarity as the source of all activity, they attributed polarity to divinity itself, thus falling into the trap of pantheistic thought. In the following discussion I present the views of three *Naturphilosophen* (Kant, Schelling, Steffens) from whose writings Coleridge drew the main issues and terminology of his advanced philosophy of nature, without, however, falling into the same errors he detected in their work. Because the texts of the *Naturphilosophen* are not easily available to English critics and because they have remained relatively unexplored in modern scholarship due to their limited scientific value and their intricate, even obscure, cosmological schemes, I provide a somewhat detailed elucidation of their systems. I focus primarily on issues to which Coleridge felt compelled to respond, and show that Coleridge's sustained efforts to produce a new philosophic system finally led him to develop a sophisticated theory of the Trinity through which he escaped some of the inconsistencies he discovered in the writings of the *Naturphilosophen*.

CHAPTER 3 ORIGINS OF COLERIDGE'S SYSTEM OF *NATURPHILOSOPHIE*

Kant's *Metaphysical Foundations of Natural Science*

The emergence of *Naturphilosophie* was intimately connected to the spectacular growth of transcendentalist thought in Germany that began with the work of Immanuel Kant. It is to Kant that we must turn in order to reconstruct the origins of this movement and comprehend its subsequent developments in the first three decades of the nineteenth century. In *Critique of Pure Reason* (1st edn, 1781; 2nd edn, 1787) Kant undertook the task of rescuing metaphysics from the inferior position into which it had fallen in his time and raising it to the level of a science in its own right. He showed that the degeneration of metaphysics was caused by two main factors. First, metaphysical studies had been dominated by the false assumption that 'knowledge must conform to objects', which made it impossible to explain how, this being the case, one could attain knowledge of objects by means of *a priori* concepts. The purpose of the *Critique* was to demonstrate that, to the contrary, objects must conform to the constitution and function of our cognitive faculties, and that 'we can know *a priori* of things only what we ourselves put into them' (Preface to the Second Edition, pp. 22–3). Second, metaphysics had lost its main claim to scientific status when it aligned itself with dogmatism, which presupposes that 'it is possible to make headway in metaphysics without a previous criticism of pure reason', which is its organ (p. 29). Kant set out to prove that the only thing that could save philosophy from becoming a pseudo-science or 'philodoxy' (p. 33) was a scrupulous analysis, not just of the powers of reason, but, more importantly, of its limitations. His aim was to bring reason to a point of complete self-exposure, which involved the recognition that its knowledge did not extend to things-in-themselves or supersensible ideas, but was confined to appearances and objects of experience. In the 'Transcendental Dialectic' of the *Critique*, Kant showed that all attempts to gain knowledge of supersensible ideas such as freedom, immortality or God, failed. While one may entertain these ideas '*in thought*', one cannot know them or furnish proof of their existence. This does not mean, however, that the existence of such ideas can be denied, for the very fact that reason has no means of ascertaining their existence speculatively 'must also suffice to prove the invalidity of all counter-assertions'. Hence, the existence of God, for example, 'while for the merely speculative employment of reason . . . remains a mere *ideal*, it is yet *an ideal without a flaw*, a concept which completes and crowns the whole of human knowledge' (p. 531). As usual in Kant, the discovery of limitations is energizing, not self-defeating. The point where reason is brought to a 'tribunal' which exposes 'all its groundless pretensions' represents the moment of its supreme triumph, and not of its failure, for reason has thereby accomplished 'the most difficult of all its tasks, namely, that of self-knowledge' (Preface to the First Edition, p. 9).

The purification of reason through self-analysis not only cures metaphysics of all of its ailments, but gives it special privileges that are unavailable to any other discipline. Metaphysics is restored to the place of honour it had once enjoyed as 'the Queen of all the sciences' (p. 7), for it is the only science that attains exhaustive knowledge 'to which no addition can be made'. It derives its principles from the thinking faculty itself and operates with certain knowledge, rather than hypotheses or opinions based on empirical evidence. Most importantly, metaphysics employs as its organ a 'self-subsistent unity', pure reason, 'in which, as in an organized body, every member exists for every other, and all for the sake of each, so that no principle can safely be taken in *any one* relation, unless it has been investigated in the *entirety* of its relations to the whole employment of pure reason' (pp. 25–6). In effect, for Kant the title of pure or authentic science must be reserved for the discipline that achieves such a self-subsistent internal structure and through it can offer complete knowledge 'of its entire field'. Since metaphysics alone can accomplish this task, any other discipline must embrace metaphysics if it is to qualify as science.

In *Metaphysical Foundations of Natural Science*, which was published between the first and second edition of the *Critique of Pure Reason* (1786), Kant took up this argument in relation to the status of natural science. Here Kant makes a clear-cut distinction between 'science *proper*' and disciplines which base their principles upon experiments, such as chemistry or empirical psychology. These disciplines 'should be rather termed systematic art than science', for only that 'can be called science *proper* whose certainty is apodictic' and whose laws are derived from *a priori* concepts. Natural science requires, therefore, a '*pure* portion', in which the principles of nature are determined according to the 'Pure cognition of the reason from mere *conceptions*' (pp. 138–9). Natural science may rely on mathematics when it proposes to show not the laws of nature in general, but 'the possibility of *determinate* natural things' which can be known through *a priori* intuition (p. 140). In fact, a major aim of Kant's treatise is to demonstrate the vital interdependence of mathematics and metaphysics in the field of natural science. But Kant insists that if the two branches of knowledge are to be combined effectively, their distinct methods and boundaries must be strictly ascertained. Mathematics, which depends on the construction of concepts rather than concepts themselves, yields an infinite number of intuitions, that is, infinite multiplicity without absolute unity. Metaphysics, on the other hand, offers a '*definite* number of cognitions, which can be fully exhausted' (pp. 143–4).[28] Since knowledge is an absolute prerequisite of true science, metaphysics must at all times remain the foundation of natural science. Its unchallenged priority ultimately guarantees the possibility of a mathematical explanation of corporeal nature.[29]

In his treatise, Kant examines the concept of matter under four headings, which correspond to the categories of the understanding (Quantity, Quality, Relation and Modality). The concept of matter thus attains the 'completeness of a metaphysical system' which can be bequeathed to posterity 'as a capital to which no addition can be made' (*Critique of Pure Reason*, p. 26). It is a system which, as Schelling thought of his own, 'time cannot touch' (*System of Transcendental Idealism*, p. 2).

The followers of Kant did not share the philosopher's assurance that his metaphysical system in general and the doctrine of corporeal nature in particular were immune to additions and alterations and that any 'attempt to change even the smallest part at once gives rise to contradictions, not merely in the system, but in human reason in general' (*Critique of Pure Reason*, p. 34). Fichte and Schelling, among others, argued that in fact contradictions were inherent in Kant's theory of knowledge and that the valuable components of Kant's critical philosophy could be passed on to posterity only within a radically new framework. The entire architectonic of Kant's theory of knowledge was based on a mistaken dualism of mind and matter, self and nature, noumena and phenomena. Both Fichte and Schelling thought that Kant's notion of the unknowable things-in-themselves was the Achilles heel of his system. A valid theory of knowledge, they claimed, must dispense with such inaccessible objects and take its starting point from the self or self-consciousness as the ground of all reality. It must also rely not on reason but on intellectual intuition by means of which the Kantian dichotomy between self and object, phenomenon and noumenon, is fully surmounted.

Kant's doctrine of corporeal nature as presented in *Metaphysical Foundations of Natural Science* also met with much adverse criticism. His followers did not contest the view that metaphysics was an indispensable part of science. Fichte, Schelling and natural scientists as well were fully persuaded that science could not survive on experiments alone and that its vitality depended on systematic knowledge derived from *a priori* principles.[30] But Kant's conception of matter was seen as basically flawed. Schelling objected to the dualistic premise in Kant's doctrine of corporeal nature, arguing that the construction of matter could not be established analytically by means of two original forces. Matter was a product of an original synthesis of two opposite forces, a synthesis which takes place in self-consciousness. Schelling pointed out that Kant's schema of the interaction between the forces of repulsion and attraction could not account for the diversity of matter and the specific differences of weight in bodies. Moreover, Kant's theory had limited applicability pertaining to mechanics only in that matter is treated as product. A genuinely dynamic conception of matter, on the other hand, must refer to the productive activity of nature.[31]

Like Schelling, Coleridge was aware of defects in Kant's metaphysics of corporeal nature that resulted from the '*barren* Dualism' of his system,[32] although he was not convinced that Schelling's synthetic elaboration of the concept of matter provided a better alternative to Kant's doctrine (marginal note to pp. 82–4). Coleridge generally found Kant's treatise to be obscure in many places and difficult to comprehend. Judging from his marginal notes, it appears that he returned to the treatise twice after the initial reading, and went over some of its parts many times without fully grasping the logic of Kant's various demonstrations.[33]

Although Coleridge admitted defeat in trying to understand some of Kant's explanations, he saw with sufficient clarity the weaknesses in the overall structure of Kant's theory of matter. Coleridge was determined not to allow himself to be 'cowed by the *term*, Grundkraft [original force] and the impossibility of rendering the same comprehensible' (marginal note to p. 61). He accepted Kant's syllogism that fundamental forces cannot be explained, because they are beyond the realm of experience, but thought that Kant's analysis of the interaction between the forces of repulsion and attraction left many unnecessary gaps and ultimately compromised the pure ideality of these forces. Why is it, for example, Coleridge wondered, that 'if the two opposite forces are equal . . . they do not destroy or suspend at least each the other? This surely should have been explained out of the nature of one or both the forces, or the power of which these are forces' (marginal note to pp. 70–1).

Coleridge also questioned Kant's ability to explain the exact mode in which the two original forces limit each other and constitute the diversity of specific matters. For Coleridge, Kant's analysis did not clarify 'what determines the specific degrees, that at once limit and determine the Attraction'. Kant emphasized the fact that the activity of the repulsive force, which is confined to the surface of matter, is independent of what happens below the surface in the area where the attractive force 'acts directly on all parts' (see *Metaphysical Foundations of Natural Science*, pp. 199–200). But, Coleridge inquired, 'if the Parts "behind the Plane of Contact" do not work, how do they resist the Attractive Power, which works immediately on all the Parts? . . . And does the Attraction *wait* until the Repulsive Expansion has *made ready* the quantum of matter in each given space? So vain is the attempt to find in a *Science* the ultimate ground of any other Science' (marginal note to pp. 82–4).

This last statement may indicate Coleridge's scepticism about the possibility of basing science on metaphysical foundations and would be a direct contradiction to his claim in *The Friend* that method in the sciences depends fully on metaphysical principles.[34] But I believe Coleridge's statement merely addresses itself to certain excesses in Kant's system that derive from Kant's attempt to demonstrate the priority of metaphysics in natural science. Kant in typical fashion carved out carefully the area in which metaphysics is applicable and the questions to which it can provide answers. In doing so, however, he left unexamined a number of problems regarding the particular interaction between the forces of attraction and repulsion that might have been solved with the help of physics.

On the other hand, Coleridge felt that Kant's doctrine of matter was not metaphysical *enough* – that, in fact, it did not sustain the ideality of the two original forces. This represents Coleridge's most serious charge against Kant and one that he levelled against most of the *Naturphilosophen*. He argued that Kant mistakenly represents matter as a moving point in space, first showing 'attraction and repulsion as two distinct powers added to matter', that is, as belonging to the metaphysical conception of matter, and then reasoning 'on these powers as being themselves Matter' (fly-leaf note referring to pp. 45–6). Hence, Kant confuses the unknown cause of a phenomenon with the phenomenon itself. He looks on repulsion and attraction alternately as the original forces which bring matter into being and as mere properties of matter. 'Again and again', Coleridge complained, 'Matter [is] assumed as a datum, the *subject* of the powers / tho' two of these powers are elsewhere taken as constituting matter!' (marginal note to pp. 103–4).

Although it is difficult to believe that Kant confuses a metaphysical cause of a phenomenon with its physical properties, there is enough slippage in some of the arguments presented in his treatise to justify Coleridge's objections. The fault may lie partly in Kant's carelessness of style. Kant applies the term 'property' (*Eigenschaft*) both to original causes and to effects. He points out, for example, that elasticity is 'an essential property of matter'.[35] Elasticity is the effect of the force of repulsion, just as weight is the effect of the force of attraction.[36] But Kant refers to repulsion and attraction also as properties of matter.[37] Further problems derive from the use of the term 'original', which is applied to elasticity and weight as well as to the cause of these phenomena, and from a series of related terms defining the same primary forces of matter, namely the force of repulsion, which is also called the force of extension or expansion. Kant appears to differentiate between the force of repulsion and extension when he states that '*the force of an extended by virtue of the repulsion of all its parts* is a *force of extension* (expansive)'.[38] This indicates that extension is a result or manifestation of the force of repulsion.[39] But Kant also established a complete equation between the two. He says that matter 'fills its spaces by the repulsive forces of all its parts, i.e., by its own force of extension, which has a definite degree, beyond which smaller or larger [degrees] can be conceived to infinity'.[40] We are thus left wondering whether the force of extension is merely the exponent of the force of repulsion in matter already constituted by the latter, or if it is itself that which, together with the force of attraction, constitutes matter. The trouble is that terms such as extension or compression make one think of physical characteristics of matter. Kant himself points out that the force of extension renders matter as 'an extended that fills its space', that is, as 'something real in the space of our external senses'. This is what Kant calls the impenetrability of matter, a property which 'rests on a physical basis', being 'nothing but the capacity of extension in matter'.[41] But the ground of impenetrability, Kant reminds us, is 'the repulsive force alone' (*Metaphysical Foundations of Natural Science*, p. 183 [*Schriften*, IV, 508]). Does impenetrability then have a 'physical basis' in the force of extension and a metaphysical ground in the force of repulsion? But if, as Kant has indicated, the force of repulsion and the force of extension are one and the same, what becomes of the distinction between the unknown cause of a phenomenon and the phenomenon itself?

Coleridge was right in perceiving that difficulties are bound to arise 'in a system which *begins* with Space' and defines powers 'by effects and products solely relative to Space and manifestable in and by Space' (marginal note to p. 61). Kant describes the '*attraction essential to all matter*' as 'an immediate effect of it on other matter, through empty space'.[42] He spells out the universal law of dynamics in terms of the variable effects of original forces related to the size of the space in which they act. This law states that 'the effect of the moving force, exercised from one point upon every other outside it, is in inverse proportion to the space in which the same quantity of moving force has had to expand itself, in order to act directly upon this point at the determinate distance'.[43] Once one admits quantity of power as dependent on the size of the space filled, it is difficult to think of these 'original' powers of matter as other than physical powers. If, as Kant notes, the force of attraction 'rests on the mass of matter in a given space, while its expansive force [rests] on the degree in which it fills it [namely, the space]' (*Metaphysical Foundations of Natural Science*, pp. 199–200 [*Schriften*, IV, 524]), does this not imply that these powers already presuppose matter as a 'datum'?

Coleridge faulted Kant with other misconceptions regarding his theory of matter, such as his definition of fluid and his assumption, which was also held by Newton, that 'Gravity is the same power as Attraction.'[44] And yet Coleridge saw that Kant's 'construction of matter by two powers, the one universal and the same in all, the other gradative and differential, and thus in each degree the ground of a specialty in matter' was a fundamental contribution to natural science that 'demanded the Admiration and gratitude of every Philosopher' (marginal notes to pp. 103–4, 80–1). Kant's doctrine of corporeal nature was a first and 'worthy attempt' to demonstrate that matter is constituted by two powers which limit each other's activity and thus determine the '*degree* of the filling of space'. He showed, however imperfectly, that the solid or 'the *real* in space' was merely the filling of space by means of the force of repulsion. In Kant, Coleridge was presented with a clear analysis of the distinction between the two powers, a distinction which he often found lacking in other *Naturphilosophen*, and which, as we shall see, he tried to maintain in his own system by differentiating strictly between the line of *being* and the line of *existence* in nature, and between constitutive and modifying powers. Yet despite Coleridge's sense of the significant merits of Kant's theory of matter, he remained profoundly distrustful of it and nervous about its possible implications.

Coleridge found the main drawback of this theory to be its disregard of the relationship between matter and spirit. He tried to assuage his discomfort with this aspect of Kant's doctrine by reminding himself that in physics or mechanics it is perfectly legitimate to talk about matter without a 'proper concern with Mind and Soul' (marginal notes to p. 37 and fly-leaf referring to p. 37). But Coleridge was unable to maintain this 'suspension of disbelief' when certain statements of Kant seemed to indicate that 'an eternity of the mundus sensibilis' could be conceived without positing a sustaining spirit. This is evident in Coleridge's response to Kant's analysis of the first law of mechanics, which states that 'With all changes of corporeal nature, the quantity of the matter remains, on the whole, the same, unincreased and undiminished.' From 'universal metaphysics', Kant argues, one can establish the proposition that 'with all changes of nature, no substance can either arise or be annihilated'. Kant demonstrates this proposition by pointing out the difference between substance taken as an object of the external sense (i.e. in relationship to *matter*) and as an object of the internal sense (i.e. in relationship to the *self*). The conception of substance in matter is confined to 'the movable in space'. Matter is made up of an infinite number of parts, each of which, being movable, becomes material substance.[45] 'Thus the amount of the matter as substance, is nothing other than the multitude of the substances of which it consists.' This quantity of matter 'cannot be increased or diminished except by new substance arising or being annihilated', which means that it always remains the same in the universe even if a particular matter 'may by addition or subtraction of its parts be increased or diminished'. Quite the contrary is the case when substance is seen as an object of the internal sense. The faculty of the soul, which is apperception, 'has a *degree* that may be greater or smaller', and the substance of the soul may be diminished to the point of extinction. 'It is no wonder therefore', Kant argues, that 'permanence of substance can be proven' of matter, 'since with matter it follows from its *conception*'. From the ego, which is the 'universal correlate of apperception and itself merely a thought', no conception of the permanence of the soul as substance can be deduced (*Metaphysical Foundations of Natural Science*, pp. 220–1).

Coleridge's reaction to this analysis was negative. To Coleridge Kant's position seemed contradictory. If, according to Kant, space is an intuition *a priori* and matter the 'sensation accompanying a specific intuition' – if 'all modes of thought' are 'purely subjective' – is matter not subjective also? And if 'matter be subjective, and the I or Subject be evanescible, must not the thought, matter, be at least equally so?' Moreover, isn't it possible to assume that the soul may have powers other than apperception, which 'during feeble consciousness' may 'be vigorously exerted' (marginal notes to pp. 117–18 and fly-leaf referring to p. 118)? But ultimately, Kant's entire argument about the indestructibility of matter appeared to Coleridge as 'a mere Sand-rope of Assertions', being 'either Atheistic' by turning substance into a 'Synonime of God', and confusing God with the sensible world, as Spinoza did, or 'nugatory, by applying y = to Matter, which has no claim to y = a – i.e. to substance in that sense'. Coleridge was willing to grant this assumption as having validity in mechanics. But, he added, 'I . . . will not let it be forced upon me, in Cosmology. Indeed, it is too near of kin to ultimate Corpuscles and empty Spaces that *really are* and yet are really Nothing' (marginal note to pp. 116–17). Notwithstanding Coleridge's assertion, he clearly did not tolerate a system that established the permanence of matter irrespective of that of spirit, even if ostensibly such a system was confined to mechanics. Coleridge could not keep 'cosmology' away from natural science, nor did he think that a system of nature could be founded by starting from the bottom instead of the top, from matter instead of the workings of the divine consciousness.

Schelling preceded Coleridge in identifying the absence of spirit in Kant's doctrine of corporeal nature as being responsible for the weakness of his dynamic system as a whole. He argued that Kant was mistaken both in establishing the concept of power (*Kraft*) as the ultimate principle of natural philosophy and in treating matter merely as a product of two powers. The concept of power as such is always something finite. Moreover, that concept always entails, as in Kant, the existence of an opposite force that limits its activity. Between opposite forces there can be a relationship either of relative equilibrium, in which case matter appears as motionless (i.e. inert), or of ongoing strife, which is alternately cancelled only to reappear again *ad infinitum*. But such a conflict would have no permanence unless there existed a third factor, which is the ground of the identity of the two powers and of their ceaseless opposition. This third factor cannot be just another power, for although power by itself does not appear in physical forms, its effects can be determined according to purely physical laws. The third factor must be a spiritual principle which is higher than power and beyond all physical laws.[46]

For Schelling nature remains unintelligible unless one perceives in it the workings of a spiritual activity that is essentially identical with the activity of a self-conscious being. Nature is both real and ideal throughout. Kant's system, by referring nature to the interaction of two powers, deals merely with physical products and does not touch on the 'inner spring-work' of nature. Hence Schelling's own system 'leaves off exactly at the point where the Dynamical Physics of Kant and his successors begins',[47] for it is concerned with nature as subject (i.e. as originally productive) and not as mere object (i.e. as product). The view that nature is thoroughly ideal, carrying within it its own final cause, and that a unifying spiritual activity lies at the root of every individual product represents the essence of Schelling's alternative to Kant's doctrine and his main contribution to the development of natural philosophy in the nineteenth century. For Coleridge, however, this alternative, though correcting some of the errors that resulted from the 'barren Dualism' of Kant's philosophy, generated a new set of problems requiring more imaginative solutions than Schelling had provided.

Nature and the Absolute in Schelling's *Naturphilosophie*

Schelling's system of nature marked an important turning point in the development of dynamic philosophy and natural science in the nineteenth century. Schelling placed upon natural science much greater demands and defined its task with closer scrutiny than Kant. For Schelling, natural science had to resolve the very questions with which all philosophic thinking began and to which the major philosophers of all ages attempted to provide adequate answers. What, for example, assures us that the representations we have of various phenomena are real – that is, correspond to actual phenomena as such? How do such representations arise in our consciousness? Are things that exist independent of the perceiver the cause of the representations we form of them? Can we ever know objects in themselves, or only the perceptions we form of them in our minds?[48] Schelling demonstrates the inadequacy of systems that assume a dualism between subject and object to explain the correspondence between our perceptions of reality and reality itself. If one considers things to be independent of the perceiver and the cause of our representations, one merely ends up permanently separating matter from spirit without making intelligible the process of cognition. The proper starting point for a coherent theory of knowledge is exclusively the assumption that between nature and self, object and subject, there exists a complete unity.

According to Schelling, in the history of philosophy there have been only two worthy, though not entirely successful, attempts to demonstrate the unity between the subjective and the objective components of knowledge. The first to show the oneness of mind and matter was Spinoza. He explained the correspondence of our perceptions and real objects by attributing both to one and the same ideal substance. But Spinoza was unable to show what produces the modifications of substance that, in turn, give birth to the world of finite things. His error was to lose himself in 'the idea of an infinite outside of us' and conceive of the individual self as one among a series of modifications of substance (*SW*, II, 20, 35–7). But one can never make cognition intelligible as long as the source of knowledge is seen as lying outside the self. We never understand anything that is external to us. We only know directly and with absolute certainty 'our own being'. The solution to the problem of knowledge is to be found only in the unity between the infinite and the finite that originates in the self.

This was precisely the direction taken by Leibnitz. Unlike Spinoza, Leibnitz understood that the principle according to which our perceptions correspond fully to real objects lies within an individual being. No external force, be it a thing or another subject, can cause any changes in an individual being. The monads, as he put it, are windowless.[49] Leibnitz dispensed not only with the idea of external causation, but also, contrary to the way Kantian philosophers viewed him, with the notion of things-in-themselves (*SW*, II, 20). For him every being possessed perceptual capacity and generated for itself an objective reality. What we call the real world is merely a form of activity in the self that acquires a boundary and thus becomes limited. And, most important, the principle according to which a being is at once limited and unlimited, active and passive, self and object, lies within its own nature. And yet

Leibnitz, although holding the key to a comprehensive theory of knowledge, in the end made no use of it. In order to explain how all beings experience the same world, Leibnitz resorted to the concept of a pre-established harmony of divine origin. This concept contradicts Leibnitz's convincing demonstration that the absolute ground of knowledge lies within an individual being, since we now are asked to think of a source of knowledge external to the self, as in the case of Spinoza's substance. By having to refer our representations to a superior being, we not only lose the possibility of claiming absolute knowledge for the self (the self being unable to know anything other than its own activity), but we also deny nature's intrinsic purposefulness. Nature can be regarded as purposeful in so far as it 'carries within itself the ground of its own existence' (*SW*, II, 38–41).

For Schelling, the task of philosophy was to bring to fruition the epistemological inquiries initiated by Spinoza and Leibnitz. The solution to the problem of knowledge lay (as the two philosophers perceived) in the unity between objects and our representations, the real and the ideal. But a system that denies finality to nature will fail to make this unity comprehensible. Schelling maintains that only the concept of the Absolute explains how we have certain knowledge of an objective world which is real in itself, though not divided from the self. The Absolute is a pure identity of subjectivity and objectivity. It is not, however, a given, like Spinoza's substance or Leibnitz's pre-established harmony, but an eternal, ongoing 'act of knowledge' and of becoming. In the process of self-knowledge, the Absolute objectifies itself in particular things, forming the world of nature, then perceives itself as pure subjectivity and as the source of all production, and finally comes to recognize its essence as the identity between the subjective and the objective, self and nature.[50] The Absolute thus expands itself into finite objects only to gather the finite back into the infinite. Nature is the form by means of which the Absolute acquires 'outness' and knows itself through another; it is a *symbol* of the Absolute which, 'like all symbols, takes on the independent life of that which it signifies'. Nature is, therefore, both real and ideal. It is at once an order of particular objects (*natura naturata*) outside the Absolute and 'the very act of absolute knowledge (*natura naturans*)', the former being the *symbol* of the latter (*SW*, II, 67).[51]

Natural philosophy is, in essence, 'the science of the Absolute' (*SW*, II, 66). Every science to qualify as such must assume as its highest principle an unconditioned reality. For natural science, the unconditioned is nature itself, perceived as a system of self-subsistent activities. The

Naturphilosoph 'treats nature as the transcendental philosopher treats the self' (*Erster Entwurf eines Systems der Naturphilosophie*, *SW*, III, 11–12 and 12 n. 2). The former begins with the objective world as the primary principle of knowledge and must explain how the subjective order can be derived from it; the latter regards the self as the sole ground of reality and must show how nature can emerge from and coincide with it. 'If, now, it is the task of Transcendental Philosophy to subordinate the Real to the Ideal, it is, on the other hand, the task of Natural Philosophy to explain the Ideal by the Real.'[52]

According to Schelling, it should be possible to think of natural science as 'thoroughly and completely realistic' for its object is nature taken as a self-subsistent system of phenomena. Its realism rests, however, on a metaphysical rather than an empirical foundation. Like Kant, Schelling maintains that *Naturphilosophie* must avoid 'the hypothetical, or merely probable', for its scientific status depends on principles that are completely certain. *Naturphilosophie* is a science of nature dealing with a 'pure knowing *à priori*' in 'the *strictest* acceptance of the term'. This does not mean that 'natural science must dispense with all experience', or that 'without any intervention of experience' it is able 'to spin all its principles out of itself'. On the contrary, natural science relies fully on data of experience, for there can be no knowledge at all except 'through experience, and by means of experience' (pp. 196–7 [*SW*, III, 276–9]).

Naturphilosophie is as little opposed to data of experience as to experimental research. Its real opponents are pure empiricism (as a doctrine concerned merely with the external appearances of nature) and a misdirected form of dynamic philosophy, as expounded by Kant. Natural science aims at understanding only what is 'original' and 'non-objective' in nature. It is interested in the 'inner spring-work' of nature and not in its outer 'surface' (p. 195 [*SW*, III, 275]). Unlike empiricism, which looks upon its object as something already constituted, natural science always produces its object in the very process of coming to know it. For natural science an experiment is an 'invasion' of nature, a production of the very phenomena that need to be observed. 'Every experiment', Schelling writes eloquently, is 'a question put to Nature to which she is compelled to give a reply. But every question contains an implicit *a priori* judgement; every experiment that is an experiment, is a prophecy; experimenting itself is a production of phenomena' (pp. 195–6 [*SW*, III, 275–6]). The invasion of nature by means of an experiment is by no means a violation of truth. Since in Schelling the *ground* of the identity of nature and the self (i.e. the Absolute) is an activity that generates its own objects of knowledge, the closer the self recapitulates this activity, the closer it will approach the inner spirit of nature. Likewise, nature becomes intelligible and approaches the life of reason only as an activity by means of which it becomes an object to itself.[53]

Schelling sees the highest principle of natural science as the original productivity of nature. Herein lies the possibility of a genuinely dynamic explanation of the laws of nature. Nature begins as an activity of infinite and continuous productivity. In this state, nature tends towards absolute formlessness because its activity is not hindered by any boundaries. If nature were to remain in this state of undifferentiated infinity, it would never become an object to itself and generate determinate products. But there is in nature a tendency that counteracts absolute productivity, and nature, like the self in *System of Transcendental Idealism*, advances from a stage of complete identity (thesis), to one of duality between its original productivity and the negation of unlimited activity (antithesis), to a moment when duality is resolved (synthesis), and finally back to its original identity. These stages are not separate, nor is there a first and a second in terms of a temporal sequence; they all occur simultaneously and are part of the same act, though they may be distinguished through philosophic analysis. In its original state of identity, nature already contains an original antithesis. But this antithesis is already permeated by a 'tertium aliquid' as 'something which is mediated by the antithesis and by which in turn the antithesis is mediated'. Only if the original antithesis of nature endures can its synthetic activity take place and vice versa (pp. 211–12 [*SW*, III, 308–9]); and only if nature returns to the original identity can the process of production by which the infinite passes over into the finite renew itself.[54] Nature is nothing but an endless circle of activity which closes in order to open again. Like 'an ever-industrious Penelope', to use Herder's metaphor, it is perpetually 'weaving and unravelling and weaving her veil'.[55]

The concept of an ideal, uninterrupted activity in nature is the *sine qua non* of dynamic physics. Schelling warned against an indiscriminate application of the denominator 'dynamic' to any theory that denied the materiality of light or the hypothesis of imponderable fluids in galvanic and electrical phenomena. Such theories are compatible with but do not by themselves reflect a genuine dynamic system of nature. Equally erroneous is the position that any system that attributes the origin of natural phenomena to the forces of attraction and repulsion automatically qualifies as dynamic philosophy. Kant, of course, made an important contribution to the development of natural science by demonstrating the failure of all attempts to derive the diverse qualities of objects from the shape of primary particles of matter. But in the end Kant did not arrive at the ground of specific qualities in objects. Kant showed that every natural phenomenon is the result of particular changes in the relationship between the forces of repulsion and attraction, but he did not explain at all what produces these changes in the first place. He looked upon qualitative changes only at the level of products, without connecting the products to the *process* from which they arose (*Erster Entwurf*, *SW*, III, 24 n. 1). If, as Kant suggested, matter is the filling of space by means of the force of repulsion, or more correctly if matter 'is the occupied space itself', one still has to account for the unconditioned principle according to which all filling of space takes place. This principle will have to be outside space and matter, and the only thing that can be conceived of outside space is 'pure intensity'. Schelling arrives at the notion of *entelechy* as the ideal ground of all qualities in objects. *Entelechy* is variously defined by Schelling as simple action, pure intensity or pure productivity that has not passed over into products; it is not something that can be explained analytically or shown to exist, but must be entertained speculatively as 'the mere *origin* of the product'. *Entelechy* represents the only simple element of nature, and the science that refers all of the phenomena of nature to it may be properly called 'dynamical atomistics'. *Naturphilosophie* is atomistic in so far as it 'affirms something simple as the basis of the explanation of quality', but it is dynamic in that it 'places the simple' not in a determinate particle of matter (i.e. in the product), but in an original productivity (*Introduction to the Outlines*, pp. 203–4 [*SW*, III, 291–4]).[56]

All of Schelling's subsequent explanations of various phenomena of nature are based on the dynamic principles enunciated above, which may be summarized as follows: (1) all processes of the phenomenal world are merely the manifestation of an original structure of activities in *natura naturans*; (2) these processes will always operate according to a law of polarity, for without a clash of opposite forces no activity can be generated; (3) antithesis presupposes synthesis, which means that as soon as a polar pair of phenomena is identified in nature, one must seek to determine the third element that constitutes their unity; (4) the pure productivity of nature, which is the basis of its permanence, is neither divorced from, nor lost in, determinate objects; the ideal is a circle that opens up into the real, the real is the same circle that closes into the ideal; (5) behind or rather contained in all of nature's multiplicity of forms is one simple action, the *entelechy*; therefore all of nature's parts in the inorganic and organic order form one single and undivided whole.

These principles generate a highly complex system of nature, and I can merely sketch here some aspects of it that pertain to Coleridge's own nature philosophy. Schelling attempts to explain the origin and operation of the entire universe from the birth of the planets to the creation of man. He contends that the cosmos emerged from an original mass of matter, namely the sun. The sun is nature's first product, marking the moment when the original duality in nature is brought to a first moment of synthesis. The sun, like any product of nature, generates its own antithesis and gives birth to the planets which are sunderings from the original mass of the sun originating from successive explosions. By causing a universal separation of matter, the sun creates the conditions for the phenomena of light and gravity without which earthly life would be impossible. Between the action of light and gravity there exists a 'secret interdependence' (*SW*, III, 136). While light creates antithesis, gravity presupposes it. Gravity, contrary to Kant's assumptions, is not related to one force only but requires the opposition between the forces of attraction and repulsion (*Introduction to the Outlines*, p. 216 [*SW*, III, 318–19 and 318 n. 1]). Light forms the *ideal* pole of the universe. It is the direct symbol of the productivity and all continuity in nature. Gravity, on the other hand, represents the *real* pole of nature, and is the symbol of matter.[57] The two poles of the universe represented by gravity and light control the primary forms of dynamic activity in nature, namely magnetism, electricity and the chemical process. In all of these one finds the same original antithesis of nature variously and 'continually rekindled'. Magnetism is the expression of the predominance of the particular over the universal, of indifference over difference. It is represented by maximum cohesion and its sphere of action is length (*Ideen*, *SW*, II, 147–52; 156–66). Electricity represents the return of duality and is 'a pure function of breadth' (*SW*, II, 150–2; cf. also II, 122–56). The chemical process enacts the synthesis of magnetism and electricity, length and breadth (*SW*, II, 175–6). Through the chemical process nature is brought back to its original state (pure identity) and begins a new series of productive acts which result in the formation of the organic world.

In the organic world, nature passes through the same stages as in the inorganic (identity–antithesis–synthesis–identity). The life of the organism is regulated by three powers, beginning with sensibility, which is the equivalent of pure productivity in *natura naturans* and the ultimate cause of all activity in the organic world. Sensibility (identity) passes over into irritability (duality), which is its first product. In turn, irritability, which 'is still something internal' and cannot fully reach an external product, passes over into the formative instinct or reproductive power (synthesis) (*SW*, III, 157, 169–72). All three powers mutually influence and presuppose one another. The organism is always a 'triplicity' (*SW*, III, 165 and n. 1). The force of reproduction is dominant in plants, irritability in lower animals and sensibility in the more developed species. But in plants as well as in the lowest animals, sensibility is never absent. 'The plant is what the animal is, and the lower animal is what the higher is. The same force that acts in the animal, acts in the plant . . .' (*SW*, III, 206). Not only are the three forces of organic nature mutually interconnected, but they are also related to the powers of inorganic nature. 'Sensibility is only the higher power of magnetism; irritability only the higher power of electricity; formative instinct only the higher power of the chemical process' (*Introduction to the Outlines*, p. 219 [*SW*, III, 325]).[58] The organic world thus recapitulates the inorganic in a more advanced form. Moreover, the opposition between the inorganic and the organic world exists only in nature viewed as object, that is, only in the realm of products. In *natura naturans*, the organic and inorganic worlds reach a higher synthesis (pp. 219–20 [*SW*, III, 325–6]). The real has once again been absorbed into the ideal, objectivity into subjectivity. With the production of the organism, nature returns once more to its original identity.

Schelling's *Naturphilosophie* exerted a great influence on the development of an organic conception of nature as a self-subsistent totality, the essence of which is a continuous activity, an infinite becoming. Of particular appeal not only to the German Romantics but also to the scientists of the time was Schelling's claim that between nature and the mind, between minute particulars and a universal Absolute, there existed an indestructible bond. 'The spirit', Steffens wrote, in a voluptuous rendition of Schelling's views, 'embraces nature, as the lover embraces his beloved; it gives itself fully to her, it finds itself in her . . . '[59] One might expect that Schelling's teaching regarding the oneness of self and nature would also be attractive to Coleridge, who in his early years advocated the doctrine of the 'one Life'. It turns out, however, that Coleridge was most uncomfortable with this principle of Schelling's *Naturphilosophie*, and for the same reasons that made him reject, however clumsily, the doctrine of 'one Life' in 'The Eolian Harp'. Although Schelling did not confuse the Absolute with nature, to Coleridge Schelling's claim that nature is a self-subsistent reality was tantamount to the pantheistic equation of God with the world. If, as Schelling asserted, nature is eternal in itself, then 'God as God' can no longer be regarded as 'the one necessary Existence'. Coleridge saw a direct contradiction between Schelling's view that nature must be perceived as having the ground of its finality within itself and the Christian position that only God is completely self-sufficient and the ground of all reality. If God, Coleridge argued, 'be Ens semper *perfectum*, and all-sufficient, the material World cannot be *necessary* – and if it be, then God is not self-sufficing – i.e. he is not GOD, but a part of the universe, nay, a product of the same' (Letter to J. H. Green of 30 September 1818, *CL*, IV, 873–4).

Coleridge did not fail to appreciate Schelling's contribution to the development of dynamic science, nor was he able to construct his system of nature without the assistance of many concepts borrowed from Schelling. He acknowledged that Schelling had been most influential in 'the revival and more extensive application of the Law of Polarity' and that he had done a permanent service to the development of philosophy by exposing the inadequacies of a mechanico-corpuscular doctrine of nature. Schelling taught Coleridge basic principles of dynamic philosophy, specifically the 'Metaphysics of Quality' (*CL*, IV, 792, 883), and helped him formulate a critical response to Kant's system of nature, particularly to his view of the two forces of matter and his conception of gravity.[60] But despite all debts to Schelling, Coleridge reacted negatively to the tenets that are the very cornerstone of Schelling's *Naturphilosophie*, namely the self-subsistent finality of nature and its unity with the Absolute. Schelling's writings on natural philosophy came as a shock to Coleridge, according to a letter he wrote to J. H. Green in September 1818, and made him regret that he made extensive use of Schelling's *System of Transcendental Idealism* in *Biographia Literaria*. Coleridge was particularly bothered by Schelling's willingness to give nature full priority over the self (*CL*, IV, 874). This is not so, however, if we look at Schelling's system as a whole. Even in *System of Transcendental Idealism* where Schelling presents natural science and transcendental philosophy as fully complementary sciences – the former subordinating the ideal to the real, the latter the real to the ideal – he emphasized the tendency of natural science to raise nature to the level of intelligence more than its concern with nature as a self-organized totality.[61] In writing to Green that Schelling all too easily passed 'the Slip' to nature (Coleridge's phrase), Coleridge was evidently overreacting to a segment of Schelling's philosophy as enunciated in *Einleitung zu dem Entwurf eines Systems der Naturphilosophie* (*Introduction to the Outlines of a System of Natural Philosophy*).[62] Still, Coleridge detected quite rightly a certain shallowness of method in Schelling evident in the facility with which Schelling applied the same conceptual schema to natural science and transcendental philosophy without any significant adaptations. The one science that Schelling claimed was constituted by the joining of natural and transcendental philosophy looked to Coleridge 'like a Candle placed horizontally and lit at both ends . . . For it will appear to the Learner, in his first perplexity, a mere Trick – viz. that one and the same Thing is called I, or Intelligence, or our Intellect (Verstand) at one end, and Nature at the other . . . ' Thus, if one starts with nature, intelligence is the effect; if one starts from the opposite end, intelligence is the cause and nature the effect. While at the time Coleridge used Schelling's *System* for *Biographia Literaria*, he may have been persuaded by the possibility of deriving the objective from the subjective, he found the reverse argument untenable. 'An unconscious activity that acts intelligently without intelligence, an intelligence that is the product of a Sans-intelligence', he argued, 'are positions calculated rather to startle or confuse the mind by their own difficulty, than to prepare it for the reception of other Truths . . . '[63] Coleridge could not tolerate a system that purported to explain the genesis of a higher order of being from a lower one. This was a point on which he frequently challenged the views of the *Naturphilosophen*.[64] In Schelling's system Coleridge detected the same violation of hierarchical standards, which he attributed to Schelling's use of opposite methods of explaining the origin of various phenomena. Schelling shows the evolution of intelligence from nature, i.e. of a higher power from a lower one, while at the same time he follows 'the method of descent, or emanation', demonstrating that the higher order is prior to and the causative ground of the lower. Such is the case with his derivation of the powers of irritability and reproduction from sensibility. This methodological instability, 'this *up* and *down* in one and the same Sphere', was for Coleridge a major drawback in Schelling's system (*CN*, III, 4449).

Coleridge voiced essentially three major objections to Schelling's *Einleitung*. The first and most serious charge concerned Schelling's equation of nature with the Absolute and his notion that polarity is present within the Absolute.[65] Coleridge's second objection pertained to Schelling's concept of *entelechy* as the primary constituent of all qualities in objects. For Coleridge the reduction of all attributes of objects to '*impossible* realities, nay, worse, hyperousian realizing powers, that are yet impossible', followed directly from Schelling's unfortunate deification of nature. Aristotle, prior to Schelling, had to invent the notion of *entelechy* 'as soon as in opposition to Plato he made Nature absolute' (*CN*, III, 4449). Moreover, the *entelechy*, as employed by Schelling, does not explain the 'idea of Multeity'. Schelling argues that the *entelechy* does not exist in actuality but 'must be *thought* as the grounds of the explanation of quality' (*Introduction to the Outlines*, p. 204 [*SW*, III, 293]). But for Coleridge the *entelechy* 'cannot be *thought*', for thought would destroy all reality; it can only be *imagined.* It is the imagination which can transform unity into multeity, 'for unity is essential to the Imagination, but at the same moment the Imagination must make it many . . . ' (marginal note to pp. 36–7 of *Einleitung*; cf. also *CN*, III, 4449).

Coleridge's third objection to *Einleitung*, and one that is of particular interest here, was directed to Schelling's treatment of the relationship between *a priori* principles and the data of experience. Schelling's argument that an 'absolute hypothesis', by means of which nature is known *a priori*, that is, a principle that 'must carry its necessity within itself', must none the less 'be brought to empiric proof' (*Introduction to the Outlines*, p. 196 [*SW*, III, 277]) appeared to Coleridge to be a contradiction in terms. If indeed natural science is to be based on principles that are certain and carry within themselves their own validity, it has every right to dispense with all experience (marginal notes to pp. 12–13; cf. *CL*, IV, 875). A mathematician, for example, who deduces the 'Truth of the Arch . . . from the essential properties of the Circle', needs no confirmation of this truth by observing its realization 'in a Bridge'. His sense of certainty about the Arch is derived 'from the Idea – which as it is not at all diminished by it's [*sic*] existing unrealizability in Experience, so neither would it be increased by the opposite' (*CL*, IV, 875). Coleridge clearly advocates Kant's definition of an *a priori* law as one requiring by necessity full independence from experiential data. Schelling's notion that 'a datum of experience' automatically becomes an *a priori* principle as soon as its internal necessity is revealed to the mind (or, in Coleridge's adaptation, an '*Anticipation . . . acquires* necessity by becoming an IDEA; but it becomes an IDEA in the moment of it's [*sic*] coincidence with an objective LAW – & vice versâ, a *constant Phaenomenon* first becomes a LAW in the moment of it's [*sic*] coincidence with an IDEA' [*CL*, IV, 876 and marginal note to pp. 12–13]) seemed to Coleridge an 'absurd' position. This position evolved from Schelling's evasive use of the term 'experience'. Schelling's protestations that '*we originally know nothing at all except through experience*' and that consequently natural science in claiming *a priori* principles is not meant to abandon experience (*Introduction to the Outlines*, pp. 196–7 [*SW*, III, 278–9]) did not convince Coleridge. He saw, and I believe quite accurately, that in this case Schelling is not referring to 'Experience ab extra', but to the 'Self-experience' of the mind – that is, to 'the *conditions* of such experience in the mind learnt by the mind' (*CL*, IV, 875; see also *CN*, III, 4445). Schelling is not, in fact, talking about objective phenomena in an empirical sense but merely about the mind's knowledge of what it itself produces from within. Within the terms of Schelling's epistemology we experience 'only the self-produced'; the so-called objective world is for Schelling exclusively a form of subjective activity that acquires a limitation.

Coleridge's regret in having adopted too rashly Schelling's *System* in *Biographia Literaria*, we can speculate, is connected with his realization, which was sharpened by his reading of Schelling's writings on natural philosophy, that the idealism of Schelling's system was *not* 'at the same time, and on that very account, the truest and most binding realism' (*BL*, I, 178) – that for Schelling a *rerum natura* or, in his terms, *natura naturata*, did not exist objectively. Coleridge appears to have been displeased by Schelling's violation of the distance between the natural world and the self as well as by the 'unreality of the Objective' in Schelling's system (*N* 36, f. 2). To say, for example, with Schelling, that 'Nature is only the visible organism of our understanding' is to imply either that nature and the understanding are one and the same, whereby 'nothing is solved', or that nature is separate from the understanding as 'an Eye-glass or pair of Spectacles from the Eye'. But if the latter is the case one must assume 'another Nature to be the stimulant, the fuel, and the Object' of the nature that is the organ of the understanding, for how can 'the Glass *be* the Landscape, seen by means of it?' (marginal note and fly-leaf note to p. 3 of *Einleitung*). For Coleridge, Schelling's *Naturphilosophie* left one with mere eye-glasses but without a landscape to behold. In equating nature with the Absolute, Schelling violated not only (in McFarland's terms) the self-sufficiency of the 'I AM', but also the reality of the 'it is'.

Coleridge's commentary on other works of *Naturphilosophie* by Schelling is not nearly as full and informative as his response to *Einleitung*,[66] though certain details are worth recording here. In his marginalia to *Erster Entwurf eines Systems der Naturphilosophie*, Coleridge singled out Schelling's notion of the solar origin of oxygen and of the earth itself as a peculiar 'Hobby-Horse'. He could not understand why, for example, hydrogen or nitrogen would not be seen as having originated from the same source as oxygen. Coleridge detected in Schelling the same partiality to oxygen that had dominated French chemical theories since Lavoisier's discoveries. Current chemical researches, however, had already exploded the 'monarchy' held by oxygen in all the vital processes in nature, showing that air was made of several gases (*N* 34, ff. 4–5); that the life of the organism depended not only on oxygen but also on carbon, as a negative condition whose '*excess* . . . it is the business of Oxygen to prevent' (marginal note to pp. 82–4 of *Erster Entwurf*); and finally, that chlorine and iodine were primary elements representing the 'Contractive Power' of nature as fully as oxygen.[67] Moreover, Schelling's enthusiasm for oxygen implicated him in a far more serious error than ignorance of current chemical theories. In arguing that oxygen was 'the principle . . . of all chemical relationships', Schelling reduced a principle to 'one Product, in which a high *Grade* of this Principle is embodied' (marginal note to pp. 137–9 of *Einleitung*). This was a fundamental error Schelling held in common with many *Naturphilosophen*. For Coleridge the chemical elements neither were actual physical bodies nor could they be confused with principles or powers of nature. They were merely ideal symbols of the operation and degree of dominance of given powers of nature.[68]

Despite such objections, Coleridge retained many features of Schelling's *Naturphilosophie* in his own system of nature. His demonstration of the dynamic interaction of space and time in his *Theory of Life* and other documents derives from Schelling.[69]. His conception of the three powers of inorganic nature (magnetism, electricity, the chemical process or galvanism) and their correspondence to the categories of length, breadth and depth, as well as his definition of the three powers of organic nature (reproduction, irritability, sensibility), are clearly indebted to Schelling. Furthermore, Coleridge's most widely used logical model for a system of nature, namely the pentad, is implicit in Schelling's presentation of the transformative acts of the Absolute, although the model as such goes back to Plato:

	Identity	
Thesis	Indifference	Antithesis
	Synthesis	

And yet, Coleridge laboured to devise a radically new framework for a system of nature within which Schellingean concepts are given new meanings. His acquaintance with Schelling's *Naturphilosophie* strengthened his awareness that the equation of nature with the Absolute does not secure a safe foundation for a dynamic philosophy of nature. Coleridge needed much clearer distinctions between the Absolute and the non-Absolute, between transformative acts in the divine consciousness and dynamic processes in the realm of nature. Such distinctions, he thought, become clearer if, instead of Schelling's terms the 'infinite' and the 'finite', one adopted such scholastic concepts as 'the real', 'the actual' and 'the potential'. These categories are one in the Godhead; they become distinct, interactive terms for the non-Absolute (*CN*, III, 4445 and *C & S*, Appendix E, p. 234). In locating all reality in the divine will, Coleridge wanted to escape from Schelling's methodological fluctuations '*up* and *down*' the scale of being (*CN*, III, 4449). He also believed that a system that established the ground of reality in God was saved from 'the unreality of the objective' in Schelling's *Naturphilosophie*, which pertained both to nature and to the finite self. Coleridge looked 'forward to the establishment' of a different kind of philosophy that maintained a distinction not only between nature and God, but also between an 'accidental' or empirical 'I', a 'self-finding' that man has in common with animals, and a 'substantial personal I' that comes to man exclusively through participation in the divine Logos. This latter and much higher self does not generate objectivity through its own activity, as Schelling claimed, but finds 'its objectivity in God'.[70]

The Simpler System: The Principle of Quadruplicity in Steffens's *Naturphilosophie*

After Schelling, the second most influential *Naturphilosoph* from whom Coleridge derived the 'inner spring-work' of his own system of nature, was Heinrich Steffens. A close follower and great admirer of Schelling, Steffens subscribed wholeheartedly to the principles of Schelling's dynamic philosophy and applied them to a wide range of geological phenomena. He hailed Schelling as the spiritual leader of the scientific community of the time and credited him with epoch-making discoveries.[71] Steffens backed Schelling's criticism of Kant's limited conception of matter and erroneous definition of gravity (*Beyträge*, pp. 216–17). Most importantly, Steffens adhered passionately to Schelling's view that man and nature share the same essence and that nature is a self-subsistent totality carrying within itself the principles of its own development. For Steffens, as for Schelling, nature is not separate from a spiritual essence, nor is there a discrepancy between *a priori* concepts and particular phenomena. The ideal spirituality of nature is never lost in objects, nor withdrawn from them. Man is himself at the centre of nature, establishing the link between particular objects and the Absolute. He willingly and without fear gives himself over to nature in an act of eternal love, sacrificing his freedom only to regain it fully by joining the world of necessity. Just as man's free spirit acquires a 'moral' identity through union with the 'divine nature', nature becomes 'alive' through union with the divine mind (*Grundzüge*, Vorrede, p. XXII).

Steffens maintains Schelling's conception of the Absolute as a completely undifferentiated identity of subject and object, being and form. There is in the Absolute 'no opposition between the inner and the outer', the particular and the universal (p. 5). The antithesis, or distinction rather, between subject and object emerges only during a particular phase of the eternal act of self-consciousness in which the Absolute, in order to know itself, takes on two separate identities, appearing as 'the eternal body, or the physical universe, or nature' at one end and as 'eternal spirit or history' at the opposite end (p. 10). The terms 'nature' and 'consciousness' or 'history' merely designate different proportions in which the subjective and objective components of the Absolute achieve dominance over one another. From the standpoint of absolute knowledge, they are identical halves of one and the same sphere.[72] History is the 'eternal prototype [*Vorbild*] of Nature, Nature the eternal duplicate [*Abbild*] . . . of History. – Nature preserves the beauty of being in an eternal form, – History the truth of form in its immortal being. Nature has in its eternally beautiful form all the truth of History, History in the truth of its eternal being has all the beauty of Nature' (pp. 11–12). Keats's grand tautology at the end of 'Ode on a Grecian Urn' renders very closely the meaning of this series of ricocheting propositions: 'Beauty is truth, truth beauty, – that is all / Ye know on earth, and all ye need to know.'

The relative differentiation of the Absolute into being and form generates two separate sciences, natural law (*Naturrecht*) or history and natural science or physics. Natural science recognizes nature as an absolute, 'self-grounded' reality. For Steffens, as for Schelling, natural science has no concern for the external appearances of nature or for any phenomenon of nature that is not truly individual, i.e. eternal in itself and a perfect mirror of the universal. The main business of natural science is to investigate the inner structure of nature, which reflects the eternal act of self-knowledge in the Absolute. This structure involves essentially three categories and three transformative processes. All of the manifestations of nature and its laws can be reduced to the 'trinity of the finite, the infinite and the eternal' and to the following, only relatively distinct acts: the metamorphosis of the infinite into the finite, of the finite into the infinite, and the reunification of both in the eternal (p. 35).

The main conceptual categories of natural science are a direct reflection of these changes in *natura naturans*. The concept of power

(*Potenz*), for example, expresses 'the relative difference of being and form with respect to the whole'. It represents an 'ideal determination', a purely formal sign that marks 'the degree of dominance of the subjective or the objective' in various phases of nature's development (p. 14). Steffens maintains Schelling's notion that each power of nature by definition involves an opposite. The dominance of the subjective over the objective in one power of nature automatically requires an inverse proportion in another power. Steffens's analysis of the relationship between space and time, the primary constituents of corporeal nature, offers a good illustration of the basic pattern of interactive powers that he employs with little variation in his entire *Naturphilosophie*. He represents the interaction between space and time by means of a sphere crossed by horizontal and vertical lines that meet in the centre. The vertical line, represented by space, is 'the line of *being*', through which the universal is actualized in particulars. The horizontal line, represented by time, is the 'line of *becoming*', through which the particular is placed under the power of the universal. The line of being corresponds to the dimension of length, the line of becoming, 'which originates in every point' yet is fixated in none, constitutes the dimension of breadth. Neither space, being and length, nor time, becoming and breadth embody reality by themselves. Reality is solely in the circle viewed in its entirety of functions; it is the identity of time and space, being and becoming, length and breadth. What we call matter is essentially 'the indifference of all dimensions'. For natural science, matter is the 'Absolute of nature', a circle whose periphery is nowhere and whose centre is everywhere (pp. 20–3).

The circle crossed by two opposite lines becomes Steffens's primary paradigm for his system of nature. Steffens identifies the lines of being and of becoming with various powers and phenomena of nature. Not only space and time, but also gravity and light, magnetism and electricity, and the chemical processes of oxidation and reduction interact in accordance with this 'simple . . . Scheme' of nature. Each of these powers represents various modes of assimilation between the infinite and the finite, and each contains a 'relative duplicity' within itself. The finite gathers at one end of these powers under the influence of an attractive force, and the infinite becomes dominant at the opposite end as a result of a repulsive force (p. 45). Each power has therefore a negative and a positive pole as well as a point where the opposition between attraction and repulsion, the finite and the infinite, relapses into indifference. Between the lines of being and of becoming, nature acquires four different poles that generate a multiplicity of relations.

Every phenomenon of nature is a mirror of this basic 'quadruplicity' of nature. Time is itself a quadruplicity, in that its own polarity is vitally connected with the polarity intrinsic to space and vice versa. Time expresses the full quadruplicity of nature, only under the determination of becoming, whereas space expresses the same quadruplicity under the determination of being. The 'real' does not consist in the 'separation of the quadruplicity of time from the quadruplicity of space, but in the identity of becoming and being, through which the opposition between these quadruplicities and with it the quadruplicity itself disappears' (p. 44).

For Steffens 'this quadruplicity of forms' and its dissolution into absolute unity constitute 'the eternal rhythm' of nature's 'own construction' that determines all modes of scientific investigation. The inner structure of nature can be represented geometrically in the form of a square inside a circle traversed by a cross:

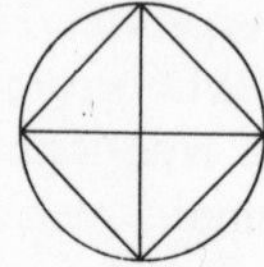

The square and the two lines inside it reflect the set of possible relations among the various powers of nature; the periphery and centre of the circle embody their permanent identity. Steffens insists now and again that the relationship between the lines of being and of becoming, as well as between their corresponding powers, is only formally speaking an opposition between A and B; in actuality they are completely identical (A = A).[73] This is not to say that natural science is meant to abandon all formal boundaries between various phenomena of nature, but only that, after setting up its conceptual categories and distinctions, it must restore them 'to the unity, in which they actually co-exist'. Natural science must follow nature's own rhythm of turning indifference into difference and of returning difference to the state from which it sprang. For the natural scientist, then, the main task is to devise the kind of conceptual framework that can duplicate the internal structure of nature.

Steffens's solution to this problem is a rather simple one. To render the basic quadruplicity of nature. Steffens resorts to three commonplace models: the cardinal points of the earth (North, South, East and West), the elemental components of the universe (earth, air, fire, water), and the primary elements in experimental chemistry (carbon, nitrogen, oxygen, hydrogen).[74] He maintains the pattern of two interactive lines with polar functions and merely superimposes on it several additional layers. Thus, the line of being corresponds to the North–South axis of the earth, and also falls under the power of gravity and of magnetism. Its attractive (North) and expansive (South) poles are marked by carbon and nitrogen or, according to ancient philosophy, by earth and air. Conversely, the line of becoming is represented by the East–West axis of the earth, by the power of light and electricity, by oxygen and hydrogen, and by fire and water. The opposition and ultimate identity between the northern and southern poles produce the hard mass of earth, while the interaction between the eastern and western poles generates fluid matter. The point of indifference in the magnetic line, where the identity of being becomes fully manifest, is constituted by precious metals. The rest of the metals form two opposite series, each occupying the northern and southern half of the magnetic line, according to their degree of coherence.[75] In the line of becoming (East–West) the point of indifference between negative and positive electricity or oxygen and hydrogen is represented by water, while the centre of indifference for the entire quadruplicity of nature, which reflects the full identity between light and gravity in the Absolute, is warmth (p. 48). Figure 3.1 provides a clearer view of Steffens's system of nature.

The relationship between the powers representing the line of being and the line of becoming is invariably described by Steffens in terms of the principles of universality and particularity. Gravity, for example, stands for the universal unity of nature in which particular forms lie dormant. Light awakens nature from its slumber, engendering movement in the place of the inertia of pure mass, and individuality of form in the place of sameness.[76] Similarly, magnetism embodies the 'victory of the universality' and 'homogeneity' of matter, electricity the triumph of the individuality and heterogeneity of forms (p. 51). The relative opposition between magnetism and electricity is abolished in the chemical process. Each chemical process is 'simultaneously magnetic and electric', embracing the full quadruplicity of nature (p. 59), although different poles of these powers may attain greater dominance in specific chemical phenomena. In processes of combustion the northern pole of the magnetic axis oscillates towards the eastern pole of the line of electricity (i.e. carbon or negative magnetism interacts with oxygen or negative electricity), whereas in processes of reduction the southern pole of the magnetic line oscillates towards the western extremity of the electric line – i.e. nitrogen or positive magnetism interacts with hydrogen or positive electricity (pp. 59–60). Accordingly, nature is divided into two interconnected hemispheres, each of which generates different

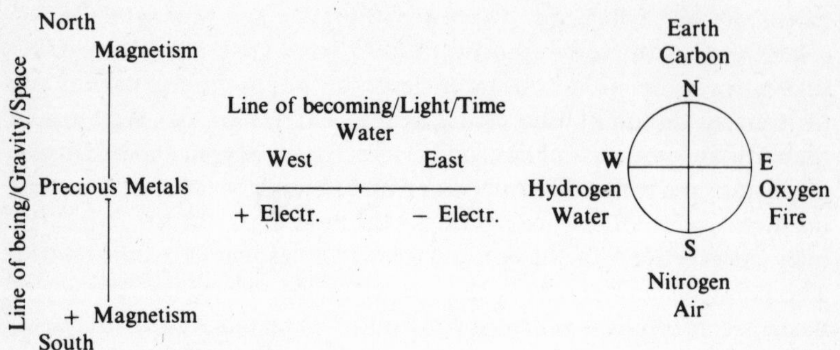

Line of being = Length Line of becoming = Breadth	Indifference = Depth
− Magnetism (North) + Magnetism (South)	Indifference = Precious Metals
− Electricity (East) + Electricity (West)	Indifference = Water
Gravity Light	Indifference = Warmth
Magnetism Electricity	Indifference = Chemical process

FIGURE 3.1

chemical transformations that define different moments in the geological history of the earth. The northeastern hemisphere is the location of the coherent metals which are susceptible to oxygenation; the southwestern hemisphere harbours the non-coherent metals which are subject to hydrogenation. This is why on our planet, land will gather towards the northeast, water towards the southwest (p. 56). In the organic world the chemical processes of the northeastern hemisphere are instrumental in the development of vegetative life, while those of the opposite hemisphere affect animal life. For Steffens all the epochs in the evolution of the planetary world, from the emergence of metals, earths and rock formations to the highest forms of animal life, represent discrete points on an infinite radius, each marking a specific degree in the inclination of the magnetic axis towards the eastern or western poles, and correspondingly, a different 'intensity' in the dominance of one power of nature over the other. Nature's grammar consists of four entities that generate an infinitude of permutations; the vast annals of the earth are contained in four hieroglyphs that hold the secret of the eternal life of each finite being.

The chemical process not only mirrors the full quadruplicity of nature in the inorganic world, but also marks the beginning of a new cycle of development in which nature attains higher forms of realization and completes its quest for self-knowledge. Each chemical process results in the creation of 'an individual life' or organism (p. 61). The most important feature of organic life is the individuality and self-determination of all its components. This is why in the organic world, as opposed to the inorganic, the identity rather than the difference between being and becoming is merely relative. The lines of being and becoming combine with one another in various degrees of intensity without reaching a point of absolute oneness (p. 62). The forces of gravity and light reemerge in the organic world, but with different functions. In fact, their identity with regard to subjectivity or objectivity is exactly the reverse of their counterpart in the inorganic world. Gravity now represents the force of particularity, i.e. the subjective side of nature, whereas light embodies the force of universality, i.e. the objective side of nature (pp. 62–3, 66–7).

Despite these and other differences, life in the organic world conforms to the same basic pattern of evolution that is reflected in inorganic nature, namely to the 'trinity' of identity, difference and indifference and to the interaction between the four poles of the lines of being and becoming. Thus, the relative identity between light and gravity under the dominance of the latter manifests itself in the power of reproduction, which determines the evolution of vegetative life; conversely, 'the assimilation between gravity and light under the power of light' constitutes sensibility, which governs animal life. The power that makes possible the manifestation of sensibility in reproduction and of reproduction in sensibility is irritability, the centre of indifference in the organism (pp. 70–1).[77] Like Schelling, Steffens maintains that in the lowest as well as the highest forms of life, the three powers are simultaneously present (p. 74). There is therefore no substantial difference, nor any discontinuity between plant and animal, or between animal and man. In man, nature achieves its highest expression of individuality. The development of the organs of nutrition in worms, of the powers of irritability and feeling in insects, and of differentiated sensory capabilities in higher animals is mirrored in man in a clearly perfected form. Steffens invites us to contemplate nature as 'one gigantic animal' in which 'every function builds a sphere of its own and leads a life of its own'. Every inhabitant of nature is a condensed image of the entire macrocosm under the determination of a particular power. Man stands in the centre of nature and 'all individual spheres of organizations must be viewed as *disiecta membra* of the human organization' (pp. 81–2). He becomes a true individual when through the development of ethical consciousness he recognizes no opposition between the infinite 'I AM' and the infinite universe. For Steffens, ethics constitutes the essence of individuality, just as in nature gravity constitutes the essence of universality. Ethical consciousness is ultimately the same as cognitive knowledge at its highest stage of development. To be moral or to know scientific truth with absolute certainty means in principle to see one's being as identical with the being of God – that is, at once as free and confined, infinite and finite. Moral consciousness further requires that nature be seen as one with the being of God, and as 'eternally free'. The inseparable unity between matter and spirit, soul and body, freedom and necessity is the great 'mystery' that underlies 'the life of individuality', a mystery that can be unravelled only through an act of unmediated intuition (pp. 203–4).

Steffens's passionate plea regarding the identity of nature, man and God fully reveals the pantheistic basis of his system of nature. Coleridge was quite aware of the 'blasphemy' implicit in Steffens's statement that the Absolute, regarded as the 'indifference of all dimensions', is the same as matter (marginal note to *Grundzüge*, p. 23 [Nidecker, p. 275]). This makes God indistinguishable from the 'absolute Something and the absolute Nothing' (*CN*, III, 4445).[78] And yet Coleridge was much harsher in his criticisms of Schelling's philosophy than of Steffens's, even though of the two, Steffens exhibits greater pantheistic tendencies. Perhaps Coleridge's severer attitude towards Schelling might relate to the fact that he had compromised himself publicly by adopting Schelling's tenets in *Biographia Literaria* and needed to put a certain distance between himself and Schelling as a way of purging his momentary identification with a pantheistic system. His borrowings from Steffens, on the other hand, were confined to his private writings. There were other reasons as well that may have influenced Coleridge's partiality to Steffens. In his writings on *Naturphilosophie* Steffens tends to be non-polemical, though he does, of course, disagree with some of the tenets of his predecessors. Still, his tone is rarely vituperative, and where he praises the contributions of other scientists he does so generously. There is also considerable warmth and emotional expressiveness in some of Steffens's statements. It is tempting to speculate that Steffens's remark that the most insignificant worm is entitled to man's eternal love (*Grundzüge*, Vorrede, pp. XI–XII, XXI–XXII) might have struck a responsive chord in the author of 'The Rime of the Ancient Mariner'.

Ostensibly, however, Coleridge appreciated Steffens because of the 'simplicity' and 'vital Schematism' of his conception of nature. Coleridge's life-long wish to evolve a 'compleat and perfectly original system' made him susceptible to the influence of philosophers who appeared to have developed a coherent system of their own, sustained by 'a sober Dignity of logical Arrangement' (fly-leaf note referring to p. 252 of Heinroth, *Lehrbuch der Anthropologie*). Steffens's works provided Coleridge with an informative and irresistible model of a fully structured scheme of nature, equipped with all the necessary terms to explain a wide variety of physical phenomena. For many years Coleridge was unable to devise a more systematic or better shaped outline for natural philosophy than what he found in Steffens. In his letters to C. A. Tulk of September 1817 and January 1818, he reproduces Steffens's *Grundzüge der philosophischen Naturwissenschaft* with the help of a number of diagrams. Coleridge retains Steffens's main geometric pattern of a circle crossed by two opposite lines, as well as the various relationships between the powers representing the lines of being and of becoming. Like Steffens, he identifies the poles of the two lines with the cardinal points, the chemical elements and the elements of the universe, situates the centre of gravity and light in the sun, and establishes the points of indifference between + and – magnetism, + and – electricity, and between light and gravity in precious metals, water and warmth respectively (*CL*, IV, 767–75, 804–9). He even repeats Steffens's schema of the distribution of land towards the northeast and water towards the southwest (*CL*, IV, 773), as well as the classification of the senses according to the four poles of nature (cf. *CL*, IV, 773–4 and *Grundzüge*, pp. 76–80, 187–92).

Coleridge's willingness to follow Steffens's 'more dynamic' conception of nature was always hampered by his recognition that, with Steffens as with Schelling, pantheism posed an implicit threat. Even in his letters to Tulk, where Coleridge's dependence on Steffens is most evident, he makes visible efforts to move away from Steffens's views, seeking to reconcile *Naturphilosophie* with religious orthodoxy. Coleridge was disturbed by Steffens's belief in the identity between nature and the Absolute – a belief that was directly opposed to the Christian notion of a transcendent, personal God – and by what he perceived as a logical fallacy in Steffens's conception of the Absolute. He did not think that Steffens, or any philosopher who presupposed a complete identity between the finite and the infinite, was able to explain how 'the Relative' connects 'with the Absolute'.[79] In Coleridge's view the connection between the Absolute and the finite world can be established only through intermediaries. This is what ensures the preservation of distinct, though not divisive, boundaries between the two realms of being. Steffens, on the other hand, eradicates all necessity or possibility of mediation by making the finite and the infinite simultaneously co-present in one another. There is evidently much at stake in Coleridge's insistence that a concept of mediation must be part of a viable system of nature. This concept is central to Coleridge's theory of symbolism and of the imagination; indeed, it informs and represents the unifying basis of his religious, philosophical and aesthetical writings. His use of mediation in his *Naturphilosophie* appears to be a protection against the violation of hierarchical norms that he perceived to be the unfortunate consequence of organic thinking among the German philosophers. Steffens, for example, shows that vegetative and animal life are parallel processes controlled by the polar activity of the forces dominant in the northeast or southwest hemisphere. For Coleridge, this theory failed to explain how vegetative life can give rise to animal life, since the two processes are presented as simultaneous, that is, as taking place 'without any intervening acts' (marginal note to p. 259 of *Geognostisch-geologische Aufsätze*). Moreover, the theory failed to account for 'the manifest chasm between the most perfect form of mineral crystallization & the meanest plant or animal' (marginal note to p. 289 of *Geognostisch-geologische Aufsätze*). Coleridge clearly wanted to maintain a separation not only between mineral and plant, plant and animal, animal and man, but most essentially between man and God. The separation is not meant to cause discontinuity between lower and higher forms of life, as is evident from the primary act of mediation, namely God's creation of Jesus Christ as his messenger among men – but to guarantee the possibility of genuine connectedness.

Steffens's conception of the Absolute threatened to violate not only a hierarchical chain of being deriving from the Deity, but also the reality of the world of nature. This seems an unfair charge against Steffens, for, like Schelling, he points to each particular of nature as vibrant with life and as fully inhabited by the Absolute. But Coleridge was disturbed by Steffens's frequent references to mere appearances in nature and by his use of the term '*Schein*' (appearance) to designate the illusory perception of a finite object. Steffens states, for instance, that natural science has no interest in the deceptive appearance (*trügerischer Schein*) of objects that do not express the whole of nature. For science such objects are a 'non-reality' (*Grundzüge*, p. 36). He also remarks that the degree of dominance of the powers of reproduction, irritability and sensibility in various forms of life 'exists only in appearance'. In reality each organization contains within itself all degrees of a given power (pp. 170–2). For Coleridge these statements were confusing. By 'appearance' Steffens ought to mean 'Manifestation' or 'Existence as distinguished from Essence', and not a deceptive or impermanent phenomenon. Coleridge could not understand why 'the Gradual', that is, the degree of dominance of the organic powers in various species from coral to the developed animals, should be regarded as 'mere appearance'. 'Is it not as real, i.e. as much an objective form of manifested Being, i.e. of Existence, as the Coral itself quoad Coral . . . ?' (marginal note to p. 172 of *Grundzüge* [Nidecker, pp. 281–2]). Coleridge perceived a paradox at the root of Steffens's conception of the Absolute. The Absolute is presented as extending itself in all particulars of the physical world, and yet there still remains such a thing called 'appearance' that can fall outside its sphere.[80] When so much burden is placed on the real as presupposing an identity with the Absolute, the danger exists that anything not absorbed by the Absolute will be discarded as an insignificant appearance. Coleridge began to fear that the reality of the objective world was as much in jeopardy in Steffens's system as in Schelling's.

Coleridge also had a number of reservations regarding the consistency of Steffens's scheme of nature. He was particularly critical of Steffens's error, not uncommon among *Naturphilosophen*, of mistaking an ideal theory of nature for an actual structure within the phenomenal world that could be verified empirically. In his eagerness to demonstrate the accuracy of his theory of metals, Steffens claimed that precious metals, because they occupy the centre of the magnetic line, will be found in greater abundance near the equator. He added that he had personally seen specimens of pure gold from the Indian islands.[81] Coleridge found this assumption fallible, if only because, notwithstanding any coincidences between theoretical and empirical observations, the place of metals in an ideal map of nature has nothing to do with the location of metals in an actual region on earth. He thought that natural science, if it is to be based on *a priori* principles, will not profit from seeking empiric verification of its laws. It has an obligation to 'dispense with all experience' in order to retain the purity of its ideal foundation.

Coleridge detected the same confusion between metaphysical and physical relations in Steffens's use of the four chemical elements. By means of these elements, Steffens defines the various powers that determine the development of inorganic and organic nature. Coleridge accepted Steffens's argument as long as the elements were represented as mere symbols of the opposite poles of magnetism and electricity, and of related powers. But Steffens inadvertently began to talk about carbon, nitrogen, oxygen and hydrogen in the same way that a chemist refers to them in experimental research. Now, oxygen viewed as a power of nature is quite different from the oxygen gas that enters into the composition of various substances. In an ideal sense oxygen is representative of a force that will become manifest not only in oxygen gas, but also in chlorine and iodine, elements commonly neglected by the *Naturphilosophen.*[82] Steffens appears to miss this distinction when he states that nitrogen is 'the characteristic substance in the lime combination' (*Beyträge*, pp. 64–5) or that 'If the metals could be chemically analysed, they would undoubtedly be found to be composed of carbon and nitrogen' (*Beyträge*, pp. 262–3).[83] Coleridge regarded it as an error to say that metals are made of carbon and nitrogen, for how can ideal powers be the same as substances forming a compound? Steffens should have said that the metals are not 'composed *of*' but 'constituted *by*' these elements, or, more accurately, by 'the Power predominant in each'. Should one contemplate the theoretical possibility of decomposing a metal, one might say without error that 'it would doubtless be found to be composed of the same Stuffs as Carbon, and as Nitrogen is composed of . . . ' When carbon and nitrogen cease to be ideal powers and become substances, they too must be seen as compounds rather than simple bodies. Every substance, Coleridge argued, echoing Schelling, is the synthetic product of opposite forces, and this applies to the chemical elements no less than to the metals. 'A simple *Body* is an absurdity.'[84] The empirical scientist may look upon substances that cannot be decomposed as simple; the speculative chemist, on the other hand, 'sees a priori, that all alike must be composite'. For Coleridge it was 'of the highest importance in all departments of Knowledge to keep the Speculative distinct from the Empirical. As long as they run parallel, they are of the greatest service to each other: they never meet but to cut and cross.'[85]

Steffens's indiscriminate approach to the difference between ideal powers and physical bodies, as well as between speculative and empirical forms of knowledge, weakened considerably his chances of 'full discovery' of the vital laws of nature.[86] His system also suffered from a flaw that, according to Coleridge, was responsible for most of the 'difficulties, *inadequacies*, and even misstatements, in which the Naturphilosophen involve themselves'. Like other scientists, Steffens overlooked the 'essential diversity' of the powers of nature. He defined the negative and positive poles of the magnetic and electrical lines in terms of the dominance of the finite or the infinite in each, and correspondingly, the action of an attractive or repulsive force. This makes the powers representing the lines of being and of becoming essentially identical. Coleridge thought that there was a real, not a merely relative, difference between them. In order to mark the distinction between the various poles of nature, Coleridge gave them different names. In his system the forces of attraction and repulsion define the activity of the N–S axis of magnetism, whereas two different forces, namely contraction and dilation, control the E–W line of electricity. There are, accordingly, five powers in nature, each of which has two opposite poles: attraction (−magnetism), repulsion (+magnetism), contraction (−electricity), dilation (+electricity) and centrality. The first, second and fifth are the 'constituent, *substantive* Powers' of nature, the third and fourth the 'modifying or adjective Powers'. The 'Powers of nature, her Hand, as it were, form a Pentad = 5 fingers, or four fingers and the Thumb'.[87]

Coleridge placed much emphasis on the difference between the substantive and modifying powers of nature. 'More and more, and by daily instance of proof', he wrote in a marginal note to Oersted, 'am I impressed with the practical no less than speculative importance of the distinction between Contraction and Attraction, Dilation and Repulsion' (marginal note to p. 24 of *Ansicht der chemischen Naturgesetze*). He vowed to devote himself to a close examination of 'the relations and complex antagonisms of the modifying to the substantial Powers' (*CN*, III, 4420). Coleridge's eagerness to devise sharper distinctions between the powers of nature appears to be motivated by his need to maintain symbolic relations in his *Naturphilosophie*. He thought that the interaction between the opposite poles of the line of magnetism (carbon and nitrogen) required by necessity 'an intermediate, which is either Oxygen and Hydrogen or both', that is, one or both of the poles of the line of electricity (*CN*, III, 4420). Steffens, too, claimed that in the production of every phenomenon nature's entire quadruplicity of powers is involved, but for Coleridge the cooperation between the four powers was predicated upon their distinctions. Only powers that are essentially, not relatively, different can act as each other's intermediaries. Where the *Naturphilosophen* emphasized the homogeneity and ultimate identity between all parts of nature, Coleridge stressed their diversity and separation from one another. Even in theories devised to explain terrestrial life and physical phenomena Coleridge wanted to keep a safe distance between various entities so as to make room for mediation and through it keep intact a hierarchical order. If nature is to approximate at all the inner life of the Absolute, its grammar must include a system of symbolic expression.

CHAPTER 4 *NATURPHILOSOPHIE* AND CHRISTIAN ORTHODOXY IN COLERIDGE'S VIEW OF THE TRINITY

In his assessment of Kant's, Schelling's and Steffens's writings on *Naturphilosophie*, Coleridge focused now and again on a single and, in its implications, most serious error that, without exception, made their systems unacceptable to Coleridge: the inability to accommodate the concept of a Christian God in an all-embracing system of the natural world. He was relentless in exposing the heresies, no less than the logical inconsistencies, resulting from the philosophers' inadequate conception of the Absolute. Schelling attempted to burn a candle at both ends by giving intelligence and nature an equal share in originating the same series of productive acts that were indigenous to the Absolute. In declaring nature a self-subsistent totality, Schelling inevitably slipped into pantheistic thought, making God 'a part of the universe, nay, a product of the same' (*CL*, IV, 873–4). Steffens fared no better when, in following Schelling's philosophy, he advocated the oneness of nature and the Absolute. Even Kant, though limiting his doctrine of nature to physics, came dangerously close to pantheism when he explained the permanence of matter without any reference to spirit. Coleridge thought that the absence of a proper theory of the Absolute in a treatise dealing with corporeal nature was potentially as damaging to dynamic philosophy as the mistaken identification of the Absolute with nature in the systems of Schelling and his followers.

Coleridge saw clearly that his main goal as a *Naturphilosoph* was to work out a viable and systematic concept of the Absolute that could accommodate the principles of dynamic philosophy without violating the Christian view of a personal God. This was a task to which he devoted many years and which preoccupied him deeply in the last decade of his life. From his earliest attempts to put together his system of natural philosophy, Coleridge had consistently begun with the biblical account of the creation of the world out of chaos, and not with an analysis of the powers of nature (see e.g. *CL*, IV, 767–75, 804–9 and *CN*, III, 4418). He started from the top of the pyramid of being, slowly working his way to the bottom through the method of descent. In his view, the only correct answer to a theory of life was a transcendent deity, and the only alternative to pantheism was a system firmly grounded in the theistic doctrine of the Trinity.[88] Coleridge spent much thought on the possible application of the Christian concept of the Trinity to a dynamic theory of nature. His later notebooks and marginalia leave no doubt that through the concept of the Trinity Coleridge hoped to resolve the major inconsistencies and inadequacies of German *Naturphilosophie* and bring dynamic philosophy within the sphere of Christian theology.[89]

Critics have generally regarded with scepticism Coleridge's efforts to reconcile German idealism and Christian orthodoxy. René Wellek's position on this subject is well known: in order to make room for his religious beliefs, Coleridge incorrigibly bends and misrepresents the radical theories of German philosophers. 'It is a truly Coleridgean inconsistency', Wellek writes, 'that he still asserts subjective idealism side by side with a belief in the Triune God and the historical creed of Christianity' (*Immanuel Kant in England 1793–1838*, p. 124). Even critics who are more favourable to Coleridge than Wellek and willing to see his departure from idealistic thought as founded on respectable and carefully scrutinized intellectual principles have interpreted his inability to complete a fully systematic philosophy of his own as indicative of his failure to synthesize German idealism and Christian values. According to Bate, the 'central difficulty that had blocked the *magnum opus* was . . . that of reconciling the "dynamic philosophy" of nature with the Christian dualism of God and the created universe'.[90] McFarland gives a somewhat different explanation of Coleridge's failure to produce a system. Coleridge, he argues, saw with increasing clarity that systems that become complete inevitably sacrifice the integrity of the 'I AM' or the 'it is' (*Coleridge and the Pantheist Tradition, passim*). I agree with Bate and McFarland that to the end of his life Coleridge was still seeking new solutions to an old problem and that something other than intellectual fatigue or the masochistic tendencies of his character kept him from publishing in coherent form the results of '20 years' incessant Thought, and at least 10 years' positive Labor' (*CL*, IV, 736). But in my view, Coleridge did *not* fail to develop a philosophic system. His writings on natural philosophy reveal the essential features of a coherent and integrated system that is thoroughly structured and even conceptually rigid, notwithstanding the fact that it is dispersed in bits and pieces throughout Coleridge's works. More importantly, Coleridge succeeded rather brilliantly in reconciling Christian religion with dynamic philosophy as his elaborations of the concept of the Trinity will show. What kept Coleridge from putting together and submitting for public review the wealth of notes in which he developed various parts of his philosophic system was a failure of self-confidence rather than of intellectual competence. Coleridge never felt sufficiently well-informed or competent to bring to completion the grand philosophic system that was to integrate and supersede all previous attempts at a synthesis of science, philosophy and religion. As *Biographia Literaria* and the *Logic* illustrate, among other works of Coleridge, it was his habit to anticipate fully an essential component of his system and postpone its elaboration, partly because he was apprehensive about the public's readiness to receive radical doctrines indebted to German writers, and partly because he was afraid of implicating himself in dangerous positions whose consequences he could not fully master. This is particularly evident in Coleridge's writings on the Trinity. Coleridge knew very well that the concept of the Trinity promised a secure basis for his own philosophic system and a solution to many of the difficulties he encountered in adopting the tenets of the *Naturphilosophen*. But although through the Trinity Coleridge discovered the key to a successful synthesis of dynamic philosophy and Christian theology, he was not ready to divulge it publicly. Coleridge was aware that any synthesis, to be genuine, can no longer resemble any of its original components. This was not a worrisome problem for Coleridge in so far as *Naturphilosophie* was concerned. He had discovered enough errors and inconsistencies in the works of the *Naturphilosophen* to welcome a thorough recasting of their systems in a new mould. But, as expected, he could not be equally comfortable with the inevitable alteration of Christian dogma after its contact with dynamic philosophy.

There is considerable anxiety in some of Coleridge's religious writings where he explores the dynamic possibilities of basic articles of faith in Christianity, such as the Trinity or the creation of the world out of chaos. The anxiety originates from Coleridge's irresistible attraction to idealistic thought and his inability to give up systematic rational analysis in his dealings with Christian theology. Wellek has presented a one-sided picture of Coleridge by arguing that he always distorts subjective idealism for the sake of Christian orthodoxy and that in his work the two philosophies stand 'side by side', unassimilated. Although it would be fruitless to deny that, in some instances, Coleridge's flights out of transcendental idealism into religious exhortations are hasty and unconvincing, much other evidence supports the view that Coleridge found a true basis of reconciliation between Christian and idealistic thought. What Wellek and other critics have missed is the extent to which Coleridge reshaped fundamental Christian tenets in order to make them compatible with the principles of dynamic philosophy. This is most evident in Coleridge's elaborations of the concept of the Trinity. Critics have often pointed out that Coleridge's treatment of the Trinity bears a distinctly unorthodox mark, though they have not been able to pin down completely the source of Coleridge's unconventional handling of this doctrine. The source is actually not that obscure. Some of Coleridge's most prominent statements on the Trinity appear in writings in which he examines various concepts of German idealism and of *Naturphilosophie* in particular. His marginalia to Boehme or Oken, as well as various notebook entries, present strong evidence that Coleridge extracted a philosophical model for the Trinity from the *Naturphilosophen*, especially from Schelling,[91] whose conception of the Absolute has as much bearing on Coleridge's notion of the Trinity as the doctrines of the Church Fathers. Critics have generally missed this point because they have taken for granted Coleridge's frequent declarations that a system based on the Trinity was directly opposed to Schelling's philosophy and to pantheism in general. But in one notebook entry Coleridge himself gives us a clue that he found close affinities between his and Schelling's idea of how a triad of powers can coexist as a full unity in the Absolute.[92] We need not distrust completely Coleridge's claim that the Trinity secured for him an alternative to Schelling's system. This alternative, however, was attractive to Coleridge precisely because, notwithstanding some of his statements to the contrary, it retained important features of Schelling's dynamic philosophy.

Coleridge's main revision of the concept of the Trinity consists in his addition of a fourth element to the traditional triad of Father, Son and Holy Ghost. Originally, Coleridge claims, God is an absolute unity of form and essence, subject and object (*CN*, III, 4427), having the ground of reality within himself (*causa sui*) and possessing simultaneously all of his ideas and attributes (*CL*, II, 1195). Coleridge names this state of undifferentiated, all-inclusive unity in divine consciousness – 'the One in all & thro all, and over all' (BÖHME, *Works* 6 [*CM*, I, 561]) – Prothesis or Identity and equates it with the absolute will, with the absolute subjectivity, and with God as divine ground (τὸ θετον).[93] Through 'an immanent Energy' in his consciousness (BÖHME, *Works* 7 [*CM*, I, 564]) God manifests his existence to himself 'in a three-fold Act, total in each and one in all' (*CN*, III, 4427), begetting the Father, the Son and the Holy Ghost. The Father represents God's primary act of self-assertion (the 'I Am in that I am') and embodies the stage of relative subjectivity in the Absolute, or 'Ipseity'. But in the very act of self-affirmation, God also begets the Son, who becomes the logos, the Word and 'the *pleroma* of being'. The Son stands for the relatively objective side of divine consciousness or 'the essential infinite in the form of the finite'. He is the *deitas objectiva*, just as at the opposite end the Father is *deitas subjectiva* (*NTP*, pp. 395–6). Coleridge clearly placed most emphasis on this phase of divine creativity. God's gesture of coming to know himself through another becomes an important example of how in a lower sphere man can attain self-consciousness and become a fully moral being. The Son is for God what another human being, 'intensely similar, yet not the same', is for man; he gives 'outness' to God and represents 'the essential Symbol' through which the Deity manifests himself to man. The Son is thus the '*Person* . . . or *real* Image, of God' (*CL*, IV, 771) and 'the sole adequate, Idea, in God, of God'. Finally, God expends a 'second Energy' (in order, not in time) to bring to full synthesis the Father and the Son, Ipseity and Alterity, the relatively subjective and the relatively objective (BÖHME, *Works* 7 [*CM*, I, 564]). God's 'three-fold' act ends with the creation of the Holy Ghost, who represents the essence of love and of the spirit of community. Figure 3.2, used by Coleridge in many notes, provides a consolidated scheme of his view of the Trinity.

The need for a clear distinction between God as ground and God as person compelled Coleridge to seek a different formula for the idea of deity from the one given in traditional Trinitarian theology. Coleridge found the best expression of his conception of the Trinity in the figure of the Tetractys by means of which Pythagoras rendered the ideal order of the universe (∴∵).[94] The Tetractys served Coleridge's purpose all too well. It accommodates both a triad of powers and a pattern of quadruplicity which, as the previous figure shows, is basic to Coleridge's presentation of the acts in divine consciousness. The Tetractys also generates the pentad, to which Coleridge often resorted in his *Naturphilosophie*, and the number ten, the Pythagorean symbol of perfection (1 +2 +3 +4 = 10). But most importantly, the Tetractys showed Coleridge the possibility of explaining the coexistence of both unity and multiplicity or distinctness within the Godhead. He was

	Prothesis			Identity	
Thesis		Antithesis	Ipseity		Alterity
	Synthesis			Community	

Identity

The Absolute Will, the Good, the Ground

Ipseity	*Alterity*
The I AM, the Father,	Truth, the Supreme Mind,
the Supreme Will	the Logos, the only begotten Word
Being	Intellect

Community

Life, Love, the Holy Spirit
Action

Prothesis

The Absolute Subjectivity

Thesis	*Antithesis*
The Relatively Subjective	The Relatively Objective
Deitas subjectiva	*Deitas objectiva*

Synthesis

The relatively subjective
united with the relatively objective

Prothesis = God as Ground (*τὸ θετον*)
Thesis, Antithesis, Synthesis = God as person (*ὁ Θεόζ*)

FIGURE 3.2

particularly fascinated by the mathematical derivation of a sequence of numbers from an original unity designated by the number 1 or 'the Monas', and he followed carefully the dialectical transformations of the

'Monas' into 'the Dyas', 'the Trias' and the 'Tetractys' (see e.g. BÖHME, *Works* 6 [*CM*, I, 562–3] and *CN*, III, 4436). The Trinity, adapted to the Pythagorean model, finally held out for Coleridge the promise of rewarding the pilgrimage he undertook in early youth to find how there can be unity in the midst of infinite diversity.[95] Coleridge was convinced that without the Tetractys, the concept of the Trinity became inconsistent. Had the Christian Fathers realized that God as Absolute Will (Prothesis) was not the same as God the Father (Thesis), they would have saved 'their exposition' from 'many inconveniences' (in Boulger, p. 133 n. 1). The idea of God, Coleridge argued, 'is impossible without producing and expanding or completing itself in the Idea of the Tetractys (A = 3 = 1) or Trinity. Again, the *το αγαθον και δ πατήρ* must be contemplated distinctly and severally as Prothesis & Thesis' so that both appear 'in the unity of the Idea. And in like manner the Idea of the Father and the Son, as Thesis and Antithesis (Ipseity ⟩-⟨ Alterity) and lastly both theses and the Idea of the H. Ghost, which occupies the place of Synthesis' must again be seen as inherent in 'the unity of the Ideas . . . ' (*N* 26, ff. 108–108^{v} [in Boulger, p. 133 n. 3]).

Why did Coleridge place so much emphasis on the distinction between God as Ground and God as person? One explanation is given by Coleridge himself. By postulating an original unity in God prior to all distinction, Coleridge wanted to avoid the error most common in the *Naturphilosophen* of placing polarity in the Absolute. He was committed to the scholastic conception of God as a pure act without any potentiality, embodying the full 'identity of the Real and the Actual' (*C & S*, Appendix E, p. 234). This statement, repeated by Coleridge in various texts, has been singularly responsible for the obfuscation of a most important source of Coleridge's view of the Trinity. Coleridge's 'Prothesis' actually has a direct equivalent in Schelling's philosophy of the Absolute. Schelling, too, claims that the Absolute is originally an undivided unity, neither subject nor object, neither essence nor form, but both simultaneously. Schelling calls this phase of the Absolute identity (A = A),[96] a term which Coleridge also uses as an alternative to Prothesis. Like Coleridge, Schelling differentiates between the original identity within the Absolute and the stage of synthesis, which is a reconstituted unity after the Absolute divides itself into subject and object. There is a remarkable resemblance between Coleridge's description of the 'threefold Act' of divine creativity and Schelling's unfolding of the series of acts by means of which the Absolute attains self-knowledge. In Schelling the Absolute progresses from the state of identity to one of antithesis, during which it perceives itself as divided into subject and object, to a stage of synthesis by which it returns to its original unity. In the following notebook entry written in 1818 Coleridge takes over Schelling's dynamic model and transplants it into the doctrine of the Trinity:

> Unitrine. Absolute Essence begotten in the Form, Absolute Form co-existing in the Essence, and the Unity of Both. Or the Subject-Object in absolute Identity neither Subject nor Object, or both in Combination, but the Prothesis or Unground of both = Τὸ *ὑπερούσιογ, O' πατηρ*.
>
> This eternal Self-position absolutely begets itself as its own Object, in which being all, it is Object-Subject . . . and again asserting the identity of the Form with the Essence, or the Essence of the Form, the Γ*ιos* affirming itself as having its Subject or Essence = God, and the Father asserting the Form identical with his Essence, there proceeds from both Father and Son, the Spirit of God, or Subject-Object. God *is* one, but exists or manifests himself to himself, at once ~~total~~ in a three-fold Act, total in each and one in all –
>
> Prothesis = God
>
> Thesis = Son Antithesis = Spirit
>
> Synthesis = Father
>
> Hence in all things the Synthesis . . . images what in God only absolutely is, the Prothesis manifested – it is a return to the Prothesis, or re-affirmation. Thus the Monas, the Dyas, the Trias, and the Tetractys are one / (*CN*, III, 4427)

The language of Coleridge's rendition of the Trinity here is unmistakably Schellingean. For Coleridge, God in effect performs an act of self-consciousness. In order to know himself God generates his own object, that is, he abandons his original unity and views himself under the separate categories of dominant subjectivity and dominant objectivity. Finally, God reasserts the unity of subject and object and returns to his original form, which is the absolute identity of both. As in Schelling, the stage of synthesis brings the Absolute full circle to its starting point.

In later writings Coleridge characteristically places the Father under the heading Thesis, the Son under Antithesis, and the Holy Ghost under Synthesis, but the pattern of simultaneous acts in divine consciousness remains basically the same. As late as 1830 Coleridge still adheres to a four-fold formula for the Trinity couched in the language of dynamic philosophy. He represents Prothesis as a state of 'absolute subjectivity', the Father as 'the relatively subjective' or the 'essential finific in the form of the infinite', and the Son as the 'relatively objective' or 'the essential infinite in the form of the finite' (*NTP*, pp. 395–6). The description of the attributes of the Father and the Son here are closely reminiscent not only of Schelling's, but more directly of Steffens's *Naturphilosophie*. All of Steffens's categories, as seen before, are expressions of the relative difference between opposite poles and of the dominance of the finite within the infinite and vice versa. Steffens's use of quadruplicity as his basic dynamic scheme of the universe also parallels Coleridge's preference for the Pythagorean Tetractys.

Coleridge is clearly attracted to the idea of a dynamic, self-conscious God who projects for man a model of continuous creativity and of self-realization through another. Without the Son, Coleridge says in a daring statement, 'in which and by which God is manifest to himself', the Deity would not attain existence 'in the same sense . . . that a circle would not be without a center & circumference' (BÖHME, *Works* 159 [*CM*, I, 679]). The separation between God the Father and the Son generates interaction and, as it were, a flow of energy. Coleridge looks upon the creation of the Trinity as a manifestation of an 'immanent Energy of the Divine Consciousness', an energy that is maintained through the dual act of division into antithetical halves and of reunion of the halves into a whole (BÖHME, *Works* 7 [*CM*, I, 564]). This again shows the influence of Schelling's view that the Absolute is essentially an act, not an entity, a ceaseless movement from identity to antithesis and from antithesis back to identity.[97] Coleridge's rejection of Unitarianism, incidentally, was not motivated solely by his need to make up for the radical opinions he held in his youth. Unitarianism denied the possibility of regarding God as a dynamic agency engaged in a series of creative acts. The Trinitarian view of God was essential for Coleridge in that it stirred in human consciousness a desire to remain active. In a marginal note to Boehme, Coleridge argues that man's development into a fully self-conscious being depends upon his imitation of God's 'three-fold Act'. There are in human consciousness 'three analogous Acts . . . or rather three dim imperfect Similitudes' of God's original creativity; and, Coleridge added, 'if ever we have a truly scientific Psychology, it will consist of the distinct Enunciation, and Development of the three primary Energies of Consciousness, and be a History of their Application and Results' (BÖHME, *Works* 9 [*CM*, I, 566]; cf. also *CL*, II, 1199).

Unquestionably Coleridge's integration of a dynamic model of activity in his definition of God fulfilled a personal need. Coleridge attributed to God two qualities that he felt he most sorely lacked and that he had previously sought in nature and some of his friends, namely productivity and will. Boulger is absolutely right in observing that Coleridge's 'unconventional . . . emphasis upon identity or manifestation of God as Absolute or Pure Will leads necessarily to a theology of doing and becoming, to a God of action known by events rather than as a subject to be contemplated' (p. 134). The potent image of a God of action held out for Coleridge the hope that, in contemplating the deity, he too would be roused from the states of indolence and paralysis to which he often fell prey. His references to the Will as the antecedent of all reality in God and as the highest faculty in man, 'deeper than Mind' or reason, can be read as the outgrowth of Coleridge's deep sense of inadequacy with regard to the 'power to do, the manly effective *Will*' (*CN*, II, 2086). But Coleridge's voluntaristic philosophy, noted by many critics, served much more than the mere satisfaction of emotional needs. As is so often the case with Coleridge, psychological factors effectively sensitized him to the pitfalls of a given doctrine and aided his speculative insights. By equating the state of identity in divine consciousness with the Will, Coleridge was able to retain Schelling's dynamic reconstruction of the transformative acts in the Absolute without incurring the risk of pantheism. Coleridge was well aware that something that is called 'Ground' can easily be confused with Spinoza's amorphous substance unless it is designated from the very beginning as Will. This is what makes God a self-sufficient and self-conscious being, substantially different from the world of nature. Will is also a quality that ensures the personeity of God prior to its actual manifestation through the Father, the Son and the Holy Ghost. As Coleridge wrote to Edward Coleridge in 1826, 'the supreme Reality, if it were contemplated abstractly from the Absolute Will, whose essence is to be causative of all *Reality*, would sink into a Spinozistic Deity' (*CL*, VI, 600).

By designating the primary state of unity in God as the Absolute Will, Coleridge sought to establish a secure foothold in orthodox religion which made it easier to retain in his system various designations borrowed from the vocabulary of subjective idealism (for example, God as absolute subjectivity, the Father as the relatively subjective, the Son as the relatively objective). But as with other such difficult philosophic moves, Coleridge could not free himself entirely of doubts concerning the viability of his positions. He found in Jakob Boehme's works the identification of an original ground in God prior to all distinctions with the Will,[98] which only alerted him to the fact that such identification does not by itself provide a sure escape from pantheism. In a marginal note to Boehme's 'Of the Election of Grace', Coleridge expressed his regret at having 'written incautiously' on the 'absolute Will as the same with the ground of the Divine Existence', noting that although the 'Will does indeed contain in itself Power' and 'Intelligence as the Identity of both', yet neither constitutes '*its essence* which is to be causative of Reality' (BÖHME, *Works* 177 [*CM*, I, 693]). Commenting on Boehme's statement that the Will is 'the *Beginning*, and is called God the Father', Coleridge pointed out that it was Boehme's error not to see that the Will is 'more and higher than the *Ground* of Deity ⟨or⟩ the Abyss' and that God did not evolve from such a ground ('the Depth begetteth not . . . ') but affirmed himself as 'the alone *Causa Sui*' through the 'Act of Self-realization' in the Trinity (BÖHME, *Works* 178 [*CM*, I, 694]). Coleridge wanted to avoid Boehme's mistake of collapsing the distinction between God as absolute unity (the Prothesis) and as manifested unity in the triad of Father, Son and Holy Ghost. He struggled hard to define the rather slippery concept of an original unity in God which is not an impersonal ground in which God's traits exist in a state of potentiality, but a pure act, a pure self-realizing Will.

Not all commentators have regarded Coleridge's attempts to introduce a fourth category (the Prothesis) in his version of the Trinity as successful. Shedd, for example, argues that by giving up 'the scheme of the Triad for that of the Tetrad' in his construction of the Trinity, Coleridge violated 'that golden position of the schoolmen that God is *actus purissimus sine ulla potentialitate*'. Coleridge's 'error in this scheme consists in this its assumption of an aboriginal Unity existing primarily by itself, and in the order of nature, *before* a Trinity – of a *ground* for the Trinity, or, in Coleridge's phrase, a *prothesis*, which is not in its own nature either triune or personal, but is merely the impersonal base from which the Trinity proper is evolved. In this way, we think, a process of development is introduced into the Godhead which is incompatible with its immutable perfection . . .' (Introduction to *AR*, p. 44).[99]

Shedd's summary of Coleridge's view of the Trinity does not give sufficient credit to Coleridge's efforts to remove the impersonality of an original ground by presenting the Prothesis as an integral part of divine consciousness under the form of the Will. There is, however, truth in Shedd's statement that a pattern of development is inherent in Coleridge's conception of the Trinity. This is a result of his attempt to retain some of the features of Schelling's dynamic philosophy. Whether or not the notion of a deity that manifests itself through a series of acts conflicts with the scholastic notion of God is an arguable point. It is possible to see that, as Coleridge himself believed, the two views are not necessarily incompatible. If God's idea of his own perfection includes a process of development through a 'three-fold Act', and if this idea is fully realized, then God still retains his identity as *'actus purissimus sine ulla potentialitate'*. All that is required by the scholastic definition is that God's ideas be always real or 'intensely actual', and that his 'Thoughts' be 'anterior to all but himself alone' (*CL*, II, 1195). Furthermore, Coleridge, by virtue of the dynamical scheme he uses, suggests the completeness of God's creative act. Nothing more can be added to or subtracted from the four phases that mark God's attainment of self-consciousness (prothesis–thesis–antithesis–synthesis). God's manifestation of his dynamic energy does not therefore preclude the idea of his 'immutable perfection'. Here Coleridge was well served by a characteristic of Schelling's philosophy – namely, the emphasis on a process of continuous activity in the Absolute, a process which, none the less, is carried out in conformity with a rigid logical model of interactive categories that is both complete and, in Schelling's estimate, unalterable by time.

A more tenuous point regarding Coleridge's revision of the concept of the Trinity concerns Coleridge's claim that the *Naturphilosophen* place polarity in the Absolute, whereas his own system, based on the Trinitarian doctrine, avoids this error. According to Coleridge, the notions of polarity and potentiality in the Absolute go hand in hand; the former generates the latter. How, then, does Coleridge succeed in circumventing this problem? The difficulty here is posed by Coleridge's use of the terms 'Thesis–Antithesis' to describe the relationship between the Father and the Son. How does this relationship differ from one of polarity as it was used by Schelling and other *Naturphilosophen*? What concerned him most was the easy collapse of polar entities into an amorphous indistinctness that eradicates all traces of their individuality. Subject and object, nature and mind, when viewed from the perspective of polarity, appear of the same essence and merge with one another. The Trinity offered Coleridge a way out of what he perceived to be a dangerous sacrifice of individuality and constant 'regression to Identity' in Schelling's system. In Schelling's version of the transformative acts in the Absolute, the same power tends to fulfil all functions. Self-consciousness is in turn an original identity, an original duality, and an original synthesis. By contrast, the Trinity, by its very nomenclature of Father, Son and Holy Ghost, promises far greater differentiation between the various phases of divine consciousness. Coleridge never tired of stressing the prominence of distinction in the kind of unity that the Trinity represented. 'The Idea of God', he argued, embodies a unity in which 'individuality is the intensest' and 'Distinction the most manifest, and indestructible of all distinctions'. This is why this model of unity must be the 'Archetype, yea, the very substance and element of all Other Unity and Union' and 'must for ever be and remain the "genera generalissima" of all knowledge' (*CL*, II, 1196). For Coleridge, the Trinity was much more than an article of faith: it was the key to method in all philosophic thinking. 'It is the doctrine of the tri-unity', he wrote, 'that connects Christianity with philosophy', making religion as indispensable to 'the philosopher' as redemption is 'to the moralist and psychologist' (*AP*, p. 288).

The need to emphasize distinctness rather than polar sameness in the Godhead drew Coleridge's attention to the figure of the Son in the dynamic scheme of the Trinity. The Son, by virtue of his double nature, human and divine, proved to be Coleridge's best means of substantiating his claim that individuality was a constitutive part of the triune God. The Son, Coleridge argued, though born out of the divine ground, possesses an inviolable identity of his own that is 'one with but not the same as' that of his divine parent. He is self-subsistent like the Father and the Absolute Will, but not 'self-originated'. Coleridge tried various ways of capturing the sensitive distinction between two essentially indivisible, yet self-subsistent powers. If, he suggested, instead of the categories 'Alter and Idem', or the Father and the Son, 'we place A = B and B = A', we can 'then explain our further meaning by saying that B is in A in another sense than A is in B. B is affirmed in A; A is presumed in B: or A *Being*, B co-eternally *becomes*' (from *Opus Max.*, f. 265 [in Boulger, p. 138]). Coleridge found this distinction to be of the greatest importance. He thought that if man could not comprehend this primordial distinction between the Father and the Logos, there was little hope that any other distinctions would make sense, particularly the 'Chasm infinitely infinite between Deity and the Creatur[e]' (BÖHME, *Works* 20 [*CM*, I, 573–4]). In fact, the lack of 'devout' attention given to 'the infinite disparateness of an eternal and creative Mind' and man's mental capacities was mainly responsible for the 'human aversion to conceive or admit the personality', which is the same thing as the 'Distinctness, of the Word and the Spirit' (BÖHME, *Works* 7 [*CM*, I, 565]).

Coleridge fully realized that, as Boulger notes, 'on the validity of the "distinctity" granted to the Logos or Alterity within the greater unity of Identity hinges the strength of a philosophical dualism of Creator and created, Absolute and individual will, God and created finite substance'

(p. 138). Moreover, a doctrine that conferred an independent reality on the Son strengthened his authority as the mediator between God and man and as man's redeemer. For man, God's loving act of manifesting himself to the finite world through the creation of the Son stirs the desire of reciprocating action. Man, too, wishes to extend his being by abandoning his finite existence and reaching out for a model of full perfection. But the possibility of unification between man and God cannot occur except through the mediation of the Son. Coleridge could not understand why this 'law of *spiritual* nature' should 'appear stranger to us . . . than the incombinableness of Oil with Water without an Intermedium in *the world of the Senses*' (BÖHME, *Works* 30 [*CM*, I, 574]).

We need not document any further the vital Christian tenets that in Coleridge's view depended on maintaining a 'devout' awareness of the separateness of the Logos from God. The question that still remains is whether Coleridge's substitution of distinctness for the law of polarity in the Absolute fully protects him from the charge of placing potentiality in the Godhead. On this question, critical opinion is likely to differ. In certain notebook entries written around 1817–18, Coleridge is strongly influenced by the dialectic of polarity as used by Schelling and other *Naturphilosophen*. His categories Thesis–Antithesis, or Subjectivity and Objectivity, applied to the Father and the Son retain the same function that they hold in Schelling (see e.g. *CN*, III, 4427). At this stage of his intellectual career, Coleridge was more intent on adapting Christian theology to the principles of dynamic philosophy than on transforming substantially dynamic philosophy to fit the tenets of Christianity. He read the first chapter of the Bible in order to corroborate the validity of a dynamic representation of the powers of nature, and in one verse he even found the exposition of 'the necessary form of Dialectic, or the evolution of Truth by means of logical Contradictions' (*CN*, III, 4418). But later Coleridge was able to refine his model of the Trinity considerably to the extent that his claim regarding his allegiance to the scholastic definition of God may be taken seriously. Coleridge's basic change is to humanize what in Schelling's system is an abstract relationship between subject and object in the second phase of the transformative activity of the Absolute. He presents the interaction between the Father and the Son as an exchange of camaraderie and affection made possible by the Holy Ghost. It would be hard to think of opposites or the law of 'Extremes Meet' with reference to a relationship in which, as Coleridge described it, love 'proceedeth from the Father to the Son', and 'is returned from the

Son to the Father' and 'this circulation constitutes the eternal unity in the eternal alterity and distinction, the life of Deity in actu purissimu' (from *Opus Max.*, f. 260^{V} [in Boulger, pp. 140–1, 260]).

Coleridge was much more comfortable with a model of activity that involved the participation of free agencies in each other's sphere of being than with strife or opposition. Some of his later formulations of the Trinity suggest that the terms of dynamic philosophy became a burden for Coleridge because they retained too many traces of the dialectic of polarity. In defining the Holy Ghost, for example, Coleridge observed that this power should not be regarded as 'a Synthesis of the Father and the Son' but as 'ens simplissimum', as 'a substantial Act proceeding from the Father and Son and the Community of the Father and the Son' (*N* 36, f. 51 [in Boulger, p. 141]). And yet Coleridge was not able to abandon completely the terms thesis, antithesis, synthesis, and equivalent categories used in dynamic philosophy. In his 'Confessio Fidei' of 1830, a document that contains a summary of Coleridge's view of the Trinity, Coleridge still mixes terms from Christian theology and dynamic philosophy (*NTP*, pp. 395–6). Undoubtedly, his most difficult problem was to ensure that the relationship between the Father and the Son is perceived as something other than polarity. But the differentiating line between polarity and distinctness with reference to God's Ipseity and Alterity is almost too thin. Coleridge's discomfort even with the term 'synthesis' in relation to the Holy Ghost indicates that he had doubts about the safety of distinctness as a constitutive feature of the Trinity within a methodological framework that retained the categories of dynamic philosophy.

This was by far the most sensitive problem Coleridge faced in trying to disentangle his system from Schellingean thought. In other matters, Coleridge was able to see quite clearly and had no trouble proving his divergence from the tenets of dynamic philosophy. He rejected vigorously and without hesitation Schelling's supposition that the Absolute can be generated from all angles of being, including nature and the finite self. He opposed Schelling's notion that nature was a self-subsistent reality. Nature is not self-originated but has its point of beginning in God, who is the sole self-subsistent reality and 'the *ground* of all things' (*CL*, IV, 770). Similarly, Coleridge was not sympathetic to systems such as Schelling's or Oken's 'in which the Intellect refuses to acknowledge a higher or deeper ground than it can itself supply, and weens to possess within itself the center of its own System' (*The Friend*, I, 522–3 n. 1; cf. Boulger, pp. 108–13). For Coleridge the finite self does not generate its own object in the way in which the Absolute creates otherness during its 'three-fold Act' of self-knowledge. Man inherits an already constituted reality in nature as well as in God. He finds his objectivity or 'substantial I' through participation in divine consciousness.

In his system of nature Coleridge's most drastic departure from the *Naturphilosophen* consists in establishing a supernatural rather than a cosmic source for the two primary forces of nature, light and gravitation. Light does not originate from the opposition between two original poles, as in Oken's theory, but is created by God. Originally the physical universe is in a 'state of Indistinction, or Fluidity', which is an amorphous 'Allness' corresponding to the Prothesis or the divine Ground (*CN*, III, 4418). This state can be imaged as total darkness or a 'transparent drop' (*CL*, IV, 770–1, 805–7; BÖHME, *Works* 6 [*CM*, I, 562]). With the creation of light by divine fiat, the original unmarked unity is divided into the first polarity, that between light and darkness, and the physical universe acquires its two primary poles, light and gravitation. From here on Coleridge retains most of the dynamic structure of the systems developed by the *Naturphilosophen*, especially by Steffens. He identifies gravity with the N–S axis of the earth, or the line of being, and light with the E–W line of becoming. From the various forms of interaction between the four poles of nature, he derives, very much like Steffens, explanations of the phenomena of magnetism and electricity, of the formation of metals and of the chemical processes of combustion and reduction. His main additions to and modifications of the systems of the *Naturphilosophen* consist in introducing clearer boundaries between powers and physical bodies, between the constitutive and modifying forces of nature, and in placing chlorine and iodine on the ideal map of nature as symbols of the power of contraction. His need for greater 'distinctity' is as evident in his conception of inorganic nature as in his view of the Trinity.

Coleridge's representation of organic nature follows the basic laws set up by the *Naturphilosophen*. Like Schelling and Steffens, Coleridge identifies the three powers of organic life as reproduction, irritability and sensibility and studies their degree of dominance in various species of animals, as well as their relationship to the corresponding forces in inorganic nature (see *TL*, esp. pp. 591–606). But in adopting the explanation of life offered by the *Naturphilosophen* Coleridge soon runs into a serious problem. For the *Naturphilosophen*, man is the apex of an evolutionary process that begins in the lowest forms of organic life. This view clearly conflicts with the biblical account of God's creation of man. Bate is right in observing that Coleridge's *Theory of Life* breaks down in the end because, just as he brings to completion the development of organic life in the highest species of animals, Coleridge realizes that he makes no provisions in his theory to account for the origin of man's soul (Bate, *Coleridge*, pp. 194–5), which is 'the principle both of Reason and Conscience' (*TL*, p. 606). In later years Coleridge found a way of getting around this difficulty by changing the number of powers in organic nature from three to five. This gives a nice balance to his system, given that Coleridge had already enumerated five powers in inorganic nature.[100] But Coleridge's primary object in multiplying the powers of organic nature was not to provide structural symmetry to his system. He was mainly concerned with establishing sharper boundaries between animal and spiritual life, so that man's soul and mind would not be seen as merely evolving out of organic nature. He wanted to show that 'Life' was not the same as 'Mind',[101] and that, in fact, the intelligibility of life depended on making mind its antecedent, not its product. Coleridge adhered strictly to the rule that in inorganic as well as organic life a lower power always derives its '*intelligibility* from the higher; and the highest must be presumed to inhere latently or potentially in the lowest' (*CL*, VI, 598).

In order to underscore the hierarchical separateness between man and animal life, Coleridge replaced the power of sensibility, which for Schelling and other *Naturphilosophen* was the highest power of organic nature, with a new triad of forces. These are (1) the self-finding, (2) the self-retaining and (3) the self-seeking powers. The self-finding power is that which man holds in common with the organic world and is the equivalent of sensibility. This power ensures the continuity of the developmental process of nature and the communal bond between man and animal life. The other two powers mark man's separation from life and full emergence into a spiritual being. By means of the self-retaining power man gains memory and self-consciousness; he becomes a 'Subject that is it's [*sic*] own Object', that is, a person who reflects upon himself. But if man were to remain in this stage he would not realize his full potential for growth. Luckily, the mind also possesses a self-seeking power by means of which it attains full self-consciousness through union with another being. The mind acknowledges a higher reality than itself, the divine Logos, through which man finds himself in God (*CL*, VI, 599–600). In adding a triad of powers in human consciousness, Coleridge is clearly trying to bring man closer to the divine creator, without, however, making him a stranger in the world of nature. The three 'primary Energies' in man are a reflection of God's 'three fold-Act' of creation, bearing witness that 'the Spirit of God created the Soul of Man as far as it was possible according to his own likeness, and if he be an omnipresent Influence, it necessarily follows, that his action on the Soul of Man must awake in it a conscience of actions within itself analogous to the divine action' (*CL*, II, 1199). In his most advanced stage of development, man reproduces, however imperfectly, the essence of the Trinity.

The concept of the Trinity represents the culmination of Coleridge's system of nature. Coleridge's elaboration of this doctrine also sets in perspective various tendencies that we have already observed in his theory of symbolism and his conception of the sublime. His use of a love relationship as a model of activity that leads to the attainment of a substantial, ideal self ties in with his description of God's act of self-consciousness, during which God finds his 'outness' in the Son and gracefully confers upon him an independent existence. We can also perceive the continuity between Coleridge's aversion to a sublime of crisis, based upon the rivalry of man and nature, imagination and reason, and his attempt, if only partially successful, to divest the Trinity of a polarized relationship between its members. In his definition of the Trinity, as in his conception of the symbol and the sublime, Coleridge seeks to demonstrate the value and energizing power of a participatory relationship between beings who retain an inalienable core of individuality yet, for that matter, seek their completion through one another. Furthermore, the Trinity also stabilized for Coleridge his conflicting attitudes towards nature.[102] Christian religion clearly established the place of nature and of man in relationship to nature. It gave full priority to the spiritual over the physical, to mind over nature. At the same time the biblical view of the creation of the world by God established the full objectivity of nature, which, Coleridge thought, was far less certain in Schelling's system, notwithstanding the philosopher's ostensible worship of nature. Yet it would be inappropriate to conclude that the Trinity, while settling many of Coleridge's philosophic difficulties, satisfied all of his needs. Even though Christian religion secured a stable place for nature in a hierarchical chain of being, it did not sanction devotion to it. It invited instead 'devout' attention to the chasm and 'infinite disparateness' between God and man and to man's chance of bridging this gap through redemption. Nevertheless, Coleridge, to the end of his life, retained a keen interest in nature, not just in its ideal powers and abstract laws as revealed by dynamic philosophy, but in its actual multiplicity of forms. *Naturphilosophie*, with its emphatic rejection of 'appearances', did not give Coleridge the concrete nature he wanted; Christianity did not allow a zealous attachment to it. In some of Coleridge's late notebook entries we still catch him in the act of 'becoming an Eye-servant of the Goddess Nature', though never with the commitment and passion of his years of picturesque travel.

The history of Coleridge's involvement with nature might best be described by means of an analogy Coleridge himself used to define the imagination in *Biographia Literaria.* He reminded readers of their experience of watching a small insect forcing its way up a stream 'by alternate pulses of active and passive motion, now resisting the current, and now yielding to it in order to gather strength and a momentary *fulcrum* for a further propulsion' (*BL*, I, 85–6). At almost every phase of his complex association with nature, Coleridge both resisted and yielded to it, sometimes with exuberance and sometimes with desperate abandonment. He regarded nature as an engulfing force, threatening the supremacy of the mind, or a pure relationship with a love object or his religious commitments, but also as a restorative power on which he could depend with greater confidence than on his friends and which protected him from falling into solipsism and extreme idealistic positions.

The full range of Coleridge's response to nature is best exhibited during the period when he felt least secure about his ties with the phenomenal world and greatly troubled about the value or possibility of maintaining such ties. This coincides with the time when in his personal life Coleridge faced repeated crises over his identity as a poet, his deteriorating friendship with Wordsworth and his unhappy love for Sara Hutchinson. I have been especially interested in pursuing the links between Coleridge's changing view of nature and his most pressing personal, poetic and speculative concerns and have found in Coleridge's writings which grow out of this period of emotional upheaval and disorientation (particularly the notebooks) the most illuminating material for my study. My aim has been to show the extent to which Coleridge held on to nature just as, like the insect struggling upstream, he prepared for yet another attempt to disengage himself from it. At no other time does nature preoccupy Coleridge as intensely or elicit reactions that swing so dramatically from amorous courtship to mistrust as in these middle years of devastating disappointments, loneliness and uncertain artistic goals. Characteristically, whenever nature claims Coleridge's allegiance, it involves him in a conflict of rival desires. The concern over what constitutes a healthy rapport with nature undoubtedly increased the friction between Coleridge and Wordsworth, and Coleridge's willingness to follow Wordsworth's programme of composing naturalistic poems merely deepened his anxieties about his insignificance as a poet. Nature also became a source of tension in Coleridge's relationship with Sara Hutchinson as Coleridge discovered that loyalty to a love object requires a renunciation of one's interest in the sensory beauty of the natural world. In his poetry Coleridge mourned the homelessness of the self in the absence of a connecting link to nature, but also expressed his grave apprehensions about the risks involved in binding the self to its physical surroundings. A similar duality in Coleridge's response to nature characterizes his emergent theory of symbolism. Through the symbol Coleridge attempted to protect the sanctity of the concrete objects of experience by insisting on their continuity with a divine essence. He found, however, that nature could impede the full manifestation of spirit in the temporal world and that a person was more likely to attain self-consciousness by identifying with a human symbol of ideality rather than a natural one. By comparison with Coleridge's utterances on nature in his middle years, the record of his later speculative writings presents a much stabler configuration of responses and concerns. Coleridge works towards securing a place for nature in a philosophic system founded on transcendentalist and Christian premises. His endeavours in this respect were by no means free from difficulties, but in general his relationship with nature remained much more serene than in previous years. Nature troubled Coleridge less because in a sense it ceased to matter as much; it did not dominate Coleridge's personal life as overwhelmingly as during the time of his close association with the Wordsworth circle. While previously a concern with nature tended to unsettle Coleridge, generating conflicting commitments, during the period when Coleridge was engaged in formulating his own system of *Naturphilosophie*, his allegiance to the natural world helped him define his views and see through the problematic tenets of German philosophers and scientists. This is not to suggest that Coleridge's involvement with nature can be described in terms of some overall progression from a period of instability and conflict to one of happy resolution. No such dialectical schema, however attractive, adequately reflects the history of Coleridge's dealings with nature. In times of greatest stress and instability, when Coleridge gave in to emotions of complete dependence on nature or extreme rejection of it, a search for balance is always evident, and occasionally Coleridge achieved the desired union of immanence and transcendence, mind and nature, self and an ideal other. Conversely, underneath the calmer speculative resolutions that Coleridge attained in some of his later writings, currents of anxieties and doubts are still present, although they do not concern his relationship with nature as much as his theological beliefs.

Writing to Gillman in 1825, Coleridge gave a spirited account of the ways in which nature and the mind, as 'rival Artists', abuse and compete with one another, and this letter represents perhaps the most concise evaluation of his complicated relationship with nature. Coleridge's confession, which dazzles the reader through its self-indulgent rhetorical spree, constitutes a powerful testimony that nature remained an activating influence on Coleridge's works from the composition of 'The Rime of the Ancient Mariner' to *Aids to Reflection*, and that it often manifested its presence in unsettling ways, challenging his certainties about the exclusive prerogative of the mind, undoing his artistic pretensions and in the end always winning:

> In Youth and early Manhood the Mind and Nature are, as it were, two rival Artists, both potent Magicians, and engaged, like the King's Daughter and the rebel Genie in the Arabian Nights' Enternts., in sharp conflict of Conjuration – each having for it's [*sic*] object to turn the other into Canvas to paint on, Clay to mould, or Cabinet to contain. For a while the Mind seems to have the better in the contest, and makes of Nature what it likes; takes her Lichens and Weather-stains for Types & Printer's Ink and prints Maps & Fac Similes of Arabic and Sanscrit Mss. on her rocks . . . ; transforms her Summer Gales into Harps and Harpers, Lovers' Sighs and sighing Lovers, and her Winter Blasts into Pindaric Odes, Christabels & Ancient Mariners set to music by Beethoven, and in the insolence of triumph conjures her Clouds into Whales and Walrusses with Palanquins on their Backs and chaces the dodging stars in a Sky-hunt! But alas! alas! that Nature is a wary wily long-breathed old Witch, tough-lived as a Turtle and divisible as the Polyp . . . She is sure to get the better of Lady MIND in the long run, and to take her revenge too – transforms our To Day into a Canvass dead-colored to receive the dull featureless Portrait of Yesterday; not alone turns the mimic Mind, the ci-devant Sculptress with all kaleidoscopic freaks and symmetries! into clay, but *leaves* it such a *clay*, to cast dumps or bullets in; and lastly . . . she mocks the mind with it's [*sic*] own metaphors, metamorphosing the Memory into a lignum vitae Escrutoire to keep unpaid Bills & Dun's Letters in, with Outlines that had never been filled up, MSS that never went farther than the Title-pages, and Proof-Sheets & Foul Copies of Watchmen, Friends, Aids to Reflection & other *Stationary* Wares that have kissed the Publisher's Shelf with gluey Lips with all the tender intimacy of inosculation! – Finis! (*CL*, v, 496–7)

Notes and References

INTRODUCTION

1. *BE*, II, 211. See *CN*, I, 174 n. The history of the hymns and their relationship to 'The Ancient Mariner' is analysed by John Livingston Lowes in *The Road to Xanadu* (Boston: Houghton Mifflin, 1927) pp. 74–9. Lowes points out that 'The Rime of the Ancient Mariner is to a remarkable degree a poem of the elements' (p. 74).
2. 'I have often thought of writing', Coleridge confessed to Sara, 'a set of *Play-bills* for the vale of Keswick – for every day in the Year – announcing each Day the Performances, by his Supreme Majesty's Servants, Clouds, Waters, Sun, Moon, Stars, &c.' *CL*, II, 825.
3. Coleridge met George Beaumont in the summer of 1803 when the artist and his wife took up lodgings at Greta Hall. The plan to transcribe some of Beaumont's drawings for a projected volume of poems must have originated at that time. In a letter of September 1803, Coleridge promised to send the artist 'three Specimens' of his translations and later produce more of them for a separate volume of poems. In February 1804, although no such poems materialized, Coleridge assured Beaumont that he intended to carry out the project. See *CL*, II, 995, 1055. The record of Coleridge's transcriptions of a total of 31 of Beaumont's drawings, oil-sketches and paintings is preserved in his booknotes. See *CN*, II, 1899 and n.
4. The lines were written during Coleridge's late tour of the Netherlands (1828) with Dora and William Wordsworth. See Kathleen Coburn, *The Self-Conscious Imagination* (London: Oxford University Press, 1974) p. 52.
5. See e.g. Charles Lamb's portrait of Coleridge in 'Christ's Hospital Five-and-Thirty Years Ago', *The Complete Works and Letters of Charles Lamb* (New York: Random House, 1963) p. 21 and Wordsworth's view of Coleridge in Book VI of *The Prelude*, ll. 294–318. (*The Poetical Works of William Wordsworth*, ed. Thomas Hutchinson [London: Oxford University Press, 1960]).
6. Joseph W. Beach, *The Concept of Nature in Nineteenth-Century English Poetry* (New York: Macmillan, 1936) p. 114.
7. Alfred Goodson, Jr, 'Coleridge and Hölderlin: Studies in the Poetics of Space', Diss. State University of New York at Buffalo, 1973, p. 14.
8. Paul D. Sheats, *The Making of Wordsworth's Poetry, 1785–1798* (Cambridge, Mass.: Harvard University Press, 1973) pp. 217–18.
9. Owen Barfield, 'Symptoms of Iconoclasm', in *Romanticism and Consciousness*, ed. Harold Bloom (New York: W. W. Norton, 1970) p. 44.
10. Earl Wasserman points out that Coleridge's ideal of a total reconciliation of subject and object, while resolving the antinomy between competing

epistemologies in Romantic literature, at the same time became inapplicable to the actual practice of poetry. It is not 'readily conceivable', Wasserman notes, 'how Coleridge's epistemology could be translated into the life of a poem', or how 'his theories of imagination and symbolism would be recognizable as shaping forces'. 'The English Romantics: The Grounds of Knowledge', *Studies in Romanticism*, 4 (1964) 29–31.

11. I deal with the impact Wordsworth had on Coleridge's relationship with nature in Part II, pp. 35–50.
12. 'On Poesy and Art', *BL*, II, 258.

PART I: COLERIDGE AND THE PICTURESQUE

1. Humphry House, *Coleridge* (London: Rupert Hart-Davis, 1953) p. 54. I am in complete agreement with House's claim that by 'minimizing the importance to Coleridge of the external world in which he lived, we run the risk of diverting attention from some of his most characteristic strengths as a writer – from his power of detailed poetic description of objects in nature; from his power of attuning moods of emotion to landscape and movements of weather; of using the shapes and shifts and colours of nature as symbols of emotional and mental states. Even his critical idealism, whether expressed in poems or in his more technical philosophy, is grounded in a minute analysis of the phenomena of sense' (p. 14).
2. *CN*, II, 2351. This note is an adaptation of the following passage from Herder's *Kalligone*, a work which Coleridge was annotating at the time (see Part III, nn. 19–25): 'sie [die Natur] schafft, indem sie zerstört, und zerstört indem sie schaffet, eine immer emsige Penelope, die ihren Schleier webt und trennt, trennt und webet'. ('she [Nature] creates as she destroys, and destroys as she creates, an ever industrious Penelope who is weaving and unravelling, unravelling and weaving her veil'.) *Herders Sämmtliche Werke*, ed. Bernard Suphan, 33 vols (Berlin: Weidmannsche Buchhandlung, 1877–1913) XXII (1880) 127. In an early fragment on nature (1783), Goethe expresses a similar perception of the continuous process of making and unmaking which goes on in the natural world: *'Sie [die Natur] schafft ewig neue Gestalten; was da ist war noch nie, was war kommt nicht wieder – Alles ist neu und doch immer das Alte . . . Sie baut immer und zerstört immer und ihre Werkstätte ist unzugänglich.' ('She [Nature] creates for ever new forms; what is now was never before, what was before will never come again – Everything is new, and yet the old . . . She builds continually and demolishes continually and her workmanship remains inscrutable.') Goethes Werke*, Hamburger Ausgabe, 14 vols (Hamburg: Christian Wegner Verlag, 1955) XIII, 45.
3. John Barrell points out that in the latter part of the eighteenth century the activity of landscape viewing according to principles of composition learned from the Italian painters was so widespread 'that it became impossible for anyone with an aesthetic interest in landscape to look at the countryside without applying them, whether he knew he was doing so or not'. *The Idea of Landscape and the Sense of Place: 1730–1840* (Cambridge University Press, 1972) p. 6. In 'Coleridge's "This Lime-Tree Bower My Prison" and

the Categories of English Landscape' (*Studies in Romanticism*, 18 [1979] 253–70), Anne K. Mellor convincingly demonstrates Coleridge's debt to the picturesque and his participation in 'the historical movement in England from an objective to a subjective aesthetics at the end of the eighteenth century' (p. 253).

4. The *locus classicus* of Wordsworth's indictment of the picturesque is Bk XII of *The Prelude*, ll. 109–39. Yet the roots of Wordsworth's early interest in the picturesque had grown much deeper than the poet acknowledges in this passage. On this issue see J. R. Watson, *Picturesque Landscape and English Romantic Poetry* (London: Hutchinson Educational, 1970) particularly pp. 93–107, and Russell Noyes, *Wordsworth and the Art of Landscape* (Bloomington: Indiana University Press, 1968).
5. Coleridge was critical, however, of certain affectations caused by the picturesque, as exemplified by a group of ladies he once saw in the Lake District who were reading Gilpin 'while passing by the very places instead of looking at the places' (*CN*, I, 760). He also took issue with specific claims advanced by individual writers of the picturesque. See for instance his marginal comments to Richard Payne Knight's *An Analytical Inquiry into the Principles of Taste* published by Edna Aston Shearer in 'Wordsworth and Coleridge Marginalia in a Copy of Richard Payne Knight's *Analytical Inquiry into the Principles of Taste*', *Huntington Library Quarterly*, 1 (1937) 63–99.
6. See *CN*, I, 1489 where Coleridge disagrees with those, meaning Wordsworth in particular, 'who hold it undignified to illustrate Nature by Art'. 'How else', Coleridge argues, 'can we bring the forms of Nature within our voluntary memory! – The first Business is to subjugate them to our Intellect & voluntary memory – then comes their Dignity by Sensation of Magnitude, Forms & Passions connected therewith.'
7. This review has been attributed to Coleridge by David Erdman. See 'Immoral Acts of a Library Cormorant', *Bulletin of the New York Public Library*, 63 (1959) 515–16.
8. Cf. *The Letters of William and Dorothy Wordsworth: The Middle Years*, ed. Ernest de Selincourt, 2 vols (Oxford: Clarendon Press, 1937) I, 2–3.
9. The annotated copy of Knight's work is in the Huntington Library. See n. 5 above.
10. Price, *An Essay on the Picturesque as Compared with the Sublime and the Beautiful*, 1st edn (London, 1794) p. 17: 'It seems to me, that the neglect, which prevails in the works of modern improvers, of all that is picturesque, is owing to their exclusive attention to high polish and flowing lines, the charms of which they are so engaged in contemplating, as to make them overlook two of the most fruitful sources of human pleasure; the first, that great and universal source of pleasure, variety . . . ; the other intricacy, a quality which, though distinct from variety, is so connected and blended with it, that the one can hardly exist without the other.'
11. For Burke's conception of the beautiful see *A Philosophical Inquiry into the Origin of Our Ideas of the Sublime and the Beautiful* (New York: Collier & Son, 1909) esp. Part III. For a discussion of Burke's theory of the sublime see Part III, pp. 102–4.
12. On the importance of play in picturesque aesthetics see Martin Price, 'The

Picturesque Moment', *From Sensibility to Romanticism*, ed. Frederick W. Hilles and Harold Bloom (Oxford University Press, 1965) pp. 270–5.

13. See e.g. *CN*, I, 1468 quoted on p. 14 above. Gilpin defined the picturesque as 'that kind of beauty which *would look well in a picture*'. *Observations on the Western Parts of England* (London, 1798) p. 238. Uvedale Price contested Gilpin's definition, arguing that it is imprecise and leads to the conclusion that all objects in art are picturesque, since 'any object in painting will please, or else the painter wouldn't have chosen it'. *An Essay on the Picturesque*, ch. III. A brief history of the various meanings of the term 'picturesque' is traced by W. J. Hipple in *The Beautiful, the Sublime, and the Picturesque in Eighteenth-Century British Aesthetic Theory* (Carbondale: Southern Illinois University Press, 1957) pp. 185–91. The entanglements between the terms 'picturesque' and 'romantic' in Germany, England and France are carefully studied by Raymond Immerwahr in *Romantisch. Genese und Tradition einer Denkform* (Frankfurt: Athenäum, 1972) particularly chs I and II. This study offers authoritative information concerning the influence of the English tradition of the picturesque on the German romantics.
14. As Patricia Ball notes, Coleridge 'is never reluctant to treat a picture as a point of departure for a verbal impression in which he can evoke and stress the animation of nature, only present in the picture by implication . . . He extols the painter's method simply because it meets his own evaluation of the importance of visual experience, epitomizing the immediacy of an encounter with the world outside the self.' *The Science of Aspects: The Changing Role of Fact in the Work of Coleridge, Ruskin and Hopkins* (London: Athlone Press, 1971) pp. 19–21.
15. See *CN*, II, 2831, and II, 1899. On Coleridge and George Beaumont see Introduction n. 3.
16. Looking at Coleridge's transcription of a waterfall from one of Beaumont's pictures, Patricia Ball remarks that 'Coleridge responds to it in a way almost indistinguishable from a personal encounter with a cataract' (*The Science of Aspects*, p. 19). In a letter to Beaumont, Coleridge himself talks about his identical response to a landscape drawing and an actual scene in nature: 'Of the poems on your Sketches, dear Sir George! I hope thus much / that they will give evidence that the Drawings acted upon my mind as Nature does, in it's [*sic*] after workings – they have mingled with my Thoughts, & furnished Forms to my Feelings' (*CL*, II, 1004). The similarity between Coleridge's descriptions of paintings and of natural objects could mean equally that he gave priority to art over nature or to nature over art. The aesthetics of the picturesque itself, despite the emphasis it placed on the study of the arts, encouraged a flexible transaction between art and nature and, as Karl Kroeber points out, brought about a 'disposition to conceive of both the natural and the artificial less as absolutes than as terms of an interactive relation'. *Romantic Landscape Vision: Constable and Wordsworth* (Madison: University of Wisconsin Press, 1975) p. 5.
17. There is in fact a connection between the 'The Rime of the Ancient Mariner' and Coleridge's interest in picturesque landscape in the years following the composition of the poem. One thinks of the marked pictorial quality of the poem's imagery, much of which Coleridge drew from Bartram's book of

travels (see Lowes, *The Road to Xanadu*, esp. pp. 513–16 and *CN*, I, 218 n.). J. R. Watson rightly intuits a link between 'The Rime of the Ancient Mariner' and Coleridge's prose descriptions, but he is wrong in suggesting that they, too, veer towards the Gothic, the 'strange and mysterious', that is, towards the eerie supernaturalism of the poem's landscapes (*Picturesque Landscape and English Romantic Poetry*, pp. 117–18). Coleridge's journal notes exhibit an intense visual imagination pressing against the boundaries of normal perception, as in 'The Rime of the Ancient Mariner', but the force of his descriptions comes from an energy directed at maintaining the natural within its proper limits rather than allowing it to slide into the vertigo of the illusory. Though the tempo of Coleridge's landscape notations may give the impression that objects are continuously being forced towards a brink from where they may fly off into some extraterrestrial dimension, in fact such experiments are conducted with the means and in the spirit of picturesque aesthetics, which is Coleridge's guarantee of a safe harbour in the natural world.

18. George Whalley, 'Coleridge's Poetic Sensibility', in *Coleridge's Variety: Bicentenary Studies*, ed. John Beer (London: Macmillan, 1974) pp. 8–9.
19. Ball, *The Science of Aspects*, p. 22. See pp. 18–34 for a general discussion of Coleridge's notebook descriptions.
20. Coleridge published only parts of his German tour, which appeared under the fictional title of 'Satyrane's Letters' in nos. 14, 16 and 18 of *The Friend* (1809) and later in *Biographia Literaria*. See *The Friend*, II, 184–96, 209–21, 236–47, and *BL*, II, 132–80. According to a letter written by Coleridge to Poole in 1801, Longman had offered to publish his tours earlier, but at that time Coleridge feared that his travels, which revealed him 'in a *personal* way, as a man who relates little adventures of himself to *amuse* people', would expose him to the 'sarcasm & the malignity of anonymous Critics' (*CL*, II, 707).
21. 'Letters from Italy', trans. A. J. W. Morrison in *The Complete Works of Johann Wolfgang von Goethe*, trans. Thomas Carlyle, Henry W. Longfellow, Sir Walter Scott *et al.*, 10 vols (New York: P. F. Collier, n.d.) IV, 71–360. See, as one instance of Goethe's interest in stories and particular individuals, his account of the adventures of Count Cagliostro (pp. 295–307).
22. *The Journals of Dorothy Wordsworth*, ed. Ernest de Selincourt, 2 vols (London: Macmillan, 1941).
23. Comparing Dorothy Wordsworth's with Coleridge's account of their journey to the island of Mount Inchdevannoch, Kathleen Coburn observes that Dorothy 'is more detailed . . . and more interested in the few persons they meet', whereas Coleridge 'is briefer, and loses himself . . . in the shapes and colours and movement of the landscape, trying with more energetic precision to articulate them' (*CN*, I, 1462 n.). There appear in Coleridge's journals of the Scottish tour scattered observations on the customs of local people, but they generally tend to occupy separate entries or segments of an entry where the descriptions of landscape are not prominent. See for instance Coleridge's note on the dress customs of the Scottish people (*CN*, I, 1437).
24. George Whalley, 'Coleridge's Poetic Sensibility', p. 9.

25. 'Letters from Switzerland', *The Complete Works of Johann Wolfgang von Goethe*, IV, 32.
26. Coleridge was keenly interested in the subject of space and time and frequently tried to define these concepts and their relationship to each other. From Kant's Inaugural Dissertation *De Mundi sensibilis atque intelligibilis forma et principiis* (1770) and the Transcendental Dialectic of the first *Critique* he adopted the view that space and time were universal forms of sensible intuition. Cf. *CN*, I, 887, *CN*, III, 3973 and nn., *CL*, IV, 851–2, *P Lect*, pp. 389–90, *L & L*, p. 121, and Coleridge's marginalia to Thomas Taylor's *Proclus* in *CN*, I, Appendix B, pp. 456–7. In later works influenced by the German *Naturphilosophen* Coleridge developed a theory of polar interaction and interdependence of space and time. Space is generally classified as the force of infinite repulsion or diffusion and time as the counterforce of attraction. Time, Coleridge argued, cannot be conceived without space and vice versa. By itself time remains a 'spaceless point' and represents the 'power of unity and active negation, *i.e.* retraction, determination, and limit, *ab intra*'. On the other hand, space without time becomes a force of 'infinite repulsion, uncounteracted and alone' which 'is tantamount to infinite, dimensionless diffusion, and this again to infinite weakness' (*TL*, p. 582). For similar views on the interaction of space and time see *The Friend*, I, 117 and n. 1, and Coleridge's letter to C. A. Tulk of September 1817, *CL*, IV, 770–5. Coleridge was also interested in mental experiences of space and time, and he recorded a curious phenomenon of metamorphosis of time into space during states of sleep, disease or opium-induced hallucinations. Cf. *CL*, II, 478 and *CN*, I, 1823. For a discussion of Coleridge's poetic representation of space see Michael G. Cooke, 'The Manipulation of Space in Coleridge's Poetry', *New Perspectives in Coleridge and Wordsworth: Selected Papers from the English Institute*, ed. Geoffrey H. Hartman (New York: Columbia University Press, 1972) pp. 165–94.
27. Lessing, *Laocoon*, trans. Ellen Frothingham (Boston: Roberts Brothers, 1890) p. 106.
28. Cf. *CN*, I, 1489 f. 56: 'The Head of Glen Nevish how simple for a Painter / & in how many words & how laboriously, in what dim similitudes & slow & dragging Circumlocutions must I give it . . . ' Commenting on this passage Patricia Ball remarks: 'Despite the "labour" and the need for "dragging Circumlocutions", Coleridge never gives up the attempt to capture what he sees verbally . . . Words may have their limitation as a means of expressing the thing seen, but his awareness that this is so is merely a measure of the premium he places on sensuous experience in itself, and he is always prepared to accept the challenge of painting words. The urge to describe is as instinctive and powerful as the readiness to see' (*The Science of Aspects*, pp. 20–1).
29. Such patterns are scattered throughout Coleridge's notebooks. For representative entries see e.g. *CN*, II, 2045 f. 13; I, 753; I, 1589 f. 56ᵛ; I, 1577 f. 53ᵛ; I, 1607; I, 357.
30. Kathleen Coburn points out Coleridge's interest in clouds. See *CN*, I, 315 n. See also Patricia Ball, *The Science of Aspects*, pp. 22–3.
31. This is an edited version of an earlier note written in November 1799. Cf. *CN*, I, 582. For an analysis of this entry see John Beer, *Coleridge's Poetic*

Intelligence (London: Macmillan, 1977) p. 230. On Coleridge's frequent use of the image of starlings see George Whalley, 'Coleridge's Poetic Sensibility', pp. 10–11.

32. Irving Massey, *The Uncreating Word: Romanticism and the Object* (Bloomington: Indiana University Press, 1970) p. 54.
33. Compare for instance the compact description of the Ramparts in *CN*, I, 346 (quoted on p. 14) with its wordy version in *The Friend*, II, 242: 'There were Woods in the distance. A rich sandy light . . . lay over these woods that blackened in the blaze. Over that part of the woods, which lay immediately under the intenser light, a brassy mist floated. The Trees on the Ramparts, and the People moving to and fro between them, were cut or divided into equal segments of deep shade and brassy light. Had the Trees, and the bodies of the Men and Women, been divided into equal segments by a rule or pair of Compasses, the portions could not have been more regular. All else was obscure. It was a fairy scene! and to encrease its romantic character, among the moving objects thus divided into alternate shade and brightness, was a beautiful Child dressed with the elegant simplicity of an English child, riding on a stately Goat, the saddle, bridle, and other accoutrements of which were in a high degree costly and splendid.'
34. Coleridge often used his journals as an outlet for his frustrated poetic pursuits. See for example the stylized description of Thirlmere in *CN*, I, 1607 and his reflections in *CN*, I, 1577 and 1616 which feature a mixture of poetic schemes, intense concentration on natural objects and private anguish.
35. Gilpin, *Observations of Cumberland and Westmoreland*, I, XXII, Quoted by John R. Nabholtz, 'Dorothy Wordsworth and the Picturesque', *Studies in Romanticism*, 3 (1964) 128.
36. The tensions caused by pantheism in Coleridge's early poetry have been analysed by Albert Gérard in *English Romantic Poetry* (Berkeley: University of California Press, 1968) ch. 3. On Coleridge's lifelong struggle with pantheism see McFarland's authoritative study, *Coleridge and the Pantheist Tradition*.
37. Cf. Martin Price, 'The Picturesque Moment', p. 277: 'The picturesque in general recommends the rough or rugged, the crumbling form, the complex or difficult harmony. It seeks a tension between the disorderly or irrelevant and the perfected form. Its favorite scenes are those in which form emerges only with study or is at the point of dissolution.'
38. Cf. W. J. Hipple, *The Beautiful, the Sublime and the Picturesque in Eighteenth-Century British Aesthetic Theory*, p. 281: 'I repeat what I have urged before, that the psychological systems of the two men [Price and Knight] are quite different, and that this difference permeates all their disputes, underlying the verbal confusions.' See also Hipple's analysis of Price's and Knight's systems in chs 14 and 17.
39. See Coleridge's criticism of Hartley's theory of association in *BL*, I, chs V–VII and *CL*, II, 706, 961, *CN*, III, 4059.
40. For his observation that dreams were caused by states of the body Coleridge may have been indebted to the theories formulated by Hobbes, Hartley and Erasmus Darwin. See David S. Miall, 'The Meaning of Dreams: Coleridge's Ambivalence', *Studies in Romanticism*, 21 (1982) 57–71.

41. Price shared many of Burke's views, a fact that he himself acknowledged in his treatise on the picturesque. On Price's debt to Burke see Hipple, pp. 204–8, 210.
42. In his marginalia to Herder's *Kalligone* and Solger's *Erwin*, Coleridge defines the beautiful as referring the mind to sense objects (a definition which is in essence Kantian) and in the former he uses the same illustration of the circle as an object of beauty. See Chapter 3, p. 118. For an early attempt to differentiate the beautiful from the picturesque see *CN*, I, 1755 and n. In *The Temple of Nature* (London: J. Johnson, 1803), Erasmus Darwin suggested that the beautiful complements the picturesque ('Additional Notes', p. 87).
43. See Knight's note to the second edition of his poem *Landscape* printed in Price, *A Dialogue on the Distinct Characters of the Picturesque and the Beautiful, in Answer to the Objections of Mr. Knight* (London, 1801) pp. 89–90.
44. Coleridge's negative response to Knight is evident from his marginal comments on Knight's *An Inquiry into the Principles of Taste*. See n. 5 above. For other critical comments on Knight see the references listed in *CN*, I, 1963 n.
45. As we have seen, Coleridge's landscapes are characterized by a movement from bounded to unbounded objects, from particularized forms to ethereal objects whose form melts into an indefinite oneness. See pp. 17–18 above. The same pattern also dominates Coleridge's landscapes in his early poetry. See especially 'Reflections on having left a Place of Retirement', ll. 27–42 and 'This Lime-tree Bower my Prison', ll. 20–43. See also Anne K. Mellor, 'Coleridge's "This Lime-Tree Bower My Prison" and the Categories of English Landscape'.
46. *BL*, II, 8. This is a favourite Coleridgean notion. For other examples see *CN*, II, 2402, 2344, 2412, 2999 and *The Friend*, I, 177 n*.

PART II: THE SELF AND THE RECEDING LANDSCAPE

1. Coleridge's tour of the Netherlands and the Rhine took place in 1828 and is recorded in N 40. I am grateful to Kathleen Coburn for lending me a transcript of this notebook.
2. See n. 4 below.
3. N Folio. This notebook is in the Huntington Library.
4. *CN*, III, 3290. Cf. 'Shakespeare's Judgment Equal to his Genius', *Sh L*, p. 55: 'Nature, the prime genial artist, inexhaustible in diverse powers, is equally inexhaustible in forms . . . and even such is the appropriate excellence of her chosen poet, of our own Shakespeare, himself a nature humanized, a genial understanding, directing self-consciously a power and an implicit wisdom deeper even than our consciousness.' Here, as elsewhere, Coleridge was influenced by Schelling's notion that nature is endowed with a creative spirit which is a manifestation of the Absolute in the form of unconscious activity. See e.g. 'Über das Verhältniss der bildenden Künste zu der Natur' in F. W. J. Schelling, *Sämmtliche Werke*, ed. K. F. A. Schelling, 14 vols (Stuttgart and Augsburg: J. G. Cotta'scher

Verlag, 1856–61) VII, 289–329. For Coleridge's debt to this essay see *CN*, III, 4397 and n. and see my discussion on pp. 54–6; 63–6 below.

5. See e.g. *CN*, II, 2453, 2543. Kathleen Coburn discusses the stabilizing, therapeutic function of Coleridge's reliance on nature in *The Self-Conscious Imagination*, pp. 56–63.
6. 'I supposed you [Wordsworth] first to have meditated the faculties of Man in the abstract . . . to have laid a solid and immoveable foundation for the Edifice by removing the sandy Sophisms of Locke, and the Mechanic Dogmatists, and demonstrating that the Senses were living growths and developments of the Mind & Spirit in a much juster as well as higher sense, than the mind can be said to be formed by the Senses –' (*CL*, IV, 574). See also the entry of 21 July 1832 in *TT*.
7. For a detailed study of the influence exerted by Coleridge and Wordsworth on their respective poetic careers see Stephen Maxfield Parrish, *The Art of the 'Lyrical Ballads'* (Cambridge, Mass.: Harvard University Press, 1973). On the differences between Coleridge's and Wordsworth's concern with nature see my Introduction, pp. 2–3, nn. 6, 7, 8, 9. For biographical studies of the Wordsworth–Coleridge relationship see H. M. Margoliouth, *Wordsworth and Coleridge, 1795–1834* (London: Oxford University Press, 1953) and William Heath, *Wordsworth and Coleridge: A Study of their Literary Relations in 1801–1802* (Oxford: Clarendon Press, 1970). See also Thomas McFarland, 'The Symbiosis of Coleridge and Wordsworth', *Studies in Romanticism*, 11 (1972) 263–303, reprinted in *Romanticism and the Forms of Ruin* (Princeton University Press, 1981) pp. 56–103 and John Beer, *Coleridge's Poetic Intelligence*, ch. 6.
8. In his notebooks Coleridge marks an event which occurred on a 'dreadful Saturday morning' of December 1806, when, apparently, he apprehended Sara Hutchinson in an intimate relationship with Wordsworth. *CN*, II, 2975 and n., III, 3328. In a later entry (*CN*, III, 3547) Coleridge rejected his original interpretation of this event as the product of jealous fantasies. For Coleridge's sense that he was never truly loved by either Sara Hutchinson or Dorothy Wordsworth, who were infatuated with Wordsworth, see *CN*, III, 3442 and 4006 ff. 22–4. For an illuminating account of Coleridge's relationship with Sara Hutchinson see George Whalley, *Coleridge and Sara Hutchinson and the Asra Poems* (London: Routledge & Kegan Paul, 1955).
9. See for example, the entry cited on p. 22 above (*CN*, II, 2346) where Coleridge tried to persuade Wordsworth about the instantaneous psychic changes resulting from contact with spatial bodies.
10. Wordsworth thought that 'The Rime of the Ancient Mariner' had been 'an injury' to the *Lyrical Ballads* due to the poem's 'strangeness' which 'deterred readers from going on'. *The Early Letters of William and Dorothy Wordsworth*, ed. Ernest de Selincourt (Oxford: Clarendon Press, 1935) pp. 226–7.
11. As Richard Haven points out, the 'notion that Coleridge left for Germany a poet and returned a philosopher' is 'at best no more than a half-truth. Some vision of an all-embracing philosophy was his before he left England, and some of his best poetry was written after his return.' *Patterns of Consciousness* (Amherst, Mass.: University of Massachusetts Press, 1969) p. 112. For a similar view and a reevaluation of Coleridge's later poetry see

Edward Kessler, *Coleridge's Metaphors of Being* (Princeton University Press, 1979).

12. See Charles Burney's unsigned review in the *Monthly Review* of June 1799, in *Coleridge: The Critical Heritage*, ed. J. R. de J. Jackson (New York: Barnes & Noble, 1970) p. 56.
13. I. A. Richards, 'Coleridge: The Vulnerable Poet', *Yale Review*, 48 (1959) 491–500. Quoted by Parrish, *The Art of the 'Lyrical Ballads'*, p. 55.
14. On the impact on Coleridge of Wordsworth's rejection of 'Christabel' see Parrish, ibid., pp. 200–1.
15. Byron regarded 'Christabel' as a more 'impressive' poem than 'even "Love" or the "Antient Mariner"'. In a letter of October 1815 Byron urged Coleridge to publish 'Christabel' in the volume of poetry he was then preparing for the press and for which he had earlier sought Byron's support. Byron also sent a copy of 'Christabel' to Murray asking him to publish the poem. See *CL*, IV, 559–63; 600–3 and nn.
16. Cited by Kathleen Coburn, 'Reflections in a Coleridge Mirror: Some Images in His Poems', *From Sensibility to Romanticism*, p. 415.
17. For such projects see *CN*, I, 1225; *CL*, II, 825, 995 and 1055. Cf. the Introduction, p. 2. Along with naturalistic poems, Coleridge also planned to write poems on *genii loci*, which indicates that his preference for supernatural subjects was by no means extinct. This project was to deal with the spirit of 'some place appearing in a Dream & upbraiding' the poet for 'omitting *him*' (*CN*, I, 1214). In another version, Coleridge planned to dramatize the eerie experience of exchanging identities with the 'Ghost of a mountain' and remaining a ghost until one could repossess one's 'Substance' (*CN*, I, 1241).
18. As late as 1828, Coleridge still felt the need to behave like a naturalist in Wordsworth's presence. Thus, during their tour of the Netherlands Coleridge resumed his activity of landscape description and tried his hand again at a topographic poem which remains fragmentary. The fragment is quoted by Kathleen Coburn in *The Self-Conscious Imagination*, p. 52.
19. See Coleridge's letter to Biggs and Cottle in *CL*, I, 637. In this letter Coleridge writes to the British publishers to advertise these poems as follows: 'Advertisement. By Persons resident in the country & attached to rural Objects, many places will be found unnamed or of unknown names, where little Incidents will have occurred, or feelings been experienced, which will have given to such places a private & peculiar Interest. From a wish to give some sort of record to such Incidents or renew the gratification of such Feelings Names have been given to Places by the Author & some of his Friends – & the following Poems written in consequence. –' Interestingly enough, Wordsworth entitled a group of his own poems 'Poems on the Naming of Places' and used exactly the same description given in Coleridge's letter. See *The Poetical Works of William Wordsworth*, ed. E. de Selincourt, 5 vols (Oxford: Clarendon Press, 1952–1959) II, p. 111. One wonders who was the original author of the advertisement for these poems, Coleridge or Wordsworth?
20. According to Wordsworth's letter to Biggs and Cottle of 10 October 1800, Coleridge did provide him with some of the poems on 'the Naming of Places', although Wordsworth's statement to the publishers might have

been based on Coleridge's promise that he would produce these poems. See *Early Letters*, pp. 255–6. Griggs does not believe that Coleridge composed any of these poems. See *CL*, I, 631 n. 2, 637 n. 2. According to Ernest Hartley Coleridge, however, one poem of the proposed collection on 'the Naming of Places' did survive. It is Coleridge's 'Inscription for a Seat by the Road Side half-way up a Steep Hill facing South'. See the editorial note to the poem in *PW*, I, 349.

21. As Kathleen Coburn points out in the n. to *CN*, I, 1610, *The Prelude* was at that time 'known to the Wordsworths as "the poem to Coleridge". Coleridge perhaps contemplated a parallel work.' Coleridge did not know *The Prelude* until after his return from Malta, although he apparently took some early drafts of the poem with him on his trip to Italy (see *CN*, II, 2092 n. and Appendix E). In January 1807 Coleridge heard Wordsworth's recitation of *The Prelude* and wrote his tribute to his friend's poetic genius in 'To William Wordsworth'. Here, as Harold Bloom perceives, Coleridge is tormented by the guilt of having failed to produce a work comparable to Wordsworth's poem, in effect asking 'where is *my* poem on the growth of my own mind?' *The Visionary Company* (Ithaca, NY: Cornell University Press, 1971) p. 230. The burden of this question for Coleridge can be better understood in the light of his earlier plan to write a replica of *The Prelude*.
22. The phrase is from Coleridge's marginal note to Adam Karl August Eschenmayer's *Psychologie* (Stuttgart & Tübingen, 1817) p. 25. The annotated copy of *Psychologie* is in the British Library.
23. Cited by Parrish, *The Art of the 'Lyrical Ballads'*, p. 41.
24. See Parrish, ibid., ch. 3, esp. pp. 90–5 which deal with Coleridge's and Wordsworth's collaboration on 'The Three Graves'.
25. See Shawcross's note in *Biographia Literaria*, II, 264–5.
26. Mark Reed points out that the number of poems Wordsworth wrote for the *Lyrical Ballads* 'seems to leave little doubt that, over and above the financial requirements of the trip to Germany, an aesthetic plan of some kind was spurring the older poet in his work' and that 'the production of the older man during this period in any case shows a distinct homogeneity when compared to that of Coleridge'. 'Wordsworth, Coleridge, and the "Plan" of the *Lyrical Ballads*', *University of Toronto Quarterly*, 34 (1965) 245, 247. On the plan and origins of the *Lyrical Ballads* see also John E. Jordan, *Why the Lyrical Ballads*? (Berkeley: University of California Press, 1976) pp. 9–32.
27. In a letter to Poole of October 1803 Coleridge speaks of his 'urgent & repeated – almost unremitting – requests & remonstrances' that Wordsworth 'go on with the Recluse exclusively' and devote himself to 'great objects & elevated Conceptions' (*CL*, II, 1013). According to Parrish, 'Wordsworth's prolonged effort to realize Coleridge's idea of philosophical poetry, though it helped to produce the *Prelude*, drew him away at last from the modes of lyrical, narrative, and dramatic utterance in which some of his most brilliant verse was cast'. *The Art of the 'Lyrical Ballads'*, p. 59.
28. From Coleridge's early letters, it appears that the study of metaphysics was always a high priority for Coleridge. Thus, the ideal community Coleridge envisioned in the days of the Pantisocracy dream was one well versed in 'History, Politics, above all, *Metaphysics*, without which no man *can*

reason but with women & children' (*CL*, I, 119). Coleridge also regarded metaphysics as an essential ingredient of all good poetry and faulted his friend Robert Southey for thinking 'too little' (*CL*, I, 294). When John Thelwall complained to Coleridge that his interest in metaphysics damaged his poetry, Coleridge replied: 'But why so violent against *metaphysics* in poetry? Is not Akenside's a metaphysical poem? Perhaps, you do not like Akenside – well – *but I do* – & so do a great many others' (*CL*, I, 215). In another letter written to John Thelwall, Coleridge explained that his poetry 'seldom exhibits unmixed & simple tenderness, or Passion' because he seldom felt 'without thinking' or expressed sentiments without blending them with 'philosophical opinions' (*CL*, I, 279). Coleridge admitted to Thelwall that he might '*think* too much for a *Poet*' (*CL*, I, 294), but this confession is free from the tormented, self-humiliating tone of Coleridge's frequent lament after the failure of the *Lyrical Ballads* project that he was only 'a kind of Metaphysician' (*CL*, I, 658).

29. See *CL*, II, 1004 where Coleridge specifically associates nature with a kind motherly protector: 'How kind Nature is to us – ! . . . I use the word "Nature" partly to avoid the too frequent use of a more awful name, & partly to indulge the sense of the *motherliness* of general Providence – when the Heart is not strong enough to lift itself up to a distinct contemplation of the Father of all things.'
30. One is reminded of Coleridge's unsuccessful attempts to finish 'Christabel' by listening to the loud wind from Skiddaw and Borrodale and taking 'many a walk in the clouds on the mountains', and his final resolution that inebriation from wine worked far better for such purposes. See *CL*, I, 643.
31. In other notebook entries written around the same period Coleridge emphasized not the mind's lordship over nature, but man's dependence on nature, on 'something more *apparently* & believedly subject to regular & certain Laws than his own Will & Reason' (*CN*, II, 2672). See also *CN*, II, 2347, 2357, 2543.
32. 'Preface to the Second Edition of *Lyrical Ballads* (1800)' in *The Prose Works of William Wordsworth*, ed. W. J. B. Owen and J. W. Smyser, 3 vols (London: Oxford University Press, 1974) I, pp. 128, 130.
33. Cf. Coleridge's later criticism of Wordsworth's 'Nature-worship's and his 'vague misty, rather than mystic, Confusion of God with the World' in *CL*, V, 95.
34. For a fuller discussion of 'Dejection' see pp. 60–3 below. For another example of Wordsworth's impact on Coleridge's poetic utterance see 'To William Wordsworth', composed after Coleridge listened to Wordsworth's recitation of *The Prelude*. In *The Visionary Company*, pp. 228–32, Harold Bloom offers a fine analysis of the poem along the lines I have pursued here.
35. Ernest de Selincourt, 'Coleridge's *Dejection: An Ode*', *Essays and Studies* (Oxford: Clarendon Press, 1937) XXII, pp. 14–15.
36. Beverly Fields, *Reality's Dark Dream: Dejection in Coleridge* (Kent State University Press, 1967) pp. 8–9.
37. For the view that the letter to Sara is not the original version of 'Dejection' but a variant of an original which has not survived see George Dekker, *Coleridge and the Literature of Sensibility* (New York: Barnes & Noble, 1978) pp. 247–50.

38. Max Schulz finds that even in the received textus, Coleridge's wish that the 'Lady' be visited by sleep 'with wings of healing' is 'superfluous' given that 'he has suggested no reason in "Dejection" for our believing that Sara might be otherwise than hale and happy'. Schulz regards this inconsistency as a 'vestige' of the theme of 'unrequited love' which Coleridge eliminated when he reworked the original version of 'Dejection', the letter to Sara. *The Poetic Voices of Coleridge* (Detroit: Wayne State University Press, 1964) p. 206. In *Coleridge and the Literature of Sensibility*, George Dekker echoes Schulz's view: 'Effective as the final stanza mostly is, surely it is a weakness that there is no preparation whatever for our discovery there that the Lady too has been ill, though not with the disease of spirit that afflicts the poet' (p. 244).
39. Irene Chayes, 'Rhetoric as Drama: An Approach to the Romantic Ode', *PMLA*, 79 (1964) 70. On the relationship between 'Dejection' and 'Lucy Gray' see Bloom, *The Visionary Company*, pp. 227–8.
40. As Irene Chayes argues, 'in terms of Coleridge's own aesthetic, the faculty at work during the experience of the storm would not be imagination but fancy, a "mode of memory"', given that the 'climactic image' of the lost child is borrowed from Wordsworth. 'Rhetoric as Drama', p. 71.
41. Suther accounts for the insistent tone of stanza IV as reflecting 'a kind of recantation' of Coleridge's earlier belief in the intrinsic power and life of nature: 'Coleridge is not content with a single image to represent the soul's contribution to the poetic transaction, but piles image upon image. It is a light, a glory, a fair luminous cloud, and later a sweet and potent voice. This multiplication of images is at least in part, no doubt, just another expression of urgency, or insistence in the repudiation of his former faith in the influxes of nature'. *The Dark Night of Samuel Taylor Coleridge* (New York: Columbia University Press, 1960) pp. 148–9. The urgency Suther sees in stanza IV may be better understood in the context of Coleridge's relationship with Wordsworth. We recall that Coleridge heard the first four stanzas of Wordsworth's 'Immortality' ode and that 'Dejection' is in part an answer to the question raised by Wordsworth in ll. 56–7 of the poem ('Whither is fled the visionary gleam? / Where is it now, the glory and the dream?'). On the relationship between 'Dejection' and the 'Immortality' ode see Fred M. Smith, 'The Relation of Coleridge's *Ode on Dejection* to Wordsworth's *Ode on Intimations of Immortality*', *PMLA*, 50 (1935) 224–34, and the interesting analysis offered by Bloom, *The Visionary Company*, pp. 222–8.
42. See Part I, pp. 21–2.
43. 'Nature' in *The Complete Essays and Other Writings of Ralph Waldo Emerson* (New York: The Modern Library, 1950) p. 6.
44. For Coleridge on the distinction between *natura naturans* and *natura naturata* or *forma formans* and *forma formata* see *CN*, III, 4397 n.; *The Friend*, I, 467 n*, 497 n. 2; *P Lect*, pp. 356, 370. For a discussion of this distinction in Coleridge see Douglas Brownlow Wilson, 'Two Modes of Apprehending Nature: A Gloss on the Coleridgean Symbol', *PMLA*, 87 (1972) 42–52, and Owen Barfield, *What Coleridge Thought* (Middletown, Conn.: Wesleyan University Press, 1971) pp. 22–5.
45. See 'Frost at Midnight', ll. 54–64, where Coleridge expresses his hope that

his son would have the privilege of being reared by nature and thus become acquainted with the alphabet of 'lovely shapes and sounds' through which divinity reveals itself.

46. In 'Nature and the Romantic Mind: Egotism, Empathy, Irony', *Comparative Literature*, 29 (1977) 193–212, Frederick Garber illustrates the various modes of the 'engagement of the Romantic self with the world', insisting that such modes 'are not single and simple but manifold and complex. Consciousness and nature, it appears, can be antagonists as well as partners, and sometimes both at once. There is no definite mode but a spectrum of them, going from a contest in which nature is used primarily to illustrate the affairs of the mind to a convergence in which consciousness may choose to blend with the universe and with another being' (p. 194).
47. Much of the poet's journey after his vision in *Alastor* is marked by a gradual disengagement from sensory experience and withdrawal within the private regions of the self. This development is poignantly marked by the moment when his eyes no longer perceive the phenomenal world but 'their own *wan light* through the reflected lines / Of his thin hair . . .' (ll. 470–71). On the recurrent image of eyes in the poem in connection with Alastor's solipsistic personality see Donald L. Maddox, 'Shelley's *Alastor* and the Legacy of Rousseau', *Studies in Romanticism*, 9 (1970) 82–98, esp. 90–2.
48. Among the critics who expressed dissatisfaction with the conclusion of 'The Eolian Harp' as being 'disappointing', 'difficult to accept', 'reverently prosaic', 'distinctly anticlimactic' or mere 'orthodox babbling' are Richard Haven, *Patterns of Consciousness*, p. 62; Humphry House, *Coleridge*, p. 77; G. Wilson Knight, *The Starlit Dome* (London: Oxford University Press, 1941) p. 99; Albert Gérard, *English Romantic Poetry*, pp. 28–9, 46–7; Harold Bloom, *The Visionary Company*, p. 202. For a defence of the ending of 'The Eolian Harp' see Ronald C. Wendling, 'Coleridge and the Consistency of "The Eolian Harp"', *Studies in Romanticism*, 8 (1969) 26–42.
49. I agree with Gérard's point that 'Sara is but a mouthpiece for something in Coleridge himself'. *English Romantic Poetry*, p. 46.
50. Paul Magnuson, *Coleridge's Nightmare Poetry* (Charlottesville: University Press of Virginia, 1974) pp. 2–3.
51. One of the earliest critics who pointed out the pantheistic dimensions of the symbol of the harp was Albert Gérard in 'Counterfeiting Infinity: "The Eolian Harp" and the Growth of Coleridge's Mind', *JEGP*, 60 (1961) 411–22, reprinted in *English Romantic Poetry*, pp. 40–63.
52. According to Humphry House, ll. 26–33 'follow admirably from the beginning', being much more 'closely connected . . . to modes of perception through the senses' than ll. 44–8 (*Coleridge*, pp. 75–6).
53. On the structural imbalance caused by the addition of ll. 26–33 see House, *Coleridge*, p. 76; Gérard, *English Romantic Poetry*, p. 42; Haven, *Patterns of Consciousness*, pp. 60–1.
54. Wilson, 'Two Modes of Apprehending Nature', p. 51.
55. The image of the moon has been variously interpreted by critics. For Richard Harter Fogle the 'moon-phenomenon' represents a 'harbinger not of disaster but of hope, for only a storm will clear the air, and only some

violence of release will rescue Coleridge from the prison-house of his dejection' ('The Dejection of Coleridge's Ode', *ELH*, 17 [1950] 74). For Marshall Suther the image of the moon epitomizes the very subject of the poem, which is the 'intimate juxtaposition of the young and promising with the wasted and worn-out', a juxtaposition 'that was wreaking destruction in Coleridge's inner life . . .' (*The Dark Night of Samuel Taylor Coleridge*, p. 120). Other critics read the image as showing 'the importance which Coleridge placed upon man's interrelation with Nature', or 'the sort of creative interaction between man and nature which has become impossible for the poet of Dejection'. See L. D. Berkoben, *Coleridge's Decline as a Poet* (The Hague: Mouton, 1975) pp. 157–8, and George Dekker, *Coleridge and the Literature of Sensibility*, p. 230. For a rather extravagant psychoanalytic reading of the moon image as suggesting a death omen connected with Coleridge's Oedipal conflicts see Beverly Fields, *Reality's Dark Dream: Dejection in Coleridge*, pp. 120–3.

56. Both Suther and Dekker have sensed that the description of the sky in stanza II of 'Dejection' is curiously well-managed for a poet who claims to have lost his link with nature. The passage, Suther notes, 'reveals very close *observation of nature*', but the details seized by the poet are 'a function of the theme of the poem', emphasizing 'the communion and kinship among the things of nature' which are no longer available to him (*The Dark Night of Samuel Taylor Coleridge*, p. 128). Dekker thinks that 'it was Coleridge's strategy to make us feel some part of the beauty which he no longer could feel. How else should his declaration of loss carry conviction? And yet we probably respond more appreciatively than Coleridge intended to the poised, precise notation' of ll. 31–8. *Coleridge and the Literature of Sensibility*, pp. 231–2.
57. M. H. Abrams, *The Mirror and the Lamp* (1953; rpt. London: Oxford University Press, 1974) pp. 67–9.
58. Suther, *The Dark Night of Samuel Taylor Coleridge*, pp. 148–9.
59. Suther believes that there is sufficient syntactical ambiguity in Coleridge's elaboration of his theory of creative joy in stanza IV to warrant a possible reading of this stanza as 'saying that the spirit and the power (the passion and the life of Stanza III) are received *from* Nature'. *The Dark Night of Samuel Taylor Coleridge*, pp. 137–9.
60. There has been considerable disagreement among critics as to whether Coleridge triumphs over his dejection at the end of the poem. In one camp are critics like Richard Harter Fogle and M. H. Abrams, who believe that in the end 'strife . . . has given way to reconciliation', as evident from the speaker's ability to turn to another, which 'argues for the rebirth of the imagination'; or that the poet 'demonstrates the power of imagination in the process of memorializing its failure' (Fogle, 'The Dejection of Coleridge's Ode', pp. 76–7 and Abrams, 'The Correspondent Breeze: A Romantic Metaphor', in *English Romantic Poets: Essays in Criticism*, ed. M. H. Abrams [New York: Oxford University Press, 1960] p. 39). In the opposite camp are critics like Suther, Max Schulz and Irene Chayes who argue that the wind has no power to revive the poet's 'genial spirits' which 'are already dead', that whatever feeling returns to the poet, 'it is not the imaginatively creative, life-giving wholeness of joy; it is still the death-

dealing fragmentation of dejection', or that what has taken place in 'Dejection' is at best 'a rehearsal of the way a revival of creativity would, or might, come about; by the time the ode ends, an actual revival is still in the future and hence still in doubt' (Suther, *The Dark Night of Samuel Taylor Coleridge*, p. 122; Schulz, *The Poetic Voices of Coleridge*, Appendix II, p. 203; and Chayes, 'Rhetoric as Drama: An Approach to the Romantic Ode', p. 71).

61. Humphry House has traced line 129 of 'Dejection' ('And be this Tempest but a Mountain Birth') to a line from Horace's *Ars Poetica* ('Parturient montes, nascetur ridiculus mus') that speaks of 'the miscarriage or failure of poetic creation'. He suggests that in this context l. 129 expresses 'a wish that the possible themes of the wind-as-poet (all terrible) may not be actualised so as to disturb Sara' (*Coleridge*, pp. 165–6).
62. For Harold Bloom, Coleridge's unwillingness to declare himself saved at the end of 'Dejection' 'evidences that his comparative damnation came because he lacked both Wordsworth's guidance (egotism, as we call it now) and Wordsworth's saving simplicity. Coleridge could not be a fanatic, even of the Imagination' (*The Visionary Company*, p. 228).
63. I agree with Bloom who suggests that the resolution of 'Dejection' 'is purely dialectical in that' it 'offers a set of assumptions that *include* the opposing Wordsworthian and Coleridgean views on the relationship between external nature and the poet's creative joy' (*The Visionary Company*, p. 224).
64. Wilson, 'Two Modes of Apprehending Nature', p. 50.
65. See the passage from Schelling's essay cited in *CN*, III, 4397 n. for a comparison of Schelling's and Coleridge's views.
66. For the source of Coleridge's quotation ('And Coxcombs vanquish Berkley with a *Grin*') in John Brown see Coleridge, *Logic*, p. 205 n. 1.
67. A different reading of the passage from Schelling is given by Hazard Adams in *Philosophy of the Literary Symbolic* (Tallahassee: University Presses of Florida, 1983). Adams warns against the 'tendency to connect Schelling too resolutely to his Neoplatonic forebears' (p. 59) that results in misrepresentations of Schelling's concept of the Absolute. In the passage under consideration, Adams points out that the terms 'ascent' and 'pure ideas', despite their Platonic origin, 'do not signify a purgation of particular mundane experience or a flying upward into the realm of Platonic ideas'. In effect, these terms 'affirm the fullness of the imaginative act' (p. 64). While Adams's interpretation of this passage might be a more truthful representation of Schelling's philosophy, Kathleen Coburn's version is closer to the way Coleridge read Schelling. The reference to Plato in Coleridge's note suggests that he must have caught the Platonic overtones of Schelling's language. One might also mention that Coleridge regarded Schelling's philosophy as heavily indebted to pagan and Christian Neoplatonists. See e.g. *CL*, IV, 874 and *P Lect*, p. 390.
68. See George Berkeley, *A Treatise Concerning the Principles of Human Knowledge*, in *The Works of George Berkeley*, ed. Alexander Campbell Fraser, 4 vols (Oxford: Clarendon Press, 1901) I, p. 261.
69. In all fairness to Berkeley, it is important to observe that he did not deny

the existence of a *rerum natura* and insisted on the distinction between external things and ideas produced by the mind (see Part I, §§ 87–8, pp. 305–7). 'Ideas imprinted on the senses' he argued, 'are *real* things, or do really exist . . . Again, the things perceived by sense may be termed *external*, with regard to their origin: in that they are not generated from within by the mind itself . . .' (§ 90, pp. 307–8). Yet for Berkeley, finally, all externality must be attributed to a spirit which produces the objects the mind perceives as generated from without, since no objects can exist independent of a perceiver.

70. Anthony John Harding in *Coleridge and the Idea of Love* (Cambridge University Press, 1974) expresses the general position regarding Coleridge's transformation of Schelling's views in *Biographia Literaria*: 'In the process of recasting Schelling, however, Coleridge shifts the focus of his attention away from epistemology and towards ontology; his footnote to Thesis VI, by one of the amazing leaps of thought which both inspire and baffle the student of Coleridge, turns Schelling's limiting concept of "das Akt des Sich-denkens" into a proof of the dependence of human existence and self-affirmation on divine existence and self-affirmation – in other words, self-consciousness becomes (in the famous phrase) "a repetition in the finite mind of the eternal act of creation in the infinite I AM". Schelling's treatment of the idea is rather less soaring; he means to use Self-consciousness only as the basis of subjective knowledge, and points out that we have been searching for a limit to our knowledge, not a passport to the infinite' (p. 180). I believe that this argument needs to be qualified. Although Schelling insists that the task of the transcendental philosopher is not to seek an absolute ground of being outside our knowledge, but to establish a principle of knowledge within knowledge itself (*System of Transcendental Idealism*, trans. Peter Heath [Charlottesville: University Press of Virginia, 1978] pp. 16–17), he describes self-consciousness as an eternal act, outside time, 'which gives all things existence, and so itself needs no other being to support it' (p. 32). However careful one wants to be not to distort Schelling's system, it is difficult not to see an analogy between this definition of self-consciousness and an absolute deity. In fact, in speaking of self-consciousness as an '*absolute act, through which everything is posited for the self*', Schelling himself compares the act of self-consciousness with God: 'If we could imagine an action in God, for example, it would have to be absolutely free, but this absolute freedom would simultaneously be absolute necessity, since in God we can think of no law or action that does not spring from the inner necessity of His nature. Such an act is the original act of self-consciousness; absolutely free, since it is determined by nothing outside the self; absolutely necessary since it proceeds from the inner necessity of the nature of the self' (p. 47). I might also add that Coleridge's view of self-consciousness as 'a repetition in the finite mind of the eternal act of creation in the infinite I AM' is not, as Harding implies, a divergence from Schelling. Schelling clearly shows that for a finite self the process of transcendental thinking is nothing but 'the free imitation, the free recapitulation of the original series of acts into which the one act of self-consciousness evolves', an act which is 'absolutely eternal, that is outside time altogether' (pp. 48–9). Where Coleridge deviates from Schelling most

sharply is not so much in mixing epistemology with ontology, but in choosing the Christian concept of a personal God instead of Schelling's abstract Absolute which, according to Coleridge, sinks his system into pantheistic thought. Cf. Orsini, *Coleridge and German Idealism* (Carbondale: Southern Illinois University Press, 1969) p. 212.

71. Critics tend to oversimplify Coleridge's philosophy of symbolism either by emphasizing too much, or by ignoring completely, the conflicts inherent in Coleridge's views. Paul de Man, for example, looks mainly at how the world of concrete particulars dissipates in Coleridge's definition of the symbol, due to Coleridge's dominant focus on the symbol's transcendental origin ('The Rhetoric of Temporality', in *Interpretation: Theory and Practice*, ed. Charles S. Singleton [Baltimore: Johns Hopkins Press, 1969] pp. 176–8). While Paul de Man gives us neither a sense of how varied and intricate Coleridge's conception of symbolism is, nor a context in which to understand Coleridge's transcendental leanings, J. Robert Barth provides us with a relevant religious background for Coleridge's views but perceives none of the tensions behind the large claims Coleridge makes for the symbol. *The Symbolic Imagination: Coleridge and the Romantic Tradition* (Princeton University Press, 1977). For a recent exposition of Coleridge's view of the symbol see M. Jadwiga Swiatecka, *The Idea of the Symbol* (Cambridge University Press, 1980) esp. ch. 2.
72. In Coleridge's concluding statement 'It' clearly stands for 'phaenomenon', which has the effect of collapsing any distinction between physical objects and the universal logos. We can speculate that if Coleridge had made the same statement in a published work he would have phrased it more cautiously as 'It is a representation of *Λογος*, of the Creator! and the Evolver!'
73. As Margery Sabin has shown, even in the extended meditation on the symbol in *SM*, Appendix C, pp. 71–3, Coleridge does not talk about the symbol in the abstract, but reproduces the very process by which the mind arrives at and creates the symbol. *English Romanticism and the French Tradition* (Cambridge, Mass.: Harvard University Press, 1976) ch. 11, pp. 202–3. The subsequent pages of this chapter are worth reading as they contain the most detailed and penetrating analysis of *The Statesman's Manual* passage offered thus far.
74. Anthony Harding, *Coleridge and the Idea of Love*, p. 121. I am indebted to this study for my analysis of the Coleridgean symbol.
75. See e.g. *CN*, III, 3962 f. 77^{v} and 4397 f. 52^{v}. Plato's theory of recollection is enunciated in *Meno* 80E–86C and *Phaedo* 72E–77A where it is linked, more explicitly in the latter, with the doctrine of the soul's pre-natal existence, its immortality, and the doctrine of transcendent forms. The theory is also present in more or less implicit forms in other dialogues of Plato, such as *Theaetetus* and possibly the *Statesman*, though the extent to which Plato retained it after *Phaedo* is a point largely disputed by critics. See R. Hackforth's commentary in *Plato's Phaedo* (Cambridge University Press, 1955) pp. 74–7.
76. In *Phaedo* 64C–67B Socrates utterly rejects any knowledge that is acquired through the senses, explaining that 'the clearest knowledge will surely be attained by one who approaches the object so far as possible by thought,

and thought alone, not permitting sight or any other sense to intrude upon his thinking'. The complete separation of the body from the soul, and of knowledge by reason from knowledge by the senses, as proposed in this section of the dialogue, is a more extreme position than Plato takes in other dialogues, or in subsequent parts of *Phaedo* for that matter, but it remains none the less a resilient component of his philosophy. (See Hackforth's commentary, pp. 48–51 and see A. O. Lovejoy, *The Great Chain of Being* [1936; rpt. New York: Harper & Row, 1960] ch. II on the tension in Plato's thought between the concept of 'otherworldliness' according to which man can find truth only through the contemplation of eternal ideas, and the concept of 'this worldliness' which holds the realm of ideas to be incomplete without its empirical counterpart.) In the theory of recollection formulated in *Phaedo* 72E–77A, Socrates clearly allows a more meaningful role for sense objects, showing that it is *through* such objects (but not *from* them) that we recover the knowledge of the ideas we possessed prior to our birth. But Socrates makes important qualifications which are worth following, for it is in such nuances that we are likely to discover the point at which Coleridge and Plato part ways. Thus, Socrates distinguishes between a lower form of recollection that commits us to the world of particulars and is for that matter inferior, and recollection of the 'thing itself' which takes us out of the realm of phenomena into the realm of essence. For example, we may, by looking at an object, be reminded of another object which is not present, as one person reminds us of another, or a 'lyre or a cloak' may bring to mind 'the form of the boy to whom it belongs'. But by this form of recollection we merely advance from one object to another, or, metonymically, from a part to a whole. In the case of the second form of recollection on the other hand, an object perceived by the senses reminds us not of another object, but of a model of perfection compared to which the qualities exhibited by the object appear to be inferior. For example, by looking at two logs of equal length, we think of equality in itself, an idea which, Socrates explains, we must already possess in the mind to conceive of it in the first place. This type of recollection involves not only objects of sense but also the intervention of judgement by which we realize that a given object 'wants to be like something else, but can resemble that other thing only defectively, as an inferior copy'. Clearly, then, objects of sense participate in the process of recollection only partially and negatively, by revealing to the mind the measure of their own deficiency. I might also add that in Plato's system, taken as a whole, knowledge is predominantly recovered through an intellectual process of reflection that relies heavily on the Socratic method of inquiry. In *Theaetetus* Socrates bluntly admits that just as children would not be born without a midwife, men would remain in utter ignorance without the benefit of his method of guiding them to take possession of their innate knowledge. If we now reexamine Coleridge's own idea of recollection in the light of the Platonic model, we notice first of all that the process by which the self is awakened to its inner truths by objects of nature is more intuitive and direct, as it does not involve the judgemental stage of comparison during which objects are found to be a defective copy of a supersensible ideal. At the end of the entry, where Coleridge attempts a more reflective explanation of his recollective experience, he again says nothing about the imperfection of natural objects, but emphasizes instead their union with the Absolute.

77. For Coleridge on outness, a notion which he borrowed from Berkeley, see *CN*, III, 3325, 3592, 3605, 4058 and nn. For an application of this notion to language see *CN*, I, 1387 quoted on p. 73 above.
78. Jean Paul Richter, *Horn of Oberon. Jean Paul Richter's School for Aesthetics*, trans. Margaret R. Hale (Detroit: Wayne State University Press, 1973) p. 210.
79. Ernst Cassirer, *The Philosophy of Symbolic Forms*, 3 vols (New Haven: Yale University Press, 1968) I, pp. 86, 89.
80. There is, however, a notable difference between Cassirer's and Coleridge's view of the symbol. For Cassirer the symbol is secularized, a product of culture, whereas for Coleridge the symbol maintains a theological referent, as my subsequent analysis shows. I am indebted to Hazard Adams for pointing out this difference to me.
81. Coleridge's earliest commentary on Kant's *Grundlegung zur Metaphysik der Sitten* is recorded in a few notebook entries written in 1803. See *CN*, I, 1705, 1710, 1711, 1717, 1719, 1723.
82. For Kant's view that any expression of love, sympathy or kindness conflicts with the principles of morality, being an example of 'pathological' feelings or maudlin sentimentality, see *Groundwork of the Metaphysic of Morals*, trans. H. J. Paton (New York: Harper & Row, 1964) pp. 66–7. See *CN*, III, 3562 and n. Schiller's objection to Kant's ethical rigorism and his concept of a moral being who is not subjected to an inner conflict between sensory and rational imperatives must have suggested to Coleridge an alternative to Kant's ethical system, which was congenial to his own beliefs (see *CN*, I, 1705 n.). In his essay 'On Grace and Dignity' (*Essays Aesthetical and Philosophical* [London: George Bell and Sons, 1916] pp. 168–223), Schiller points out that without the cooperation and most intimate harmony between duty and inclination, moral conduct can never be secure. The principles of morality based, as in Kant, on the repression of man's sensuous nature by reason, are always threatened by instability since under the conditions of violent conflict, the repressed party will always resist and possibly overturn the oppressor. 'The enemy', Schiller writes, giving as usual a passionate, if not slightly neurotic, psychological or political twist to Kant's arguments, 'which only is overturned can rise up again, but the enemy reconciled is truly vanquished.' This is to say that only if reason makes a concession to instinct can it maintain its sphere of influence safely. For Schiller 'the moral perfection of man cannot shine forth except from this very association of his inclination with his moral conduct . . . It is only when he gathers, so to speak, his entire *humanity* together, and his way of thinking in morals becomes the result of the united action of the two principles, when morality has become to him a second nature, it is then only that it is secure . . .' (pp. 199–200). A man who has achieved a true moral being can abandon himself 'with a certain security to inclination, without having to fear being led astray by her. That proves in fact that with him the two principles are already in harmony – in that harmony . . . which constitutes that which we understand by a noble soul'

(pp. 202–3). For Coleridge's conception of the relationship between duty and inclination see Laurence S. Lockridge, *Coleridge the Moralist* (Ithaca, NY: Cornell University Press, 1977) pp. 130–45. See p. 139, n. 91 for Schiller's influence on Coleridge. See also Harding, *Coleridge and the Idea of Love*, pp. 112–14. For the influence of Schiller's essay on Wordsworth's 'Ode to Duty', see Newton P. Stallknecht, *Strange Seas of Thought* (Bloomington: Indiana University Press, 1958) pp. 212–22 and *passim*.

83. Coleridge insisted on the distinction between 'being' and 'doing', if only because he perceived all too often that his purest aspirations were betrayed by morally reprehensible acts. See *CN*, I, 1705 n., Lockridge, *Coleridge the Moralist*, pp. 40–5 and *passim*, and especially Harding, *Coleridge and the Idea of Love*, pp. 37–43, 101–5 and *passim*.
84. The importance of love in the attainment of a unified self is amply documented by Harding in *Coleridge and the Idea of Love*. For Coleridge's revision of Kant's and Schelling's notion of 'apperception' and 'self-consciousness' see pp. 117–21, 170–4, 179–94 and *passim*.
85. Coleridge was well aware that sensuality could easily deteriorate into lust. For his frequent analysis of the difference between love and lust see e.g. *CN*, I, 448, 1822; *CN*, II, 2495; *CN*, III, 3284, 3293 f. 17, 3729, 3746, 3777 and n., 3873, 3989, 4019; and *CL*, III, 305.
86. *CN*, II, 2495. For Coleridge's conception of physical love as aiding man's spiritual development see Harding, *Coleridge and the Idea of Love*, pp. 98–9, 110–14, and *passim*.
87. On the concept of the ideal self see again Harding who refers to this subject throughout his study. See pp. 89–91 for an analysis of entry 2540, *CN*, II, quoted above.
88. Cf. Nathaniel Brown's discussion of Shelley's search for likeness in *Sexuality and Feminism in Shelley* (Cambridge, Mass.: Harvard University Press, 1979) *passim*.
89. Coleridge's notebooks and letters, particularly those occasioned by his difficulties with Wordsworth and Sara Hutchinson, powerfully portray Coleridge's keen sense of isolation, which was clearly deepened by the high value he placed on companionship. See, for example, his frequent use of encaged birds as emblems for his self (*CL*, II, 782 and *CN*, III, 3314 and n.) or of the pathetic figure of a blind Arab in poems such as 'The Blossoming of the Solitary Date-tree', or 'Love's Apparition and Evanishment'.
90. The analogy of two clocks keeping perfect time with one another was used by Leibnitz to demonstrate his theory of pre-established harmony. See the *Third Explanation of the New System* in Leibnitz, *The Monadology and Other Philosophical Writings*, trans. Robert Latta (London: Oxford University Press, 1925) pp. 331–3.
91. Quoted by Harding, *Coleridge and the Idea of Love*, p. 116.
92. 'Letter to Richard Woodhouse' of 27 October 1818 in *The Letters of John Keats*, I, 387.
93. For an earlier instance of Coleridge's distinction between copy and imitation see *CN*, II, 2211 and n. For a later and fuller development of this distinction see 'On Poesy or Art' in *CN*, III, 4397. See also Emerson R. Marks's discussion of the distinction between copy and imitation in *Coleridge on the Language of Verse* (Princeton University Press, 1981) chs III and IV.

94. Cf. *CN*, III, 4397 f. 50: 'It is sufficient that philosophically we understand that in all Imitation two elements must exist, and not only exist but must be perceived as existing – Likeness and unlikeness, or Sameness and Difference . . . the Artist may take his point where he likes – provided that the effect desired is produced – namely, that there should be a Likeness in Difference & a union of the two . . .' Cf. *Phaedo* 74–6 where Socrates points out that a particular object as a copy of an eternal form will look both like and unlike the original, will strive to resemble it, but will always resemble it 'defectively'.
95. Cf. *The Friend*, I, 177 n*: 'Distinct *notions* do not suppose different *things*. When we make a threefold distinction in human nature, we are fully aware, that it is a distinction not a division . . .' Coleridge was fond of reiterating the notion that distinctness (a quality which also defines individuality) did not conflict with unity but was basic to it. He was also fond of observing personal experiences which confirmed this view. See e.g. *CN*, II, 2402, 2344, 2412, 2999. The compatibility of distinction and unity was also basic to Coleridge's doctrine of 'one life'. Cf. *SM*, p. 31: 'In the Bible every agent appears and acts as a self-subsisting individual: each has a life of its own, and yet all are one life.'
96. Cf. *The Friend*, I, 155–6: 'I should have no objection to define Reason . . . as an organ bearing the same relation to spiritual objects, the Universal, the Eternal, and the Necessary, as the eye bears to material and contingent phaenomena.'
97. *SM*, p. 68 n. 3. Coleridge frequently denounced the inadequacy of an impersonal conception of God, as advocated by Greek philosophers, Deists or Spinozists, maintaining that Christianity is the only religion which affirms 'a living God . . . *our* God, not only the God of the universe, but the Lord God whose voice our parents heard walking in the garden . . .' *P Lect*, p. 223. For similar statements on the 'living God' of the Scriptures see *SM*, pp. 32–3, *The Friend*, I, 522 n. – 523, *N*, 28 f. 36. See also Harding, *Coleridge and the Idea of Love*, pp. 137–46 and *passim*. For a discussion of the impersonal nature of Spinoza's conception of God see McFarland, *Coleridge and the Pantheist Tradition*, pp. 63–70.
98. See e.g. *SM*, p. 46 n. 3 where the editor points out that 'It is not always understood that C[oleridge] sought a moderate position between the extremes of minimizing and maximizing the mysteriousness of spiritual truths.' Cf. also 'The Eolian Harp', ll. 58–9: 'For never guiltless may I speak of him / The Incomprehensible! . . .'
99. Coleridge often maintained that the highest spiritual truths are available only to intuition rather than abstract logic. Intuition for Coleridge is at times equivalent to faith, or to Schelling's 'intellectual intuition' in some contexts. By intuition Coleridge generally means 'an immediate spiritual consciousness' of a given object, such as 'the idea of God, as the One and Absolute' (*SM*, p. 32). In *BL*, II, 230, Coleridge states that he 'restored the words, *intuition* and *intuitive*, to their original sense – "an intuition", says Hooker, "that is, a direct and immediate beholding or presentation of an object to the mind through the senses or the imagination"'. Coleridge praised the Neoplatonists for grounding their system in 'the assertion of intellectual intuitions – or *immediate* Beholding of supersensuous Objects' instead of

arriving at 'transcendancies by mere purification of Conceptions', like Plato and Kant. See the marginal note to Tennemann's *Geschichte der Philosophie*, VI, 45, quoted in *P Lect*, p. 425. In *BL*, ch. XII (*BL*, I, 166–8, 172–3) Coleridge cites Plotinus for his belief in intuition, while at the same time he employs Schelling's concept of intellectual intuition. Schelling defines the organ of transcendental thinking as a 'knowing . . . that is not arrived at by way of proofs, or inferences, or any sort of aid from concepts, and is thus essentially an intuition . . . an intuition freely reproductive in itself, and in which the producer and product are one and the same' (*System of Transcendental Idealism*, p. 27). For Coleridge on intuition see also *SM*, pp. 46, 90; *CM*, I, 632 (BÖHME, *Aurora* 95, and 95 nn. 3 and 4); *The Friend*, I, 493 and n. 2, 519.

100. Cf. Coleridge's fragmentary poem 'Reason' (1830) which suggests that a proper connection between self and pure spirit requires the dispersion of all material intermediaries: 'Whene'er the mist, that stands 'twixt God and thee, / Defecates to a pure transparency, / That intercepts no light and adds no stain — / There Reason is, and then begins her reign!' (ll. 1–4). See Kessler's analysis of this poem in *Coleridge's Metaphors of Being*, pp. 43–4.
101. Cf. Sabin, *English Romanticism and the French Tradition*, pp. 204–5, 208.
102. Quoted by Earl R. Wasserman, 'The English Romantics: The Grounds of Knowledge', pp. 29–30.
103. Kessler, *Coleridge's Metaphors of Being*, p. 41.
104. On the development of the journey pattern in Coleridge see Haven, *Patterns of Consciousness*, ch. II.
105. This is not to say that Coleridge's later poetry is of a peaceful, reconciled character, or that it is devoid of tensions. Some of these tensions have been well defined by Kessler in *Coleridge's Metaphors of Being* as related to Coleridge's struggle to liberate poetry from metaphor and pure being from material phenomena.
106. The scene of the meeting of waves on the surface of the river does not lead to another spell of erotic fantasies but becomes the occasion of a controlled analogy between the parting and rejoining of waves and 'love's brief feuds' (ll. 122–34). The immediate sequel to the scene is perhaps the speaker's most positive encounter with the natural world during the entire journey: 'I pass forth into light . . . How bursts / The landscape on my sight! Two crescent hills / Fold in behind each other, and so make / A circular vale . . . How solemnly the pendent ivy-mass / Swings in its winnow: All the air is calm' (ll. 135–48).
107. I am indebted for this observation to my student Judith Peck.
108. I disagree with Kessler's reading that in 'The Picture' Coleridge meant to expose both nature and art as 'phantoms of Being, one a "watery idol," the other a "relique" which can only testify to a life that has already moved on' (pp. 61–2). The picture by itself carries a positive message, reinforcing the speaker's desire to resist illusion and get a firm grasp of the objective reality around him. Coleridge does not criticize here the unsubstantial reality of art or of nature for that matter, but the way in which a subject may misrepresent both by projecting his own fantasies onto them.
109. One other poem might be mentioned here, the sonnet 'To Nature', probably composed in 1820 (*PW*, I, 429). In this poem the speaker begins by

expressing doubt about the possibility of deriving joy from intercourse with natural objects and ends by deifying nature as 'the only God'. The poem contains echoes of Keats's 'Ode to Psyche'. 'Earnest piety' of l. 5 calls to mind the 'happy pieties' of ancient times whose loss Keats deplores in the Ode (l. 41). Coleridge's appraisal of his 'poor' abilities in worshipping nature (l. 14) bears a certain resemblance to Keats's modest address to Psyche in the opening lines of the Ode (ll. 1–4), while Coleridge's decision to 'build an altar in the fields' and become nature's priest reminds one of the last stanza of the Ode, in which Keats vows to be Psyche's priest and create a place of worship for the goddess in his mind.

110. See e.g. the speaker's journey at the beginning of the poem through the uninspiring landscape of 'weeds', 'thorns', 'matted underwood' and rustling snakes (ll. 1–6).

111. Such is the image of the 'Helmsman on an ocean waste and wide' reminiscent of 'The Rime of the Ancient Mariner' (ll. 23–4) and the Brocken-Spectre phenomenon which brings about the controversial ending of the poem. For an analysis of this poem and especially of the ambiguous meaning of the Brocken-Spectre emblem see Stephen Prickett, *Coleridge and Wordsworth: The Poetry of Growth* (Cambridge University Press, 1970) pp. 22–45, and Kessler, *Coleridge's Metaphors of Being*, pp. 127–37.

112. At the beginning of 'The Garden of Boccaccio' the poet finds himself in a state of unredeemed vacancy and emotional paralysis, familiar to us from 'Dejection', which he finally overcomes when a gracious friend places before him an 'exquisite design' of Boccaccio's garden. As the picture steals upon his 'inward sight', the poet abandons himself, first to a stream of associative fancies about his personal past, as in 'Frost at Midnight', and subsequently to Boccaccio's own artistic world and the civilization to which it belongs. An experience of nature in this poem is absorbed into a recreation of an imagined past, both personal and historic. See e.g. ll. 35–6, 60–4, 75–92. 'The Garden of Boccaccio' represents Coleridge's sole indulgence in the kind of populous mythological landscape we most commonly associate with Keats's poetry, with nymphs and fauns, Grecian urns and maidens pursued by lovers.

113. The episode of the old man gazing at the moon in 'Limbo' (ll. 19–30) has been adequately described by Harold Bloom as 'one of the great and genuinely difficult passages in Coleridge's poetry' (*The Visionary Company*, p. 234). For an interpretation of this episode see Stephen Prickett, *Coleridge and Wordsworth: The Poetry of Growth*, p. 201, and Daniel Deneau, 'Coleridge's "Limbo": A Riddling Tale', *The Wordsworth Circle*, 3 (1972) p. 102.

114. Beverly Fields argues that Coleridge could not entertain a sexual relationship with a women he actually loved, which explains his inability to propose to Mary Evans and his marriage to Sara Fricker. See *Reality's Dark Dream*, ch. 3, esp. pp. 50–6.

115. 'Letters from Switzerland', *The Complete Works of Johann Wolfgang von Goethe*, IV, p. 10.

116. Cf. Coleridge's observation recorded by Julius Charles Hare, 'in reference to those who almost deify' nature: 'No! Nature is not God; she is the devil in a strait waistcoat.' Quoted in *SM*, p. 71 n. 6.

117. Compare e.g. *CN*, II, 2543 (discussed on p. 21) and *CN*, I, 1356; III, 3767 analysed on pp. 95–8 above.
118. See Orsini, *Coleridge and German Idealism*, pp. 219–20: 'The fact that Coleridge incorporated so much of Schelling in his own book, [*Biographia Literaria*] either by translation or adaptation, simply means that, at that time, he accepted Schelling's arguments and adopted his philosophy . . . At this time Coleridge was an absolute or transcendental idealist. Historically, this is more than remarkable. It is a unique phenomenon in early nineteenth century England, which has not yet been completely recognized even by historians of philosophy.'

PART III: COLERIDGE'S CONCEPTION OF THE SUBLIME

1. Friedrich Schiller, 'On the Sublime', in *Essays Aesthetical and Philosophical*, p. 132.
2. Kant, 'Analytic of the Sublime', p. 89.
3. See Burke, *A Philosophical Inquiry into the Origin of Our Ideas of the Sublime and the Beautiful*, p. 114; Kant, 'Analytic of the Sublime', p. 83; Schiller, 'On the Sublime', p. 133.
4. For a history of the sublime see Samuel H. Monk's seminal study *The Sublime: A Study of Critical Theories in Eighteenth Century England* (New York: Modern Language Association of America, 1935). Among many other studies on the sublime see W. J. Hipple, *The Beautiful, the Sublime and the Picturesque in Eighteenth-Century British Aesthetic Theory*; Marjorie Nicolson, *Mountain Gloom and Mountain Glory: The Development of the Aesthetics of the Infinite* (Ithaca, NY: Cornell University Press, 1959); Ernest Tuveson, 'Space, Deity, and the "Natural Sublime"', *Modern Language Quarterly*, 12 (1951) 20–38; Albert O. Wlecke, *Wordsworth and the Sublime* (Berkeley: University of California Press, 1973).
5. *A Philosophical Inquiry*, p. 58: 'That power derives all its sublimity from the terror with which it is generally accompanied, will appear evidently from its effect in the very few cases, in which it may be possible to strip a considerable degree of strength of its ability to hurt. When you do this, you spoil it of everything sublime, and it immediately becomes contemptible.' Hence, for Burke domestic animals which present no threat to man also inspire contempt, for love, Burke remarks, 'approaches much nearer contempt than is commonly imagined' (p. 59).
6. For Burke's physiological explanation of the effect of pain and terror on the mind see *A Philosophical Inquiry*, pp. 110–14. In *An Analytical Inquiry into the Principles of Taste*, 3rd edn (London, 1806), Richard Payne Knight criticized Burke for his defective physiology and optical theories. See Pt I, pp. 59–60, Pt III, ch. 1, esp. pp. 376–8.
7. There are a few places in Burke's treatise in which the emotion of 'delight' does not have terror as its source, but a feeling of 'inward greatness'. For instance, in speaking about ambition, Burke remarks that it 'tends to raise a man in his own opinion', and 'produces a sort of swelling and triumph that is extremely grateful to the human mind; and this swelling is never more perceived, nor operates with more force, than when without danger we are

conversant with terrible objects; the mind always claiming to itself some part of the dignity and importance of the things which it contemplates' (p. 46). The delight Burke describes here comes from man's realization of his own superior might appropriated, as it were, from the power that originally dominated him. In this version of the sublime, the balance of power changes dramatically: powerlessness gives way to power, and the weak party grows strong proportionally with the challenge of an opponent's strength. We seem to move here out of a sublime predicated by the code of sheer physical force and violence and to approach a form of sublimity keyed to man's passion for excellence and self-admiration.

8. See also Kant, 'Analytic of the Sublime', pp. 104–5. For Schiller on the moral education fostered by the sublime see 'On the Sublime', pp. 130–1 and *passim*.
9. See e.g. 'Analytic of the Sublime', p. 100, where Kant points out that the state of joy one arrives at in the dynamical sublime, arising from 'the cessation of an uneasiness' experienced in the presence of a fearful object, is accompanied and secured by 'the resolve that we shall no more be exposed to the danger; we cannot willingly look back upon our sensations [of danger], much less seek the occasion for them again'. For Schiller the sublime becomes such a radical assertion of freedom that in some cases it even legitimates suicide. See the discussion of Schiller's sublime on pp. 106–8 below and Thomas Weiskel, *The Romantic Sublime* (Baltimore: Johns Hopkins Press, 1976) p. 48. On this point Wordsworth most diverges from Burke and is closest to the German writers. He makes the sublime dependent on a process of mediation through memory, self-conscious reflection, and imagination, whereby it becomes a special event, saved from the amnesia that new experiences produce in a Burkean world. For Wordsworth, as for the German writers, the sublime becomes possible only at a certain stage of adulthood when one develops the ability to view experiences of 'pain and fear' as a required discipline by which one can recognize 'A grandeur in the beatings of the heart' (*The Prelude*, Bk I, ll. 412–14). The sublime for Wordsworth does not have the immediacy that it owns in Burke's system but is delayed, as it were, until the mind can fully comprehend and sort out the events it has encountered. Thus, neither the 'thoughtless youth' of 'Tintern Abbey' nor the child who steals the boat in Book I of *The Prelude* has access to the sublime properly speaking. The former lives in a Burkean present of sensations and is thus excluded from the 'sense sublime' requiring the 'remoter charm, / By thought supplied' ('Tintern Abbey', ll. 81–2) – that is, mediated experience; the latter, like Kant's uneducated man, will know only the fearful side of nature, which leaves him in a state of 'blank desertion' and loneliness. It is the adult who, contemplating events from childhood, can find in them a purposiveness that renders them truly sublime. Moments of the past which have been screened by memory and assigned a place in an ongoing process of personal growth become for Wordsworth uniquely individual and permanent sources of sublime feelings to which the mind can always return. Wordsworth, unlike Burke, sees no value in exposing the mind to a bombardment of continuously novel experiences that remain unmarked by recollective awareness and are lost in a temporal stream of consecutive sensations.

10. See 'Analytic of the Sublime', p. 97, where Kant points out that the aesthetical judgement of the sublime 'represents the subjective play of the mental powers (imagination and reason) as harmonious through their very contrast. For just as imagination and *understanding*, in judging of the beautiful, generate a subjective purposiveness of the mental powers by means of their harmony, so [in this case] imagination and *reason* do so by means of their conflict.'
11. Although like Kant, Schiller views nature negatively, as a force from which man must liberate himself in order to fulfil his human destiny, he also looks upon it as a companion who helps man complete his moral education. 'Nature herself', Schiller states, 'has actually used a sensuous means to teach us that we are something more than mere sensuous natures. She has even known to make use of our sensations to put us on the track of this discovery – that we are by no means subject, as slaves, to the violence of the sensations' (p. 134). Hence, for Schiller intercourse with natural objects is beneficial to man and conducive to the formation of the sublime frame of mind. As soon as, through free contemplation, man feels immune to the violence of blind physical nature and discovers 'something permanent in his own being', the once 'coarse agglomeration of nature that surrounds him begins to speak in another language to his heart, and the relative grandeur which is without becomes for him a mirror in which he contemplates the absolute greatness which is within himself . . . The sight of a distant infinity – of heights beyond vision, this vast ocean which is at his feet, that other ocean still more vast which stretches above his head, transport and ravish his mind beyond the narrow circle of the real, beyond this narrow and oppressive prison of physical life' (pp. 137–8). In such celebratory passages about 'the great spirit of nature', Schiller unmistakably displays a sense of nature's positive influence on the quality of man's spiritual life for which there is simply no parallel in Kant.
12. At the end of his essay Schiller recommends the union of the sublime with the beautiful as the ideal goal one should pursue, since the beautiful, although removing man from the chaos of physical nature, none the less binds him to it. But this marriage of the beautiful to the sublime remains unconvincing, for all along Schiller has implied an insurmountable dichotomy between morality and a comfortably harmonious relationship with nature. Although it is desirable to 'be in good relations with physical nature, without violating morality', it is not always possible or 'convenient' to 'serve two masters' (p. 141). And when the choice is between the beautiful and the sublime, a noble soul must choose the latter. 'Beauty', Schiller reminds us, 'under the shape of the divine Calypso, bewitched the virtuous son of Ulysses', and made him a 'slave of sense'; but luckily, by a sudden 'impression of the sublime in the form of Mentor', he 'remembers that he is called to a higher destiny – he throws himself into the waves, and is free' (p. 136). If anything, this story teaches not the happy union of the beautiful with the sublime, but the treacherous influence of the former and the supreme dignity of the latter. There is finally only one option for man if he wishes to be a free 'citizen of a better world' (p. 140), and this option, which the sublime makes possible, necessitates a tragic conflict between man's natural and spiritual desires.

13. In his study *The Romantic Sublime*, Thomas Weiskel extends Schiller's misgivings to the entire genre of the sublime and its main practitioners, including Kant and Burke, as well as pre-Romantic and Romantic poets. Weiskel, like Schiller, examines the darker reality of human sacrifice that hides beneath the promise of man's victory through transcendence guaranteed by the sublime. But while Schiller can still make a passionate plea for the sublime, obviously finding value in man's choice of his spiritual destiny, tragic as that might be, Weiskel makes it his task to reveal the seductive charms the sublime exercised on so many nineteenth-century writers and to expose its most sinister implications. For Weiskel the sublime, irrespective of its variants, leads either to dead ends or to highly suspect moral and political attitudes. But Weiskel's study is not, properly speaking, about the Romantic sublime, but specifically about modernism and its loss of the values that had made the sublime meaningful in its time. Weiskel makes painfully clear that for modern man – who cannot console himself with the religion of transcendence, who has been sensitized enough by Freudian psychology to see through the mystique of power and heroic gestures, and who no longer trusts that the undoing of one fiction can lead to anything one might call 'truth' without blushing – the sublime is equivalent to bad faith. Weiskel's study, in other words, gives credence to the nostalgic sentiments expressed by some critics that Romanticism is no longer with us. See my review of Weiskel in *The Wordsworth Circle*, 9 (1978) 110–20.
14. John Baillie, 'An Essay on the Sublime', *The Augustan Reprint Society*, no. 43 (Los Angeles: William Andrews Clark Memorial Library, 1953).
15. *The Letters of John Keats*, ed. H. E. Rollins, 2 vols (Cambridge, Mass.: Harvard University Press, 1958) I, p. 185.
16. See Edna Aston Shearer, 'Wordsworth and Coleridge Marginalia in a Copy of Richard Payne Knight's *Analytical Inquiry into the Principles of Taste*' (cited in Part I, n. 5 above), p. 89.
17. Knight himself regards taste as individual, varying according to nations and even temporary fashions. He agrees with Hume that beauty 'is no quality in things themselves: it exists merely in the mind, which contemplates them, and each mind perceives a different beauty' (*An Analytic Inquiry*, p. 16).
18. Richter, 'Theory of the Sublime', in *Horn of Oberon: Jean Paul Richter's School for Aesthetics*, p. 74.
19. Herder, *Kalligone*, 3 vols (Leipzig, 1800) II, Pt III, pp. 5–150. A copy of Coleridge's annotated copy is in the British Library.
20. *Kalligone*, pp. 39, 41: '. . . nicht Gegensätze sind das Erhabne und Schöne, sondern Stamm und Aeste Eines Baums; sein Gipfel ist das erhabenste Schöne . . . das Gefühl des Erhabnen ist dem Gebiet des Schönen *Anfang* und *Ende*.' (' . . . the sublime and the beautiful are not opposites but the stem and branches of the same tree; its peak is the most sublime beauty . . . the feeling of the sublime is the *beginning* and *end* of the sphere of the beautiful.') The tendency to unite the beautiful with the sublime also surfaces in Schleiermacher. In *Vorlesungen über die Aesthetik* Schleiermacher mentions that 'sublimity and tenderness are only the vanishing points of the line of beauty'. Quoted by E. F. Carritt, *The Theory of Beauty* (London: Methuen, 1914) p. 175. Elinor Shaffer in 'Coleridge's Revolution in the Standard of Taste', *Journal of Aesthetics and Art Criticism*, 28 (1969) 213 and n. 2, finds

traces of an attempt to reconcile the beautiful with the sublime in Schelling's *System des transcendentalen Idealismus* and more prominently in his *Philosophie der Kunst*, a series of lectures published after Coleridge's death. She argues that Coleridge was 'more radical' than the Germans in eradicating the distinction between the beautiful and the sublime 'by absorbing the beautiful into the sublime and making the sublime the single aesthetic category' (p. 213). But it seems to me that the most relevant source of Coleridge's views is not Schelling, but Herder, who is no less radical than Coleridge in claiming that the sublime is 'the *beginning* and *end* of the sphere of the beautiful'. As we shall see in the following discussion, Coleridge developed his theory of the sublime in his marginalia to Herder's *Kalligone*, and although he reacted negatively to Herder's attack on Kant, he was none the less susceptible to some of Herder's views.

21. Coleridge's own beliefs were congruent with Herder's view that a striving for form can be perceived in all aspects of nature, even chaos itself. As Coleridge once remarked, 'In nature all [is] harmony' (*CN*, I, 418), and it is indeed the discovery of unity within a complex variety of objects which dominates his numerous descriptions of natural scenery in his travel journals and letters.
22. Although Coleridge has his own disagreement with Kant, he had a deep admiration for the German philosopher and was prompt to defend him whenever his work met with adverse criticism. (See e.g. Coleridge's negative reaction to Christoph Friedrich Nicolai's attack on Kant in *Über meine gelehrte Bildung, über meine Kentniss der kritischen Philosophie und meine Schriften dieselbe betreffend, und über die Herren Kant, J. B. Erhard, und Fichte* (Berlin and Stettin, 1799). Coleridge's annotated copy of this work is in the British Library.) Coleridge's antagonism to Herder for his extreme anti-Kantian attitudes is evident in some of the vituperative comments he made about *Kalligone*. Coleridge referred to the first volume of *Kalligone*, which he took with him to Malta, as the most 'disgusting' work he had ever read, dragging the system of a profound thinker into the '6-inch-deep Gutter of muddy Philosophism'. He found the second volume, including the section on the sublime, more tolerable, but he remained critical of Herder's gross misunderstanding of Kant's views and his blind partiality to the Greeks. Herder's statement that only objects and not ideas of reason can arouse feelings, as well as his inability to grasp Kant's point that the 'ideas of reason which, although no adequate presentation is possible for them, by this inadequateness that admits of sensible presentation are aroused and summoned into the mind' ('Analytic of the Sublime', p. 84), convinced Coleridge that Herder 'never possessed an *Idea*' in his mind (marginal note to *Kalligone*, III, 48–9). For an analysis of Coleridge's opposition to Herder see G. A. Wells, 'Man and Nature: An Elucidation of Coleridge's Rejection of Herder's Thought', *Journal of English and Germanic Philology*, 51 (1952) 314–25.
23. See pp. 124–5 below.
24. Coleridge's marginalia to Herder's *Kalligone* have been published in part by J. Shawcross in 'Coleridge Marginalia', *Notes and Queries*, 4 (1905) 341–2. The full text of the marginalia will become available in vol. II of *Marginalia*, forthcoming.

25. Marginal note to *Kalligone*, III, 59–62, cited in Shawcross, 'Coleridge Marginalia', p. 342. In a passage recorded by Allsop in his *Recollections*, Coleridge explains that 'the grand' is defined by the predominance of parts that diminishes one's 'attention to the whole', while in the case of 'the majestic', the 'impression of the whole, i.e. the sense of unity predominates so as to abstract the mind from the parts'. On the other hand, the sublime occurs when 'neither whole nor parts [are seen and distinguished] but unity, as boundless or endless *allness*'. The passage is reprinted in *BL*, II, 309 and in a fuller version in Clarence DeWitt Thorpe, 'Coleridge on the Sublime', *Wordsworth and Coleridge: Studies in the Honor of George McLean Harper*, ed. Earl Leslie Griggs (Princeton University Press, 1939) p. 195.
26. Shawcross, 'Coleridge Marginalia', p. 342.
27. Thorpe, 'Coleridge on the Sublime', p. 195.
28. *The Friend*, I, 106 and n*. This passage is analysed by Wlecke, *Wordsworth and the Sublime*, pp. 77–9.
29. Cf. Wlecke, *Wordsworth and the Sublime*, p. 78: 'Coleridge here postulates for the world of ideas what we have already seen him postulating for the world external to the mind: the proposition that "nothing that has a shape can be sublime," and this proposition's corollary that "those objects whose shape most recedes from shapeliness are commonly the exciting occasions"'.
30. See *BL*, I, 202. On the term 'esemplastic' which is Coleridge's coinage, see *BL*, I, 107; *CN*, III, 4176 and n. and BÖHME, 46 n. 4 (*CM*, I, 595).
31. *CN*, I, 921. For a fine analysis of this entry see Wlecke, *Wordsworth and the Sublime*, pp. 82–5.
32. On light and translucence as constituent qualities of the Coleridgean symbol see Part II, p. 69.
33. T. M. Raysor, 'Unpublished Fragments in Aesthetics by S. T. Coleridge', *Studies in Philology*, 22 (1925) 532–3.
34. *Wordsworth and the Sublime*, p. 84. It is a pity that Wlecke, who provides an excellent commentary on Coleridge's conception of the sublime in the early part of his essay ('Intuitions of Existence', *Wordsworth and the Sublime*, ch. 4), takes one wrong turn in his argument and distorts the meaning of Coleridge's sublime. Wlecke argues that sublime consciousness for Coleridge involves an 'intuition of absolute existence', a 'glorious vision' of a divine 'I AM' which is 'a vision of existence without essence' (pp. 86–7). Such an existentialist reading is a gross misrepresentation of Coleridge's religious views which underlie his conception of the sublime. For Coleridge the movement towards an 'I AM' is clearly a movement towards an absolute essence which is 'the *ground* of all things' and from which all things derive 'their existence' (*CL*, IV, 770). Coleridge described the state of existence without essence as that of living in a world of 'coloured shadows, with no greater depth, root, or fixture, than the image of a rock hath in a gliding stream or the rain-bow on a fast-sailing rain-storm' (*SM*, p. 78). It is true that, as Wlecke indicates, Coleridge borrowed the scholastic definition of God as 'actus purissimus sine ulla potentialitate' (*BL*, I, 94), but he surely does not mean by this that God is pure existence without essence. Rather, for Coleridge existence and essence are one in God. 'What ever is *real* in God', Coleridge wrote, 'is likewise *ACTUAL* and this is the true Idea of the

Eternal: of whatever truly IS, and can truly BE, the simultaneous Act, Fruition, and *very* Being!' (*C & S*, Appendix E, p. 234). It is precisely this union in God of being and act, essence and existence, which in turn becomes the ground of all temporal things.

35. The essay is printed in *The Prose Works of William Wordsworth*, II, 349–59. Subsequent references to this essay include line numbers.
36. The degree to which Wordsworth and Coleridge formulated their respective aesthetic theories in collaboration with one another is most vividly illustrated by their marginal comments on Richard Payne Knight's *Analytical Inquiry into the Principles of Taste*. Although most of the notes are in Wordsworth's hand, the question of authorship is far more difficult to determine. See Edna Aston Shearer, 'Wordsworth and Coleridge Marginalia', p. 65. Some critics have used the notes to document Coleridge's theory of the sublime, being persuaded by Julius Ira Lindsay's claim that they were written by Wordsworth at Coleridge's dictation. See Elinor Shaffer, 'Coleridge's Theory of Aesthetic Interest', *Journal of Aesthetics and Art Criticism*, 27 (1969) 404, 408 n. 33.
37. From the very beginning Wordsworth is trying to present the sublime as a less sensational and privileged event than it was commonly regarded by his contemporaries. Unlike Addison, Baillie or Burke, Wordsworth does not make the sublime dependent on novelty of experience. He argues that through repeated exposure to the same objects one's 'conceptions of the sublime, far from being dulled or narrowed by commonness or frequency, will be rendered more lively & comprehensible by more accurate observation and by encreasing knowledge' ('The Sublime and the Beautiful', ll. 1–7). His insistence that familiarity with objects prepares the mind for an encounter with sublimity – a claim to which he returns at the end of the essay (ll. 288–344) – is an undisguised attempt to remove the sublime from the realm of the extraordinary and bring it within the sphere of 'common incidents'. This is Wordsworth's most original contribution by far to the theory of the sublime in the nineteenth century. No other writer to my knowledge made as strong a case for the necessity of engaging the mind in a 'preparatory intercourse' with an object in order to experience the sublime.
38. See Owen and Smyser's editorial note to ll. 68–9 of the *Prose Works* (p. 453).
39. See Coleridge's marginal note to Solger's *Erwin*: 'Nothing not shapely . . . can be called beautiful: nothing that has a shape can be sublime . . . ' (Raysor, 'Unpublished Fragments in Aesthetics', p. 533). The question of individual form is also tackled by Kant who states that while the beautiful 'is connected with the form of the object', the sublime 'is to be found in a formless object' ('Analytic of the Sublime', p. 82). It is also worth noting that one of Uvedale Price's claims regarding the superiority of the picturesque over the sublime is that the former 'requires variety of form' which relieves the formless monotony of the sublime (*An Essay on the Picturesque*, pp. 80–1). Wordsworth in effect appropriates for the sublime a quality which for Price was exclusive to the picturesque, and which for Kant and Coleridge pertained to the beautiful.
40. Cf. ll. 218–220: 'Individuality of form is the primary requisite: and the form must be of that character that deeply impresses the sense of power.' On the importance of power for Wordsworth see W. J. B. Owen, *Wordsworth as*

Critic (University of Toronto Press, 1969) pp. 195–228. The view that the sublime is always connected with power is, of course, recognizably Burke's. But Wordsworth appears to be uncomfortable with Burke's restrictive principle that 'power derives all its sublimity from the terror with which it is generally accompanied' (*A Philosophical Inquiry*, p. 58). For Wordsworth power does not merely condition a response of 'dread and awe', but can also produce 'sympathy and participation'. Similarly, he claims that a mountain whose lines 'may flow into each other like the waves of the sea, and, by involving in such image a feeling of self-propagation infinitely continuous and without cognizable beginning', may 'thus convey to the Mind sensations not less sublime than those which were excited by their opposites, the abrupt and the precipitous' (ll. 97–102). While Wordsworth would have found in Burke the connection between the sublime and infinity, he significantly dissociates the experience of infinity from terror. (For Burke's view that infinity inspires terror see *A Philosophical Inquiry*, p. 64.) Wordsworth is clearly interested in diversifying the sublime, especially in showing its gentler side, which does not threaten one's existence but produces an effortless expansion of the mind and a 'feeling of self-propagation infinitely continuous'. In this Wordsworth approaches Baillie's perspective on the sublime and is moving closer to Coleridge's views. We can infer that the mind is not subject here to any pain or displeasure, but is experiencing a purely positive sense of infinite growth. The mind is also less conscious of the individual form of the object it contemplates and – to borrow Coleridge's terms – encounters the dissolution of all shape into the shapelessness of infinity, 'without cognizable beginning' or end.

41. Duration remains a loose term in Wordsworth's essay and finally drops out of view. In ll. 216–20, for example, where Wordsworth again lists the qualities that render the mountain an object of sublimity, he mentions individuality of form and power, but not duration.
42. A further difficulty pertains to Wordsworth's claim that a child or person unfamiliar with a certain landscape can still experience the sublime, even when duration is absent and only fear or wonder prevails. Wordsworth is convinced that 'a Child or an unpracticed person whose mind is possessed by the sight of a lofty precipice . . . has been visited by a sense of sublimity, if personal fear & surprize or wonder have not been carried beyond certain bounds' (ll. 136–40). But earlier in his essay Wordsworth states that the impression of sublimity depends on the coexistence of all three elements, individual form, duration and power, and 'if any one of them were abstracted, the others would be deprived of their power to affect' (ll. 69–72). Wordsworth appears to want it both ways: to define the sublime with precision, yet at the same time to enlarge its sphere so as to exclude no possible variant or person of whatever age or condition. In the process his tools of analysis fail him. Wordsworth is unable to show consistently how the three elements of the sublime work together.
43. See the editorial note to ll. 140–4 (pp. 454–5). For Coleridge on the suspension of the exercise of comparison see pp. 124–5.
44. The two forms of sublimity – one involving participation and sympathy with power, the other submission to power – can be found in Burke, although

Burke places greater emphasis on the latter. (On Burke's sublime of participation see n. 7 above.) But Burke is not interested, like Wordsworth, in intense unity as 'the head and front of the sensation', of sublimity, an interest that is central to Coleridge's and Kant's conception of the sublime.

45. The passage also poses an interesting question concerning Coleridge's influence on Wordsworth's conception of the sublime. I suspect that Coleridge raised with Wordsworth the problem he tackles here regarding the possible incongruity between the mind's consciousness of two powers and the desired experience of unity requiring the extinction of the comparing power. On this issue, as on many others, the two friends took opposite sides. Coleridge, as we have seen earlier, consistently refused to include in the experience of sublimity any barriers that needed to be overcome or that could produce pain. He also excluded the double agency of imagination and reason on which the Kantian sublime is based. Again, Wordsworth turns out to be more in tune with Kant's philosophy than the very man who supposedly taught him the principles of transcendental aesthetics. But just as Wordsworth takes a different position on the sublime from Coleridge in describing the attitude of resistance to power, he describes in parenthesis the sublime of participation in terms with which Coleridge would have been entirely sympathetic. In fact, Wordsworth sums up best the essence of Coleridge's sublime in defining the sublime of participation as a 'manifest approximation towards absolute unity'. And thus Wordsworth has allowed us to perceive more clearly that Coleridge's sublime is one of participation, conceived as a movement of the mind towards an impression of 'total completeness'.
46. Wordsworth is approaching here, however tentatively, Kant's notion regarding the universality of the aesthetic judgement.
47. See e.g. the illustration immediately following the Kantian passage of ll. 223–36 (analysed on pp. 132–3 above) where Wordsworth clearly returns to empirical considerations, examining how a waterfall acts upon the senses and the imagination (ll. 236–55).
48. Marginal note to Solger, *Erwin* in Raysor, 'Unpublished Fragments in Aesthetics', p. 533.
49. Wlecke, *Wordsworth and the Sublime*, p. 77.
50. Cf. Thorpe, 'Coleridge on the Sublime', p. 216: 'With Coleridge, sublimity begins with a species of emphatic response to a great, complex, or otherwise inspiring object . . . and culminates in an intuition of the mystery and greatness of the absolute one and all of Deity.'
51. *CN*, II, 2064. For Coleridge on the natural sublime see Shaffer, 'Coleridge's Revolution in the Standard of Taste', pp. 216–17.
52. Quoted by Thorpe, 'Coleridge on the Sublime', p. 217.
53. For Coleridge's debt to Burke and his success in fusing Burke's and Kant's aesthetic theories see Shaffer, 'Coleridge's Theory of Aesthetic Interest'.
54. See *CN*, II, 2093. For Coleridge's criticisms of association theories see Part I above, n. 39.
55. Weiskel, *The Romantic Sublime*, p. 59.

PART IV: COLERIDGE'S SYSTEM OF *NATURPHILOSOPHIE*

1. McFarland, *Coleridge and the Pantheist Tradition*, p. 192. On the *magnum opus* see also McFarland, *Romanticism and the Forms of Ruin*, ch. 6 (pp. 342–81).
2. In *CL*, IV, 589 Coleridge referred to the 'Logosophia' as a work on the divine and human logos, made up of six treatises, the fourth of which was to provide a 'detailed Commentary on the Gospel of St John – collating the *Word* of the Evangelist with the Christ crucified of St Paul. –' I do not mean to suggest here that Coleridge's *magnum opus* can be confined to his writings on natural philosophy. As McFarland has shown, other works by Coleridge, such as *Biographia Literaria* or *Aids to Reflection*, were conceived as parts of the *magnum opus* (*Romanticism and the Forms of Ruin*, pp. 342–81).
3. For Coleridge's extensive interest in science at various stages of his career see Trevor H. Levere's informative study *Poetry Realized in Nature: Samuel Taylor Coleridge and Early Nineteenth-Century Science* (Cambridge University Press, 1981).
4. For an analysis of the *Theory of Life* see Levere, *Poetry Realized in Nature*, pp. 42–5, 161–6, 215–19.
5. As Levere points out (*Poetry Realized in Nature*, Introduction, n. 12), most of Coleridge's scientific speculations are to be found in vols 3 and 4 of *CN* and the forthcoming edition of *Shorter Works and Fragments*, ed. H. J. Jackson and J. R. de J. Jackson (vol. 11 in the Bollingen edition of *The Collected Works of Samuel Taylor Coleridge*). To these sources one must add Coleridge's annotations of many works by the *Naturphilosophen* which will appear in the five vols of the *Marginalia*.
6. Modern scholarship has produced only a handful of studies on the general aims and directions of *Naturphilosophie*. For an introduction to natural science and philosophy in the nineteenth century see Alexander Gode-von Aesch, *Natural Science in German Romanticism* (New York: Columbia University Press, 1941); J. B. Stallo, *General Principles of the Philosophy of Nature* (Boston: Wm. Crosby and H. P. Nichols, 1848); Barry Gower, 'Speculation in Physics: The History and Practice of *Naturphilosophie*', *Studies in the History and Philosophy of Science*, 3 (1972–3) 301–56; H. A. M. Snelders, 'Inorganic Natural Sciences 1797–1840: An Introductory Survey', *Studies in Romanticism*, 9 (1970) 193–215; Walter D. Wetzels, 'Aspects of Natural Science in German Romanticism', *Studies in Romanticism*, 10 (1971) 44–59. For a good, select bibliography of German and English studies on *Naturphilosophie* and individual *Naturphilosophen* see Marshall Brown, *The Shape of German Romanticism* (Ithaca, NY: Cornell University Press, 1979) pp. 227–33. For an early attempt to present Coleridge's system of *Naturphilosophie* see Craig W. Miller, 'Coleridge's Concept of Nature', *Journal of the History of Ideas*, 25 (1964) 77–96. On the importance of polarity in Coleridge's work and German *Naturphilosophie* see McFarland, 'A Complex Dialogue: Coleridge's Doctrine of Polarity and Its European Contexts', in *Romanticism and the Forms of Ruin*, pp. 289–341. Elinor Shaffer has pointed out the scarcity of studies dealing with Coleridge's interest in *Naturphilosophie*. See 'Coleridge and Natural

Philosophy: A Review of Recent Literary and Historical Research', *History of Science*, 12 (1974) 284–98. Recently, this gap has been filled by Levere's study *Poetry Realized in Nature*.

7. See Gower, 'Speculation in Physics', esp. pp. 327–9, Snelders, 'Inorganic Natural Sciences', esp. pp. 199–206 and Robert C. Stauffer, 'Speculation and Experiment in the Background of Oersted's Discovery of Electromagnetism', *Isis*, 48 (1957) 33–50.
8. Kant's *Prolegomena and Metaphysical Foundations of Natural Science*, trans. Ernest Belfort Bax (London: George Bell and Sons, 1883) pp. 210–11.
9. On these Newtonian concepts see Arnold Thackray, *Atoms and Powers: An Essay on Newtonian Matter-Theory and the Development of Chemistry* (Cambridge, Mass.: Harvard University Press, 1970) esp. pp. 17–18.
10. In Query 31 to the *Opticks*, which in its extended form did not appear until the revised 1717 edition (see Thackray, *Atoms and Powers*, pp. 18–24 on Newton's additions to and revisions of his *Opticks*), Newton expressed reservations regarding the corpuscular explanation of how particles of solid bodies cohere with one another. He speculated that there might be a force, as yet not identified by experimental research, that causes these particles to stick together. See Trevor H. Levere, *Affinity and Matter: Elements of Chemical Philosophy 1800–1865* (Oxford: Clarendon Press, 1971) pp. 6–8. Both Levere and Thackray discuss the impact of Newtonian theories on the development of a dynamical conception of matter.
11. In his *Zur Farbenlehre* (Tübingen, 1810) Goethe points out that in his theory of colours Newton was 'mistaken in his observations as an experimentalist' and 'employed the whole force of his talent to give consistency to this mistake' (p. xiv). For Goethe's dynamic system of colours see esp. pp. 187–8, 289, 300. Steffens in 'Ueber die Bedeutung der Farben in der Natur' (*Schriften*, 2 vols (Breslau, 1921) ii, pp. 8–9) and Schelling in *Erster Entwurf eines Systems der Naturphilosophie* (*Sämmtliche Werke*, iii, 36 n. 1), attack Newton's conception of colours and praise Goethe's dynamic theory.
12. Oken, *Erste Ideen zur Theorie des Lichts* (Jena, 1808) p. 11.
13. Originally, Oken claims, the universe is filled by primal matter (*Urmaterie*), which occupies all space and must be conceived geometrically as an infinite sphere. The ether represents the part of the primal matter remaining in the cosmos after the formation of the planets.
14. On Oken's theory of light and colour and its influence on Coleridge see Levere, *Poetry Realized in Nature*, pp. 154–6.
15. See the chapter 'Vital Force' in von Aesch, *Natural Science in German Romanticism*, esp. pp. 191–3.
16. In *Elementa Medicinae* (1780), Brown argued that the property which differentiates living from dead matter is 'excitability', i.e. the capacity to respond to external or inner stimuli. All diseases are the result of either excessive excitement or deficient stimulation (*The Works of John Brown*, 3 vols (London, 1804) esp. ii, pp. 10–15, 134–47, 179–81). Although Brown did not offer his principle of plus and minus excitability as a full clarification of the source of life, 'that was precisely what his German followers expected from it or at least what they tried to develop out of its principles' (von Aesch, p. 191).

17. Some identified the agent of life as the irritability of the muscle, others located it in the sensibility of the nerves, and others looked on both irritability and sensibility as the offsprings of a universal 'vital force'. See the quotation from Oskar Walzel's *Deutsche Romantik* cited by von Aesch, p. 191, n. 34.
18. Among the *Naturphilosophen*, Ritter possessed an intensely analogical imagination. In *Beweis, dass ein beständiger Galvanismus den Lebensprocess in dem Tierreich begleite*, Ritter set out to demonstrate that galvanic properties were present throughout nature and that galvanism was at the root of physiological processes in the human organism (see Wetzels, 'Aspects of Natural Science in German Romanticism', pp. 52–9 and Gower, 'Speculation in Physics', pp. 327–39). In further experiments Ritter studied the similarity between plants and animals with regard to galvanic sensibility. He discovered that the parts of the mimosa plant, when stimulated by positive or negative electricity, reacted in similar ways to the organs of a frog. On the mimosa plant as a bridge between plant and animal life see Robert M. Maniquis, 'The Puzzling *Mimosa*: Sensitivity and Plant Symbols in Romanticism', *Studies in Romanticism*, 8 (1969) 129–55.
19. Oersted's account of his discovery of electromagnetism as presented in his *Autobiography* and in an article published in *The Edinburgh Encyclopedia* is cited by Robert C. Stauffer in 'Speculation and Experiment in the Background of Oersted's Discovery of Electromagnetism', Appendix I and II (pp. 48–50).
20. As Coleridge wrote, opposite poles 'are, of course, antitheta ejusdam essentiae'. Marginal note to J. C. Heinroth, *Lehrbuch der Anthropologie* (Leipzig, 1822) pp. 252–5. In his note to pp. 406–7 of this work, Coleridge reacted negatively to Heinroth's assumption that the body and the soul were opposed to one another. Coleridge realized that this assumption implied the identity of the soul and the body according to the principle of polarity, thus jeopardizing the autonomy of the spirit.
21. On the various meanings of the circle and centrality in the works of *Naturphilosophen* and of the Romantics see Marshall Brown's stimulating study *The Shape of German Romanticism*.
22. See Modiano, 'Coleridge's Views on Touch and Other Senses', *Bulletin of Research in the Humanities*, 1 (1978) 28–41.
23. Schelling, 'Kritische Fragmente', in *Jahrbücher der Medicin als Wissenschaft*, 3 vols (Tübingen: J. G. Cotta'scher Buchandlung, 1805–8) II, pp. 287–303, esp. 291.
24. Steffens, *Beyträge zur innern Naturgeschichte der Erde* (Freyberg, 1801) p. 312. Cf. Coleridge, *TL*, 596.
25. Karl Christian Wolfart, *Erläuterungen zum Mesmerismus*, vol. II of *Mesmerismus: Oder System der Wechselwirkungen* (Berlin, 1814–1815) § 94, pp. 210–15. On the inner sense see §§ 94–5 (pp. 215–22). On the importance of the inner sense for the *Naturphilosophen* see von Aesch, *Natural Science in German Romanticism*, pp. 176–82. For a discussion of attempts by English writers to represent the interaction of various senses see ch. 1 of Glen O'Malley, *Shelley and Synaesthesia* (Evanston, Ill.: Northwestern University Press, 1964).
26. Eschenmayer's theory of the senses appears in his article 'Spontaneität =

Weltseele' published in *Zeitschrift für Speculative Physik*, ed. Schelling, 2 vols (Jena and Leipzig, 1800–1801) II, pp. 39–58. See esp. pp. 50–3.

27. *CL*, IV, 806. A similar reaction against the sensuous cosmos of the *Naturphilosophen* and their inability to distinguish properly between physical and spiritual qualities appears in Coleridge's marginal note to Wolfart, *Erläuterungen zum Mesmerismus*, II, p. 154.
28. Cf. Kant, *Critique of Pure Reason*, p. 577: '*Philosophical* knowledge is the *knowledge gained by reason from concepts*; mathematical knowledge is the knowledge gained by reason from the *construction* of concepts. To *construct* a concept means to exhibit *a priori* the intuition which corresponds to the concept . . . The latter must, as intuition, be a *single* object, and yet none the less, as the construction of a concept (a universal representation), it must in its representation express universal validity for all possible intuitions which fall under the same concept.' On the differences between mathematical and metaphysical knowledge see also Kant's pre-critical essay *Untersuchungen über die Deutlichkeit der Grundsätze der natürlichen Theologie und der Moral* (1763), *Vermischte Schriften* (Halle, 1799) II, pp. 1–54 and *Critique of Pure Reason*, pp. 21 ff., 577–91 and *passim*.
29. Kant, *Metaphysical Foundations of Natural Science*, p. 142: 'But to render possible the application of mathematics to the doctrine of body, by which alone it can become natural science, principles of the *construction* of conceptions belonging to the possibility of matter in general must precede. Hence a complete analysis of the conception of a matter in general must be laid at its foundation; this is the business of pure philosophy . . .'
30. On this see Gower, 'Speculation in Physics'.
31. See Schelling, *Erster Entwurf eines Systems der Naturphilosophie*, *Sämmtliche Werke*, III, p. 101.
32. Marginal note to Kant, *Metaphysische Anfangsgründe der Naturwissenschaft* (Riga, 1787) pp. 80–1. Subsequent quotations from Coleridge's marginal notes refer to this edition.
33. On pp. 117–18 of *Metaphysische Anfangsgründe der Naturwissenschaft* there are three marginal notes written at three different times, the second and the third being dated July 1811 and August 1819.
34. In 'Essays on the Principles of Method' (*The Friend*, I, 448–524), Coleridge argues that science cannot be based on mere empirical observation but must derive its principles from 'pure reason, the spirit' or 'intellectual intuition' (*The Friend*, I, 491).
35. Kant, *Metaphysical Foundations of Natural Science*, pp. 172–3: 'The expansive force of a matter is termed *elasticity*. Now as the former is the basis on which the filling of space, as an essential property of all matter, rests, this elasticity must be termed *original*; seeing that it cannot be derived from any other property of matter. All matter is accordingly originally elastic.' ('Die expansive Kraft einer Materie nennt man auch *Elasticität*. Da nun jene der Grund ist, worauf die Erfüllung des Raumes als eine wesentliche Eigenschaft aller Materie beruht, so muss diese Elasticität *ursprünglich* heissen, weil sie von keiner anderen Eigenschaft der Materie abgeleitet werden kann. Alle Materie ist demnach ursprünglich elastisch.') For this part of my discussion it will be necessary to include references to

the German text, given that I am following Kant's conceptual language. I quote from *Kant's Gesammelte Schriften*, 24 vols (Berlin: Georg Reimer, 1910–1955) IV, pp. 467–565, henceforward referred to as *Schriften*.

36. Kant, *Metaphysical Foundations of Natural Science*, p. 193: '*The effect* of the universal attraction, which all matter exercises directly upon all [matter] and at all distances, is termed gravitation; the endeavour to move itself in the direction of the greater gravitation is *weight*. The effect of the thorough going repulsive force of the parts of each given matter is termed its *original elasticity*.' *Schriften*, IV, p. 518: '*Die Wirkung* von der allgemeinen Anziehung, wie alle Materie auf alle und in allen Entfernungen unmittelbar ausübt, heisst die *Gravitation*; die Bestrebung in der Richtung der grösseren Gravitation sich zu bewegen ist die *Schwere*. Die Wirkung von der durchgängigen repulsiven Kraft der Theile jeder gegebenen Materie heisst dieser ihre ursprüngliche Elasticität.'
37. Kant, *Metaphysical Foundations of Natural Science*, p. 183: 'With this transition from one property of matter to another specifically different from it, [i.e. from the force of repulsion to the force of attraction] which yet equally belongs to the conception of matter, *although it is not contained therein*, the attitude of our understanding must be more closely considered.' *Schriften*, IV, p. 509: 'Bei diesem Übergange von einer Eigenschaft der Materie zu einer andern, specifisch davon unterschieden, die zum Begriffe der Materie eben sowohl gehört, *obgleich in demselben nicht enthalten ist*, muss das Verhalten unseres Verstandes in nähere Erwägung gezogen werden.'
38. Kant, *Metaphysical Foundations of Natural Science*, p. 172. *Schriften*, IV, p. 499: '*Die Kraft aber eines Ausgedehnten vermöge der Zurückstossung aller seiner Theile ist eine Ausdehnungskraft* (expansive).'
39. Cf. *Metaphysical Foundations of Natural Science*, p. 176: 'Matter is impenetrable by its own original force of extension (proposition 3); but this is only the result of the repulsive forces of each point in a space filled with matter.' *Schriften*, IV, p. 503: 'Die Materie ist undurchdringlich und zwar durch ihre ursprüngliche Ausdehnungskraft (Lehrs. 3), diese aber ist nur die Folge der repulsiven Kräfte eines jeden Punkts in einen von Materie erfüllten Raum.'
40. Kant, *Metaphysical Foundations of Natural Science*, p. 172. *Schriften*, IV, p. 499: 'Die Materie erfüllt ihre Räume durch repulsive Kräfte aller ihrer Theile, d. i. durch eine ihr eigene Ausdehnungskraft, die einen bestimmten Grad hat, über den kleinere oder grössere ins Unendliche können gedacht werden.'
41. Kant, *Metaphysical Foundations of Natural Science*, p. 182. *Schriften*, IV, p. 508: 'Die Undurchdringlichkeit als die Grundeigenschaft der Materie, wodurch sie sich als etwas Reales im Raume unseren äusseren Sinnen zuerst offenbart, ist nichts als das Ausdehnungsvermögen der Materie (Lehrsatz 2).'
42. Kant, *Metaphysical Foundations of Natural Science*, p. 187. *Schriften*, IV, p. 512; '*Die ursprüngliche und aller Materie wesentliche Anziehung* is eine unmittelbare Wirkung derselben auf andere durch den leeren Raum.'
43. Kant, *Metaphysical Foundations of Natural Science*, p. 198. *Schriften*, IV, p. 522: 'Das allgemeine Gesetz der Dynamik würde in beiden Fällen dieses

sein: die Wirkung der bewegenden Kraft, die von einem Punkte auf jeden anderen ausser ihm ausgeübt wird, verhält sich umgekehrt wie der Raum, in welchem dasselbe Quantum der bewegenden Kraft sich hat ausbreiten müssen, um auf diesen Punkt unmittelbar in der bestimmten Entfernung zu wirken.'

44. Fly-leaf note referring to p. 66. For Coleridge gravity is the synthesis of the forces of attraction and repulsion. It is 'not a compound' but 'a higher Third' (*SM*, pp. 81–2). For another attack on Kant's conception of gravity see *CL*, IV, 808. Coleridge's objection to Kant's concept of gravity is derived from Schelling. See n. 60 below.
45. For Kant's definition of material substance see *Metaphysical Foundations of Natural Science*, p. 176.
46. Schelling, *Ideen zu einer Philosophie der Natur* (henceforward cited as *Ideen*), *Sämmtliche Werke* (henceforward cited as *SW*), II, pp. 49–50.
47. *Einleitung zu dem Entwurf eines Systems der Naturphilosophie oder über den Begriff der speculativen Physik und die innere Organisation eines Systems dieser Wissenschaft*, *SW*, III, 326.
48. Schelling discusses these questions in the introduction to *Ideen*, *SW*, II, 11–73.
49. *SW*, II, 20–1, 37–8. For Leibnitz's view that the monads are windowless see *The Monadology*, p. 219.
50. On the Absolute see *Ideen*, *SW*, II, 57–73. The various metamorphoses of the Absolute are presented in Schelling's *System of Transcendental Idealism*.
51. Frederick Copleston notes that Schelling does not make the 'relation between the infinite and the finite, between the Absolute in itself and its self-manifestation, crystal clear. We have seen indeed that *Natura naturata*, considered as the symbol or appearance of *Natura naturans*, is said to be outside the *Absolute*. But Schelling also speaks of the Absolute as expanding itself into the particular. Clearly, Schelling wishes to make a distinction between the unchanging Absolute in itself and the world of finite particular things. But the same time he wishes to maintain that the Absolute is the all-comprehensive reality.' *A History of Philosophy*, 8 vols (New York: Doubleday, 1965) VII, p. 137. See also p. 154.
52. Schelling, *Introduction to the Outlines of a System of Natural Philosophy; or On the Idea of Speculative Physics and the Internal Organization of a System of This Science*, trans. Tom Davidson, *Journal of Speculative Philosophy*, 1 (1867) 194 (*SW*, III, 272).
53. Cf. Schelling, *System of Transcendental Idealism*, p. 6: 'Nature's highest goal, to become wholly an object to herself, is achieved only through the last and highest order or reflection, which is none other than man; or, more generally, it is what we call reason, whereby nature first completely returns into herself, and by which it becomes apparent that nature is identical from the first with what we recognize in ourselves as the intelligent and the conscious.'
54. Schelling provides a useful illustration of the perpetual metamorphosis of nature's productivity into products. What we see in nature is 'not really the subsisting of a product, but only the continual process of being reproduced'. The best analogy for this process is the relationship between a

stream and a whirlpool. The stream, where it flows in a straight line, is '*pure identity*' (i.e. the symbol of nature's productivity). When the stream 'meets resistance, there is formed a whirlpool' (the equivalent of products of nature). The whirlpool 'is not anything abiding, but something that every moment vanishes, and every moment springs up anew. – In Nature there is originally nothing distinguishable; all products are, so to speak, still in solution, and invisible in the universal productivity. It is only when retarding points are given, that they are thrown off and advance out of the universal identity. – At every such point the stream breaks (the productivity is annihilated), but at every step there comes a new wave which fills up the sphere' (p. 202; *SW*, III, 289). The same illustration is used in *Erster Entwurf eines Systems der Naturphilosophie* (*SW*, III, 18 n. 2).

55. See Part I above, n. 2.
56. Schelling's use of the Aristotelian notion of *entelechy* is derived from Leibnitz. Leibnitz had already adapted Aristotle's *entelechy* to mean not so much a state of perfection in which the realization of the potentiality of a given thing is completed, as a simple force or substance that carries within itself the principles of its own activity. For Leibnitz the monads are the 'real atoms of nature', indivisible and indestructible at the same time. See *The Monadology*, §§ 1–5 (pp. 217–18) and § 18 where Leibnitz defines the monads as *entelechies*. On the differences between Leibnitz's and Aristotle's use of *entelechy* see *The Monadology*, p. 229 n. 32.
57. Cf. *Ideen* (*SW*, II, 107–10) where Schelling examines the relationship between light and matter, and light and gravity. He argues that since light and matter are one in the higher synthesis that takes place in *natura naturans*, 'light is the same as matter and matter the same as light, only one represents the real, the other the ideal' (p. 107). Those who argue for the immateriality of light which they oppose to the reality of matter do not understand that matter is not purely material, nor light purely immaterial, for light 'is also matter itself' (p. 109). The relationship between gravity, as the symbol of the real, and light can be represented as that between a motherly, receptive principle and an active generative principle (pp. 109–10).
58. On the interaction between the three powers of organic nature and between these and the powers of inorganic nature see Schelling, *Erster Entwurf*, *SW*, III, 196–220.
59. Heinrich Steffens, *Grundzüge der philosophischen Naturwissenschaft*, Introduction, p. XXI.
60. Coleridge's complaint that Kant failed to consider why the two forces of matter do not annihilate each other when they become equal and his objection to Kant's derivation of gravity from the force of attraction (see p. 157 above) had been already voiced by Schelling. For Schelling's attack on Kant's concept of the two powers and of gravity see *Ideen*, *SW*, II, 49–50, 231–41; *Erster Entwurf*, *SW*, III, 24 n. 1, 261–8; *Introduction to the Outlines*, p. 220 (*SW*, III, 326).
61. See Schelling, *System of Transcendental Idealism*, pp. 5–6. In his adaptation of this passage from *System* in *BL*, I, 175–6, Coleridge retains Schelling's emphasis on the tendency of natural science to elevate itself to the objectives of transcendental philosophy.

62. *CL*, IV, 874. Coleridge's response to *Einleitung* appears in three documents: in his marginalia to this work, in a set of notebook entries (*CN*, III, 4449, 4450, 4453), and in his letter to J. H. Green (*CL*, IV, 873–6). Some of Coleridge's arguments overlap in these works. Coleridge's annotated copy of *Einleitung* (Jena and Leipzig, 1799) is in Dr Williams's Library.
63. Marginal note and fly-leaf note to p. 3 of *Einleitung*. The candle illustration also appears in *CL*, IV, 874.
64. In his marginal note to Heinroth, *Lehrbuch der Anthropologie*, pp. 36–7, Coleridge points out that one of the most frequent errors in *Naturphilosophie* and the 'cause of its failure' is the derivation of a higher power from a lower one.
65. *CL*, IV, 874: 'Our first point therefore is – steadily to deny and clearly to expose, the Polarity as existing or capable of existing in the unity of a perfect Will or in the Godhead as ens realissimum.'
66. Coleridge also annotated Schelling's *Ideen zu einer Philosophie der Natur* (Landshut, 1803), *Erster Entwurf eines Systems der Naturphilosophie* (Jena and Leipzig, 1799), and various essays that appeared in *Jahrbücher der Medicin als Wissenschaft*, ed. A. F. Marcus and F. W. J. Schelling, 3 vols (Tübingen, 1805–8) and in *Zeitschrift für speculative Physik*, ed. Schelling, 2 vols (Jena and Leipzig, 1800–1).
67. Marginal note to pp. 137–9 of *Einleitung*. In various writings on *Naturphilosophie* Coleridge includes chlorine and iodine as primary symbols of the contractive power of nature. See e.g. *CN*, III, 4420, *CL*, IV, 773 and marginal note to vol. I, pp. 2–4 of Oken's *Lehrbuch der Naturgeschichte*, 6 vols (Leipzig and Jena, 1813; Jena, 1816–26). Coleridge's inclusion of these elements in his scheme of nature was no doubt influenced by Davy's view that chlorine and iodine were simple bodies and not compounds, as French chemists maintained. For Davy's researches on chlorine see *Elements of Chemical Philosophy*, in *Collected Works*, ed. John Davy, 9 vols (London, 1839–40) IV, pp. 173–80 and his papers read before the Royal Society, *Collected Works*, V, pp. 284–357, 524–7. On iodine see *Collected Works*, V, pp. 437–77; 492–502; 510–16.
68. Cf. the important note to I, pp. 2–4 of Oken's *Lehrbuch der Naturgeschichte*: 'When a Philosopher shews me Carbon in its purest form of Diamond or Quarz, as the Body in which the . . . Power of Attraction or Astriction is best represented & most predominant; and Nitrogen, as the Body in which the Power of Repulsion or Self-projection is paramountly represented . . . I know and understand what he means, and can give to the Ideal what subsists as Idea, and to the Real or ⟨Phaenomenal⟩, what exists as Phaenomena.' See also *CN*, III, 4420; *TL*, 583; *CL*, IV, 772–3, 808–9.
69. See e.g. *TL*, 580–3 and Schelling's *Ideen*, *SW*, II, 228–33.
70. *N* 36, ff. 172–3. Quoted by Harding, *Coleridge and the Idea of Love*, pp. 193–4.
71. Steffens was particularly impressed by Schelling's important discovery of the relationship between magnetism and the dimension of length. According to Steffens, it was Schelling who first saw that the negative pole of the magnetic line represented the point of maximum coherence in matter. See Steffens, *Beyträge zur innern Naturgeschichte der Erde* (Freyberg, 1801) p. 155 n. 212.

72. Like Schelling, Steffens defines 'intellectual intuition', the organ of philosophic knowledge, as the 'identity of thought and being', subjectivity and objectivity (Steffens, *Grundzüge*, p. 5).
73. See e.g. Steffens, *Grundzüge*, pp. 22, 40.
74. See esp. ibid., ch. 3, pp. 36–65.
75. Ibid., pp. 46–7. On the classification of metals see ch. 6, esp. pp. 88–95. In the line of electricity the correspondent of the two groups of coherent and non-coherent metals is constituted by two series of earths, the silica series that occupies the contractive side of the line (from the centre to the East pole) and the lime series that occupies the opposite side of the line (from the centre to the West pole).
76. On the relationship between light and gravity see *Grundzüge*, pp. 25–30 and *passim*. According to Steffens, the representative of the complete unity between gravity and light in the planetary world is the sun. The visible sun is, however, only 'the reflex of the true sun which exists in each planet and in each organization', namely of the unity between individuality and universality. In the human organization light is 'the highest principle' of individuality, gravity the 'deepest principle' of universality, while the inner centre of unity between the two, the place of 'absolute truth and clarity', is reason (pp. 28–9).
77. On the relationship between the three powers and the development of organic life in various species of animals see also *Grundzüge*, pp. 71–82, 169–94.
78. Coleridge criticized the *Naturphilosophen* severely for their equation of the Deity with absolute nothingness. He found this error most frequently in Oken, who based his system on 'the highest mathematical idea', namely the original zero of all numerical series, explicitly identifying the zero with the primordial being (*Ousia*). See Oken, *Lehrbuch der Naturphilosophie* (Jena, 1809) esp. Pt I (*Mathesis*), BK I (*Theosophie*). On p. 15 of this work Oken states: 'God is the self-conscious nothingness, or the existing (self-conscious) nothingness is God.' ('Gott ist das selbstbewusste Nichts, oder das seiende (selbstbewusste) Nichts ist Gott.') For Coleridge's reactions to this pantheistic position see his comments to pp. 2, 4–6, 15, 20, 41 of *Lehrbuch der Naturphilosophie* and *CN*, III, 4429.
79. Marginal note to pp. 46–7 of *Grundzüge* (Nidecker, *Revue de Littérature Comparée*, 11 (1931) 278).
80. Copleston notes the same problem in Schelling's system. See n. 51 above.
81. Steffens, *Beyträge zur innern Naturgeschichte der Erde*, pp. 170–1. For Coleridge's comment on this passage see Nidecker, *Revue de Littérature Comparée*, 12 (1932) 864.
82. Fly-leaf notes referring to pp. 243 and 250 of Steffens, *Geognostisch-geologische Aufsätze*. For Coleridge's view of chlorine and iodine see n. 67 above. Coleridge also charged Oken with the same confusion between ideal powers and physical bodies. Responding to Oken's claim that the 'elements of which the planet consists, such as earth, water, air and finally also fire or aether, are not particulars, nor bodies but universals', Coleridge wrote: 'But these very Elements are <either> mere Hypotheses . . . or they are Personifications of the Powers and Forces manifested in Bodies . . . When a Philosopher shews me Carbon in its purest form of Diamond or Quarz, as

the Body in which the . . . Power of Attraction or Astriction is best represented & most predominant; and Nitrogen, as the Body in which the Power of Repulsion or Self-projection is paramountly represented – and in like manner the power of Contraction in Oxygen, and of Dilation in Hydrogen, allotting to other Bodies, as Chlorine, Iodine &c the intermediate points in this Compass of Powers: – I know and understand what he means, and can give to the Ideal what subsists as Idea, and to the Real or ⟨Phaenomenal⟩ what exists as Phaenomena.' Marginal note to Oken, *Lehrbuch der Naturgeschichte*, I, pp. 2–4.

83. It must be said to Steffens's credit that he is not unaware of the differences between bodies and powers and that he specifically points out that carbon and nitrogen are not identical with the forces of attraction and repulsion, but merely the representatives of these powers in hard bodies. See *Beyträge*, pp. 260–2. In the following passage Steffens draws clear distinctions between powers, 'Stuffs' and the chemical elements: ' . . . *die Kräfte*, deren Ausdruck die Metalle, *das Thätige* in dem *ruhenden* Körper sind, welches *die Grenze sucht: die Stoffe* hingegen *das Ruhende* in dem *thätigen* Körper, welches die *Grenze gefunden hat. Stickstoff* und *Kohlenstoff* erscheinen nur als *Kräfte*, so lange sie *unmittelbar verbunden sind*, und daher ihr ganzes Daseyn durch die Tendenz zur Trennung offenbaren. – *Repulsivkraft* und *Attractivkraft* erscheinen nur als *Stoffe*, wenn die *Trennung* ein *Maximum erreicht* und die *Grenze* gefunden ist.' (' . . . *the powers*, which are expressed through metals are the *active principle* in the *passive* body that *seeks a boundary*: *substances*, on the other hand, are the *passive principle* in the *active* body that *has found a boundary*. *Nitrogen* and *Carbon* appear only as *powers*, as long as they *are directly connected with one another*, and therefore they manifest their being entirely through the tendency to separation. – *The repulsive* and *attractive power* appear only as *substances*, when their separation *reaches* a *maximum* and the *boundary* is found.')
84. Marginal note to pp. 262–3 of *Beyträge* (Nidecker, *Revue de Littérature Comparée*, 12 (1932) 867). For Schelling's view that no body, not even a chemical element, is simple see *Erster Entwurf*, *SW*, III, 34–9, esp. 34 n. 1 and 38 n. 1.
85. Marginal note to pp. 42–3 of Oersted, *Ansicht der chemischen Naturgesetze, durch die neuern Entdeckungen gewonnen* (Berlin, 1812). See Nidecker, *Revue de Littérature Comparée*, 13 (1933) 680.
86. Marginal note to *Beyträge*, pp. 64–5 (Nidecker, *Revue de Littérature Comparée*, 12 (1932) 859).
87. Fly-leaf note to *Beyträge* (Nidecker, *Revue de Littérature Comparée*, 11 (1931) 283–5). Cf. also Coleridge's classification of the five powers of nature in *CN*, III, 4420, 4435, 4436.
88. 'Even while my faith was confined in the trammels of Unitarianism . . . ', Coleridge wrote in a note to Boehme's *Aurora*, 'I saw clearly, as a truth in philosoph~~ly~~y, that the Trinitarian was the only consequent Medium between the Atheist and the Anthropomorph.' *CM*, I, 566. See also BÖHME, *Works*, 110, 159 (*CM*, I, 645–6, 679) and McFarland, *Coleridge and the Pantheist Tradition*, pp. 227–8.
89. For discussions of Coleridge's concept of the Trinity see McFarland, *Coleridge and the Pantheist Tradition*, pp. 191–255; James D. Boulger,

Coleridge as Religious Thinker (New Haven: Yale University Press, 1961) esp. pp. 94–142; J. Robert Barth, *Coleridge and Christian Doctrine* (Cambridge, Mass.: Harvard University Press, 1969) esp. pp. 85–104; and Craig W. Miller, 'An Examination of the Key Terms in Coleridge's Prose Writings', Diss. University of Washington, 1956, pp. 7–43.

90. Walter Jackson Bate, *Coleridge* (New York: Collier, 1973) p. 214.
91. See e.g. *CN*, III, 4427, 4428, 4429; BÖHME, *Works*, 6, 7, 111, 159 (*CM*, I, 562–5, 646–7, 679). In his marginal notes to Oken's *Lehrbuch der Naturphilosophie* Coleridge comments on both the inadequacy of Oken's conception of the Absolute as well as on the possible adaptations of his views to an orthodox rendition of the Trinity. See esp. Coleridge's note to vol. I, p. 19 of *Lehrbuch* (cited in *CN*, III, 4428 n.) where Coleridge detects some positive signs of a possible convergence between *Naturphilosophie* and Christian orthodoxy.
92. *CN*, III, 4428. At the end of this entry Coleridge equates his name with Schelling: 'S. T. C. = Schelling'. The connection between Coleridge's *Naturphilosophie* and his view of the Trinity has been adequately perceived by Levere (*Poetry Realized in Nature*, pp. 1, 6, 15, 36, 55, 104, 109, 116–18, 120–1, 126–9), although Levere does not offer an analysis of Coleridge's concept of the Trinity as I do here.
93. On the distinction between God as divine ground and God as person see BÖHME, *Works* 6 and 6 n. 5 (*CM*, I, 561).
94. On the Tetractys see BÖHME, *Works* 6 and 6 n. 10 (*CM*, I, 563) and Bate, *Coleridge*, p. 217.
95. See *CN*, I, 556, 1561. Cf. McFarland, *Coleridge and the Pantheist Tradition*, pp. 228–30.
96. See Schelling, *System of Transcendental Idealism*, pp. 34–50 and *passim*. See also pp. 162, 164 above. The act of self-consciousness, Schelling writes, which is one and the same as the Absolute is 'ideal and real, simultaneously and throughout. By means of it, what is posited as real is also immediately posited as ideal, and what is posited as ideal is likewise posited as real.' The Absolute is therefore the '*thoroughgoing* identity of ideal and real positedness . . . ' (*System of Transcendental Idealism*, p. 42). Boulger has noticed the coexistence of subjective idealism or the 'identity-philosophy' and 'other traditional or scholastic assumptions' in Coleridge's conception of the Trinity, but does not show the parallels between Schelling's view of the Absolute and Coleridge's idea of God. See *Coleridge as Religious Thinker*, pp. 108–9, 142.
97. For his conception of a dynamic Absolute Schelling was much indebted to Boehme. See Robert F. Brown, *The Later Philosophy of Schelling: The Influence of Boehme on the Works of 1809–1815* (Lewisburg, Pa.: Bucknell University Press; London: Associated University Presses, 1977).
98. The development of the concept of an original ground in Boehme's works is discussed by Brown, *The Later Philosophy of Schelling*, pp. 31–82.
99. Boulger in *Coleridge as Religious Thinker*, p. 134 and Bate in *Coleridge*, p. 217 also argue that Coleridge introduces potentiality and becoming in God.
100. These powers are gravitation, light, magnetism, electricity and galvanism. See e.g. *CN*, III, 4420. For a different view of the number of powers in nature see BÖHME, *Works* 137 (*CM*, I, 660).

101. On the difference between life and mind see *N* 36, ff. 3–3^{v}. 31^{v}, in Boulger, *Coleridge as Religious Thinker*, pp. 119–20 and 120 n. 8.
102. For the view that for Coleridge 'one of the prime functions of Christianity was to reconcile man with nature', see McFarland, *Coleridge and the Pantheist Tradition*, p. 205.

Bibliography

Abrams, M. H. *The Mirror and the Lamp* (1953; rpt. London: Oxford University Press, 1974)

——. 'The Correspondent Breeze: A Romantic Metaphor', in *English Romantic Poets: Essays in Criticism*, ed. M. H. Abrams (New York: Oxford University Press, 1960) pp. 37–54

Adams, Hazard. *The Philosophy of the Literary Symbolic* (Tallahassee, Florida: University Presses of Florida, 1983)

Aesch, Alexander Gode- von. *Natural Science in German Romanticism* (New York: Columbia University Press, 1941)

Baillie, John. 'An Essay on the Sublime', *The Augustan Reprint Society*, no. 43 (Los Angeles: William Andrews Clark Memorial Library, 1953)

Ball, Patricia. *The Science of Aspects: The Changing Role of Fact in the Work of Coleridge. Ruskin and Hopkins* (London: Athlone Press, 1971)

Barfield, Owen. *What Coleridge Thought* (Middletown, Conn.: Wesleyan University Press, 1971)

——. 'Symptoms of Iconoclasm', in *Romanticism and Consciousness*, ed. Harold Bloom (New York: W. W. Norton, 1970) pp. 41–6

Barrell, John. *The Idea of Landscape and the Sense of Place: 1730–1840* (Cambridge University Press, 1972)

Barth, J. Robert. *Coleridge and Christian Doctrine* (Cambridge, Mass.: Harvard University Press, 1969)

——. *The Symbolic Imagination: Coleridge and the Romantic Tradition* (Princeton University Press, 1977)

Bate, Walter Jackson. *Coleridge* (New York: Collier, 1973)

Beach, Joseph W. *The Concept of Nature in Nineteenth-Century English Poetry* (New York: Macmillan, 1936)

Beer, John. *Coleridge's Poetic Intelligence* (London: Macmillan, 1977)

Berkeley, George. *A Treatise Concerning the Principles of Human Knowledge*. In *The Works of George Berkeley*, ed. Alexander Campbell Fraser, 4 vols (Oxford: Clarendon Press, 1901) I, pp. 211–347.

Berkoben, Lawrence David. *Coleridge's Decline as a Poet* (The Hague: Mouton, 1975)

Bloom, Harold. *The Visionary Company* (Ithaca, NY: Cornell University Press, 1971)

Boulger, James D. *Coleridge as Religious Thinker* (New Haven: Yale University Press, 1961)

Brown, John. *Elements of Medicine*. In *The Works of John Brown*, 3 vols (London, 1804)

Brown, Marshall. *The Shape of German Romanticism* (Ithaca, NY: Cornell University Press, 1979)

Brown, Nathaniel, *Sexuality and Feminism in Shelley* (Cambridge, Mass.: Harvard University Press, 1979)

Brown, Robert. *The Later Philosophy of Schelling: The Influence of Boehme on the Works of 1809–1815* (Lewisburg, Pa.: Bucknell University Press; London: Associated University Presses, 1977)

Burke, Edmund. *A Philosophical Inquiry into the Origin of Our Ideas of the Sublime and the Beautiful* (New York: Collier & Son, 1909)

Carritt, E. F. *The Theory of Beauty* (London: Methuen, 1914)

Cassirer, Ernst. *The Philosophy of Symbolic Forms*, 3 vols (New Haven: Yale University Press, 1968)

Chayes, Irene. 'Rhetoric as Drama: An Approach to the Romantic Ode', *PMLA*, 79 (1964) 67–79

Coburn, Kathleen. *The Self-Conscious Imagination* (London: Oxford University Press, 1974)

——. 'Reflections in a Coleridge Mirror: Some Images in His Poems', in *From Sensibility to Romanticism*, ed. Frederick W. Hilles and Harold Bloom (Oxford University Press, 1965) pp. 415–37

Cooke, Michael G. 'The Manipulation of Space in Coleridge's Poetry', in *New Perspectives in Coleridge and Wordsworth: Selected Papers from the English Institute*, ed. Geoffrey H. Hartman (New York: Columbia University Press, 1972) pp. 165–94

Copleston, Frederick. *A History of Philosophy*, 8 vols (New York: Doubleday, 1965)

Darwin, Erasmus. *The Temple of Nature* (London: J. Johnson, 1803)

Davy, Humphry. *Collected Works*, ed. John Davy, 9 vols (London, 1839–40) vols IV–V

Dekker, George. *Coleridge and the Literature of Sensibility* (New York: Barnes & Noble, 1978)

de Man, Paul. 'The Rhetoric of Temporality', in *Interpretation: Theory and Practice*, ed. Charles S. Singleton (Baltimore: Johns Hopkins Press, 1969) pp. 173–209

Deneau, Daniel. 'Coleridge's "Limbo": A Riddling Tale', *The Wordsworth Circle*, 3 (1972) 97–105

Emerson, Ralph Waldo. 'Nature', in *The Complete Essays and Other Writings of Ralph Waldo Emerson* (New York: The Modern Library, 1950) pp. 3–42

Erdman, David. 'Immoral Acts of a Library Cormorant', *Bulletin of the New York Public Library*, 63 (1959) 433–54; 515–30; 575–87

Eschenmayer, Adam Karl August. *Psychologie* (Stuttgart and Tübingen, 1817)

——. '*Spontaneität = Weltseele*', in *Zeitschrift für Speculative Physik*, ed. F. W. J. Schelling, 2 vols (Jena and Leipzig, 1800–1801) II, pp. 39–58

Fields, Beverly. *Reality's Dark Dream: Dejection in Coleridge* (Kent State University Press, 1967)

Fogle, Richard Harter. 'The Dejection of Coleridge's Ode', *ELH*, 17 (1950) 71–7

Garber, Frederick. 'Nature and the Romantic Mind: Egotism, Empathy, Irony', *Comparative Literature*, 29 (1977) 193–212

Gérard, Albert. *English Romantic Poetry* (Berkeley: University of California Press, 1968)

——. 'Counterfeiting Infinity: "The Eolian Harp" and the Growth of Coleridge's Mind', *JEGP*, 60 (1961) 411–22

Gilpin, William. *Observations on the Western Parts of England* (London, 1798)

Goethe, Johann Wolfgang von. *Goethes Werke*, Hamburger Ausgabe (Hamburg: Christian Wegner Verlag, 1955) vol. XIII

——. 'Letters from Switzerland. Travels in Italy', vol. IV of *The Complete Works of Johann Wolfgang von Goethe*, trans. Thomas Carlyle *et al.* (New York: P. F. Collier, n. d.)

——. *Zur Farbenlehre* (Tübingen, 1810)

Goodson, Alfred Jr. 'Coleridge and Hölderlin: Studies in the Poetics of Space' (Diss. State University of New York at Buffalo, 1973)

Gower, Barry. 'Speculation in Physics: The History and Practice of *Naturphilosophie*', *Studies in the History and Philosophy of Science*, 3 (1972–3) 301–56

Harding, Anthony John. *Coleridge and the Idea of Love* (Cambridge University Press, 1974)

Haven, Richard. *Patterns of Consciousness* (Amherst, Mass.: University of Massachusetts Press, 1969)

Heath, William. *Wordsworth and Coleridge: A Study of their Literary Relations in 1801–1802* (Oxford: Clarendon Press, 1970)

Heinroth, Johann Christian. *Lehrbuch der Anthropologie* (Leipzig, 1822)

Herder, Johann Gottfried von. *Kalligone*, vol. XXII of *Herders Sämmtliche Werke*, 33 vols, ed. Bernard Suphan (Berlin: Weidmannsche Buchhandlung, 1877–1913)

——. *Kalligone*, 3 vols (Leipzig, 1800)

Hipple, W. J. *The Beautiful, the Sublime, and the Picturesque in Eighteenth-Century British Aesthetic Theory* (Carbondale: Southern Illinois University Press, 1957)

House, Humphry. *Coleridge* (London: Rupert Hart-Davis, 1953)

Immerwahr, Raymond. *Romantisch: Genese und Tradition einer Denkform* (Frankfurt: Athenäum, 1972)

Jackson, J. R. de J. (ed.) *Coleridge: The Critical Heritage* (New York: Barnes & Noble, 1970)

Jordan, John E. *Why the Lyrical Ballads*? (Berkeley: University of California Press, 1976) pp. 9–32

Kant, Immanuel. *Critique of Judgement*, trans. J. H. Bernard (New York: Hafner Press, 1951)

——. *Critique of Pure Reason*, trans. Norman Kemp Smith (London: Macmillan, 1976)

——. *Groundwork of the Metaphysic of Morals*, trans. H. J. Paton (New York: Harper & Row, 1964)

——. *Metaphysische Anfangsgründe der Naturwissenschaft*. In Kant's *Gesammelte Schriften*, 24 vols (Berlin: Georg Reimer, 1910–55) IV, pp. 467–565

——. *Metaphysische Anfangsgründe der Naturwissenschaft* (Riga, 1787)

——. *Prolegomena and Metaphysical Foundations of Natural Science*, trans. Ernest Belfort Bax (London: George Bell and Sons, 1883)

——. *Untersuchungen über die Deutlichkeit der Grundsätze der natürlichen Theologie und der Moral* (1763), in *Vermischte Schriften*, 4 vols (Halle, 1799) II, pp. 1–54

Kessler, Edward. *Coleridge's Metaphors of Being* (Princeton University Press, 1979)

Knight, G. Wilson. *The Starlit Dome* (London: Oxford University Press, 1941)

Knight, Richard Payne. *An Analytical Inquiry into the Principles of Taste*, 3rd edn (London, 1806)

Kroeber, Karl. *Romantic Landscape Vision: Constable and Wordsworth* (Madison: University of Wisconsin Press, 1975)

Lamb, Charles. *The Complete Works and Letters of Charles Lamb* (New York: Random House, 1963)

Leibnitz, Gottfried Wilhelm, Freiherr von. *The Monadology and Other Philosophical Writings*, trans. Robert Latta (London: Oxford University Press, 1925)

Lessing, Gotthold Ephraim. *Laocoon*, trans. Ellen Frothingham (Boston: Roberts Brothers, 1890)

Levere, Trevor H. *Poetry Realized in Nature: Samuel Taylor Coleridge and Early Nineteenth-Century Science* (Cambridge University Press, 1981)

——. *Affinity and Matter: Elements of Chemical Philosophy 1800–1865* (Oxford: Clarendon Press, 1971)

Lockridge, Laurence S. *Coleridge the Moralist* (Ithaca, NY: Cornell University Press, 1977)

Lovejoy, Arthur O. *The Great Chain of Being* (1936; rpt. New York: Harper & Row, 1960)

Lowes, John Livingston. *The Road to Xanadu* (Boston: Houghton Mifflin, 1927)

Maddox, Donald L. 'Shelley's *Alastor* and the Legacy of Rousseau', *Studies in Romanticism*, 9 (1970) 82–98

Magnuson, Paul. *Coleridge's Nightmare Poetry* (Charlottesville: University Press of Virginia, 1974)

Maniquis, Robert M. 'The Puzzling *Mimosa*: Sensitivity and Plant Symbols in Romanticism', *Studies in Romanticism*, 8 (1969) 129–55

Manwaring, Elizabeth Wheeler. *Italian Landscape in Eighteenth-Century England* (London: Oxford University Press, 1925)

Margoliouth, H. M. *Wordsworth and Coleridge, 1795–1834* (London: Oxford University Press, 1953)

Marks, Emerson R. *Coleridge on the Language of Verse* (Princeton University Press, 1981)

Massey, Irving. *The Uncreating Word. Romanticism and the Object* (Bloomington: Indiana University Press, 1970)

McFarland, Thomas. *Coleridge and the Pantheist Tradition* (Oxford: Clarendon Press, 1969)

——. *Romanticism and the Forms of Ruin: Wordsworth, Coleridge and Modalities of Fragmentation* (Princeton University Press, 1981)

——. 'The Symbiosis of Coleridge and Wordsworth', *Studies in Romanticism*, 11 (1972) 263–303

Mellor, Anne K. 'Coleridge's "This Lime-Tree Bower My Prison" and the Categories of English Landscape', *Studies in Romanticism*, 18 (1979) 253–70

Miall, David S. 'The Meaning of Dreams: Coleridge's Ambivalence', *Studies in Romanticism*, 21 (1982) 57–71

Miller, Craig W. 'An Examination of the Key Terms in Coleridge's Prose Writings' (Diss. University of Washington, 1956)

——. 'Coleridge's Concept of Nature', *Journal of the History* of *Ideas*, 25 (1964) 77–96

Modiano, Raimonda. 'Coleridge's Views on Touch and Other Senses', *Bulletin of Research in the Humanities*, 1(1978) 28–41

——. 'Coleridge and the Sublime: A Response to Thomas Weiskel, *The*

Romantic Sublime', *The Wordsworth Circle*, 9 (1978) 110–20

Monk, Samuel Holt. *The Sublime: A Study of Critical Theories in Eighteenth-Century England* (New York: Modern Language Association of America, 1935)

Nabholtz, John R. 'Dorothy Wordsworth and the Picturesque', *Studies in Romanticism*, 3 (1964) 118–28

Nicolai, Friedrich Christoph. *Über meine gelehrte Bildung* (Berlin and Stettin, 1799)

Nicolson, Marjorie. *Mountain Gloom and Mountain Glory: The Development of the Aesthetics of the Infinite* (Ithaca, NY: Cornell University Press, 1959)

Nidecker, Henri. 'Notes Marginales de S. T. Coleridge', *Revue de Littérature Comparée*, 11 (1931) 274–85; 12 (1932) 856–71; 13 (1933) 676–86

Noyes, Russell. *Wordsworth and the Art of Landscape* (Bloomington: Indiana University Press, 1968)

Oersted, Hans Christian. *Ansicht der chemischen Naturgesetze, durch die neuern Entdeckungen gewonnen* (Berlin, 1812)

Oken, Lorenz. *Erste Ideen zur Theorie des Lichts* (Jena, 1808)

——. *Lehrbuch der Naturgeschichte*, 6 vols (Leipzig and Jena, 1813; Jena, 1816–26)

——. *Lehrbuch der Naturphilosophie*, 3 vols (Jena, 1809)

O'Malley, Glen. *Shelley and Synaesthesia* (Evanston, Ill.: Northwestern University Press, 1964)

Orsini, Gian N. G. *Coleridge and German Idealism* (Carbondale: Southern Illinois University Press, 1969)

Owen, W. J. B. *Wordsworth as Critic* (University of Toronto Press, 1969)

Parrish, Stephen Maxfield. *The Art of the 'Lyrical Ballads'* (Cambridge Mass.: Harvard University Press, 1973)

Plato. *Plato's Phaedo*, trans. R. Hackforth (Cambridge University Press, 1955)

Price, Martin. 'The Picturesque Moment', in *From Sensibility to Romanticism*, ed. Frederick W. Hilles and Harold Bloom (Oxford University Press, 1965) pp. 259–92

Price, Uvedale. *An Essay on the Picturesque as Compared with the Sublime and the Beautiful*, 1st edn (London, 1794)

——. *A Dialogue on the Distinct Characters of the Picturesque and the Beautiful, in Answer to the Objections of Mr. Knight* (London, 1801)

Prickett, Stephen. *Coleridge and Wordsworth:* The Poetry of Growth (Cambridge University Press, 1970)

Raysor, T. M. 'Unpublished Fragments in Aesthetics by S. T. Coleridge', *Studies in Philology*, 22 (1925) 529–37

Reed, Mark. 'Wordsworth, Coleridge, and the "Plan" of the *Lyrical Ballads'*, *University of Toronto Quarterly*, 34 (1965) 238–53

Richards, I. A. 'Coleridge: The Vulnerable Poet', *Yale Review*, 48 (1959) 491–500

Richter, Jean Paul, *Horn of Oberon: Jean Paul Richter's School for Aesthetics*, trans. Margaret R. Hale (Detroit: Wayne State University Press, 1973)

——. *Kampaner Thal* (Erfurt, 1787)

Rollins, H. E. (ed.) *The Letters of John Keats*, 2 vols (Cambridge, Mass.: Harvard University Press, 1958)

Sabin, Margery. *English Romanticism and the French Tradition* (Cambridge, Mass.: Harvard University Press, 1976)

Schelling, Friedrich Wilhelm Joseph. *Einleitung zu dem Entwurf eines Systems der Naturphilosophie. Oder über den Begriff der speculativen Physik und die innere Organisation eines Systems dieser Wissenschaft* (1799). In *Sämmtliche Werke*, 14 vols (Stuttgart: J. G. Cotta'scher Verlag, 1856–61) III, pp. 269–326

——. *Erster Entwurf eines Systems der Naturphilosophie* (1799). *Sämmtliche Werke*, III, pp. 3–268

——. *Ideen zu einer Philosophie der Natur* (1803). *Sämmtliche Werke*, II, pp. 1–343

——. *Introduction to the Outlines of a System of Natural Philosophy: or On the Idea of Speculative Physics and the Internal Organization of a System of This Science*, trans. Tom Davidson. *Journal of Speculative Philosophy*, 1 (1867) 193–220

——. 'Kritische Fragmente', in *Jahrbücher der Medicin als Wissenschaft*, ed. A. F. Marcus and F. W. J. Schelling, 3 vols (Tübingen: J. G. Cotta' scher Buchandlung, 1805–8) II, 283–304.

——. *System of Transcendental Idealism*, trans. Peter Heath (Charlottesville: University Press of Virginia, 1978)

——. 'Über das Verhältniss der bildenden Künste zu der Natur', *Sämmtliche Werke*, VII, pp. 289–329

——. (ed). *Zeitschrift für speculative Physik* (Jena and Leipzig, 1800–1)

Schiller, Friedrich. *Essays Aesthetical and Philosophical* (London: George Bell and Sons, 1916)

Schulz, Max F. *The Poetic Voices of Coleridge* (Detroit: Wayne State University Press, 1964)

Selincourt, Ernest de. *The Letters of William and Dorothy Wordsworth. The Middle Years*, 2 vols (Oxford: Clarendon Press, 1937)

——. *The Early Letters of William and Dorothy Wordsworth* (Oxford: Clarendon Press, 1935)

——. 'Coleridge's *Dejection: An Ode', Essays and Studies* (Oxford: Clarendon Press, 1937) XXII, pp. 7–25

Shaffer, Elinor. 'Coleridge's Revolution in the Standard of Taste', *Journal of Aesthetics and Art Criticism*, 28 (1969) 213–21

——. 'Coleridge's Theory of Aesthetic Interest', *Journal of Aesthetics and Art Criticism*, 27 (1969) 399–408

——. 'Coleridge and Natural Philosophy: A Review of Recent Literary and Historical Research', *History of Science*, 12 (1974) 284–98

Shawcross, John. 'Coleridge Marginalia', *Notes and Queries*, 4 (1905) 341–2

Shearer, Edna Aston. 'Wordsworth and Coleridge Marginalia in a Copy of Richard Payne Knight's *Analytical Inquiry into the Principles of Taste', Huntington Library Quarterly*, 1 (1937) 63–99

Sheats, Paul D. *The Making of Wordsworth's Poetry, 1785–1798* (Cambridge, Mass.: Harvard University Press, 1973)

Smith, Fred M. 'The Relation of Coleridge's *Ode on Dejection* to Wordsworth's *Ode on Intimations of Immortality', PMLA*, 50 (1935) 224–34

Snelders, H. A. M. 'Inorganic Natural Sciences 1797–1840: An Introductory Survey', *Studies in Romanticism*, 9 (1970) 193–215

Stallknecht, Newton P. *Strange Seas of Thought* (Bloomington: Indiana University Press, 1958)

Stallo, J. B. *General Principles of the Philosophy of Nature* (Boston: Wm. Crosby and H. P. Nichols, 1848)

Stauffer, Robert C. 'Speculation and Experiment in the Background of Oersted's Discovery of Electromagnetism', *Isis*, 48 (1957) 33–50

Steffens, Heinrich. *Beyträge zur innern Naturgeschichte der Erde* (Freyberg, 1801)

——. *Geognostisch-geologische Aufsätze* (Hamburg, 1810)

——. *Grundzüge der philosophischen Naturwissenschaft* (Berlin, 1806)

——. *Schriften*, 2 vols (Breslau, 1821)

Suther, Marshall. *The Dark Night of Samuel Taylor Coleridge* (New York: Columbia University Press, 1960)

Swiatecka, M. Jadwiga. *The Idea of the Symbol: Some Nineteenth Century Comparisons with Coleridge* (Cambridge University Press, 1980)

Thackray, Arnold. *Atoms and Powers: An Essay on Newtonian Matter-Theory and the Development of Chemistry* (Cambridge, Mass.: Harvard University Press, 1970)

Thorpe, Clarence DeWitt. 'Coleridge on the Sublime', in *Wordsworth and Coleridge: Studies in the Honor of George McLean Harper*, ed. Earl Leslie Griggs (Princeton University Press, 1939) 193–19

Tuveson, Ernest. 'Space, Deity, and the "Natural Sublime"', *Modern Language Quarterly*, 12 (1951) 20–38

Wasserman, Earl. 'The English Romantics: The Grounds of Knowledge', *Studies in Romanticism*, 4 (1964) 17–34

Watson, J. R. *Picturesque Landscape and English Romantic Poetry* (London: Hutchinson Educational, 1970)

Weiskel, Thomas. *The Romantic Sublime* (Baltimore: Johns Hopkins Press, 1976)

Wellek, René. *Immanuel Kant in England 1793–1838* (Princeton University Press, 1931)

Wells, G. A. 'Man and Nature: An Elucidation of Coleridge's Rejection of Herder's Thought', *Journal of English and Germanic Philology*, 51 (1952) 314–25

Wendling, Ronald C. 'Coleridge and the Consistency of "The Eolian Harp"', *Studies in Romanticism*, 8 (1969) 26–42

Wetzels, Walter D. 'Aspects of Natural Science in German Romanticism', *Studies in Romanticism*, 10 (1971) 44–59

Whalley, George, 'Coleridge's Poetic Sensibility', in *Coleridge's Variety: Bicentenary Studies*, ed. John Beer (London: Macmillan, 1974) pp. 1–30

——. *Coleridge and Sara Hutchinson and the Asra Poems* (London: Routledge & Kegan Paul, 1955)

Wilson, Douglas Brownlow. 'Two Modes of Apprehending Nature: A Gloss on the Coleridgean Symbol', *PMLA*, 87 (1972) 42–52

Wlecke, Albert O. *Wordsworth and the Sublime* (Berkeley: University of California Press, 1973)

Wolfart, Karl Christian. *Erläuterungen zum Mesmerismus*, vol. II of *Mesmerismus*. Oder System der Wechselwirkungen (Berlin, 1814–15)

Wordsworth, Dorothy. *The Journals of Dorothy Wordsworth*, ed. Ernest de Selincourt, 2 vols (London: Macmillan, 1941)

Wordsworth, William. *The Poetical Works of William Wordsworth*, ed. Thomas

Hutchinson (London: Oxford University Press, 1960)
——. *The Poetical Works of William Wordsworth*, ed. E. de Selincourt, 5 vols (Oxford: Clarendon Press, 1952–9) vol. II
——. 'The Sublime and the Beautiful', in *The Prose Works of William Wordsworth*, ed. W. J. B. Owen and J. W. Smyser, 3 vols (London: Oxford University Press, 1974) II, pp. 349–59

Index